Advance Praise for

Repertoires of Racial Resistance:
Pedagogical Dreaming in Transborder Educational Spaces

"*Repertoires of Racial Resistance* is an essential read for anyone committed to social justice. This timely volume, comprising 15 compelling chapters, brilliantly highlights the imaginative and transformative strategies that communities of color employ to resist and combat inequities. Featuring contributions from an intergenerational group of current college students, practitioners, and academics, the book showcases how youth and their allies harness creativity and leadership to drive meaningful social change. This book is a powerful testament to the resilience and ingenuity of marginalized communities in the face of oppressive forces that seek to silence and erase them. This volume is a vital resource for educators, scholars, and activists dedicated to improving the material conditions of our most marginalized."

—*Dr. Royel M. Johnson,*
Associate Professor of Education and Social Work at University of Southern
California, Director of the National Assessment of Collegiate Campus Climates

"*Repertoires of Racial Resistance* is an excellent collection of essays focusing on how young people of color's re-imaginings have the potential to transform the education system in pursuit of racial justice. While theoretically informed, a major strength of the volume is that the voices of young people are front and center, underscoring that they are legitimate producers of knowledge with the potential to create change in the educational environment. *Repertoires of Racial Resistance* is a must read for anyone interested in the future of America's multiethnic educational system."

—*Leo R. Chavez*
Distinguished Professor Emeritus of Anthropology,
University of California, Irvine

"In *Repertories of Racial Resistance*, Abad and Conchas provide a brave and timely volume to address the role of education that both instructs us about the challenges that exist in our social ecologies, while also recognizing the transformative possibilities of education, particularly for historically marginalized communities. Rooted in Freireian pedagogy, and others, Abad and Conchas assemble a slate of scholars who are dedicated to these principles and provide students, educators, and scholars with a set of tools to help them dream and imagine the true transformative possibilities of education."

—*Louie F. Rodriguez, Professor of Education,*
University of California Riverside

"As a Black race scholar activist who leads a youth centered organization focused on racial identity development and intergenerational healing, and racial justice, I am beyond elated and honored to be invited to affirm the labor and wisdom put into this book. This book unveils and further illuminates content that is needed amidst our sociopolitical context for educators, researchers, P-20 professionals, workforce development designers, and beyond. From racial identity affirmation and navigation, this book further enhances and invigorates the work needed toward the actualization of racial healing."

—*Dr. Janiece Z. Mackey PhD,*
Co-Founder and CEO,
Young Aspiring Americans for Social and Political Activism (YAASPA)

"Youth are our best teachers. This collection is beautifully written and illustrates the power of learning from and with BIPOC young people and the adults who understand their brilliance. This volume is urgently needed. It invites a rethinking of the theories we engage and methods we use, drawing attention to multiple sites where racial resistance is occurring in and beyond classrooms. Through incisive methodologies, the essays remind us of the worlds young people are creating and our role in supporting them."

—*Edward R. Curammeng,*
Associate Professor, College of Education,
California State University, Dominguez Hills

Repertoires of Racial Resistance

Ethnic Studies Revival

Edited by *Gilberto Q. Conchas and Mahmoud Suleiman*

The mission of the **Ethnic Studies Revival** series is to present volumes of current research and work focused on praxis and the effective implementation of critical ethnic studies educational experiences in diasporic communities of color and Indigenous communities while making connections between the local, national, and transnational settings. The book series seeks to provide an interdisciplinary intellectual space that inspires educators in schools and outside-of-schools to transform inequities based on race, ethnicity, nationality, gender, sexuality, ability, class, and the intersections among them, while advancing visions of social, political, economic justice, and decolonial understandings of the global world. In particular, the series amplifies transformative ethnic studies models that seek to affirm the intellectual, social, racial, ethnic, and cultural being of ALL diverse groups [such as, but not limited to, Pan African Americans, Pan Asian American, Indigenous Americans, Latinas/o/xs, and Muslim Americans]. The book series draws attention to these groups' intersectional identities, histories, plights, and contributions and educators' dynamic roles in advancing efforts to pluralize the curriculum and instruction reflective of the diverse educational and social expectations of all learners in democratic schools and societies.

Repertoires of Racial Resistance:
Pedagogical Dreaming in Transborder Educational Spaces (2024)
Edited by Miguel N. Abad and Gilberto Q. Conchas

Forthcoming Titles:
Somos Hija/o/xs del Maíz/We are Children of the Corn:
Pillars of Hope, Resistance, and Latina/o/x Educational Success
Edited by Gilberto Q. Conchas, Nancy Acevedo, and Victor DeAlba

The State of Latinxs and Education:
Maintaining Continuity and Enhancing Equity
Edited by Gilberto Q. Conchas, Mahmoud Suleiman, and Victor DeAlba

If you are interested in submitting a proposal for publication consideration, please send your prospectus (https://myersedpress.presswarehouse.com/publishers/stylus/myers/files/Prospectus%20Guidelines%20MEP%202023.pdf) to the series editors, Gilberto Q. Conchas (gqc5330@psu.edu) or Mahmoud Suleiman (msuleiman@csub.edu) along with your current CV.

Repertoires of Racial Resistance

Pedagogical Dreaming in Transborder Educational Space

EDITED BY *Miguel N. Abad, and Gilberto Q. Conchas*

Myers
Education
Press

Gorham, Maine

Contents

ACKNOWLEDGMENTS

We want to express our gratitude to all the authors and collaborators included in this book. This has been a collaborative process, and we are grateful and fortunate to have been able to work with talented scholars and skillful practitioners. Also, a big thank you to Victor DeAlba for supporting the editors behind the scenes - your contributions have been invaluable.

Ethnic Studies Revival

In a world grappling with deep-rooted and persistent manifestations of racialized inequities, the need for insightful exploration and understanding of diverse racioethnic experiences has never been more urgent (Conchas, 2024). This is particularly true in PreK-12 schools and higher education institutions wherein the wrath of extreme racism, nativism, xenophobia, sexism, and homophobia in today's America is most palpable (Conchas & Acevedo, 2020). The book you hold in your hands, *Repertoires of Racial Resistance*, is not just a collection of chapters; it is a beacon of enlightenment, a testament to the power of knowledge in combating bigotry and fostering inclusivity.

This informative, timely, and sincere book focuses on the problems and possibilities of marginalized populations in U.S. society and schools, namely youth of color and adult allies. *Repertoires of Racial Resistance* explores the integral role of dreaming and imagination in pursuing educational justice in distinct transborder educational spaces. The illuminating case studies in this book highlight how youth and adults utilize Transformative Methodologies not only to generate knowledge, but also to empower communities, combat all forms of inequality, and promote social change.

The chapters demonstrate how researchers, practitioners, and youth utilize methodologies such as participatory action research, testimonio, counternarratives, and critical storytelling to make sense of social inequalities, and envision futures rooted in liberation and justice. This text considers the intimate relationship between youth leadership and empowerment with dreaming and imagination. The book includes case studies based in diverse transborder educational contexts such as PreK-12 schools, community-based settings, and higher education. Moreover, the edited volume specifically highlights how BIPOC young people leverage their imaginations as part of their efforts to advocate for justice in their communities, families, and schools. This book demonstrates the importance for researchers and practitioners to leverage youth imagination and freedom dreams in creating culturally-sustaining educational settings and promoting transformative youth leadership. This hopeful book is in line with the major tenets of the **Ethnic Studies Revival Series**.

The mission of the **Ethnic Studies Revival Series** is to present volumes of current research and work focused on praxis and the effective implementation of critical ethnic studies as part of educational experiences in diasporic communities of color and Indigenous communities while making connections among the local, national, and transnational settings. The book series seeks to provide an interdisciplinary intellectual space that inspires educators in schools and outside-of-schools to transform inequities based on race, ethnicity, nationality, gender, sexuality, ability, class, and the intersections among them, while advancing visions of social, political, economic justice, and decolonial understandings of the global world. In particular, the series amplifies transformative ethnic studies models that seek to affirm the intellectual, social, racial, ethnic, and cultural being of ALL diverse groups (such as, but not limited to, Pan African Americans, Pan Asian American, Indigenous Americans, Latinas/o/xs, Arab Americans, and Muslim Americans). The book series draws attention to these groups' intersectional identities, histories, plights, and contributions and educators' dynamic roles in advancing efforts to pluralize the curriculum and instruction reflective of the diverse educational and social expectations of all learners in democratic schools and societies.

The timeline and underlying rationale for the **Ethnic Studies Revival Series** is based on the growing cycles of ignorance, intolerance, racism, nativism, xenophobia, sexism, islamophobia, and homophobia, and all forms of *phobia-isms* in today's America that must be confronted through promoting inclusive and global perspectives to empower all students and their communities. The book series is rooted in the understanding that Ethnic Studies paradigms and epistemologies contribute to educators, students, and educational leaders' development of a critical consciousness and can also be utilized to contextualize and understand the experiences of Students of Color and other marginalized groups in the institutions of PreK-12 schooling and higher education. This series will provide a thoughtful and rigorous platform for social justice-oriented educators to acquire and grapple with the knowledge and skills, and empower themselves with the political will to cultivate the community cultural wealth of all participants in a global society—including, but not limited to, the diverse educational experiences of students of color, under-resourced students, language minority students, students with disabilities, immigrant students, and other minoritized populations, such as LGBTQ+ students.

Drawing from the rich legacies of scholars such as Noam Chomsky (2003), Paulo Freire (2000), and their "dangerous" epistemologies, this series endeavors to transcend the boundaries of traditional education by embracing a pedagogy of liberation—a praxis that intertwines critical reflection with transformative action. Chomsky's insights into linguistic and political analysis, Freire's pedagogy of the oppressed, and our approach on the ubiquity of wars and the importance of literacy intersect to underscore the urgency of multicultural education and cultural proficiency in confronting systemic injustices (Suleiman, 2024). We hope this series will serve as a poignant reminder of the interconnectedness of global phenomena and local realities. In a world marked by conflicts and violence, the pursuit of education becomes not only a means of personal empowerment, but also a pathway to peace and understanding (Suleiman & Huber, 2022). By shedding light on the complex relationship between warfare, literacy, and cultural identity, we seek to recognize the profound impact of local and geopolitical forces on educational practices and to engage in critical, courageous, and, yes, dangerous dialogue aimed at fostering a culture of peace and cooperation.

At the heart of this endeavor lies the principle of praxis—an iterative process of emancipatory reflection and action that empowers individuals to become agents of change in their own lives and communities (Suleiman, 2024). This requires our serious engagement in courageous and dangerous discourse that is good and necessary. As we navigate the complexities of ethnic studies and multicultural education, we are called not only to interrogate existing systems of oppression but also to actively participate in the creation of more just and equitable alternatives (Conchas & Acevedo, 2020). Through the good danger of praxis, theory is not divorced from practice; rather, it serves as a catalyst for transformative action, informed by the lived experiences and aspirations of those most affected by injustice.

We recognize that landmark research in the field of multicultural education has provided compelling evidence of its efficacy in fostering academic achievement, promoting positive intergroup relations, and nurturing the development of critical consciousness among students. For example, studies by researchers such as James A. Banks and Cherry M. Banks (2019), Sonia Nieto (2008), Gloria Ladson-Billings (2022), and Geneva Gay (2010) have underscored the importance of integrating diverse perspectives and experiences into the curriculum to enhance students' cultural competence and promote social justice (see also Muhammad, 2020; López & Sleeter, 2023; Sleeter & Grant, 1991). As such, we intend to establish continuity in transformative actions across the educational spectrums and provide new lenses that amplify the core elements of universal human needs and expectations that educators are drafted to champion regardless of their diversity.

Thus, central to the principles of the **Ethnic Studies Revival Series** is the recognition of the interconnectedness of race, identity, ethnicity, culture, and power. As such, this series endeavors to explore the intersecting dimensions of identity and inequality, offering nuanced insights into the complex dynamics of privilege and oppression that shape our social realities. By amplifying and centering the voices and experiences of historically marginalized communities, the volumes in the series will illuminate the often-overlooked contributions and struggles that have shaped our collective history.

As you embark on this journey through the myriad cultures, histories, and struggles presented in the series volumes, we hope to inspire readers and expand their intellectual horizons to engage actively in the pursuit of social change and empowerment. Each insight gained, each perspective embraced, brings us closer to a world where diversity is celebrated, and all individuals are valued for their inherent worth. In the spirit of inclusivity and solidarity, we delve into this series with open minds and compassionate hearts, knowing that through our collective efforts, we can build a more equitable and harmonious society for generations to come.

The field of Ethnic Studies is not just an academic discipline; it is a call to action, albeit dangerous but necessary. It challenges us to confront uncomfortable truths, to interrogate systems of power and privilege, and to amplify voices that have been marginalized for far too long. It is through this critical examination that we can begin to dismantle the structures of oppression and forge a path toward genuine empathy, equity, and justice.

Gilberto Q. Conchas, State College, PA &
Mahmoud Suleiman, Bakersfield, CA

Reference

Banks, J. A., & Banks, C. M. (2019). *Multicultural education: Issues and perspectives.* Wiley.

Chomsky, N. (2003). *Chomsky on democracy and education.* Routledge.

Conchas, G. Q. (2024). *The color of success 2.0: Race and transformative pathways for high-achieving urban youth* (2nd ed.). Teachers College Press of Columbia University.

Conchas, G. Q., & Acevedo, N. (2020). *The Chicana/o/x dream: Hope, resistance, and educational success.* Harvard Education Press.

Freire, P. (2000). *Pedagogy of the oppressed.* Bloomsbury Academic.

Gay, G. (2010). *Culturally responsive teaching: Theory, research, and practice.* Teachers College Press.

Ladson-Bilings, G. (2022). *The Dreamkeepers: Successful teachers of African American children* (3rd ed.). Jossey-Bass.

López, F., & Sleeter, C. E. (2023). *Critical race theory and its critics: Implications for research and teaching.* Teachers College Press.

Muhammad, G. (2020). *Cultivating genius: An equity framework for culturally and historically responsive literacy.* Scholastic Incorporated.

Nieto, S. (2008). *Affirming diversity: The sociopolitical context of multicultural education.* Pearson.

Sleeter, C. E., & Grant, C. A. (1991). Race, class, gender, and disability in current textbooks. *Theory Into Practice, 30*(1), 42-49.

Suleiman, M. (2024). The ubiquity of wars and the "good danger" of praxis. *Journal of Leadership, Equity and Research, 10*(1), 1-3.

Suleiman, M., & Huber, T. (Eds.). (2022). *Beyond provincialism: Promoting global competencies in teacher and educator preparation.* Information Age Publishing.

Introduction:
Repertoires of Racial Resistance and Pedagogical Dreaming from the Classroom to the Streets

Victor DeAlba, Gilberto Q. Conchas, and Miguel N. Abad

> *The idea of dreaming—and in many Black scholars' views, radical dreaming—isn't a fluffy notion. Being rooted in our dreams has served the most innovative leaders of yesterday and today. If we look at some of the people who have inspired generations and catapulted us forward, they have often been dreamers—people who had a vision for a world that did not yet exist.*
>
> Jamila Dugan, 2022

THIS TIMELY ANTHOLOGY interrogates modern social theory and policy's most critical and pressing issues: racial inequity, social inequity, and educational opportunity. More poignantly, how education spaces, those in both communities and schools, are contested spaces of race, power, and resistance. The book interrogates popular discourse of educational success—cultural explanations—as a hegemonic device pitting racialized groups against one another and how transformative methodologies are utilized to resist inequitable power relations and the status quo. The aim is to illuminate how these approaches facilitate social justice-driven resistance led by ethnically and racially minoritized young people, families, communities, and their educator allies.

The volume speaks to social transformation theories, theories of racialization, and critical social scientific thought. A critical inquiry examines the ways in which education can both reproduce and disrupt systems of racial oppression. On the macro-structural level, schooling is a specific educational process that is associated with the reproduction of ethnoracial, class, sexuality, and gender stratification. At the same time, educators, students, and progressive scholars have also demonstrated how education can facilitate individual, interpersonal, and collective struggles for social justice in their communities. This book will focus on resistant efforts in education highlighted by transformational methodological approaches. We define transformative methodologies as approaches to research and knowledge production that explicitly (a) center the perspectives, experiences, and expertise of BIPOC youth and communities as essential to research, (b) challenge conventional social science frameworks that relegate communities to being "objects" of inquiry, and (c) facilitate ethnically and racially minoritized young people to leverage their educational opportunities to express their agency, imagine emancipatory futures, and embody social change.

This book explores how ethnically and racially minoritized young people engage in diverse forms of resistance and develop into social and historical actors (Gutierrez et al., 2019). Through a collection of theoretical chapters and praxis-driven U.S. case studies based on cutting-edge methodological approaches, this anthology interrogates how young people connect educational inequities with other intersecting oppressions and injustices in their communities. This book illustrates how young people engage in collective activism, organizing, and quotidian forms of individual and interpersonal resistance within schools and other community-based contexts. These case studies will bring together empirically-driven narratives that highlight a wide range of contexts (urban, suburban, and rural), ethnic and racialized communities (BIPOC), gender diverse communities (LGBTQIA+), and their intersections that lead to transformational change through pedagogical dreaming. Additionally, this anthology contains insights from the critical reflections of school leaders and other adult allies who have collaborated with and supported youth in enacting transformational change. Through this lens, chapter authors interrogate both the particularities of some structural barriers to educational justice, as well as the cross-cutting factors and practices that resonate across disparate contexts and communities.

Youth resistance scholars have highlighted how youth resistance can be understood as a constellation of techniques, associations, and relationships young people engage in as an individual expression of agency or as part of larger social justice projects. While much of youth resistance literature has been occupied with how young people learn to engage in critical analysis of society, our book is also concerned with imagination, critical hope, and praxis. As expressed in the quote by Dugan (2022), shared at the opening of this section, we highlight the ways in which young people today are radically dreaming, conceptualizing, asserting, and inhabiting more socially-just educational futures through participation in social movements and in their everyday lives with their families, peers, and neighborhoods. Moreover, our book highlights the work of innovative educators who partner with and inspire young people to facilitate transformational educational praxis—what we coin as repertoires of resistance. In fact, "radical dreaming—isn't a fluffy notion" (Dugan, 2022, para. 9).

These original theoretically-informed chapters and praxis-driven case studies explore and interrogate five interrelated conversations with respect to education as emancipation:

1. How might resistance and imagination contribute to our current understandings of educational justice?

2. What kinds of educational projects—broadly defined—can support ethnically and racially minoritized young peoples in imagining and asserting their freedom dreams for themselves and their communities?

3. What modes of educational resistance, imagining, and dreaming are young people engaging in as they respond to injustices in their communities? In what ways are young people becoming historical actors in the process? How do educational practitioners support these processes?

4. What does educational inequity and transformative resistance look like comparatively between and within geographic contexts, race, ethnicity, gender, sexuality, and social class?

5. How are young people and their adult allies engaging in solidarity-building praxis across the physical and social barriers that separate structurally vulnerable communities?

These counterspaces begin to fill the cracks in the opportunity structure that create ethnic and racial disparity and failure. Through their transformative visions and direct action, the radical dreamers highlighted in this book continue to catapult us forward and inspire generations to come.

The Power and Significance of Transformative Methodologies

Black, Indigenous, People of Color (BIPOC) have historically found themselves challenging institutional and sociopolitical forces that attempt to silence them. Additionally, academic research and the overall U.S. schooling system has exacerbated this dynamic by focusing on Eurocentric approaches to learning while excluding those of scholars of color, often referred to as the apartheid of knowledge (Bernal & Villalpando 2002; Pérez Huber, 2009). Despite these systems of oppression, BIPOC have created unique and innovative ways to expand conventional notions of knowledge production by challenging established research norms and prominently featuring their voices, experiences, and perspectives (Smith, 1999). Existing literature highlights the effort by scholars of color to decenter white dominant logic and amplify voices and ideas from historically marginalized and oppressed groups. Transformative methodologies are promising tools that have been utilized by BIPOC for decades, allowing them to share their stories, amplify their ideas, document their history, and create their own narratives.

This section will provide a better understanding of the potential that transformative methodologies have in amplifying the voices of BIPOC students, advancing liberation, and promoting social justice in education. In so doing, we aim to provide a brief overview of the roots and origins of transformative methodologies and how scholars in the field define and conceptualize them. We also identify some key elements of transformative methodologies that can provide guidance for enacting meaningful change in educational policy, practice, and research. We describe the main theoretical underpinnings that scholars credit for the development and evolution of these transformative methodologies. We look to existing scholarship to highlight the importance of these methodologies in educational research and their potential as methodological and pedagogical approaches to lift up the individual and collective experiences of marginalized groups. Lastly, we discuss the implications of these transformative methodologies on future works in educational research.

Roots and Origins of Transformative Methodologies

As scholars, educators, and educational leaders seek to utilize transformative methodologies to analyze and understand the experiences of ethnically and racially minoritized groups, it is important to first acknowledge the significance of how and where these transformative methodologies originated. While many different types of methodologies can be labeled as "transformative," this chapter will focus on those used throughout the book and most often employed in existing literature. Transformative methodologies encompass *testimonios*, youth participatory action research (YPAR), counternarratives, counter stories, and critical storytelling. While each of these approaches is unique in its own way, many are similar in origin, utilization, and intent. Although it is difficult to determine the exact origin of each of these methodologies, we look to the existing scholarship to credit those that have paved the way for this type of research and practice to flourish.

The *testimonio* genre has a long and varied history that can be traced back to Latin America, with roots in Latin American Studies dating back to the 1970s (Blackmer Reyes & Curry Rodríguez, 2012; Booker, 2002; Pérez Huber, 2009). Its origins are tied to social movements of liberation and resistance and most utilized by Latin American and Chicana/o/x groups. *Testimonios* are said to first be used to share the experiences and ongoing struggles of those who were persecuted by their governments and other sociopolitical forces in Latin American countries (Delgado Bernal et al., 2012). There are plenty of literary works from people directly impacted by historical events that provide an account from their perspective. These examples show how *testimonios* have been aimed at centering voices from the margins. Of these *testimonios* in the 1970s and 1980s, many of them were from "indigenous representatives and labor and guerilla leaders" (Zimmerman, 2004, p. 1119). Throughout the 1990s, *testimonios* also reflected the experiences of oppression, marginalization, and resistance of folks from other social movements that supported human rights, women's rights, and LGBTQIA+ rights.

YPAR has similar roots, as it stems from participatory action research (PAR), which has been utilized since the 1970s and has traces in Indigenous communities in Africa, Asia, Latin America, and the South Pacific (Desai, 2019). Colombian sociologist Orlando Fals-Borda (1987) conceptualized participatory action research as a step towards promoting a people's science that could democratize knowledge production and support the agency of marginalized communities in advocating for positive change and social justice. Notable scholars, such as Paulo Freire (1982), whose work focuses on amplifying the voices of marginalized communities, have also been linked to the foundations of PAR. Youth participatory action research builds on PAR but focuses on conducting this type of research in collaboration with youth. Caraballo et al. (2017) credit the field of critical psychology and, more specifically, Alice McIntyre's (2000) study with urban youth, as the first to specifically utilize YPAR. Counternarratives, critical storytelling, and counter stories came in the mid- to late-1990s among scholars in the fields of social work, Latina/o/x Studies, and critical pedagogy (Miller, et al., 2020). Many scholars credit their origins to critical legal studies (CLS) and critical race theory (CRT), which were developed to counter the structure and application of law that was disproportionately impacting BIPOC within the U.S. judicial system. Counternarratives, critical storytelling, and counterstories gained popularity in the field of education to capture the narratives and experiences of BIPOC students as they navigate through their educational journeys. These transformative approaches have evolved to encompass art, poetry, photography, and many other forms of creative expression.

It is important to understand the roots of all these transformative methodologies because they underline the historical significance of this continuous effort to amplify the voices of those experiencing oppression. These methodologies were cultivated by scholars and people from structurally vulnerable communities, often as forms of resistance against epistemic violence from Western regimes of knowledge that aimed to silence non-Eurocentric perspectives (Dotson, 2011; Spivak, 1988). At the same time, these methodologies reflect not only a reaction to oppression but also a radical imagination rooted in overcoming oppression and creating a new and better world (Kelley, 2002). In the following section, we provide an overview of how these transformative methodologies are defined by the scholars who have paved the way.

Definitions and Conceptualizations

Testimonios.

The uniqueness of transformative methodologies can make them a challenge to define. Their definitions and conceptualizations span the fields of anthropology, education, ethnic studies, humanities, psychology, women's studies, and beyond; however, we will attempt to engage in this critical discussion.

Testimonios are often defined as a method (Latina Feminist Group, 2001; Pérez Huber, 2009), methodology, and methodological tool, but also as pedagogy and a pedagogical tool. *Testimonios* can be conceptualized as a process (Cienfuegos & Monelli, 1983) and a practice (Blackmer Reyes & Curry Rodríguez, 2012). While there are many definitions and conceptualizations of *testimonios,* scholars have identified a few key elements of *testimonios* to consider. Rodriguez-Campo (2021) makes the point that using a single definition to describe *testimonios* would not do them justice because of the many forms they may take. She shares that every *testimonio* is comprised of the "recounting of specific memories that speak to collective experiences related to oppressive conditions" (Rodriguez-Campo, 2021, p. 2). Cindy Cruz (2012) has argued that *testimonio* is not only a research methodology but that it also reflects a pedagogical framework that can disrupt neoliberal narratives of education by recentering dispossessed communities and social justice movements. Blackmer Reyes and Curry Rodríguez (2012) define *testimonios* as an oral or written account from the first-person perspective that draws on experiences and self-consciousness of an important topic or issue to which someone bears witness. They also emphasize that *testimonios* should be told from the first-person perspective of the real protagonist or someone who witnessed the events.

Additionally, they share that the account must be with the intention to empower those who have experienced or are currently experiencing similar situations. Brabeck (2003) goes into detail by providing four distinct features that can build on the definition of *testimonios.* These four distinct features are: (1) *testimonios* are given from the perspective of a representative individual that offers a collective identity/understanding, which provides researchers a different way of thinking about representing "the Other"; (2) *testimonios* do not make claims of universal representation, but rather aim to provide an understanding of the experiences within a particular community; (3) *testimonios* challenge the standards of what is often accepted as knowledge production. Rather than continuing the narrative that "experts" and "scientists" who use "rational" and "objective" methods are the producers of knowledge, *testimonios* emphasize the validity of experiential knowledge and lived experiences as valuable sources of information (p. 256); and 4) *testimonios* provide westerners greater context for understanding the experiences of "the Other" which couldn't accurately be described if not having ever experienced it. Brabeck (2003) adds that this allows researchers the opportunity to have important and impactful discussions about those experiences to inform research in a way that creates bridges of solidarity and collaboration.

Youth participatory action research (YPAR).

Another methodology that is featured prominently within this project is youth participatory action research (YPAR). Anyon et al. (2018) conducted a review of research to examine common principles, characteristics, and conceptualizations of YPAR in studies published after 2009. Of the 63 distinct studies they analyzed, they found that most of them identified participatory (93.7%) and transformative (88.9%) as key principles for YPAR. Additionally, they found that many of these studies (90.5%) underscored the need for a method of social action used by the participants (Anyon et al., 2018). To provide more specificity for defining YPAR, we can look to the characteristics provided by Cammarota and Fine (2010). They list the following: (a) The researcher is not alone but operates with others in a collective; (b) Stakeholders should not be limited or defined narrowly; (c) Participating stakeholders should adhere closely to the tenet of intersectionality; (d) Knowledge gained should be critical in nature; (e) Knowledge gained is active, not passive; and (f) YPAR is explicitly pedagogical, but has implications for education and youth development.

Just as importantly, YPAR projects explicitly position young people as legitimate producers of knowledge who have the power and agency to effect change in their material realities (Torre et al., 2017). Said differently, YPAR methodologies position young people not as "objects" of inquiry but as valuable co-creators of theoretical and empirical insights for addressing social problems. While YPAR is a collaboration between young people and adults, young people drive the inquiry by sharing decision-making responsibilities with adult researchers around creating research questions, creating data generation plans, analyzing data, drawing inferences and conclusions, and planning interventions based on their research conclusions (Mirra et al., 2015). Additionally, YPAR scholars have written in depth about the politics of intersubjectivity and the nuances of relationality that occur as adult scholars and youth researchers collaborate to generate knowledge toward addressing social issues that are relevant to local communities (Lac et al., 2022; Ritterbusch, 2019). In other words, YPAR is more than a collection of methods for doing social science research because it also reflects an ethic and philosophy for engaging in research projects that are driven by and accountable to communities.

Counternarratives, critical storytelling, and counter stories.

Counternarratives have taken many different forms, but some early scholars have characterized them as a competing understanding of an existing narrative or form of knowledge (Lather, 1998). Although counternarratives were often spoken about in terms of scholars countering information published by others in research or academia, their conceptualization has evolved to include more practical implications. When it comes to critical storytelling, Cooper (1994) describes them as a critical perspective that "starts with the stories of the least advantaged and allows a critique of the larger society through the stories about their experiences" (p. 135). In Cooper's definition, the storytelling had to include the perspective of students to critique educational practices and improve the overall educational system. Counter stories have been defined as a powerful resistance to the white hegemony and a way to link experience, research, community, and social change (Delgado Bernal, 1998; Villenas et al., 2019). It is also important to note that some scholars use counternarratives, critical storytelling, and counter stories interchangeably due to their roots and origins and the similarities in the way they are defined.

The overarching themes of transformative methodologies.

Transformative methodologies can be a powerful tool for voicing individual experiences of oppression, injustice, and resistance that also represent the stories of a larger group's experience. Because of the varying definitions and conceptualizations of these transformative methodologies, they can take many forms, such as speeches, journal or diary entries, interviews, spoken word, and other forms of writing, but their origin is narrative in form (Blackmer Reyes & Curry Rodríguez, 2012). The power of voicing these individual experiences allows the narrator to "[seek] empowerment" (Blackmer Reyes & Curry Rodríguez, 2012, p. 527) and construct a collective discourse of solidarity (Pérez Huber, 2009). Whatever form they may take, they recount a personal experience of oppression or injustice and are used as a tool for bringing about justice and social change; they are political and intentional (Blackmer Reyes & Curry Rodriguez, 2012; Delgado Bernal et al., 2012).

As demonstrated in which was just detailed, many scholars assign these transformative methodologies varying, but often overlapping themes. The chapters in this book will provide a glimpse into the utilization of these types of transformative methodologies in a way that helps us continue the work. For the purposes of this anthology, we provide several key tenets that we believe are essential for transforming policy, practice, and research in education.

- The descriptions are first-hand accounts (Dixson and Rousseau Anderson, 2018) and/or recount specific memories that speak to collective experiences related to oppressive conditions (Rodriguez-Campo, 2021);

- They "further [challenge] traditional interpretations of what constitutes knowledge and who has the ability to produce it" (Brabeck, 2003, p. 3) and/or counteract the narratives of the dominant group (Delgado, 1989);

- They can take many forms such as speeches, journal or diary entries, interviews, spoken word, and other forms of writing (Blackmer Reyes & Curry Rodríguez, 2012); and

- The personal experience of oppression or injustice is used as a tool for bringing about justice and social change, and it is intentional and political (Blackmer Reyes & Curry Rodriguez, 2012; Delgado Bernal et al., 2012).

These key tenets serve as a guide for better understanding the transformative approaches taken by the authors throughout this book. In addition to the roots and origins, we must also recognize the theoretical underpinnings of these approaches that have built the foundation for the scholarship as we know it today.

Theoretical Underpinnings

As mentioned in the roots and origins section, many of these transformative methodologies are interdisciplinary but stem from similar ambitions to amplify the voices at the margins. Counternarratives, critical storytelling, and counter stories are said to have come from the field of critical legal studies (CLS) to contest the structure and application of law within the United States by understanding the experiences of those who are disproportionately impacted by the judicial system.

Critical race theory (CRT), which also stems from CLS, is often associated with many transformative methodologies due to one of its main tenets being to challenge dominant narratives. Dixson and Rousseau Anderson (2018) share how counternarratives have been an important function of CRT scholarship by giving BIPOC the opportunity to challenge stereotypes of their identity/ies but also to highlight their stories of success that are often excluded from the dominant narrative. Scholars have since expanded the theoretical structure of these transformative methodologies, with their ties to CRT and CLS, into fields of social work, Latina/o/x Studies, critical pedagogy, and education. Many of the scholars already discussed in this chapter provide their own understanding of the theoretical underpinnings of YPAR and *testimonios* and their development.

Although the first YPAR study conducted was credited to the field of critical psychology, Cammarota and Fine (2010) share that the lens through which we examine YPAR is found in critical youth studies. They go on to share that "the pedagogical philosophy on which YPAR is based derives from Freire's (1993) notion of praxis—critical reflection and action. Students study their social contexts through research and apply their knowledge to discover the contingent qualities of life" (Cammarota & Fine, 2010, p. 6). Moreover, YPAR is also influenced by participatory action research movements (PAR) in 20th Century post-colonial societies such as Latin America and Africa, which aimed to democratize knowledge production and support local communities in forwarding local social justice projects (Fals-Borda, 1987; Nabudere, 2008). Regarding *testimonios*, Brabeck (2003) provides context for how they have been used in multidisciplinary studies throughout the field of social science and beyond educational research. Blackmer Reyes and Curry Rodríguez (2012) share how Chicana scholars were empowered by Patricia Hill Collins and other members of the Memphis Center for Women to use *testimonios* as "emerging power" that makes them "agents of knowledge" allowing them to "speak to the importance that oppression [and] the importance that knowledge plays in empowering people" (p. 527). As with YPAR, they share that *testimonios* are situated in the liberationist pedagogy, which was inspired by Paulo Freire (1970). This pedagogy aims to approach writing and other narrative forms to liberate from oppression.

The foundational aspect or theoretical underpinning of *testimonios* is that they aim to bring awareness to the readers and listeners and liberate those experiencing injustice and oppression. Blackmer Reyes and Curry Rodríguez (2012) share, "like Freire's (1970) *Pedagogy of the Oppressed*, testimonio empowers the speaker or narrator to transform the oral to its written representation not as an act of oppression and ignorance but rather as an acknowledgment of the revolutionary aspect of literacy" (p. 527). Conchas and Acevedo (2020) credit Anzaldúan concepts and Chicana feminist theories for their use of *testimonios* to examine institutional mechanisms that shape aspirations, expectations, and achievements of Chicana/o/x students who grew up in marginalized communities and navigated unequal school contexts. Similarly, Jupp, Berumen, and O'Donald refer to Anzaldúa's (1987) work on Chicana and Indigenous identities for the eventual emergence of U.S.-based *testimonio* research in education. They go on to cite the Latina Feminist Group (2001) and Delgado Bernal (1998) for the development of what they call the two largest "taproots" for *testimonio* work. They credit the Latina Feminist Group for producing a "literary, multivocal, collective, narrativized approach to testimonio" (p. 20). Delgado Bernal is credited for emphasizing the purpose of this work as developing "agents of knowledge who participate in intellectual discourse that links experience, research, community, and social change" (p. 21). All these scholars point out important scholarship that contributed to the development and evolution of *testimonios*.

Due to its roots in Latin American Studies, scholars have also linked the theoretical underpinnings of *testimonios* to Latina/o/x Critical Theory (LatCrit) as well as CRT. LatCrit is similar to CRT, but LatCrit is concerned with a progressive sense of a coalitional Latina/o/x pan-ethnicity (Valdes, 1996), and it addresses issues that may not be examined by critical race theorists. Lat-Crit is a theory that elucidates Latina/o/x multidimensional identities and can address the intersectionality of racism, sexism, classism, and other forms of oppression. Pérez Huber (2009) explains, "CRT allows us to focus the research lens on communities of color; LatCrit narrows that lens to focus on Latina/o communities" (p. 394). Considering that the major tenets within LatCrit are also to address issues of injustice and oppression, this theoretical framework uniquely aligns with *testimonios*.

Pérez Huber (2009) provides five points that link *testimonios* with LatCrit: (1) A LatCrit lens exposes structural conditions that contribute to oppression, and *testimonio* allows for people to describe the experiences of that oppression; (2) LatCrit and *testimonio* both operate with the intent to challenge dominant Eurocentric ideologies; (3) *Testimonios* are developed from the experiences of BIPOC, and a LatCrit framework works to validate their experiential knowl-edge: (4) Both LatCrit and *testimonio* aim to represent the collective oppression of a community as opposed to an individual struggle; and (5) LatCrit and *testi-monio* serve to end injustices and advance social justice. As highlighted by these scholars, the theoretical foundation of *testimonios* is comprised of challenging dominant Eurocentric ideologies, amplifying the voices of BIPOC, and creating avenues to dismantle oppressive and unjust systems. In the next section, we look to scholars who have built on these underpinnings and contributed to the evo-lution of transformative approaches through their work in educational research.

Transformative Methodologies in Educational Research

At the start of this chapter, we defined transformative methodologies as approaches to research and knowledge production with three distinct charac-teristics. First, they aim to center the perspectives, experiences, and expertise of BIPOC youth and communities as essential to research. This ensures a com-prehensive, accurate, and inclusive representation of BIPOC in an area that has often deliberately excluded them. The second characteristic challenges what has been called "traditional" or "conventional" social science research that has treated communities of color as "objects" of inquiry. This is a key characteris-tic because it underscores the importance of treating communities of color as the producers of knowledge and ensures they get the recognition they deserve. The third and final characteristic is that they facilitate ethnically and racially minoritized youth to leverage their educational opportunities to express their agency, imagine emancipatory futures, and embody social change. By doing so, these approaches help to foster radical dreaming and imagining that has contributed to monumental social change throughout our nation's history. There are many examples of transformative methodologies used in the field of education and for educational research. For this chapter, we highlight various examples from scholars who have directly utilized transformative methodologies in their research or have cited examples of them in their work.

Scholars, Kinoch et al. (2020), describe their work as an academic counternarrative that examines how Black youth resist dominant discourses within their schools and communities. Through interviews and conversations with BIPOC students who have recently experienced injustice, they create three different research vignettes that serve as counter stories and/or counternarratives that they argue will support the need for a pedagogical agenda that supports social justice. In a 1.5-year participant ethnography conducted by Jimenez (2020), she finds that critical and culturally relevant pedagogies in the classroom can counter deficit perspectives and create a space where students feel comfortable sharing their migrant and English Language Learner experiences. Those experiences ultimately serve as counternarratives to misconceptions and stereotypes that are often placed on these students. Another example of counternarratives is McCarty et al.'s (2006) ethnographic study of Native youth to understand language loss and their effort to revitalize language and culture within education. Their study not only provides the counternarratives of Native youth but helps to support the case for the utilization of transformative methodologies for challenging negative stereotypes or misinformation and preserving language and culture. While the scholars within these examples specify counternarratives, it is important to note that its similarities to counter stories and critical storytelling can lead them to be used interchangeably.

As for *testimonios*, Blackmer Reyes and Curry Rodríguez (2012) provide examples of how they have been used as short narratives to understand the experiences of undocumented students. The students reject the labels that are often placed on them and challenge them by creating their own narratives. The examples demonstrate how institutions of higher education can also adopt *testimonios* as a formal tool to understand, acknowledge, and actively intervene in systems of exclusion. A more recent example of the use of *testimonios* is found in Larios (2020), which shows how *testimonios* coupled with technology can add to their empowering nature. While many other scholars have acknowledged that *testimonios* can come in many different forms, Larios' use of digital *testimonios* demonstrates how they can be used as a process for healing, but also how technology can increase the visibility and impact of the stories that seek to resist systems of oppression and injustice. Larios (2020) states:

> The process of creating a digital testimonio is a process of great reflection and patience with oneself, an essential tool for others to also initiate a healing journey. Creating digital testimonios allows space to reflect on our experiences and to communicate those experiences in a way that honors the storytellers. Having the autonomy to share our *testimonios* is very empowering and generates the conversation of who deserves to hear *nuestras* voices. The method/methodology of digital testimonios is a powerful way to share the experiences of those who have been forced into the margins to speak up and to reclaim their voices and testimonios on their own terms, which from my own experiences, has been a liberating process. (p. 322)

Another unique approach to *testimonios* is found in Montes and Castro (2020), which shows how two school principals utilized *testimonios* as *conversaciones* among each other to better understand the impact of COVID-19 on their role as educational leaders tasked with supporting or promoting student learning. They coupled their *conversaciones* with asynchronous journaling to help them reflect and capture information about their personal accounts that may not have been captured in their *conversaciones*. Their use of *testimonios* also helped them better understand their role as principals and their responsibility to reassess and transform their policies and practices. Montes and Castro (2020) share, "It is imperative that we not remain passive or silent and we take this opportunity to use our privilege and examine our current practice and our educational philosophy and values. Part of moving forward starts with a level of acknowledgment, considerable introspection, and collective work to reassess and revisit what we do, why we do it, in the best interest of whom, and according to whom" (p. 4). Both Larios (2020) and Montes and Castro (2020) demonstrate how *testimonios* can be versatile and how *testimonios* can be used in a way that is most comfortable for the person sharing their story.

We can also look to Conchas and Acevedo's (2020) book, *The Chicana/o/x Dream*, which utilized narratives and *testimonios* to understand the experiences of Chicana/o/x students participating in several unique research projects at community colleges and at four-year universities. Their use of this transformative approach uncovered how existing colonial mechanisms within the U.S. schooling system create barriers for Chicana/o/x students to reach their educational goals. Despite the constraints they faced, the *testimonios* show these students empowered themselves by turning adversities into opportunities with the support of emotional, aspirational, social, and cultural capitals. Conchas and Acevedo (2020) show how the use of *testimonios* captures the way Chicana/o/x students moved beyond the realities surrounding them to perceive positivity, potential, and success in their present and future selves.

Lastly, Rodriguez-Campo (2021) points us to the collective work of Moraga and Anzaldúa (2015), which has sought to decenter hegemonic methodologies and legitimize transformative approaches. She goes on to say that, "21st century *testimonio* has been used by education researchers to critically examine the education and *educación* of Latina/o/x people in every stage of the schooling pipeline through the work of Delgado Bernal et al. (2012), Pérez Huber (2009), and in *Telling to Live: Latina Feminist Testimonios* by the Latina Feminist Group (2001)" (p. 4). Additionally, she highlights the growing prevalence of *testimonios* in educational research and the amount of literature that has already been developed to prove their effectiveness as a research tool for empowerment. She shares, "additional research is required to understand the extent to which *testimonio* can serve as a method, methodology, and pedagogy for healing across the PK–20 spectrum" (Rodriguez-Campo, 2021, p. 9).

Testimonios, YPAR, counternarratives, critical storytelling, and counter stories are all approaches or methodologies that allow BIPOC to reflect on the traumatizing experiences of injustice and provide the opportunity for them to challenge the stereotypes or narratives that augment injustice. Additionally, they provide scholars and educators with the necessary information to decenter whiteness in their research, curriculum, and pedagogical decisions. In the next section, we introduce the idea of love, imagination, and freedom dreaming and discuss the role of transformative methodologies in amplifying these notions, which we use to organize this book.

Repertoires of Racial Resistance Around Three Themes

One cannot discuss transformative works and movements without acknowledging the role of Kelley's (2002) seminal piece on transformative vision, aspiration, and dreaming. Kelley discusses the impact of imagination on empowering youth and adult allies to envision a future they wish to create and live within. His concept of freedom dreaming has inspired educators, policymakers, and scholars to reimagine education as a space of opportunity and transformation. For educators and practitioners, it has led to the development of pedagogies that aim to give voice to and empower historically marginalized groups of students. For policymakers, freedom dreaming encourages equitable policies and systemic reform. For scholars, Kelley's ideas have sparked critical discussions around radical imagination and hope for contributing to transformative change for liberating BIPOC within U.S. schooling systems.

Prominent BIPOC scholars have continued to build on this notion through their use, development, and evolution of transformative approaches that have changed how we view and conduct research. As Mayes et al. (2022) explain, "freedom dreaming engages a radical imagination that recognizes and catalyzes by the struggle for change while working toward a new future where humanity is restored and freedom, liberation, and joy are centered" (p. 5). Through this lens, we've examined the innovative approaches taken by the authors throughout this book to organize and craft an anthology that complements and strengthens the existing foundational works of literature.

The three themes that organize this book represent a comprehensive exploration of transformative methodologies used to examine topics in education, resistance, and social activism. These themes delve into the critical role of empowering young voices, the innovative approaches of school leaders, and the creation of transformative spaces that empower BIPOC students. At the heart of these themes is an overarching focus on resistance and freedom dreaming, transformative leadership, and supportive environments for serving as catalysts to social and educational transformation. The themes highlight the need to amplify the voices of youth, strengthen adult allyship, and cultivate safe spaces in and outside of schools. Together, these themes offer a multifaceted perspective.

Theme 1: Transformative Methodologies and Centering Youth Voice as a Catalyst for Social Change

This theme focuses on the critical role that young people's experiences and perspectives play as the driving forces for transformative change in and out of school. Considering that youth have often been excluded from having a voice in educational decision-making, there is a gap in the literature that captures the authentic experiences of these students. This theme, as underscored in the chapters, emphasizes the importance of youth as not just beneficiaries but as active agents and contributors to social change. Each chapter within this theme explores different aspects of how youth voices can be centered and empowered to effect meaningful change.

Theme 2: Transformative Methodologies and Critical Reflections of School Leaders

This theme explores the innovative and thoughtful strategies school leaders and adult allies utilize to support and empower historically marginalized student groups. Adult allies play a critical role in supporting, encouraging, and amplifying the voices of BIPOC students as they navigate their educational journeys. The chapters within this theme offer a unique perspective on how school leaders can and have implemented transformative practices and policies to transform the existing U.S. schooling system. The transformative methodologies used within this section include critical reflection and action on the part of adult allies to acknowledge and intervene in the systemic inequities faced by marginalized students.

Theme 3: Transformative Methodologies and Spaces for Fostering Youth Empowerment

This theme offers the organizational lens and emphasizes the necessary step of creating and fostering transformative spaces that empower and support young people. Such spaces have historically been undermined and underfunded but have persevered as hubs of culture, community, and resistance. This empowerment is seen as a key to enabling youth to both resist systemic inequity and to dream of a better world they wish to see. The chapters in this theme provide insights from an organizational perspective, offering practical steps that can be employed by other institutions and groups that seek to facilitate this type of transformative change and empowerment.

Organization of the Anthology

The book is comprised of this introduction and 15 chapters. The book is organized around three themes, with five chapters in each part. We chose these three themes based on a thorough analysis of 95 chapters submitted to our call for chapter proposals. All the chapters speak to the conceptual framework of repertoires of racial resistance and pedagogical dreaming. The chapters present empirically informed studies that paint a picture of systematic inequity within the context of history, policy, and structures of education and society. Within this picture, the bleak outlook of normative inequities is contrasted and challenged by success stories of minoritized young people and their adult allies who utilize their educational opportunities to advocate for social justice within their schools and communities. These chapters aim to offer a clearer sense of how young people from different racial, ethnic, and geographic backgrounds resist structural and cultural barriers to their education and aspirations.

Theme I, *Transformative Methodologies and Centering Youth Voice as a Catalyst for Social Change*, includes chapters that center on the experiences and voices of students as critical components for transformative change. In Chapter 1, Orubba Almansouri, through the creation of counterspaces, explores how a group of Yemeni boys organized together to advocate for themselves to establish a sense of belonging in their transnational community. These students utilized their agency to ensure that they were part of both the inner community of their high school and a larger transnational community in New York City. Considering that Yemeni migrants make up the 6th-largest ethnic Arab group in the U.S., capturing the experiences of students within this often-underrepresented community has profound implications for transformative educational change.

In Chapter 2, Rachel Brand utilized Youth Participatory Action Research (YPAR) to examine the pervasive problem of food insecurity among college students in California. Utilizing these student-centered research methods, the author engages in conversations with students to assess what strategies they would employ to tackle this pressing issue. Collaborating with a group of undergraduate students to develop a YPAR project, the findings show that this transformative approach gave students an opportunity to grapple with both food insecurity and their own role as changemakers. Through resistance to their university's food system and engagement in collective action, the students who participated in this project developed a newfound sense of agency, allowing them to dream of new possibilities for a food-secure campus. This chapter looks at how dreaming collectively changed the students themselves and offered new insights into strategies to address food insecurity at their college and beyond.

In Chapter 3, Brianna R. Ramirez utilizes a *plática* methodology, which draws from Chicana feminist epistemologies and engages students as collaborators and co-constructors of knowledge production. This approach captures and documents how Chicana/x and Latina/x daughters from mixed-status immigrant families in California engage in activating their agency and resistance to support their families and collective survival and success in everyday life. The author focuses on the critical discussions with Latina and Chicana undergraduate students as a way to explore how spirituality shapes their care and their activism in their families and communities. Drawing from Delgado Bernal and Aleman (2017), Ramirez explains how spirituality promotes transformative ruptures, or moments of interruption, of systemic marginality, chipping away at the white supremacist, heteropatriarchal, and colonial ideologies and systems. Furthermore, the chapter offers a novel framework for situating spirituality as a powerful catalyst for resistance to oppression and a pathway to conceptualize educational transformation and radical futures.

In Chapter 4, Jie Y. Park, Borodine Chery, Eric J. DeMeulenaere, Elsabet Franklin, Leyla Knight, Zabrina Richards, and Chloe Wing Ching Yau use critical co-constructed autoethnography to foreground the role of care, community, and relational practice in racial justice work at a predominantly white university in the Northeast of the United States. The authors utilize Black fugitivity as theory and method, arguing that through care work that builds kinship and intimacy, activists, students, and social justice organizers can create humanizing communities for larger-scale freedom dreaming. The chapter shows how university faculty and undergraduate students can collaborate to facilitate a race dialogue program on their campus.

In Chapter 5, Ma. Glenda Lopez Wui presents the counternarrative of Mina (pseudonym), a female Muslim American student leader from a Southern city of the U.S., whose imaginings and dream for social justice for her fellow Muslims led to her founding the Muslim Student Association in high school to counter Islamophobia. The author shares how Mina continued her civic engagement in college and her dreams of serving Muslim communities in adulthood through medical missions. Mina's imaginings and civic engagement were nurtured by her Muslim identity and supportive familial and school environments. This chapter captures Mina's educational journey by amplifying her voice and providing insight into the impact of in-school and out-of-school support systems.

Theme II, *Transformative Methodologies and Critical Reflections of School Leaders*, offers a lens into the perceptive and innovative approaches of educational leaders and other adult allies that aim to support historically marginalized student groups. In Chapter 6, Anna Mei Gubbins and Aubry Threlkeld use collaborative autoethnography to share how they collaborated with two student groups to organize around social identity and social justice missions (Cumming-Potvin, 2023) at a private liberal arts college in the Northeastern United States. The two student groups represent people from historically marginalized groups: members of the 2SLGBTQIA+ community (mostly racialized as white) and students who identify through their advocacy for racial justice (predominately BIPOC students). The authors share their process of reflecting and encouraging each other's active support of students on campus. This chapter presents a collaborative autoethnography (Bochner and Ellis, 2016) focused on Black feminist theories of intersectionality (Bilge and Collins, 2016; Combahee River Collective, 1977; Crenshaw, 1989), wherein the authors, as adult allies with a range of identities, come to a deeper understanding of their collective commitment and joy while simultaneously navigating challenges from within a centrist/conservative predominantly white-serving institution (PWI).

In Chapter 7, Ava Jackson and Corey Winchester present their theorizations and imaginings, dialectical conversations, and critical dialogue to explore how teaching and learning in a high school history class in a Midwest suburb outside of Chicago transformed normative enclosures of teacher-student dichotomies. The authors employed critical pedagogical practices in the classroom to encourage young people to use historical thinking as a practice of social dreaming. The authors explain this process and how it was made possible through an axiologically-driven research-practice partnership.

In Chapter 8, Reva Jaffe-Walter and Kathleen Rucker use interviews from two larger ethnographic studies conducted within a network of high schools in New York that exclusively serves multilingual immigrant youth from 119 countries to provide examples of solidarity, in which school leaders and teachers have come together to resist incoherent policies and to dream of more responsive policies and practices for their students. In doing so, the authors consider how creative policy negotiation can support more humanizing schools for immigrant multilingual learners and their teachers.

In Chapter 9, Jorge F. Rodriguez, PhD, Bernadine Cortina, and Jessica Tonai utilize storytelling to share the experiences of students and community members from a youth media advocacy and research project. The authors share how the project has developed a media platform where youth and community members tell their stories and advocate for their community using any medium of expression (Kelner & Share, 2005, 2013; Quijada et al., 2013). The authors use media and feminist theory to interpret, document, and perceive young people's expressions to be dreamweaving that supports and prepares them to navigate oppressive systems that often engage youth toward erasure and marginalization.

In Chapter 10, Simona Goldin, Danita Mason-Hogans, Justin Clyburn, and Shelby Freeman outline the work of organizing a course for college freshmen at a Southern university, with the course being centered around multiculturalism and the histories of racial violence and injustice in the university town. The project and the chapter are a collaboration between a university researcher, a local historian, an undergraduate student, and a local educator. The chapter describes the authors' pedagogical approach, including *testimonios* from long-standing community members. The chapter shares an excerpt from Mason-Hogans' lecture to university students, which recounts the historical memories of injustice and the extractive relationship between the university and the town and its

Black community. Moreover, the chapter showcases student-led research and analysis of the course outcomes, which revealed broadly promising but uneven ways racial literacy developed among individual students in the class. This chapter underscores how university spaces can provide powerful opportunities for community and student collaborations toward racial justice, even as those institutions are implicated in local histories of racial injustice

Theme III, *Transformative Methodologies and Spaces for Fostering Youth Empowerment*, emphasizes the importance of the creation of spaces for empowering youth to resist and dream. These chapters provide an organizational lens for how to contribute to transformative change. In Chapter 11, Charlotte Austria, Chelsea Chhem, J Jimenez, May Lin, and Madison San Luis share their experiences with art-making as Cambodian and Filipino American artists and youth organizers. The authors explore how art can be conceptualized as a form of dreaming that connects us with ancestors who have always waged resistance against imperialism and neo-colonialism. The authors express that by making time to practice art collectively, we prefigure our future dreams, showing that youth are powerful in their present creativity. In this chapter, the authors imagine and make possible alternative futures shaped by imagination, joy, and collectivity.

In Chapter 12, Carlos R. Casanova, PhD and Eric Alvarez employ critical ethnography to examine an after-school program in rural Iowa serving Latina/o/x youth. In this chapter, the authors highlight three youth space practices that emerged when Latina/o/x youth and adult youth workers collaborated on co-creating and implementing a youth space designed to promote Latina/o/x youth's critical understanding of social injustice and taking action. Within the chapter, the authors underscore that when Latina/o/x youth reimagine a positive vision of the world, their vision includes a youth space that centers on their history of activism, a pedagogy guided by reflection, dialogue, and adult staff who stand in solidarity with Latinx youth at social protests.

In Chapter 13, Olga M. Correa shares the process of developing a virtual counterspace with students in Northern New Jersey. The author expresses how the virtual youth-led space outside the traditional classroom promoted Kelley's (2002) idea of freedom dreams and highlighted the assets that Black and Latina/o/x students embody. The author engages in conversations with Black and Latina/o/x students as they express their concerns about navigating these unjust realities during the COVID-19 pandemic. The chapter contributes to scholarship that examines how school segregation reinforces stereotypes of inferiority among students and fosters racial and ethnic biases about under-represented groups.

In Chapter 14, David Flores utilizes oral history to examine the role of religion during the Chicana/o/x movement in East Los Angeles. Using archival data and oral interviews with some of the principal organizers of the Chicana/o/x movement, the author shows how the Church of Epiphany should be remembered as one of the most critical spaces of *el movimiento* that helped spark the radical imagination of Chicana/o/x youth during the Mexican American Civil Rights Movement of the late 1960s. The author discusses what we are missing by ignoring the potential of religious institutions and leaders uniquely positioned to support young people to dream, cultivate, and enact a more just future.

In Chapter 15, Gerardo Mancilla shares the collaborative process of developing a pre-college program with undocumented students in Wisconsin. The author describes how the program went from dreaming to actualization, from the creation of the curriculum to the implementation of the various modules that addressed different aspects of applying for college. He shares how the ten high school students who participated left with more knowledge and preparation to navigate their educational journeys. The chapter discusses the important lessons learned during the program and insights from the conversations and resources that were shared.

Paving New Directions

The illuminating chapters in this book highlight needs and promises within education through transformative methodologies. As we specify throughout this chapter, transformative methodologies center the perspectives, experiences, and expertise of BIPOC youth and their communities. They counter traditional social science frameworks that have often treated communities of color as "objects" to be studied. Additionally, they promote an active and participatory role for BIPOC in research by empowering them to leverage their educational opportunities to express their agency, imagine emancipatory futures, and embody social change. ***We hope to have made our point clear: that*** *transformational education research need not be associated with one method of research only or with a finite set of theoretical frameworks.*

This timely collection of chapters elevates different types of transformative methodological approaches to paint a more vivid picture of problems and promises within the system. Research in the field of education still has many areas of inquiry left unexplored, and this book proposes several considerations for scholars to engage in ongoing discussion. We hope that organizing these chapters within the three themes—Transformative Methodologies and Centering Youth Voices as Catalysts for Social Change, Transformative Methodologies and Critical Reflections of School Leaders, and Transformative Methodologies and Spaces for Fostering Youth Empowerment—fosters productive understanding, discussion, and movement toward transformative components of educational experiences for BIPOC students. The aim is to promote imagination and dreaming among students despite the continuing issues of inequity within the U.S. schooling system.

The authors in this provocative anthology provide a critical examination of the effort and resistance of young people as they stand up to the inequity that continues to plague disenfranchised populations. In so doing, this book goes beyond presenting critical case studies of resistance and adult allyship and (a) takes a rare look at in-school and out-of-school success stories on a comparative level instead of those depicting only failure. For example, in Chapter 1, Almansouri highlighted the creation of counterspaces in school by a group of Yemeni boys aiming to foster self-advocacy and belonging. These students exercised their agency to integrate into the school's core community and connect with a larger transnational community in New York City; (b) explores the social and cultural processes that enable BIPOC students to escape the unequal structures of U.S. schooling to perform well in school. For instance, in Chapter 3, Ramirez gave a glimpse into the critical discussions with undergraduate Latina and Chicana students who sought to examine the role of spirituality in shaping their care and their activism in their families and communities. The author introduces a novel framework that posits spirituality as a powerful catalyst for resistance to oppression and outlines a vision for transformative educational change and radical futures; (c) illuminates how educators and schools can address these issues by becoming increasingly attuned to the sociocultural worlds in which their students live. For example, in Chapter 6, Gubbins and Threlkeld presented an autoethnography of two adult allies who collaborated with and supported students belonging to two historically marginalized groups—the 2SLGBTQIA+ community and BIPOC community. The authors shared their process of reflection and how they actively supported each other as adult allies; and (d), paves the way toward overcoming challenges that historically disadvantaged groups face to receive equitable, high-quality education. For instance, in Chapter 8, Jaffe-Walter and Rucker provided examples of solidarity in which school leaders and educators came together to resist inequitable policies and envision more responsive policies and practices for their students. Through this analysis, the authors explored the potential of creative policy negotiation to foster more nurturing school spaces for immigrant multilingual learners and their educators.

In the face of the social, institutional, and economic barriers that exist within the paradoxical system that is the U.S. schooling system, it is crucial to also underline the agency and resilience of ethnically and racially marginalized groups as they work to survive and take up the roles of historical actors by making positive social change locally and globally. For instance, in Chapter 12, Casanova and Alvarez highlighted an after-school initiative in rural Iowa dedicated to serving Latina/o/x youth through collaboration between youth and adults. Through their distinct practices, they create and implement spaces that enhance critical awareness among Latina/o/x youth to actively intervene in injustice and promote social justice. Rather than focusing on top-down solutions to educational and social inequity, this book centers on grassroots and community-centered examples of resistance and social change within diverse educational settings. In Chapter 14, for example, Flores explored the role of religion and the Church of Epiphany in East Los Angeles as a critical space of culture, community, and resistance during the Chicana/o/x Movement. Through the personal experiences of principal organizers of the movement, the authors reveal how this critical space helped to spark the radical imagination of Chicana/o/x youth in the midst of their resistance efforts of the late 1960s. Developmental scholars have described how grassroots youth organizing can provide ethnically and racially minoritized young people crucial opportunities to become individual civic actors and develop the civic capacity of their communities and neighborhoods.

This anthology's exploration into the multifaceted nature of resistance, agency, allyship, imagination, and dreaming among BIPOC youth and communities as they stand up against inequities offers important insights for policy, practice, and research. The practical implications of these authentic accounts can significantly benefit educators and educational leaders and encourage them to adopt and implement more nuanced, culturally-responsive, and transformative approaches. By highlighting stories of success, engagement, and empowerment, this book can serve as a guide for reimagining educational spaces that are tailored to the needs and aspirations of historically marginalized students. Additionally, the case studies in this book break through the barriers created by traditional research by acknowledging that BIPOC students and communities are experts in their experiences and a central component for understanding and transforming education. The anthology, therefore, not only helps to fill existing gaps in literature but also serves as a critical resource for the development and evolution of educational practices and policies by grounding them in equity, respect, and the collective struggle for a socially-just society.

Furthermore, this book also highlights the need to understand hope and dreaming as concomitant to concepts of youth resistance. At the same time, resistance is a necessary but insufficient condition for social justice. As historian Robin D. G. Kelly (2002) reminds us, dreams and imagination provide much of the essential raw material for emancipatory projects, both big and small, and individual and collective. As such, this book specifically focuses on examples where ethnically and racially minoritized young people and their adult allies engage in pedagogical dreaming as part of their resistance efforts. The achievement cases provide a road map toward educational opportunity and success in communities and schools. We believe that the case studies will make you think, and we hope, make you act, and help us reclaim education as truly the best hope to achieve the American dream.

"The idea of dreaming—and in many Black scholars' views, radical dreaming—isn't a fluffy notion," as Dugan (2022, para. 9) reminds us. Dugan (2002) goes on to say, "If we look at some of the people who have inspired generations and catapulted us forward, they have often been dreamers—people who had a vision for a world that did not yet exist" (para. 9). A truly remarkable feat that we hope this anthology illuminates through the voices of youth and their adult allies.

Reference

Anyon, Y., Bender, K., Kennedy, H., & Dechants, J. (2018). A systematic review of youth participatory action research (YPAR) in the United States: Methodologies, youth outcomes, and future directions. *Health Education & Behavior, 45*(6), 865-878.

Anzaldúa, G. (1987). *Borderlands/la frontera: The new Mestiza.* Aunt Lute Books.

Bernal, D. D., & Villalpando, O. (2002). An apartheid of knowledge in academia: The struggle over the" legitimate" knowledge of faculty of color. *Equity & excellence in education, 35*(2), 169-180.

Blackmer Reyes, K., & Curry Rodríguez, J. E. (2012). *Testimonio:* Origins, terms, and resources. *Equity & Excellence in Education, 45*(3), 525–538. https://doi.org/10.1080/10665684.2012.698571

Bilge, S. & Collins, P. H. (2016) *Intersectionality.* Polity Press.

Bochner, A. P., & Ellis, C. (2016). *Evocative autoethnography: Writing lives and telling stories.* Routledge.

Booker, M. (2002). Stories of Violence: Use of Testimony in a Support Group for Latina American Battered Women. In L. H. Collins, M. R. Dunlap, & J. C. Chrisler (Eds.), *Charting a new course for feminist psychology* (pp. 307-321). Prager.

Brabeck, K. (2003). IV. Testimonio: A strategy for collective resistance, cultural survival and building solidarity. *Feminism & Psychology, 13*(2), 252–258. https://doi.org/10.1177/0959353503013002009

Cammarota, J., & Fine, M. (2010). Youth participatory action research: A pedagogy for transformational resistance. In J. Cammarota & M. Fine (Eds.), *Revolutionizing Education: Youth participatory action research in motion* (pp. 9-20). Routledge.

Caraballo, L., Lozenski, B. D., Lyiscott, J. J., & Morrell, E. (2017). YPAR and critical epistemologies: Rethinking education research. *Review of Research in Education, 41*(1), 311-336.

Cienfuegos, A. J., & Monelli, C. (1983). The testimony of political repression as a therapeutic instrument. *American Journal of Orthopsychiatry, 53*(1), 43–51. https://doi.org/10.1111/j.1939-0025.1983.tb03348.x

Combahee River Collective (1977). *The Combahee River collective statement. United States.* [Web Archive] Retrieved from the Library of Congress, https://www.loc.gov/item/lcwaN0028151/

Conchas, G. Q., & Acevedo, N. (2020). *The Chicana/o/x dream: Hope, resistance, and educational success.* Harvard Education Press.

Cooper, C. S. (1994). Storytelling in the Basic Course for the Promotion of Cultural Diversity.

Crenshaw, K. (1989) Demarginalizing the intersection of race and sex: A Black Feminist critique of antidiscrimination doctrine, feminist theory and antiracist politics. *University of Chicago Legal Forum*. Article 8. https://chicagounbound. uchicago.edu/uclf/vol1989/iss1/8

Cruz, C. (2012). Making curriculum from scratch: *Testimonio* in an urban Classroom. *Equity & Excellence in Education, 45*(3), 460-471, DOI: 10.1080/10665684. 2012.698185

Cumming-Potvin, W.M. (2023). *LGBTQI+ allies in education, advocacy, activism, and participatory collaborative research*. Routledge.

Delgado, R. (1989). Storytelling for oppositionists and others: A plea for narrative. *Michigan Law Review, 87*(8), 2411–2441. https://doi.org/10.2307/1289308

Delgado Bernal, D. (1998). Using a Chicana feminist epistemology in educational research. *Harvard Educational Review, 68*(4), 555-583.

Delgado Bernal, D. & Alemán, E. (2017). *Transforming Educational Pathways for Chicana/o Students: A Critical Race Feminista Praxis*. Teachers College Press.

Delgado Bernal, D., Burciaga, R., & Flores Carmona, J. (2012). Chicana/Latina *testimonios*: Mapping the methodological, pedagogical, and political. *Equity & Excellence in Education, 45*(3), 363–372. https://doi.org/10.1080/10665684.2012 .698149

Desai, S. R. (2019). Youth participatory action research: The nuts and bolts as well as the roses and thorns. In K.K. Stunk & L. A. Locke (Eds.), *Research Methods for Social Justice and Equity in Education* (pp. 125-135).

Dixson, A. D., & Rousseau Anderson, C. (2018). Where are we? Critical race theory in education 20 years later. *Peabody Journal of Education, 93*(1), 121-131. https:// doi.org/10.1080/0161956X.2017.1403194

Dotson, K. (2011). Tracking epistemic violence, tracking practices of silencing. *Hypatia, 26*(2), 236-257.

Dugan, J. (2022, October 1). *Radical dreaming for education now*. ASCD. https://www. ascd.org/el/articles/radical-dreaming-for-education-now

Fals-Borda, O. (1987). The application of participatory action-research in Latin America. *International sociology, 2*(4), 329-347.

Freire, P. (1970) *Pedagogy of the Oppressed*. Translated by Myra Bergman Ramos, Continuum.

Freire, P. (1982). Creating alternative research methods: Learning to do it by doing it. In B. Hall, A. Gillette, & R. Tandon (Eds.), *Creating knowledge: A monopoly* (pp. 29-37).

Freire, P. (1993). *Pedagogy of the Oppressed*. Continuum.

Gutiérrez, K. D., Becker, B. L., Espinoza, M. L., Cortes, K. L., Cortez, A., Lizárraga, J. R. Rivero, E., Villegas, K., & Yin, P. (2019). Youth as historical actors in the production of possible futures. *Mind, culture, and activity, 26*(4), 291-308.

Jimenez, R. M. (2020). Community cultural wealth pedagogies: Cultivating autoethnographic counternarratives and migration capital. *American Educational Research Journal, 57*(2), 775–807. https://doi.org/10.3102/0002831219866148

Jupp, J. C., Berumen, F. C., & O'Donald, K. (2018). Advancing testimonio traditions in educational research: A synoptic rendering. *Journal of Latinos and Education, 17*(1), 18-37.

Kelley, Robin D. G. (2002). *Freedom dreams: The Black radical imagination.* Beacon Press.

Kellner, D., & Share, J. (2005). Toward critical media literacy: Core concepts, debates, organizations, and policy. *Discourse: studies in the cultural politics of education, 26*(3), 369-386.

Kinloch, V., Penn, C., & Burkhard, T. (2020). Black lives matter: Storying, identities, and counternarratives. *Journal of Literacy Research, 52*(4), 382–405. https://doi.org/10.1177/1086296X20966372

Lac, V. T., Antunes, A. C., Daniel, J., & Mackey, J. (2022). What is the role of adult facilitators in critical participatory action research? Employing affective labor while navigating the politics and the perils alongside minoritized youth researchers. *Educational Policy, 36*(1), 142-168.

Larios, S. E. (2020). Digital Testimonios: A personal journey towards healing and empowerment. *Journal of Curriculum and Pedagogy, 17*(3), 318-322.

Lather, P. (1998). Critical pedagogy and its complicities: A praxis of stuck places. *Educational theory, 48*(4).

Latina Feminist Group. (2001). *Telling to live: Latina feminist testimonios.* Duke University Press.

Mayes, R. D., Edirmanasinghe, N., Ieva, K., & Washington, A. R. (2022). Liberatory school counseling practices to promote freedom dreaming for Black youth. *Frontiers in Education 7.*

McCarty, T. L., Romero, M. E., & Zepeda, O. (2006). Reclaiming the gift: Indigenous youth counter-narratives on Native language loss and revitalization. *American Indian Quarterly, 30*(1/2), 28-48.

McIntyre, A. (2000). Constructing meaning about violence, school, and community: Participatory action research with urban youth. *The Urban Review, 32*, 123-154.

Miller, R., Liu, K., & Ball, A. F. (2020). Critical counter-narrative as transformative methodology for educational equity. *Review of Research in Education, 44*(1), 269-300.

Mirra, N., Garcia, A., & Morrell, E. (2015). *Doing youth participatory action research: Transforming inquiry with researchers, educators, and students.* Routledge.

Montes, I. R., & Castro, L. P. (2020). Finding hope, healing and liberation beyond covid-19 within a context of captivity and carcerality. *Penn GSE Perspectives on Urban Education, 18*(1).

Moraga, C., & Anzaldúa, G. (Eds.). (2015). *This bridge called my back: Writings by radical women of color.* SUNY Press.

Nabudere, D. W. (2008). Research, activism, and knowledge production. *Engaging contradictions: Theory, politics, and methods of activist scholarship,* 62-87.

Pérez Huber, L. (2009). Disrupting apartheid of knowledge: *Testimonio* as methodology in Latina/o critical race research in education. *International Journal of Qualitative Studies in Education, 22*(6), 639–654. https://doi.org/10.1080/09518390903333863

Quijada Cerecer, D. A., Cahill, C., & Bradley, M. (2013). Toward a critical youth policy praxis: Critical youth studies and participatory action research. *Theory into practice, 52*(3), 216-223.

Ritterbusch, A. E. (2019). Empathy at knifepoint: The dangers of research and lite pedagogies for social justice movements. *Antipode, 51*(4), 1296-1317.

Rodriguez-Campo, M. (2021). Testimonio in education. *Oxford Research Encyclopedia of Education.* https://doi.org/10.1093/acrefore/9780190264093.013.1346

Smith, L. T. (1999). *Decolonizing methodologies: Research and indigenous peoples.* Zed Books.

Spivak, G. C. (1988). Can the subaltern speak? In C. Nelson & L. Grossberg (Eds.), *Marxism and the interpretation of culture* (pp. 21–78). University of Illinois Press.

Torre, M. E., Stoudt, B. G., Manoff, E., & Fine, M. (2017). Critical participatory action research on state violence: Bearing wit(h)ness across fault lines of power, privilege, and dispossession. In N. K. Denzin & Y. S. Lincoln (Eds.), *The SAGE Handbook of Qualitative Research* (5th ed.) (pp. 492–515).

Valdes, F. (1996). Latina/o ethnicities, critical race theory, and post-identity politics in postmodern legal culture: From practices to possibilities. *Berkeley La Raza Law Journal, 9*(1), 1.

Villenas, S., Deyhle, D., & Parker, L. (2019). Critical race theory and praxis: Chicano (a)/Latino (a) and Navajo struggles for dignity, educational equity, and social justice. In L. Parker, D. Deyhle, & S. Villenas (Eds.), *Race Is… Race Isn't: Critical Race Theory and Qualitative Studies in Education* (pp. 31-52). Routledge.

Zimmerman, M. (2004). Testimonio. In M.S. Lewis-Black, A. Bryman, & T. Futing Liao (Eds.), *The Sage Encyclopedia of Social Science Research Methods,* Sage Publication, California.

CHAPTER 1

Fostering Belonging:
How Yemeni Boys Create Counterspaces in a NYC High School

Orubba Almansouri

Introduction

IMMIGRANT YOUTH NOW make up 25% of the United States (U.S.) population that is under the age of eighteen (Duong et al., 2016). According to the National Center for Education Statistics, in the 2022-2023 school year, there were five million English Language Learners (ELL) enrolled in K-12 schools across the U.S. (National, 2023). This chapter explores Yemeni youth's sense of belonging in a New York City (NYC) public school that was encouraged through a process of dreaming and imagining a collective identity. To establish this sense of belonging, a simple assimilation is not sufficient. Hall (2004) argues that immigrant youth are not adopting cultural traditions in the process of forming their identity; rather, there is a continuous process of negotiation that happens within their affinities to negotiate belonging. For the Yemeni boys in this study, belonging comes in what Abu El-Haj (2007) refers to as multilayered affiliations. These affiliations transcend U.S. borders to create transnational communities through the development of multilayered identities and affiliations. These transnational communities are fueled by the boys' imagined community and by their dreams of fitting into a new space while remaining connected to their Yemeni identity. In this chapter, I argue that in order to establish a sense of belonging to their perceived transnational community,

Yemeni boys utilized their agency to create counterspaces in their high school to ensure that they are part of both the inner community of the school and a larger transnational community.

In their work on counterspaces, Solórzano and Yosso (2002) and Yosso (2006) describe counterspaces as spaces where marginalized People of Color can come together to build community and solidarity with one another while challenging deficit discourses about their communities. Through my work with youth, specifically in this project with Yemeni boys, I aim to push this definition deeper and argue that counterspaces offer youth a tool to build transnational communities while fostering a sense of belonging in their new environments, all while building and maintaining networks of support that allow youth to continue dreaming. I built my understanding of transnational communities from the works of Abu El-Haj (2007, 2010), Anderson (1983/1991), Castles (2004), and Portes (1999). In his definition of transnational activities, Portes explains that they "take place on a recurrent basis across national borders and … require a regular and significant commitment of time by participants. Such activities … may be initiated by more modest individuals such as immigrants and their home country kin and relations. These activities are not limited to economic enterprises but include political, cultural and religious initiatives" (p. 464), as we will see the Yemeni students carry out in this study.

My work on belonging draws on the work of Abu El-Haj (2007, 2010, 2015), Jaffe-Walter and Lee (2018), and Yuval-Davis (2011). According to Yuval-Davis (2011), there are three factors that play a role in the construction of belonging: (1) social locations, (i.e., race, gender, or class); (2) people's "identifications and emotional attachments to various collectivities and groupings" (p. 12), which become more dominant when they feel their individual or collective identities are threatened; and (3) ethical and political value systems that play a role in the individual degree of belonging for themselves or those around them, hence how attachments and actions are assessed and valued by the self and others. This chapter is organized into four parts. First is a brief methodology section, followed by a three-part deep narrative analysis and discussion. After that is a summative discussion section followed by a conclusion.

Methodology

This chapter draws on ethnographic work from a larger research project that explores how alums of a New York City high school reflect on navigating learning in a new language, a new culture, and a new land, all while preparing for college and career paths. The school is a public high school in New York City that serves recently arrived immigrant youth and English Language Learners. It is part of a larger network of international public schools that serves immigrant ELL youth through a non-traditional model of education.

Taking into consideration Yuval-Davis's (2011) three facets of belonging: social locations, identification and collective grouping, and ethical and political value systems, this research aims to answer the following questions:

a. How do alumni students of this NYC high school reflect on their schooling experience through their identities as language learners and immigrants?

b. What, if any, are the shared experiences of these alumni that allowed them to successfully complete graduation requirements for NYC high schools and go forward into college or career paths?

This chapter will focus on data collected from one of the focus groups, which was done with five Yemeni male students who are recent alumni of the school in focus, as well as follow-up interviews with each of them. To gather data for the project on alumni experiences, there was a call through the school's alumni network, asking for participants to join the focus group. As a previous educator at the high school, I had access to this network. The students in this focus group had been friends since they started at school and continued their friendship after graduation. When they heard I was conducting the project, the five boys volunteered to do a focus group together. After the focus group was conducted, I spoke individually with each participant and invited them to schedule optional follow-up interviews, to which they all agreed.

The boys had met in the mixed ninth-tenth grade classrooms of the high school. They were all relatively new to the country, migrating from Yemen to live in New York with family members or relatives. Even before the focus group started and the hallway as a counterspace came to life, the desire to volunteer and do the focus group together reflects the boys' continuous dreams to work towards a collective identity and transnational belonging.

Manbi Al Afkar, Source for Ideas

In the focus group, the students were given colored pencils and paper and were prompted to answer the following question: When you think about your time in high school, what images or words pop into your head? Malik began sharing what he drew in his image:

Here is the hallway corner where we always gathered (*everyone seemed to recognize the corner and started chuckling*). Like even when you know the teacher says it's time to switch class we always come to this corner to see everyone. It was like three minutes between classes but we have to.

His friend Ziyad jumps in:

That was our *manbi al afkar* (source for ideas), Ms., like you know all our good and bad ideas came from that corner. *Ziyad added as he pointed to a similar drawing in his paper. Tell me more about that, I asked.* You know we all come to the school and some of us know a little English because we went to middle school, like me, but most of us didn't know a lot of English. It was like we needed to know we were all good and check in. Our classes, everyone is not from America but, umm, there are a lot of Spanish people and they always help and talk to each other and we want to make sure that we can help each other too. Like even some teachers know Spanish but no one knows Arabic.

All five boys in the focus group included a version of this gathering on their map. In these narrow hallways right across from the main office the boys had established a system to congregate in between classes, at the start of the day and dismissal. In the high school, there are four teams. Two teams have mixed ninth and tenth-grade students in the classes, an eleventh-grade team and a twelve-grade team. The demographics of the student population shift every year depending on larger U.S. and global migration patterns. For instance, over half the school population in the last four years has been comprised of students from Central and South America. All the Yemeni boys in the focus group and interview were from team A, and there were ten Yemeni males on their team.

In these moments of community building, the Yemeni students had established many rituals. They had a system to know who would be late or absent and who would be responsible for telling the teachers and delivering assignments to their friends. These times were used differently, from critical community building, including questioning equity and equality in teacher and student relations, inclusion and exclusion of materials and demographics in the curriculum, to simply making lunch plans. Salim shares:

> We never ate school lunch, and we were always late coming back from outside after lunch because by the time we go to the store to get the lunch it would be packed. Sometimes we used to be late and we haven't eaten yet. I don't remember who gave this idea but I think it's Emad. He made friends with the guys that run the deli near the school and got their numbers. After we got in trouble several times for being late we made a system. The period before lunch we would gather in our spot and we would say what we wanted. Someone would type it up in the chat and then it was either Emad or Ziyad that would call the deli a half hour before lunch and place all our orders. Then two of us took turns to go pick up the food right when the period finished. (*How did they call the deli in the middle of the class?*) They would ask to use the bathroom and call from there. Some of the teachers I think knew, but they were never really late so it didn't bother them, I think. (*Where is your spot for eating?*) It was outside of the gym in the hallway and then sometimes in the hallway by the elevator or in the library. (translation, mine, from Arabic to English)

This counterspace was also their support network, where they checked on one another to see how they were doing throughout the day. These hallways were their counterspace that allowed the boys to congregate and build together the network that they had through high school and still maintain today. This space afforded the boys an opportunity to speak freely in Arabic, to share resources, to vent, and more importantly, to navigate and work towards a belonging that did not strip them of their social locations and collective transnational identity.

In their work on imagined communities and sense of belonging, Abu El-Haj (2007) and Yuval-Davis (2011) explore how immigrants position themselves in spaces physically and emotionally based on their connections to various national identities. Abu El-Haj (2007) urges us to "examine how this positioning regulates immigrants' capacity to mobilize rights and resources that facilitate participation in the economic, social, cultural, and political spheres of the nation in which they now reside. Schools play an important role in the construction of the symbolic boundaries of the nation—in constructing who is and is not a member of the nation—and in the provision of resources with which immigrant youth learn to belong to and navigate their new society" (p. 288). The gatherings that the Yemeni students had were often loosely structured, youthful, loud and joyful, and assisted them in creating roadmaps for navigating their new spaces and acquiring their identities. That is, until they needed to be otherwise.

An important image came up from the mapping exercise in the focus group of a poster board with students around it. Both Ziyad and Malik had this on their maps. Once Ziyad described a few things on his map, he looked around at the group, asking "Tthkro?" *Do you remember?* He started then explaining:

> I was in ninth grade but I think it was tenth grade for some of us, we had like an argument with one of the teachers. Umm no, I don't think "argument" is right, it was like we felt like they didn't understand us or know anything about us like they did about other kids. We wanted them to, umm, think about how life before we came here like how we went to school. So we worked on a presentation about school and our life in Yemen *(he pointed to the presentation board he drew)*. We did it not in class time but we all got together and we asked one teacher to help us get the stuff and the room to work in. When everything was ready, like [after a] few weeks, we invited all our teachers to come hear our presentation. And I think from that point for me at least, *(he said looking around)*, things changed.

In *Towards Human Agency*, Heesoon (2006) argues that philosophy is a part of education through the lens of agency. He argues that agency is cultivated to allow people to enact their freedom, which is grounded in personal knowledge and ethics. Therefore, there needs to be a cultivation of autonomy in education if we want to develop a society that thinks on its own and makes decisions on its own. This autonomy is felt through Ziyad's reflection, *From that point for me at least, things changed.* There needs to be a reimagining of not just what curriculum is being taught but also what supports and opportunities are afforded to students as they maneuver new spaces and negotiate their identities. This is what happened to this group of Yemeni students when they were equipped with the tools to utilize their agency in an effort to foster their sense of belonging and educational experience in their NYC high school.

Disseminating Knowledge from Counterspaces to Posterboards

The idea of having this presentation to disseminate knowledge to their teachers about what it means for them to be Yemeni boys was born in one of the three-minute counterspace gatherings and was revisited several times due to circumstances that would arise. For some, it was the fact that they did not feel comfortable holding girls' hands in dance class; for others, it was the way teachers addressed their behaviors in class compared to those of their peers; and for all, it was struggling to fit in. In her work on the experiences of Palestinian Youth in education, Abu El-Haj (2007) argues that it goes beyond the incorporation of youth into socioeconomic and racial and ethnic orders in the U.S. to make them identify as being part of the nation. National belonging is produced, and needs to be maintained through the different factors that allow for it to be constructed and negotiated in the first place. Educational spaces and educators play a crucial role in the negotiation process. This collective gathering that gave rise to this self-led project was possible because of the work that the students had already put into their counterspace and the work that the school had put in to foster students' sense of belonging. The willingness of teachers to support the creation of this presentation and spend their lunch learning from the students enabled the Yemeni boys to feel included in the larger school culture while accepting their transnational identities.

Once Ziyad paused, the boys started talking about that day. *"They even said the Yemeni anthem with us,"* Salim excitedly added. Looking around, there were smiles on their faces as they remembered that day. I asked them to share some of the things that they included in their presentation. They shared that they wanted to do the presentation Yemeni-style. Salim looked at me and said, *"but Ms., we didn't do it exactly like the ethaa (morning assembly) in Yemen."*

Most schools in Yemen start the day with line ups and exercises in the yard, followed by an assembly. The assembly rotates daily to include every class throughout the year. They start with the pledge to the flag; an abridged Yemeni anthem, followed by a reading from the Holy Quran; a Hadith, a saying from the Prophet; a creative sketch which is open to scenes from a play; stand-up comedy sketches, moral virtues, sharing of jokes, or trivia; then there is a section on literature which is a poem or a short literary excerpt followed by announcements.

In their presentation, the students took their teachers through a day of schooling in Yemen, going over small changes that might differ if you went to school in the village versus if you went to school in the city. One important thing that they covered was that schools in Yemen were gendered. They brought up that one of the reasons there was tension at the beginning of the year was due to misunderstandings between working in groups with female students. Tawfik shares: "The girls tell the teacher that I don't talk to them and I don't look respectful when I talk to them because I don't look at them."

For someone like Tawfik, who had only been around women in his family in the village, it was a culture shock for him to be around girls in a new culture and environment. According to boys, one of the reasons for this misunderstanding was that other Yemeni boys did not seem to have an issue working or talking with the girls in their classes. This presentation allowed the students to showcase that even though they all come from Yemen, depending on their diverse experiences and environment and whether they went to middle school in the U.S., their behaviors and characteristics will be different, especially at the beginning of the year.

In her work, *The Politics of Belonging,* Yuval-Davis (2011) draws a distinction between belonging and the politics of belonging. She argues that belonging is mostly driven by the emotional attachments to spaces and feelings of "being at home" (p.10). While the politics of belonging come into play when the home is being threatened in some way, "the politics of belonging comprise specific political projects aimed at constructing belonging to particular collectivity which are themselves being constructed in these projects in very specific ways and in very specific boundaries" (Yuval-Davis, 2011, p.10). The Yemeni students' experience of belonging both in their NYC high school and belonging in the sense of the transnational community of Yemenis may have felt threatened or weakened during the time they decided to take this on.

This presentation afforded the Yemeni students an opportunity to use their agency to shape what and how they wanted to learn. Part of their presentation covered what schooling and life in Yemen is like during Ramadan. This led to a follow-up meeting with their dance teacher, who was open to ideas about how to incorporate body movement exercises and routines into the curriculum that does not include music. Being one of the holiest and spiritual months that strengthens the Muslims imagined community across the globe, students felt extra pressure to reexamine their belonging to American society during that month. This was more eminent for students whose first experience in American schools was at the NYC high school. Emad shares:

> Another important thing I think that really helped us was talking with the dance teacher. We like dancing but in Ramadan we try to stop listening to music and dance. Mosh kasal (*not laziness*) we play soccer every day. But like, you know, in Ramadan you want to be a better Muslim and we, we have to not listen to music you know, Ms., it's part of fasting.

It was clear from the group that they loved their dance teacher, which had a lot to do with her ongoing efforts to learn more about them and negotiate with them about what they were willing and unwilling to engage in. In her work on student agency and educators' role in fostering and enabling agency in their students, Stetsenko (2019) concludes, "agency is paramount to teaching-learning if the latter is understood to be about meaningful, active, and passionate knowing-being-doing by people as actors of history and agents of the world-in-the-making" (p. 37). The recognition of their teacher fostered several opportunities in which the Yemeni students collaborated with her for dance shows and art festivals, sharing with the school many of their traditional dances and cultural clothing throughout the years, far beyond their being in her dance class. In the follow-up interviews, Tawfik noted that he changed with time in school:

I was shocked at first, everything was so different from home. But when I started working in the store and then going to school and getting more comfortable I realized that it's not about not being Yemeni; it's like, I can be Yemeni in a different way, you know. *(Can you give an example?)* Like I was one of the students that had problem making eye contact with the girls and with the female teachers; like, I didn't want to be close to them. But after time with group work, dance class, and working in the store, I felt more comfortable around women than before. Like I didn't have to touch them but, umm, I can still be with them in class and talk to them, but I didn't do that for like a year.

Because agency is always in transition, and our identities are not static, they are interconnected and interdependent on many other systems in various communities. For example, culture and agency are linked in all spaces across the globe. Pacheco (2012) writes, "culture—and its concomitant tools, artifacts, and signs—is viewed not as fixed and finite but as dynamic and processual. That is, individuals and groups do not possess culture but live culturally" (p. 122). Therefore, agency is also alive and in transition, just as culture, and it is crucial to recognize this in both structured and non-structured educational spaces. An example is Tawfik's utilization of his agency to explain to his teachers the different cultural norms between genders, and even though he reflects on changing throughout the years, he sees that change as agentic because he needed that time to negotiate with himself elements of cultural shifts and experiences that grew with his sense of transnational identity and belonging at his NYC high school.

What these teachers at the high school did for these students followed in line with Abu El-Haj's (2007, 2015), Delgado Bernal's (2002), Ladson-Billings' (1992, 2004), and Nieto's (2015) call for teachers to see immigrant, multicultural, and multilingual students as a resource for learning about the diversity of cultures and societies. This will help them build relationships with their current students and can be an asset to how they think about interdisciplinary work across their teaching. Some of Team A's teachers invited the Yemeni boys to share their presentation with their classmates and teach them about the culture and schooling in Yemen.

Each Other's Light in the Darkness

The Muslim students at the NYC high school have often come together to celebrate Eid. This event is student-led, with support from clubs and advisors. Students bring food, dress in cultural attire, and invite their friends and classmates to celebrate with them. It is a time when students' imagination comes to life in the school cafeteria or gym. It is a time in which Muslim students, including the Yemeni boys, forge a sense of belonging to the larger community of the high school, all while strengthening their collective identity as Muslims and their transnational connection to their home countries and ethnic communities. Simultaneously, it is a time when students who share similar social and ethical beliefs come together to plan, organize, and carry out this celebration. For the Yemeni boys, this became an opportunity to take what they had been gathering, creating, and dreaming of in their counterspaces for years into a larger space and share it with others. It allowed them to take the reliable support network they had built for themselves within their small group and utilize it to support a larger project while continuing to be there for one another.

While the Eid celebration was a happy and celebratory memory for most of the boys in the focus group, for Ziyad, that day marked one of his hardest moments in school. On the day of the Eid celebration, he was assisting in preparing for the party when the assistant principal called him to her office.

> When she told me that my father collapsed and he had a heart attack and they took him to Mount Sinai, I didn't know what to say. I remember that I was so excited for the party, but it's like someone just shut off the light. *Alhamodollah*, my dad got treatment and he's now doing okay. But that day she told me I had to go to the hospital; I didn't know what to do. When I left her office, Emad was standing there. *(How did he know?)* He heard that the assistant principal called me, and he and Ismail came up. *(Is this usually a thing?) He smirked adding* Good and bad we don't leave each other alone, Yemenieen *(Yemenis)*. They didn't know it was about my dad being sick; they thought maybe something happened, but it's what we do, you know. A lot of the students and the teachers always talk and say why we are always together in the hallway or lunch or library. When we know that someone is in the office or in a ... it's like

qalaq (anxiety evoking), like I know what it feels to be there and not understand or know what I can say or how or what the rules are we try to support. It's not just language, it's knowing what or what not to say or do. (*What happened when you saw your friends?*) I told them what happened and Emad put his arm around me and he told Ismail to tell the others we had to go, but they should stay and make sure that they do their part, and he will text the group. Then before I could make sense of anything the Uber dropped us off at Mount Sinai and we went to look for my family.

Ziyad's reflection on his memories demonstrates why, in the mapping exercise, all five boys had the word family on their papers. The counterspace that they have established has afforded them a strong relationship that formed into a brotherhood, reinforcing a sense of shared belonging into the physical space of the high school and into a transnational community that they identified with. They took each other to the nurse's office when needed and they accompanied one another to speak with the assistant principal and principal when issues arose. They translated for each other and they shared resources for both in- and out-of-school life. All the boys worked to support their families in deli stores throughout high school, and all are still working in delis today. Three of them are full-timers, and two are part-timers as they take college classes. As the years went by, they became networks for their peers seeking job opportunities, and many of them ended up working for one another's family member or in the same neighborhoods during and after high school. These networks were afforded to them because of the counterspace they created in the hallways that allowed them to meet in one physical space to discuss things that class time was not allocated for.

Discussion

What started as a three-minute hallway gathering grew into a counterspace that afforded the boys both a physical and imagined space to build and foster a community for themselves. This counterspace allowed them to dream, grow, develop, and create without dissociating from their social locations, ethnic, or collective identities, all while fostering a sense of belonging in their new environments. It is important to recognize that this counterspace gave life to a network of support that transcends school walls and allows the boys to continue to support one another's dreams long after leaving their safe space in the hallways of their high school.

Knowing that they belonged to a transnational community, a culture, a people that shared their way of life, customs, and beliefs strengthened the role and life of the counterspace the boys had created. It reassured them that the knowledge they came with and the toolbox they have are important and valid. Moreover, it allowed them to navigate belonging in a new culture and environment while utilizing their agency to create and disseminate knowledge that may shift the way others in this community perceive them. Both the structure of the high school and the educators in it allowed for the creation of productive counterspaces that allow for students to utilize their own toolboxes and knowledge to speak to and engage with the community they are trying to belong in without stripping them of their connection to their larger imagined transnational community. The support of educators, whether through giving up lunch periods to listen to a presentation, inviting students to present in the class, or working with students to create new curriculum, the educators at the high school played a role in acknowledging the validity and important role that the counterspaces created for the boys.

Conclusion

Fujino et al. (2018), Olitsky (2006), and Rodriguez (2019) use different pedagogical approaches that lead to a re-envisioning of education and knowledge and examining, critiquing, and understanding its connection to various systems we live in. They call for a decolonial approach that centers first on the individual and their experience in the community to which they belong and then on their work and connection to the larger society. Understanding the Yemeni students' agency and identity and providing them with opportunities to create and lead counterspaces in schools equip them with tools to navigate and enhance both their local and transnational belonging. Murrell (2009) shares, "The implication for understanding the identity development of young people in school settings is then that we are not looking for a state of being as much as we are seeking to understand a process of development. More concretely, we are looking at development of young people's agency in doing—their developing capacity for engaging and negotiating the demands of their lives, particularly schooling" (p. 100). Revisiting our ideas and definitions for what we consider education, knowledge, and identity is crucial to how we as educators fulfill our duty to the young people we work with. Particularly the recognition that identity is continuously in formation and part of it develops based on the interactions and roles that are provided for students to occupy and construct in spaces of knowledge and counterspaces. By supporting the creation of these counterspaces, we as educators are encouraging students to radically dream and create a physical space where they not only fit and thrive but where they can create a deeper sense of belonging that transcends any geographic location.

In the follow-up interview with Emad, he tells me that in his previous middle school, something like the presentation and the collaboration with the dance teacher would not have happened. He felt that the teachers need to already have a buy-in into their students' lives to be willing to spend their lunch period eating and listening to a presentation. As a language learner, he felt that the NYC high school offered him a place to learn with respect and participation. Although the Yemeni students might not reflect and reference their experiences in terms that we as educators know to be culturally relevant teaching, equity in education, or counterspaces, and how they reflect on lived experiences demonstrates their understanding of these processes and the need for shifting of educational pedagogies in our schools.

References

Abu El-Haj, T. R. (2007). "I was born here but my home it's not here": Educating for democratic citizenship in an era of transnational migration and global conflict. *Harvard Educational Review* 77(3), 285-316.

Abu El-Haj, T. R. (2010). "The beauty of America": Nationalism, education and the "war on terror." *Harvard Educational Review* 80(2), 242-274.

Abu El-Haj, T. R. A. (2015). *Unsettled belonging: Educating Palestinian American youth after 9/11*. University of Chicago Press.

Anderson, B. (1991). *Imagined communities: Reflections on the origin and spread of nationalism*. Verso. (Original work published 1983)

Castles, S. (2004). Migration, citizenship, and education. In J.A. Banks (Ed.), *Diversity and citizenship education* (pp. 17-48). Jossey Bass Publishers.

Delgado Bernal, D. (2002). Critical race theory, Latino critical theory, and critical raced-gendered epistemologies: Recognizing students of color as holders and creators of knowledge. *Qualitative Inquiry, 8*(1), 105-126.

Duong, M. T., Badaly, D., Liu, F. F., Schwartz, D., & McCarty, C. A. (2016). Generational differences in academic achievement among immigrant youths. *Review of Educational Research, 86*(1), 3-41.

Fujino, D., Gomez, J., Lezra, E., Lipsitz, G., Mitchell, J., & Fonseca, J. (2018). A transformative pedagogy for a decolonial world. *Review of Education, Pedagogy, and Cultural Studies, 40*(2), 69-95.

Hall, K. D. (2004). The ethnography of imagined communities: The cultural production of Sikh ethnicity in Britain. *Annals of the American Academy of Political and Social Science, 595*, 108–121.

Heesoon, B. (2006). Philosophy for education: Towards human agency. *Paideusis, 15*(1), pp. 7-19.

Jaffe-Walter, R., & Lee, S. J. (2018). Engaging the transnational lives of immigrant youth in public schooling: Toward a culturally sustaining pedagogy for newcomer immigrant youth. *American Journal of Education, 124*(3), 257–283.

Ladson-Billings, G. (1992). Culturally relevant teaching: The key to making multicultural education work. In C.A. Grant (Ed.), *Research and multicultural education* (pp.106-121). Falmer Press.

Ladson-Billings, G. (2004). Culture versus citizenship: The challenge of racialized citizenship in the United States. In J. A. Banks (Ed.), *Diversity and citizenship education: Global perspectives* (pp. 99–126). Jossey-Bass.

Murrell, P. C. (2009). Identity, agency, and culture: Black achievement and educational attainment. In L. C. Tillman (Ed.), *The sage handbook of African American education* (pp. 89–106). Sage.

National Center for Education Statistics. (2023). *English Learners in Public Schools* [Interactive map]. U.S. Department of Education, Institute of Education Sciences. https://nces.ed.gov/programs/coe/indicator/cgf

Nieto, S. (2015). *Why we teach now.* Teachers College Press.

Olitsky, S. (2006). Structure, agency, and the development of students' identities as learners. *Cultural Studies of Science Education, 1*, 745–766.

Pacheco, M. (2012). Learning in/through everyday resistance: A cultural-historical perspective on community resources and curriculum. *Educational Researcher, 41*, 121–132.

Portes, A. (1999). Conclusion: Towards a new world—the origins and effects of transnational activities. *Ethnic and Racial Studies, 22*(2), 463-477.

Rodriguez, A. J. (2019). (Re)engaging our ethical commitments and becoming activists in our own backyards. *Journal for Activist Science & Technology Education, 10*(1), 12-22

Solórzano, D., Ceja, M., & Yosso, T. (2000). Critical race theory, racial microaggressions, and campus racial climate: The experiences of African American college students. *Journal of Negro Education, 69*(1/2), 60-73.

Solórzano, D. G., & Yosso, T. J. (2002). A critical race counterstory of race, racism, and Affirmative Action. *Equity & Excellence in Education, 35*(2), 155–168.

Stetsenko, A. (2019). Radical-transformative agency: Continuities and contrasts with relational agency and implications for education. *Frontiers in Education,* (4). https://doi.org/10.3389/feduc.2019.00148

Yosso, T. J. (2006). *Critical race counterstories along the Chicana/Chicano educational pipeline.* Routledge.

Yuval-Davis, N. (2011). *The politics of belonging: Intersectional contestations.* Sage

Youth Participatory Action Research and Student Resistance: Envisioning for College Food Security for All

Rachel Brand

Introduction

THE IMAGE OF the struggling student who subsists on ramen noodles has become a normalized depiction of college life in the United States. While higher education promises to offer students an opportunity for upward mobility, the college experience remains deeply unequal (Shipley & Christopher, 2018; Willis, 2019). Many students enter college without the financial support necessary to cover their material needs, such as food, books, and housing (Broton, 2020). Studies show that around 40% of college students in the United States suffer from some degree of food insecurity (Nazmi et al., 2019), a condition defined by the USDA as "the limited or uncertain availability of nutritionally adequate and safe foods or limited or uncertain ability to acquire acceptable foods in socially acceptable ways" (USDA, n.d.).

Food insecurity has vast implications for college students, including feelings of stigma, embarrassment, or shame (Henry, 2020), social isolation (Brand, 2023), and mental and physical health impacts such as high stress or trouble with sleep (El Zein et al., 2019). In addition, food insecurity most heavily impacts students from marginalized populations (Broton, 2020; Willis, 2019), including Black, Indigenous, People of Color (BIPOC), LGBTQ+, first-generation, and low-income students (Shipley & Christopher, 2018; Willis, 2019). Due to the severity of this problem, colleges have employed various strategies to assist their students. The most common include short-term solutions such as food pantries, vegetable gardens on campus, cooking classes, and assistance with the Supplemental Nutrition Assistance Program (SNAP) registration process (Watson et al., 2017; Willis, 2019). However, even with such resources in place, the problem persists, and students often navigate food insecurity on their own.

Hagedorn-Hatfield et al. (2022) note that research about college food insecurity lacks student-based research approaches, which could offer important ideas for interventions. Students themselves are best equipped to speak about their own experiences. To address the lack of student-centered research, I conducted a youth participatory action research (YPAR) project with a group of 38 undergraduate students at a private college in California. The objective of this study was to examine college students' perceptions about and experiences with food insecurity and to identify student-centered strategies to address the problem.

Throughout the YPAR process, the students conducted original research, analyzed the problem collectively, and devised innovative action projects. As a result of their findings, they created a framework to address food insecurity that centered their peers and worked to combat the individualized approach toward food insecurity. The students critiqued and resisted the strategies used by their university as they built new relationships and dreamed together.

Youth Participatory Action Research and Resistance Theory

Participatory action research (PAR) is a community-based research approach that centers those most impacted by a given issue (Rodriguez & Brown, 2009). PAR validates the knowledge of community members who are closest to the problem and deems their experiences and ideas important (Koirala-Azad & Fuentes, 2009). YPAR (participatory action research conducted with youth) mirrors PAR and often takes place in educational contexts. Throughout the semester, students used the terms PAR and YPAR interchangeably when referring to our project. YPAR supports students in their development as academic learners and agents of social change. To carry out a YPAR project, participants identify a problem, research the problem, analyze the problem, develop and implement a plan of action, and evaluate their actions (Duncan-Andrade & Morrell, 2008). As such, YPAR is an active process that can result in action for social change as students develop their academic and critical thinking skills.

While the YPAR cycle guided this project, I also utilized resistance theory to understand where students experienced tension and resistance to the food systems on their campus. Resistance theory offers the opportunity to "understand more thoroughly the complex ways in which people mediate and respond to the interface between their own lived experiences and the structures of domination and constraint" (Macleod, 2008, p. 21). Within this context, students' lives hold meaning that can be analyzed and used to change systems of power, including at their educational institutions. Solórzano and Delgado Bernal (2001) argue that resistance indicates that people are not only acted upon but have agency to negotiate and make meaning of their lives. YPAR reinforces the importance of locating student agency, centering the voice of marginalized youth, and building students' critical consciousness.

Aronowitz and Giroux (1985) note that resistance is not simply defiance or oppositional behavior but also "must have a revealing function that contains a critique of domination and provides theoretical opportunities for self-reflection and struggle in the interest of social and self-emancipation" (p. 233). This aligned with the YPAR process, where the students named and analyzed the problem, reflected on and critiqued the responses by their university, and gained a collective sense of agency to enact change.

As students engaged in resistance and action, they experienced a deep sense of transformation and began to dream of a better future for themselves and their peers. As they worked with their peers, they gained a newfound sense of agency and belief that they could make change. This process served as an account of transformative resistance (Cammarota, 2017), as it was "political, collective, conscious and motivated by a sense that individual and social change is possible" (Solórzano & Delgado Bernal, 2001, p. 320). While initially many students were resistant to the project itself and did not believe in their own agency, this shifted by the end of the semester. Students felt empowered by their experiences and built a sense of hope and belief in the possibility of a student-led, food secure campus.

The YPAR Project

I implemented this YPAR project with undergraduate students at a private university in Northern California where I was both an adjunct professor and a graduate student. Throughout the semester, I reflected on my positionality as the students' professor and co-researcher. PAR promotes horizontal relationships and analysis of power dynamics (Koirala-Azad & Fuentes, 2009), and I engaged students in many discussions about my role and limitations as their professor, as well as the complexities of being both an adjunct professor and student myself. In alignment with PAR, I sought to create mechanisms where students would not be in competition around assignments and grades, but rather work as a community. For instance, all of our group work took place during class hours, and homework included readings and individual reflections in order to ensure that students had equal time and capacity for our group action projects. We worked as a team throughout the semester, and I regularly checked in with the students individually and as a group.

My overall goal for this project was to understand how students would approach college food insecurity when engaged in action research. I was curious to see if this process would yield innovative results that could be replicated at other universities. I had taught within higher education for many years, and knew many students experienced food insecurity. I was interested in the students perspectives on both food insecurity overall and their university's strategies to combat the problem. Given the lack of community-based research methods used to study this problem, I hoped the YPAR process could inspire new strategies and actions centered on students' lived experiences.

I implemented the YPAR project with undergraduate students from two course sections. The students collaborated across sections on their work. All of the data is from August 2021- December 2021. At the start of the semester, I gave students a detailed description of the PAR cycle and how it would apply to our course, and we spent a few weeks on each stage of the cycle. The students decided on their projects collectively and I supported their ideas through grant funding and networking to help actualize their plans. While the students carried out their research, analysis, and action projects, I analyzed their conversations, decisions, and experiences.

I received Institutional Review Board approval for this PAR project, and each student signed an agreement that their participation allowed me to use their materials, such as homework, journals, interviews, and recordings of our class discussions. The students were informed that their decision to participate in the study (or not) would in no way affect their overall grade in the course, and they could opt out of the study at any time. I use pseudonyms throughout this study to maintain students' privacy.

According to *U.S. News & World Report* (n.d.), as of fall 2022, the population of the school was 6,018 undergraduate students, with a total student body of 9,688 students. Of the total students, 35% were listed as male and 65% female (no other gender categories listed). Statistics for fall 2022 racial demographics of the entire student body were Asian (26%), African American (8%), Hispanic (21%), Two or more races (10%), International (10%), and white (24%) (U.S. News & World Report, n.d.).

This course fulfilled the university's Community Engaged Learning requirement, and as a result, students from all majors and disciplines joined the course. The following chart lists the demographics of the students and how they self-identify in regard to race, food insecurity, and gender identity through their own words. In some cases, students chose not to answer.

Table 2.1 *Breakdown of the Students in Section One of the Course*

Student Pseudonym	Year in College	Major	Race	Have you faced food insecurity?	Gender Identity
Brad	Senior	—	White	No	Male
Julie	Senior	Accounting	Asian	No	Female
Nina	Senior	Environmental Studies	White	No	Genderfluid
John	Senior	Computer Science	White	No	Male
Olivia	Senior	International Studies	White	Yes	Female
Ben	—	Computer Science	Asian	No	Male
Alex	Senior	Finance	Mexican	No	Male
Owen	Senior	Entrepreneurship	Asian	Yes	Male
Sara	—	Sociology	Mixed race	Yes	Female
Grace	Senior	Politics	White	No	Female
Tamara	Senior	Chemistry	Asian	Yes	Female

Victoria	—	International Studies	Latina	No	Female
Laura	Senior	Environmental Studies	Asian American	No	—
Tristan	Junior	International Studies	—	No	Non-binary
Caroline	Senior	Accounting	Asian	No	Female
Lola	Sophomore	Environmental Studies	Mixed race	No	Female
Gina	Senior	Environmental Studies	White	No	Non-binary
Lucy	Freshman	Philosophy	White	Yes	Female
Cody	Senior	Communication	White	No	Male

Table 2.2

Breakdown of the Students in Section Two of the Course

Student Pseudonym	Year in College	Major	Race	Have you faced food insecurity?	Gender Identity
Danny	Senior	Entrepreneurship	Asian	No	Male
Ashley	Senior	Biology	Asian	No	Female
Joshua	Senior	Computer Science	Asian	No	Male
Julian	Senior	Environmental Studies	White	No	Male
Emory	Junior	Biology	Mixed race	No	Female
Tori	Junior	Economics	African American	Yes	Female
Bella	Sophomore	Environmental Studies	White	No	Female
Jane	Sophomore	Environmental Studies	White	Yes	Female
Andre	Junior	Media Studies	—	No	Non-binary
Monty	Senior	—	White	No	Male
Fiona	Senior	Chemistry	Filipina	No	Female
Kate	Junior	Chemistry	White	No	Female
Dave	Senior	Biochemistry	White	Yes	Male
Martin	Junior	Environmental Science	Mixed race	Yes	Non-binary
Ellie	Senior	Chemistry	Mexican	Yes	Female
Michael	Sophomore	Environmental Studies	—	Yes	Male

Jasmine	Senior	Biology		Asian	No	Female
Jaco	Senior	Chemistry		Mixed race	Yes	Male
Hope	—	—		—	No	—

Students joined the project with different levels of awareness of and experiences with food insecurity. Those who had experienced food insecurity themselves voluntarily played a leadership role in this project. This role emerged from their desire to speak to their experiences. In alignment with YPAR, the students built research questions and projects around the first-hand experiences of those who were food insecure.

To date, there is no large-scale survey administered about food insecurity on the university's campus. However, through conversations with students and other community members, it was clear that food insecurity affected students at the university. While the university has food resources in place, such as a campus food pantry, students were eager to add more resources that met the needs of the student community.

Findings

At the start of the semester, the students in the course decided that college food insecurity would be the basis for our YPAR project. This interest developed after we spent two weeks studying several different food system-related problems. The students created their research questions, which included: (a) How can we improve food security on campus? and (b) How do we give a platform to food-insecure students to address this issue? To obtain their data, the students conducted and transcribed 28 in-depth interviews with peers that each lasted between 20-30 minutes. To create interview questions, the students who had experienced food insecurity came up with questions they thought were most important to ask, followed by additional questions from the rest of the class. Three students from the class also gave testimonials about their own experiences with food insecurity. After collecting the data from their interviews, the students collectively analyzed their findings in small groups, discussing the themes they found while maintaining the confidentiality of their peers. These themes informed the direction of their action projects.

The students' action projects were geared towards institutional change, including a short write-up about food resources to include in syllabi across campus, the development of a campus-wide food security coalition, and collaborations with administrators on campus. They also created short-term resource-based actions, such as food giveaways, websites pointing students to local free food, and educational resources. These projects were intentionally embedded in an explicit framework of joy and celebration to highlight the importance of community-wide awareness about food insecurity. The students felt the university's solutions were too hidden (such as an anonymous food pantry) which they felt perpetuated notions of shame. In resistance to this idea, the students offered community meals in a public space on campus to highlight the pervasiveness of food insecurity.

After completing their action projects, the students reflected on their overall experience individually and collectively. While a wealth of information came from these projects, this chapter highlights the centrality of resistance and dreaming to the positive outcomes that students experienced. It shows how using YPAR helped to facilitate and encourage student agency and collective action, which led to students' ability to dream. The following description shows how YPAR enabled students to (a) collectively analyze food insecurity at their school, (b) grapple with their role as changemakers, and (c) develop a framework of hope and community care based on their dreams for the future.

Collective Analysis Of College Food Insecurity

At the start of the YPAR process, the students discussed their personal experiences with food insecurity and came to recognize that this was a widespread problem on their campus. Joshua, a college senior, noted:

> I know many people who struggle to buy food because we're college students. I was surviving off ramen for a solid week until payday because my bank account was so low. Ramen tastes so nasty to me now, but it's cheap and fills you up.

As students engaged in these conversations, they realized the pervasiveness of food insecurity and how normalized the problem had become. Tori, a college junior, remarked, "I knew that a lot of students struggled to afford food and basic necessities, but I've always been conditioned to think that was just a normal part of the college experience." Our class conversations were the first time many of the students had spoken openly about this experience or felt that the issue was taken seriously.

Most of the students had friends or acquaintances who were food insecure, and they discussed what they had observed amongst their peers. Laura, a college senior, said:

> Over the past few years, I've noticed that many students experience food insecurity, especially low-income students of color. Many students work multiple jobs, as well as apply for government aid programs or seek help from local food pantries near them. With the cost of housing, annual tuition increases, educational materials each semester, transportation, and bills, food and grocery expenses are often put at a lower priority at the expense of students' health and overall well-being. We all just figure out how to make things work.

This depiction was very relatable to the students. They understood food insecurity as a normal part of being a student no matter if you lived on or off campus.

As they discussed food insecurity, the students grappled with the issues they experienced with their campus cafeteria as well. Tori explained:

> They raised the prices of food in the cafeteria and so now a lot of people are running low on money. It's heartbreaking because a lot of my friends and I have started skipping meals just so that we don't have to buy food off campus at the end of the semester. We have a meal plan and yet we're still worried about our next meal in that we don't know if we're going to have enough money left. I personally was eating three meals a day at the beginning of the semester and then I realized I was going to run out of money so now I eat one meal a day. Am I hungry? Yes. Am I going to end up having to spend extra money that I don't have at the end of the semester? No.

Due to the prevalence of food insecurity, students said they often engaged in small acts of resistance to combat this problem. They shared their meal plans or took cafeteria food to friends, yet they had never organized collectively to approach the university about its dining policies.

As students became more aware of the problem, they began to see their role in making demands to the university. Jane, a college senior, explained the cost difference between food on and off campus. According to Jane, "This package of granola they have is $10 for one bag; you can get the same bag at Safeway for $8 less, so that's $2. No matter what economic principle you apply, nothing explains that level of inflation. Period." This conversation inspired the students to push for more transparency in food costs at their institution. They felt that the university's food system was entrenched in a philosophy of making money rather than looking out for student needs, and wanted to feel that they were part of a caring community rather than feeling like consumers. These convictions led the students towards building their agency as changemakers.

Students' Role As Changemakers

As students moved through the YPAR project, they considered how to resist the injustices they named in their critiques. Nina, a college senior, grappled with the changes she wanted to see:

> I want to go back to the idea that colleges have become businesses; we are paying to get a degree. I think in general higher education needs to stop being treated as a business and more like a center for learning and advancement of growing young people into adults and into functioning members of society, not just taking advantage of them.

As students shared these problems and experiences with one another, many became inspired to take action.

However, while some students felt empowered to work towards change, others were conflicted about their role. As they conceived of their action plans, students grappled with their frustration in taking on these projects due to the lack of agency for students in general. In one discussion, Victoria, a college senior, noted, "Students don't have control over the food system, we must buy from monopolies. How do we address that? How do we give people control over their food?"

In response to Victoria's question, Tamara, a college senior, stated:

> I think the university needs to help students out. The food is expensive, tuition is expensive, and there is no way that everyone can afford all of that. I know people who can only eat one meal a day because they have to make sure they also have enough to pay for books and tuition. If we are paying for our education, the university should help us afford to eat.

Olivia agreed with this sentiment and said, "If PAR means working with the most vulnerable, how come we, the food insecure students, have to make the changes? Shouldn't this be on the university?" This perspective was common as many of the students felt that the university, rather than students, should work to solve campus issues.

While the students were not able to resolve this tension, the experience of creating action projects, working with peers, and seeing their successes actually helped students move into a place of empowerment. YPAR was a mechanism that gave them a voice and a chance to resist, resulting in a sense of agency. In reflecting on the experience, Tori stated:

> This project made me realize the impact I could have on my community. My whole life I've been made to believe that change requires waiting for someone with more power to speak up, but the PAR project made me realize that we, the community, are the people with the power. It only takes a group of passionate people and the determination to improve issues in our community to make a difference.

The students began to feel that the community cared much more about food insecurity than they had previously realized. YPAR helped students find their agency, analyze and resist common ideas about food insecurity, and work as a collective. In the final stage of the project, the students worked together with a new vision and dream for a food secure campus.

The Chance To Dream

As students began to dream together, they rejected the idea that short-term solutions such as food pantries were enough. They pushed for transparency about the cafeteria prices and strived to create an inclusive food system embedded in joy and care. They wanted the university to address the high costs of being a student and the prevalence of food insecurity. Several students met with the campus provost in order to put forward their collective goals for food security, which included:

a. Transparency about the meal plan.

b. Trust between students and administrators regarding food systems on campus.

c. A culture of community care that decreases stigma and takes food insecurity seriously.

d. Student agency and empowerment regarding issues on campus.

e. Students, administrators, and faculty united in solidarity for change.

f. A deeper understanding of students' stories and experiences related to food insecurity.

g. A more robust web of resources for students regarding basic needs.

To meet these goals, the students developed several action projects that were embedded in food sovereignty, relationship building, and attention to vulnerable students. They took a desire-based approach (Tuck, 2009) that looked at the skills and knowledge the community had to offer. These frameworks resisted the norms around food that they felt were detrimental to student well-being.

Within their vision for food security, students centered their own lives and their family knowledge. Reinforced by YPAR and community cultural wealth (Yosso, 2005), students used their cultural backgrounds to bolster their work. Laura discussed how her family knowledge informed her approach to campus food security: "Learning about my family's farming background and pre-colonial agricultural practices has highlighted how important it is to be an active part of creating and supporting locally controlled food systems that serve communities rather than profit off them." Students used the assets and knowledge of their communities to create a critical approach to food insecurity.

John spoke about how the project reflected the unique characteristics and knowledge of the class community. He said, "I hope our project will be to seek to reveal what our community has already built, to improve awareness and accessibility of the assets we already possess, believing that this will unlock even greater possibilities in the future."

As students worked on their projects, they created a vision for food security on campus based on their hopes and dreams. At the beginning of the semester, students had discussed small-scale resistance, such as sharing meal cards, yet the YPAR process helped them dream of a new food system entirely, based on relationships, trust, and equitable resources. The students' collective vision was described by Laura, who said:

> We hope to allow food insecure students to be nutritionally-and socially -supported by the campus community in a way that lets them take control of their narrative, their needs, and their solutions. I would also expand this to include welcoming the entire campus community to engage in conversations and destigmatize the topic of food insecurity, as all students should feel comfortable to seek help in assessing nutritional food without the fear of judgment.

In addition to a framework of trust and community care, students pushed to make changes to the meal plan and create more transparency in how prices are set. Students also petitioned for longer hours for the school food pantry and for students to be represented in decision-making about food vendors.

A new conception of what a food-secure campus could look like was very important to students and resulted in a feeling of camaraderie. They felt that the process of creating projects with their class community served as an example of the approach they hoped for from the university. As Tristan explained:

> We have so many skills and talents and ideas on how to improve our situation and make our college a more food secure place. We are working to increase student awareness and involvement in this issue, and the process of strategizing is a community building practice in and of itself.

> We are utilizing our skills to build upon structures already in place, and
> in addition, attempting to make changes within the system for future
> student generations.

Through the YPAR process, the students began to believe in their own knowledge and experiences as a means to address a community problem. Students
took pride in their approach and framework to address food insecurity. Community was at the heart of their design, and their projects were based on care
and action.

In speaking about their projects, the students expressed a newfound sense
of hope and trust in their university. Andre said, "I think this project gave me
hope. It allowed me to see that my voice can be heard and that our university is
willing to make changes." In the end, students found that the project gave them
a sense of support and belief in possibilities for the future.

Discussion

This study offers insight into the innovative ways that students approach
college food security when they are involved in action research and the importance of utilizing student knowledge when addressing campus issues. Student
engagement in deep analysis of and resistance to college food insecurity was
central to this project. As students envisioned a food-secure campus, they developed a new framework, along with specific action projects, to actualize their
dream of an equitable, food secure campus.

The students critiqued the university's short-term strategies to alleviate
food insecurity, they created a vision for food security that included care for
the community. They challenged an individualized approach to food insecurity
that leaves students negotiating their eligibility for short-term resources and
grappling with how to prioritize their many financial burdens.

To confront college food insecurity, the students openly discussed the
problem itself, and their role as changemakers. Their original research and personal experiences served as the starting point for their work as they unpacked
the pervasiveness and complexities of the issue. At first, many students were
frustrated by their involvement in this project and felt it put an extra burden

on the students. In the end, however, students saw the experience as an opportunity to come together as a community and work for change.

While this study utilized YPAR to address food insecurity, this methodology could be implemented on college campuses to address other pressing issues, as well. Going through this process helped students name the tensions and resistance they felt towards their university, and helped students believe in their agency. The focus on action gave students a lived experience to validate that they could make change in their community. In the future, scholars might look at how the agency derived from YPAR can be sustained in the long term and how universities can support the projects accomplished by their students. While this project was conducted over a semester, a follow-up study could investigate what students would gain by participating for a longer period of time. Another follow-up study could examine how YPAR can help shift students' overall relationship with their university.

The students in this study received accolades from the university's provost and faculty and staff across campus. This support was unexpected, as they had thought that the school administrators "didn't care." This experience and collaboration bolstered the students' sense of agency and excitement for action. Unfortunately, many of the students in this course were in their final year in college and graduated soon after the semester ended. However, even in just one semester, they had the chance to see that their projects greatly expanded the conversation about food insecurity on campus.

Conclusion

This study demonstrates the importance of catalyzing student resistance and community-based research methods to address campus issues. This process resulted in resistance that was transformative as the students engaged in oppositional behavior as a means toward social change. Through discussions, projects, and engagement with administrators, students worked hard to shift food systems embedded in the university. This study shows the possibilities that arise by centering students' voices and offering opportunities like YPAR to help students' visions come to fruition.

To enact long-term change, universities should include students in discussions about their campus food systems and be transparent about food costs, choices of food purveyors, and the decisions the university grapples with in its food procurement. When students are not included in this process, they can feel frustrated and or taken advantage of and are left without a meaningful lens through which to understand this problem. Student-centered research methods offer a starting point through which to analyze campus food insecurity, where students' voices and concerns can be heard and valued.

This research is significant in its innovative approach to addressing campus food insecurity. It includes a unique investigation examining the nuances of students' resistance to and reflections on food insecurity at their university. The outcomes of this project show that transparency in campus food is not a threat to the university but rather makes students feel included in the process and that their university cares for their overall well-being. Students often hope to build relationships and feel connected to and supported by their university. Campus food systems can serve as a space where the university community supports students to resist and dream.

References

Aronowitz, S. and Giroux. (1985). *Education under siege: The conservative, liberal, and radical debate over schooling.* Routledge.

Brand, R. (2023). Students as co-researchers: Using participatory action research to address college food insecurity. *Journal of Agriculture, Food Systems, and Community Development, 12*(2), 47–62. https://doi.org/10.5304/jafscd.2023.122.017

Broton, K. M. (2020). Food insecurity in higher education. In K. M. Broton & C. L. Cady (Eds.), *Food insecurity on campus: Action and intervention* (pp. 12–32). Johns Hopkins University Press.

Cammarota, J. (2017). Youth participatory action research: A pedagogy of transformational resistance for critical youth studies. *Journal for Critical Education Policy Studies (JCEPS), 15*(2), 188–213.

Duncan-Andrade, J. M. R., & Morrell, E. (2008). *The art of critical pedagogy: Possibilities for moving from theory to practice in urban schools.* Peter Lang. https://doi.org/10.3726/b12771

El Zein, A., Shelnutt, K. P., Colby, S., Vilaro, M. J., Zhou, W., Greene, G., Olfert, M. D., Riggsbee, K., Morrell, J. S., & Mathews, A. E. (2019). Prevalence and correlates of food insecurity among U.S. college students: A multi-institutional study. *BMC Public Health, 19*(1), 660.

Hagedorn-Hatfield, R. L., Hood, L. B., & Hedge, A. (2022). A decade of college student hunger: What we know and where we need to go. *Frontiers in Public Health, 10* (Article 827724). https://doi.org/10.3389/fpubh.2022.837724

Henry, L. (2020). *Experiences of hunger and food insecurity in college.* Palgrave Pivot.

Koirala-Azad, S., & Fuentes, E. (2009). Introduction: Activist scholarship—Possibilities and constraints of participatory action research. *Social Justice, 36*(4), 1-5. https://www.jstor.org/stable/29768557

Macleod, J. (2008*). Ain't no makin' it: Aspirations and attainment in a low-income neighborhood* (3rd ed.). Westview.

Nazmi, A., Martinez, S., Byrd, A., Robinson, D., Bianco, S., Maguire, J., Crutchfield, R. M., Condron, K., & Ritchie, L. (2019). A systematic review of food insecurity among US students in higher education. *Journal of Hunger & Environmental Nutrition, 14*(5), 725–740. https://doi.org/10.1080/19320248.2018.1484316

Rodriguez, L. F., & Brown, T. M. (2009). From voice to agency: Guiding principles for participatory action research with youth. *New Directions for Youth Development, 123,* 19–34.

Shipley, G., & Christopher, M. (2018). Food insecurity on college campuses: Collateral damage of a societal crisis. *Journal of College and Character, 19*(4), 309–315.

Solórzano, D. G., & Delgado Bernal, D. (2001). Examining transformational resistance through a critical race and latcrit theory framework: Chicana and Chicano students in an urban context / Les étudiants hispano-américains dans un environnement urbain. *Urban Education, 36*(3), 308–342.

Tuck, E. (2009). Suspending damage: A letter to communities. *Harvard Educational Review, 79*(3), 409–428. https://doi.org/10.17763/haer.79.3.n0016675661t3n15

U.S. Department of Agriculture [USDA]. (n.d.). *Food security in the U.S.* Retrieved on December 24, 2022, from https://www.ers.usda.gov/topics/food-nutrition assistance/food-security-in-the-u-s/measurement/

U.S. News & World Report. (n.d.). *University of San Francisco.* Retrieved on May 16, 2024, from https://www.usnews.com/best-colleges/university-of-san-francisco-1325

Watson, T. D., Malan, H., Glik, D., & Martinez, S. M. (2017). College students identify university support for basic needs and life skills as key ingredients in addressing food insecurity on campus: Food insecurity is a persistent stressor for some students; food literacy may help improve student well-being. *California Agriculture, 71*(3), 130–138.

Willis, D. E. (2019). Feeding the student body: Unequal food insecurity among college students. *American Journal of Health Education, 50*(3), 167–175.

Yosso, T. (2005). Whose culture has capital? A critical race theory discussion of community cultural wealth. *Race, Ethnicity and Education, 8*(1), 69-91.

CHAPTER 3

Making *Mundo Nuevo:* Chicana/Latina Daughters Enacting Chicana/a/o/x and Latina/o/x Immigrant Educational Futurities and Possibilities Through Spiritual Activism and Transformative Ruptures

Brianna R. Ramirez

Introduction

> "I inherited my mother's belief that the map to a new world
> is in the imagination, in what we see in our *third eyes* rather
> than in the desolation that surrounds us."
> (Kelley, 2022, p. 3)

THIS CHAPTER AIMS to center spirit and spirituality as sources for youth agency and resistance in education. Kelley (2022) points to the metaphysical root of liberation, locating freedom within the capacity to see, imagine, dream, and prophesize a different world for all peoples and communities beyond the historical and contemporary oppressive realities. Central to pursuing freedom is following and living by what one sees through the "third eyes," allowing the vision and dream of freedom to guide everyday agency and resistance (Kelley,

2022 p. 3). Aligned with the intent to explore the metaphysical root of liberation, this chapter bridges spiritual activism (Anzaldúa, 2002) and transformative ruptures (Delgado Bernal & Alemán, 2017) to center spirit and spirituality as a source for Chicana/Latina student resistance and their contribution to cultivating educational possibilities and futures. Anzaldúa (2002) considers spirit to be "a presence, force, power, and energy within and without. Spirit infuses all that exists- organic and inorganic- transcending the categories and concepts that govern your perception of material reality" (p. 558). Anzaldúa argues that centering and enacting on and through spirit is at the core of making *mundo nuevo*, creating a new, just, liberated, and free world.

Chicana/Latina Spiritual Activism and Transformative Ruptures in Education

The centering of spirit and spirituality in resistance is rooted in Women of Color feminist theorizations that aim to challenge the Western ways of knowing that fragment "bodymindspirit" (Lara, 2005, p. 11) and splinter the embodied intersecting marginalities that result in dehumanization and objectification of the racialized body (Cruz, 2001). Chicana feminists situate fragmentation of the bodymindspirit (Lara, 2005, p. 11) within existing ideologies, structures, and systems of oppression that construct, categorize, restrict, harm, and marginalize the body, mind, and spirit (Hurtado, 2003; Moraga & Anzaldúa, 2002). Eurocentric and Western paradigms center knowledge in science, rationality, and objectivity over the knowledge produced through everyday life, instinct, intuitive knowledge, and intuition (Lara, 2002). The body, in particular the racialized and gendered body, is de-centralized within Eurocentric and Western thought and society, yet Women of Color feminist scholars situate the body as the material site through which intersecting systems of marginality are experienced and also upheld and produced (Cruz, 2001; Dillard, 2000; Moraga & Anzaldúa, 2002). Feminist scholars also point to the holistic connection of bodymindspirit (Lara, 2005), situating their whole selves as the site of constructing truth rooted in our everyday lives (Dillard, 2000) and as sites of transformation and resistance (Lara, 2005).

Chicana/Latina scholars in education have uncovered the systemic, structural, and spiritual harm experienced by Chicanas/Latinas in educational systems that results in the separation and segmentation of bodymindspirit and dehumanization in these contexts (Espino, 2021). The split and fragmentation of bodymindspirit can impact the physical and mental health and well-being of Chicana/Latina students, administrators, and faculty (Espino, 2021; Ramirez & Puente, 2021). Chicana/Latina feminisms in education aim to center Chicana/Latina bodymindspirit through centering their whole selves, experiences, and ways of knowing that stem from all parts of their being, to inform everyday navigation and resistance, and to transform research, systems, and practice (Delgado Bernal, 1998). In resisting the fragmentation of bodymindspirit in educational systems and contexts, Chicanas/Latinas create new possibilities for pursuing education and lives as their whole selves (Delgado et al., 2006; Espino, 2021).

The following section reviews the framework and application in educational scholarship that advance a bridging of Chicana/Latina feminist and critical race *feminista* orientation for Chicana/Latina student resistance and contribution to Chicana/o/x/Latina/o/x educational pathways.

Spiritual Activism

This chapter applies and builds on scholarship that advances spiritual activism in education to center spirit and spirituality as a source for imagining and enacting agency and justice. Kelley (2022) situates freedom within seeing, dreaming, and imagining a possible just and liberated world, free of marginalities, harms, and injustices. Central to freedom dreaming is pursuing one's sensitivity and capacity for imagination and vision beyond one's present reality to see and create a new world and future that is first possible only through the imagination. To deeply understand one's present realities and struggles and to create meaning and vision beyond one's current perceptions is a spiritual undertaking (Anzaldúa, 2002). Anzaldúa situates agency and liberation in the spiritual realm, as the promise and commitment to transformation and activism stem from the nexus of "the imaginal knowings derived from viewing life through the third eye, the reptilian eye looking inward and outward simultaneously" (2002, p. 542), pointing to the creation of imagined alternatives and possibilities.

This chapter proposes spiritual activism (Anzaldúa, 2002) as a resistance framework that centers the physical and nonphysical worlds, imagined possibilities, and deep knowing and connection for a liberated future to understand how Chicana/Latina undergraduate daughters navigate educational systems and processes on behalf and alongside their families, contributing to interrupting the systems of marginality that Chicana/o/x/Latina/o/x families experience in schooling and educational systems in the United States. Spiritual activism is part of Anzaldúa's seven stages of "*Conocimiento*" framework (p. 540) that offers a lens for understanding the journey of coming to *saber* (to know) and growth in consciousness that Chicanas/Latinas and folks who live at the intersection of marginality experience in making meaning of the complexity of everyday life, challenges, and systems. Spiritual activism is defined by Anzaldúa (2013) as "the ability to recognize and endow meaning to daily experience …[which] furthers the ability to shift and transform" (p. 568). This framework situates activism and resistance in an imaginal knowing that is in the realm where one's connection to the larger physical and nonphysical worlds intersects with an understanding of one's position, reality, and navigation of daily life and society, and is woven together with a potential vision that transcends the present reality as a guide for agency and resistance (Elenes, 2013). Acting on this imaginal knowing "motivates you to work actively to see that no harm comes to people, animals, ocean- to take up spiritual activism and the work of healing. *Te entregas a tu promesa*[1] to help your various cultures create new paradigms, new narratives" (Anzaldúa, 2013, p. 558). Therefore, spiritual activism contributes to making *mundo nuevo* or a new world (Anzaldúa, 2002) through advocating, challenging, and resistance for educational and social justice rooted and guided by an imaginal knowing that stems from one's embodied and everyday existence (Acevedo-Gil & Madrigal-Garcia, 2018; Elenes, 2013; Keating, 2005). Spiritual activism is situated within Black feminist and Chicana/Latina feminist scholars that theorize about the fragmentation of bodymindspirit (Lara, 2005) and the pursuit and journey of agency, healing, and transformation (Salazar Pérez & Saavedra, 2020). Centering spiritual activism is aligned with challenging the removal and fragmentation of spirit and spirituality in the Eurocentric and Western world. Lara (2002) calls us to "heal the de-spiritualization of the academy … the de-politicization of the spiritual … [and] our separation from ourselves, each other, and the visible and invisible world" (p. 437). Spiritual activism politicizes spirit and spirituality, the deep connection and foresight within and between physical and nonphysical worlds, and the straddling of historical, contemporary, and a not-yet-present liberated future as a root, catalyst, and guide for transcending and creating a new reality through everyday action, agency, and resistance.

Chicana/Latina feminist educational scholars have applied spiritual activism as a lens for exploring student agency and resistance in educational spaces and contexts. Acevedo-Gil and Madrigal-Garcia (2018) show how Latina/o/x graduate student scholars enact and embody spiritual activism through peer mentorship rooted in shared navigation, reciprocity, and validation of each other's experiences for cultivating relationships rooted in their collective belonging and care. Spiritual activism has also been considered with Latina community college students (Acevedo et al., 2021) and undergraduate students (Ramirez, 2023). Through spiritual activism, Acevedo et al. (2021) demonstrate the process of navigating, resisting, and healing from the marginality that Latina community college students in STEM experience. Acevedo et al. (2021) identified the connection between spiritual activism as a process and journey that can support a sense of belonging for Latina community college students in STEM pathways. Ramirez (2023) advances spiritual activism in higher education by centering Chicana/Latina undergraduates in their roles as daughters and sisters within mixed status and immigrant familial and community contexts. Spiritual activism for Chicana/Latina students intersects with educational, familial, and societal contexts as students negotiate within the racist, sexist, and nativist systems and processes they and their families experience and navigate in the United States (Ramirez, 2023). This perspective advances a Chicana/Latina feminist understanding of the agency and resistance of Chicana/Latina undergraduates within and against the intersections of their personal and familial experiences and positionalities to promote collective support, survival, and resistance (Ramirez, 2023; Ramirez & Carrola, 2021). The present chapter builds on scholarship bridging spiritual activism within educational spaces and processes (Acevedo-Gil & Madrigal-Garcia, 2018; Acevedo et al., 2021; Ramirez, 2023). This chapter advances spiritual activism in education to explore how Chicana/Latina undergraduate students contribute and shape their families' and communities' educational experiences, trajectories, and navigation. Through their spiritual activism, students follow their deep knowledge of power and allow their potential vision for change and a different future to guide their everyday acts of agency and resistance against structures designed to work against Chicana/o/x/Latina/o/x students.

Transformative Ruptures

To make visible how spiritual activism engages in interruption and intervening on power, this chapter also bridges transformative ruptures, a framework theorized through a critical race *feminista* orientation (Delgado Bernal & Alemán, 2017) that braids together the tenets and offerings of critical race theory with Chicana/Latina feminist epistemologies and principles. Critical race theory is intended to interrogate, uncover, and interrupt how race, racism, and intersectional systems of oppression shape and underlie the lives of People of Color in the United States (Solórzano & Yosso, 2001). Through the bridging of spiritual activism (Anzaldúa, 2002) and transformative ruptures (Delgado Bernal & Alemán, 2017), conceptualizations, and scholarship, this chapter makes the contribution of students' spiritual activism for advancing Chicana/o/x/Latina/o/x educational possibilities and futurities. Transformative ruptures are incidents, experiences, and moments where systemic and intersectional marginalities are interrupted in the educational trajectories and experiences of Chicana/o/x/Latina/o/x students (Delgado Bernal & Alemán, 2017). Rooted in racial realism (Bell, 1991), transformative ruptures recognize the pervasiveness and permanence of racism and marginality in U.S. society yet argue that we can interrupt and intervene on how power traditionally functions. Delgado Bernal and Alemán (2017) argue that these moments of interruption of systemic marginality chip away at the white supremacist, heteropatriarchal, and colonial ideologies and systems.

An emerging body of scholarship has applied transformative ruptures to recognize the interruption of educational structural inequities. Delgado Bernal (1998) considers how pedagogies of the home, the knowledge systems, lessons, and *consejos* (advice) taught within Chicana/o/x/Latina/o/x student homes, families, and communities cannot destroy racism and other intersecting systems of oppression. However, these familial and community resources contribute to transformative ruptures by interrupting Eurocentric and white normative forms of knowledge bases and navigation. Transformative ruptures also make visible how parenting and mothering through a critical race *feminista* orientation (Delgado Bernal & Alemán, 2017) create possibilities for transformative ruptures within critical, reflective, and humanizing raising and socialization of Chicana/o/x/Latina/o/x children and learning in the home (Delgado Bernal, 1998). Souto-Manning (2021) explored the COVID-19 pandemic and response in education as a space and possibility for transformative rupture in disrupting the racial, capitalistic system. Furthermore, Hannegan-Martinez et al. (2022) have explored student resistance as a potential for transformative ruptures and offer pedagogical ruptures to recognize the moments, experiences, and interactions that nurture transformative student agency and resistance.

In the bridging of spiritual activism and transformative ruptures for understanding Chicana/Latina student resistance, this chapter has three central goals. First, through contextualizing spiritual activism in the systems of marginality that Chicana/o/x/Latina/o/x immigrant families experience, this chapter re-frames Chicana/Latina undergraduates as agents of change and resistance in U.S. society in their conscious and intentional everyday roles as daughters, sisters, and community members. Second, this chapter makes visible how student spiritual activism contributes to transformative ruptures, in the interruption, even momentarily, in the functioning of systems of marginality in the educational trajectories of Chicana/o/x/Latina/o/x students. This chapter argues that Chicana/Latina undergraduate resistance creates opportunities for Chicana/o/x/Latina/o/x educational pathways and futures.

Methodology and Pláticantes

This chapter draws from a series of *pláticas* with ten Chicana/Latina students who are daughters of Chicana/o/x/Latina/o/x immigrants in the United States and attending various four-year universities in California. *Pláticas* methodology centers on producing knowledge through the "everyday talk" of Chicana/o/x/Latina/o/x as a data source (Fierros & Delgado Bernal, 2016; Gonzalez, 2001) rooted in Chicana feminist epistemologies (Delgado Bernal, 1998). A *pláticas* methodology engages students as collaborators and co-constructors of knowledge production (Fierros & Delgado Bernal, 2016). *Pláticas* provide space for a fluid discussion, welcoming collaborators to bring their whole selves, histories, and experiences to data collection (Fierros & Delgado Bernal, 2016). As a research methodology, *pláticas* challenge the Eurocentric perspective that research has to be neutral and unbiased (Fierros & Delgado Bernal, 2016).

The ten Chicana/Latina undergraduate *pláticantes* are from Chicana/o/x/ Latina/o/x, mixed-status immigrant families, and were born or raised in California. Three of the students emigrated from México, and two of the immigrant students were undocumented. The *pláticantes* in this study all have younger siblings, and many of the student *pláticantes* are the oldest daughters in their nuclear families. Students described that their families navigate intersectional systems of marginality in the United States, particularly concerning race/ethnicity, gender, immigration status, socio-economic status, and language. Many of the Chicana/Latina students are either the first in their families to experience and graduate from the K-12 school system in the United States and are all first-generation college students. The student *pláticantes* varied in their majors, with many in the social sciences, physical sciences, and applied sciences. At the time of data collection, the Chicana/Latina undergraduates were in their second, third, or fourth year at their institution. With the centrality of knowledge produced in the everyday lives of Chicana/Latinas, *pláticas* methodology supports capturing and documenting how Chicana/Latina daughters engage in activating their agency and resistance to support their families and collective survival and success in the U.S. everyday.

Findings

A spiritual activism framework uncovers how Chicana/Latina undergraduate daughters consciously engage in actions and roles within their families because the intersecting systems of marginality they and their families navigate in the United States necessitate their action and response to support community access and success in education. These include (a) being called on by parents to take the lead in decisions about the educational trajectories of younger siblings; (b) serving as educational advisors and femtor[2] to family and community; and (c) sharing *consejos* and strategies for agency and resistance from their lived experience and navigation. In doing so, this makes visible how

Chicana/Latina undergraduates engage in spiritual activism in their everyday lives that contributes to transformative ruptures (Delgado Bernal & Alemán, 2017) in the moments and situations in which they challenge, interrupt, and act against how power aims to function against their families and communities within U.S. education institutions. These forms of spiritual activism also make visible the contradictions and challenges that Chicana/Latina undergraduate daughters negotiate, as their spiritual activism is essential for their families' survival and navigation, yet undeniably situated within gendered and cultural norms (Ramirez, 2023).

Leading Younger Siblings' Educational Trajectories

One example of spiritual activism that Chicana/Latina undergraduate daughters practice is rooted in serving a central role in leading, guiding, and making decisions about their younger siblings' educational trajectories. This form of spiritual activism is situated in navigating systems and identities as the first in their families to go to college and navigate the K-12 educational system in the United States. Celeste is the oldest daughter of previously undocumented Mexican immigrants, a first-generation college student who grew up in Los Angeles County and is now attending a four-year university. In the *plática*, she shared that her parents rely on her to make most decisions about her younger sister's educational trajectory. She shared the following:

> For example, for my sister, even when we were choosing her high school, me and my sister sat down and did research on different high schools in the area; I took her to visit the schools, and I literally would write down dates for visits or open houses. *I think it's important we see the schools if we can because I know from my experience that all high schools, even in the same city, are not resourced the same.* And when I couldn't go because I had a class or work, I would tell my parents or my husband to go with her in my place and to bring back the information they gave at school to me. And so, for the high school application everyone would call me and they're like, what do we put here? And I'm like, everyone is there, and no one can help? And I'd be like, in the middle of doing my homework and answering and be like, okay, show me a picture of the … So, everything would

fall on me. *It can be frustrating and hard for me, but it's really important, and I do it because I myself didn't know how to read certain things fully like official documents until I was in college.* I didn't know how to read articles, it would take me so long, it still takes me long. And so, for me, that was something important to show up for my family in that way.

For my parents, I know, they weren't able to go to school and like, learn these things, like, so I share a lot of these things with them. *I just feel responsible because I consider a formal education and now college education as a huge privilege. And I know that my parents weren't able to get that and I feel really responsible to share everything that I'm learning with them and use it to contribute to my family.*

Celeste shares the central role she holds in supporting her sister and parents in navigating the K-12 educational system in the United States. She aims to strategically navigate the educational system alongside her family, cognizant of the inequities in funding, resources, and opportunities in schooling. Celeste makes visible the challenges tied to this experience on her time, energy, and capacity as she negotiates her college and familial contexts. Yet, she recognizes that these actions and roles become necessary within the systemic and hierarchal systems she and her family navigate and experience in the United States.

Taking the lead on decisions shaping her sister's educational trajectory is a form of spiritual activism. Celeste is cognizant of her own lived experiences and the intersectional reality that her family navigates as a mixed-status family that requires strategic navigation and advocacy in her sister's educational trajectory. She recognizes how inequities shape the everyday experiences of her family, including the challenges and barriers with researching and preparing to submit a high school choice application, and acts to facilitate and support these processes. Celeste leads her family through educational processes in recognizing that her parents experience U.S. systems and structures as undocumented and monolingual Spanish-speaking people whom these systems were not designed to serve or support. Celeste's conscious actions in supporting her sister's educational journey result in a transformative rupture in her sister's and family's journey by interrupting how intersectional systems of oppression, including racism, classism, and nativism, traditionally shape educational pathways of

Chicana/o/x/Latina/o/x students in the United States. Through everyday decisions and navigation, Celeste leverages the privileges and opportunities she has experienced to interrupt how inequities underlie the educational process for students like her sister, and intentionally navigates intersectional systems and processes to set up her sister in educational contexts and pathways that will support her to thrive.

Serving as Educational Advisors and Femtors to Family and Community

The *pláticas* revealed that Chicana/Latina undergraduates also engage in spiritual activism when serving as advisors and femtors to their families and communities, particularly in navigating educational systems and processes. Denise is a queer Chicana majoring in environmental science, the oldest daughter in her family, and the first to pursue a higher education. Denise shared how she supports her younger sister with navigating the college application process and college choice process:

> I talk to my sister all the time on the phone because she's applying to college and more like *mentoring her and guiding her* even though I can't be there in person. My sister calls me up all the time. Like literally for anything that she does she's like, "Oh my god, I don't know how to do this. Can you help me?" Like … I was helping her sign-on. So she committed … to a California university, so she's going to be starting there next fall. And just like throughout the entire process, I was helping her like, "You gotta do this, you gotta do that," and during that time, I was going home more often just because I wanted to be there in person to kind of guide her through it. I'll talk to her often just because I feel she needs the most guidance and *because I've been through the process already … like I definitely want to give her insight on what I struggled in … but then also because I had mentors and I had advisors that kind of held my hand through the process because then honestly how would I know how to do any of this?* I did grow up with a single mom in an all-female household; my mom is my rock. The only person who has been able to support me at home has been my mom. With my sister, I take on the role of supporting because I feel she is going through a moment where a lot

of stressors are definitely building up and having me kind of guide her through that process [helps]. I hope to kind of lift off her shoulders some of that stress which in turn also helps my mom not having that stress on top of everything else she does for us as a single mom. *It's a cycle I am trying to interrupt.*

Denise shares that she consciously takes on "mentoring" and "guiding" her younger sister through the college application and transition process. She recognizes the role of mentors and advisors in her own college access and choice experience as a first-generation college student and the oldest daughter raised in an all-female household. Denise intentionally takes on this role in her younger sister's educational journey as she recognizes the structural and systemic information and resource gap in accessing college in her community. Growing up in a single-parent household with her mother as the primary income and support, Denise also situates closely and intimately supporting her sister in navigating this critical educational transition as direct support to her mother. These efforts potentially alleviate an additional stressor that their mother would have to take on in addition to working multiple jobs as the only source of income within their family during this educational transition. Through her spiritual activism, Denise interrupts how racism, sexism, and classism shape educational and life opportunity processes and structures for Chicanas/Latinas in the United States. Denise states, "It is a cycle I am trying to interrupt," as she is cognizant of the inequitable challenges and barriers from her lived experience and aims to interrupt them in her sister's educational journey. Denise is also intent on alleviating the stressors that the college access and transition experience can cause for students and families navigating this experience. In doing so, Denise politicizes the role of sister, daughter, mentor, and advisor, situating these roles as having the potential to intervene in how these systems function and underlie the trajectories of Chicana/o/x/Latina/o/x students.

Sharing "Consejos" and Strategies for Agency and Resistance

The student *pláticantes* also made visible that a third form of spiritual activism they engage in centers the importance of sharing *consejos* and strategies for agency, resistance, and navigation with their families, in particular, resources and information they gained access to within higher education or institutions that their families have not had an opportunity to access and experience. This form of spiritual activism was evident in Maribel's experience as a first-generation college student who grew up in a low-income neighborhood and household. Maribel shared how she leveraged and shared advice and navigational strategies with family:

> So basically, from undergraduate and my time here in college, *there is a lot I learned [about] how the process works from school and my own experience.* For example, applying to school, or unemployment benefits or navigating college and documents for getting to college. Like those documents and stuff … My family has always used social welfare programs and things like that; they're always getting food stamps and things like that. But oftentimes there's things that for whatever reason, the food stamps would get canceled, or they weren't eligible anymore, and we never questioned that, you know, why is this happening, we were just like okay and took it as fact. But I'm not just okay with things like that anymore, because now that I have that understanding. *I can't just take things as how they are anymore because I can understand why, oh, it's because of this, or you didn't turn in this. And then I was able to help them. Also with my younger siblings, telling them about college and how applying to college works and how to apply for financial aid, and why it's important now to focus on school, because it's going to determine this and that step and the requirements like A-G classes … that all matters and no one tells us it matters and that everything we do shapes our opportunities for college.*
>
> Honestly, I feel like the Latina culture is very family-oriented. And I've always cared deeply for my family. And sometimes, in the beginning, this was my every day and all the time to the point where it wasn't healthy for me. But I feel like now that I've learned to establish boundaries and stuff … *And I've seen the ways, not only just institutional, like systemic inequities, that have impacted my family, and I know that it's not their fault, and if I have access or experiences that can help my family out, then I will use [them] to help them.*

Maribel describes how she shares advice and strategies for navigating institutions and processes such as unemployment, social services, and higher education with her family, including younger siblings and parents. She recognizes that her *consejos* are informed by the privilege to access particular institutions, such as a four-year university, and her lived experience of navigating U.S. systems alongside her family since she was young. As the first in her family to pursue higher education, Maribel is the first family member to navigate the higher education system and access particular educational resources. She explicitly recognizes the complexity and contradictions inherent in taking on this role with her family. Maribel describes how supporting family is situated within cultural, ethnic, and gendered expectations for Latinas. She also explicitly states how she intentionally shares advice and strategies with her family due to the institutional and systemic inequities that impact her family, making this form of advocacy and resistance necessary. Her spiritual activism supports her in negotiating these contradictions, recognizing the agency and capacity of her family, and understanding how systemic and structural inequities necessitate intentional interruption in her family's everyday challenges and navigation. Her spiritual activism interrupts the pattern of Chicana/o/x/Latina/o/x immigrant students and families falling through the cracks of educational and social service systems in the United States (Pérez Huber et al., 2015).

Towards a Framewok of Chicana/Latina Spiritual Activism and Chicana/O/X and Latina/O/X Educational Futurities

Student experiences documented in the *pláticas* show how Chicana/Latina undergraduates contribute to Chicana/o/x/Latina/o/x educational futurities through their spiritual activism and transformative rupturing of normative power (see Figure 3.1). The student *pláticas* demonstrate how Chicana/Latina undergraduate daughters engage in spiritual activism through everyday and intentional actions that support their families' strategic navigation of inequities, challenges, and barriers within educational systems and processes. Kelley's (2022) theorization of freedom dreaming is rooted in "living through our third eyes" (p. 3), the capacity to see, imagine, and envision possibilities of a liberated world and future and embodying, enacting, and creating that freedom and world. Kelley (2022) points to the need for deep connection, understanding, and the possibility of imagining a different future, a possibility that stems from a deep understanding of one's present reality and the world to "see the poetic and prophetic in the richness of our daily lives" (p. 2). In exploring student resistance through the centering of spiritual activism, this chapter challenges the "de-spiritualization of the academy" and "the de-politicization of the spiritual" (Lara, 2002, p. 437) by arguing that resistance is innately a spiritual undertaking and that the spiritual is by default political. Students' deep knowledge of their present realities, intuitive and embodied experiences, and the ability to envision and enact a future that transcends the present possibilities and boundaries within systemic and structural oppression is the spiritual root of their everyday resistance. This chapter connects the inner workings of the mind and spirit, dreaming and visionary work, to the outer world of action, allowing the metaphysical to guide resistance in creating a *mundo nuevo* (Anzaldúa, 2002).

The student *pláticantes* in this research demonstrate their capacity to understand and make meaning of complex contradictions and negotiations with how racism, sexism, nativism, and cultural norms shape Chicana/Latina roles and expectations within their families, while also grappling with and attending to the systemic inequities rooted in those same systems of marginality that underlie the lives of their families that necessitate interruption (Ramirez, 2023). Spiritual activism is rooted in the students' ability to recognize how systems of marginality shape their families' lives and educational pathways and take action to transform the inequities (Anzaldúa, 2002). Chicana/Latina students from mixed-status and immigrant families know intimately how these oppressive systems function because the systems often work against them and their families as they exist, negotiate, and resist within and against them. Anzaldúa (1987) considers how racial and gendered outsiders in U.S. society have the capacity "to see in surface phenomena the meaning of deeper realities, to see the deep structures below the surface" (p. 62). Students possess *la facultad* as they hold the sensitivity for seeing, feeling, and recognizing structural inequities that require attention, attending to, and interrupting.

Figure 3.1

Chicana/Latina Spiritual Activism and Chicana/o/x/Latina/o/x Educational Futurities

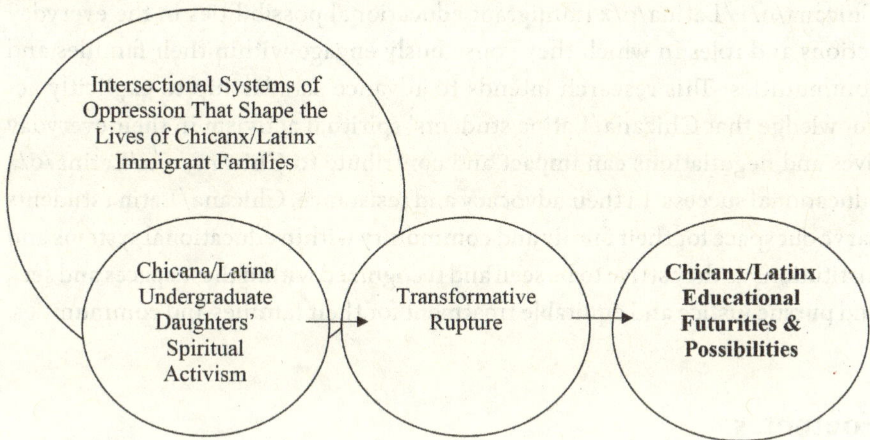

With spiritual activism, students interrupt how racism and intersectional marginalities function against Chicana/o/x/Latina/o/x students and families in K-12 schooling and higher education. Educational (in)opportunities are shaped by upholding racial and intersectional inequities in educational systems, processes, and practices (Camargo Gonzalez et al., 2021; Nava & Martinez, 2023). Through this intimate and everyday form of spiritual activism, Chicana/Latina undergraduate daughters intervene in the intersectional systems of marginality that are upheld by schooling and higher education systems as Chicana/o/x/Latina/o/x students experience these systems as *atravesada/o/xs*, outsiders within a system and institution not designed for Chicana/o/x/Latina/o/x students to succeed and thrive (Conchas & Acevedo, 2020). The experiences of the student *pláticantes* in this study make visible how student spiritual activism (Anzaldúa, 2002) can contribute to transformative ruptures (Delgado Bernal & Alemán, 2017) within Chicana/o/x/Latina/o/x educational pathways through interrupting and intervening, even if momentarily, in how power traditionally functions and restricts opportunity. The students in this research intervene in the racism and marginality present in their siblings' and family members' educational experiences, pathways, and transitions and contribute to creating openings, possibilities, and bridges for educational success and futures (see Figure 3.1).

The bridging of spiritual activism and transformative ruptures framework in this chapter supports an uncovering of how Chicana/Latina daughters within immigrant families in the United States contribute to imagining and enacting Chicana/o/x/Latina/o/x immigrant educational possibilities in the everyday actions and roles in which they consciously engage within their families and communities. This research intends to advance scholarship to explicitly acknowledge that Chicana/Latina students' spiritual activism in their everyday lives and negotiations can impact and contribute to Chicana/o/x/Latina/o/x educational success. In their advocacy and resistance, Chicana/Latina students carve out space for their family and community within educational systems and institutions as they strive to be seen and recognized within these spaces and seek and pursue justice and equitable treatment for their families and communities.

Footnotes

[1] You follow your promise.

[2] I use femtor in my writing to challenge patriarchal assumptions inscribed in the normative use of language such as mentor and mentee, and to center and make visible the gender identities of women involved in these relationships and the gendered labor that women, and in particular women of color, engage in within academia.

Reference

Acevedo-Gil, N., & Madrigal-Garcia, Y. (2018). Mentoring among Latina/o scholars: Enacting spiritual activism to navigate academia. *American Journal of Education*, 124(3), 313-344.

Acevedo, N., Nunez-Rivera, S., Casas, Y., Cruz, E., & Rivera, P. (2021). Enacting spiritual activism to develop a sense of belonging: Latina community college students choosing and persisting in STEM. *Journal of Women and Gender in Higher Education*, 14(1), 59-78.

Anzaldúa, G. E. (1987). *Borderlands: La Frontera*. Aunt Lute Books.

Anzaldúa, G. E. (2013). Now let us shift … the path of conocimiento … inner work, public acts1. In *This bridge we call home* (pp. 540-578). Routledge.

Anzaldúa, G. E. (2002). Now let us shift … the path of conocimiento … inner work, public acts. In G. E. Anzaldúa & A. Keating (Eds.), *This Bridge We Call Home* (pp. 554-592). Routledge.

Bell, D. (1991). Racial realism. *Connecticut Law Review, 24,* 363.

Camargo Gonzalez, L., Ramirez, B.R., Burciaga, R., Pérez Huber, L., & Solórzano, D.G. (2021) Latina/o Education (In)Opportunity. In E. G. Murillo, Jr., S. A. Villenas, R. T. Galván, J. S. Muñoz, C. Martínez, & M. Machado-Casas (Eds.), *Handbook of Latinos and Education: Theory, Research, and Practice.*

Conchas, G. Q., & Acevedo, N. (2020). *The Chicana/o/x dream: Hope, resistance, and educational success.* Harvard Education Press.

Cruz, C. (2001). Toward an epistemology of a brown body. *International Journal of Qualitative Studies in Education, 14*(5), 657-669.

Delgado Bernal, D. (1998). Using a Chicana feminist epistemology in educational research. *Harvard Educational Review, 68*(4), 555-583.

Delgado Bernal, D. & Alemán, E. (2017). *Transforming Educational Pathways for Chicana/o Students: A Critical Race Feminista Praxis.* Teachers College Press.

Delgado Bernal, D., Elenes, C. A., & Godinez, F. E. (Eds.). (2006). *Chicana/Latina education in everyday life: Feminista perspectives on pedagogy and epistemology.* State University of New York Press.

Dillard, C. B. (2000). The substance of things hoped for, the evidence of things not seen: Examining an endarkened feminist epistemology in educational research and leadership. *International Journal of Qualitative Studies in Education, 13*(6), 661-681.

Elenes, C. (2013). Nepantla, spiritual activism, new tribalism: Chicana feminist transformative pedagogies and social justice education. *Journal of Latino/Latin American Studies, 5*(3), 132-141.

Espino, M. M. (2021). Pathways to healing BodyMindSpirit for Latina-identified college students, administrators, and faculty in higher education. *Journal of Women and Gender in Higher Education, 14*(1), 1-4.

Fierros, C. O., & Delgado Bernal, D. (2016). Vamos a pláticar: The contours of pláticas as Chicana/Latina feminist methodology. *Chicana/Latina Studies,* (15)2, 98-121.

Gonzalez, F. E. (2001). Haciendo que hacer-cultivating a Mestiza worldview and academic achievement: Braiding cultural knowledge into educational research, policy, practice. *International Journal of Qualitative Studies in Education, 14*(5), 641-656.

Hannegan-Martinez, S., Mendoza Avina, S., Delgado Bernal, D., & Solorzano, D. G. (2022). (Re) Imagining Transformational Resistance: Seeds of Resistance and Pedagogical Ruptures. *Urban Education,* 00420859221092973.

Hurtado, A. (2003). Theory in the flesh: Toward an endarkened epistemology. *International Journal of Qualitative Studies in Education, 16*(2), 215-225.

Keating, A. (2005). Shifting perspectives: Spiritual activism, social transformation, and the politics of spirit. In A. Keating (Ed.), *EntreMundos/AmongWorlds: New Perspectives on Gloria E. Anzaldúa* (pp. 241-254).

Kelley, R. D. (2022). *Freedom dreams: The Black radical imagination*. Beacon Press.

Lara, I. (2002). Healing sueños for academia. In G. Anzaldúa & A. Keating (Eds.), *This bridge we call home: Radical visions for transformation* (pp. 433-438). Routledge.

Lara, I. (2005). Bruja positionalities: Toward a Chicana/Latina spiritual activism. *Chicana/Latina Studies*, (4)2, 10-45.

Moraga, C. L., & Anzaldúa, G. E. (2002). *This bridge called my back: Writings by radical Women of Color*. Third Woman Press.

Nava, P., & Martinez, R. (2023). Critical junctures along the Chicanx/Latinx educational pipeline: Interdisciplinary and intersectional perspectives. *Association of Mexican American Educators Journal*, 17(2), 4-10.

Pérez Huber, L., Malagón, M. C., Ramirez, B. R., Gonzalez, L. C., Jimenez, A., & Vélez, V. N. (2015). *Still Falling through the Cracks: Revisiting the Latina/o Education Pipeline*. UCLA Chicano Studies Research Center.

Ramirez, B. R., (2023). Collective survival, love, and resistance: The spiritual activism of Latina undergraduate daughters from mixed status immigrant families. In M. J. Villasenor & H. Jimenez (Eds.), *Latinx experiences: Interdisciplinary perspectives*. Sage Publishing.

Ramirez, B. R., & Carrola, M. (2021). Chicana/Latina immigrant undergraduate mujeres and the survival and prosperidad of their familias. In B. Pletcher, F. Bruun, R. Banda, K. Watson, & A. Perez (Eds.), *Empowering student researchers: Critical contributions by emerging 21st century scholars*. Texas A&M University.

Ramirez, B.R., & Puente, M. (2021). Avanzando Juntas: Chicana/Latina Pedagogy of Sisterhood in Graduate School. *About Campus*. https://doi.org/10.1177/10864822211058247

Salazar Pérez, M., & Saavedra, C. M. (2020). Spiritual activism as a means for social transformation: Womanist and Chicana feminist possibilities. *Equity & Excellence in Education*, 53(3), 315-323.

Solórzano, D. G., & Yosso, T. J. (2001). Critical race and LatCrit theory and method: Counter-storytelling. *International Journal of Qualitative Studies in Education*, 14(4), 471-495.

Souto-Manning, M. (2021). The pandemic as a portal: On transformative ruptures and possible futures for education. *Occasional Paper Series, 2021*(46), 2.

CHAPTER 4

Community, Care, and Relational Practice:

Reimagining Freedom Dreaming in a Difficult Dialogues Program

Jie Y. Park, Borodine Chery, Eric J. DeMeulenaere, Elsabet Franklin, Leyla Knight, Zabrina Richards, and Chloe Wing Ching Yau

THIS CHAPTER DRAWS on our *praxis* in the Difficult Dialogues on Race and Racism program (DD) at a predominantly white university in the Northeast of the U.S. DD is a student-run, intergroup dialogue program in which Eric (white man) and Jie (Asian woman) serve as faculty advisors. A group of ten-to-twelve Black, Indigenous, People of Color (BIPOC) and white undergraduate DD fellows design and facilitate antiracist dialogues on campus. Over the last three years, DD fellows have hosted dialogues for students, faculty, and staff on racial microaggressions, inclusion and belonging, and relationships across race lines. DD emerged from Eric and Jie's yearning for a more racially-just campus in the wake of the murders of George Floyd and Breona Taylor. The call for chapters for *Repertories of Resistance* prompted Jie and Eric to grapple with whether DD was a space for "freedom dreaming" (Kelley, 2002/2022). From this conversation, Jie invited 11 DD fellows to a series of dialogues and to co-author the chapter. Five accepted: Borodine, Chloe, Elsabet, Leyla, and Zabrina are all Students of Color (two Asian and three Black).

An Unusual Opening: Integrating Our Conceptual Framework with Our Epistemological Stance and Methodological Approach

In a speech at the Second Sex Conference, Audre Lorde (1984) offered the now famous line, "The master's tools will never dismantle the master's house" (p. 112). She recognized that liberation requires not only new ideas, but new practices and modes of representation as well. A decade earlier, Paulo Freire (1970) in *Pedagogy of the Oppressed* offered processes for building knowledge for education that mirror the humanizing ideals for which we strive. He argued that revolutionary praxis and building knowledge must be done collectively, in solidarity with people. We, as students and activists for racial liberation, recognize alongside Lorde and Freire that our quest for liberation must not only apply to our ideals, but also to our practices and processes. Thus, we begin our chapter by aligning our journey with the destination, or more concretely, by revealing the synergies among our theoretical frame, epistemology, methodology, and our approach to writing.

Theoretically, we situate our dialogue and writing within a set of critical tensions in the scholarship on Black fugitivity (Gross-Wyrtzen & Moulton, 2023; Harney & Moten, 2013; Lewis, 2023; Moten, 2003). The first tension is the in-betweenness of the flight *from* oppressive spaces and flight *towards* liberation. Lewis (2023) highlights, "Fugitivity is a process of prolonged liminality—the period between what was and what is to become. Thus, the most apt way to understand the Black condition as an experience and phenomenon is to linger with the in-between" (p. 1389).

In the dialogues with all seven of us, which is also our method of analysis, we sought to showcase and make sense of this liminal tension. Where and how do we situate our gaze? Is it looking over our shoulders at the systems of oppression and the traumas from them (Kelley, 2018), or do we look ahead, toward our imaginations of the promised land (Kelley, 2002/2022)? And in Freire's (1998) terms, how can we denounce oppression while simultaneously announcing our humanizing possibilities?

Addressing that question, we turn again to Black fugitivity, which deconstructs the either/or gaze of behind or ahead, simultaneously holding not only the past and future but also the present—the journey itself. Grace Lee Boggs underscores the importance of the journey and trust-filled connections with those beside us on the journey (Boggs & Kurashige, 2012). Framing our work within fugitivity reminds us to attend to the journey itself and recognize that in the interpersonal spaces and alongside others on the journey, we can forge small and intimate spaces that enable us to not only imagine liberatory futures but seed their emergence (brown, 2017).

Just as we refuse the either/or construction of the backward gaze and the forward gaze, we challenge the dichotomous framing of caring for the self and caring for the collective. Gross-Wyrtzen and Moulton (2023) assert, "Intimacy, kin-making, and care work are central to contemporary fugitive practices of freedom for racialized, sexualized people struggling to survive" (p. 1265). Guided by Black fugitivity, we embrace the tensions embedded in caring for ourselves and caring for the collective. We seek not the middle ground but the dialectical space that embraces both/and.

Importantly, we conceive of fugitivity not only as theory but as method (Gross-Wyrtzen & Moulton, 2023). Fugitivity as a method enables us to dive into the messy work of forging community and kin-making in the "under-commons" (Harney & Moten, 2013). It is simultaneously a refusal to become disciplined by "an institution incapable of loving [us]—of loving anyone, perhaps" (Kelley, 2018, p. 154). In other words, it "is about becoming undisciplined" (Gross-Wyrtzen & Moulton, 2023, p. 1264).

We embrace this call to be undisciplined, to refuse the master's tools, not only in our theorizing, but in how we collectively build knowledge and convey that knowledge-building in writing. We do this by writing a critical co-constructed autoethnography (Cann & DeMeulenaere, 2012)—a powerful tool for fugitivity as method. Garrett-Walker et al. (in press) identify three components that make autoethnography critical. First is methodological. They write, "autoethnography came about as a critique to research that distanced the researcher from the researched" (Cann & DeMeulenaere, in press, p. 8). Furthermore, as we reject the false dichotomy of looking behind and ahead, autoethnography complements this by integrating the inward with the outward gaze. In autoethnography, "we look inward—into our identities, thoughts, feelings and experiences—and outward—into our relationships, communities, and cultures" (Adams et al., 2015, p. 46).

Relying on critical autoethnography is one way we become undisciplined and subversive. But methodology alone does not make it critical. Critical autoethnography is also disruptive of what bell hooks has called the "white supremacist capitalist patriarchy" (Garrett-Walker et al., in press, p. 9). But even that is still insufficient. We also need praxis, or "an activist commitment to change the material conditions caused by oppression" (Garrett-Walker et al., in press, p. 9).

To further link critical autoethnography to fugitivity as method, we add the "*co-constructed*" component to our methodology (Cann & DeMeulenaere, 2012, p. 146), linking back to Gross-Wyrtzen and Moulton's (2023) concept of "kin-making" (p. 1265). This chapter is authored by seven of us, making our voices heard together and conveying the very human process by which we used dialogue to make sense of freedom dreaming. The narrative dialogues included in this chapter reveal moments of profound insight intertwined with differences and uncertainty. We also include quotidian moments, suggesting that learning occurs communally and within the pace and breadth of lived lives. The type of writing we engage with provides "a tool that can reveal the love and respect coupled with critique, the humor even within the spaces of pain" (Cann & DeMeulenaere, 2020, p. 37). If our activist and pedagogical work strives to humanize ourselves and those with whom we work, we assert that our research methods and writing should strive to operate in concert with such convictions. We seek, in this method of writing, to not only be "undisciplined," but also to use our writing to capture and show the journey, the flight from fugitivity if you will, rather than just tell about it. Thus, we invite readers to first enter into our dialogue space. After sharing a series of dialogues, we offer an analysis of them, highlighting everyday forms of care, community, and relational practices in racial justice work like the Difficult Dialogues program.

Checking Into Difficult Dialogues

Eric logs onto Zoom a little before 6:30 p.m. It has been two months since he has seen the fellows. Eric looks at the desktop screen with a broadening smile as lonely black frames transform into summered faces.

"Nice to see you, Zabrina! Are you calling from home?" Eric asks.

"Nice to see you too" she replies, "I am in Los Angeles for my summer internship."

Another face fills the screen. "Hi!" Chloe chimes in.

"Hello, Chloe! What time is it there?" Eric asks.

"It is 6:30 in the morning in Hong Kong, I just woke up and I'm really tired." Elsabet, Borodine, and Jie soon check into the digital space.

"Hi everyone, sorry I am late," Jie says. "It looks like everyone is here except Leyla. Has anyone heard from Leyla?"

"I'll text them," Eric offers.

As Eric turns to his phone, Jie begins the process of having everyone check in.

Jie is the last to share, "I definitely resonate with what many of you said about energy levels. I just had a knock-down, drag-out power struggle with my five-year-old. So yeah, just feeling it right now." She leans back into her chair.

There is a pause. Eric was about to start the agenda, but he let the silence hang, then offered,

"What Jie said reminds me—in these Zoom spaces, we're like in different worlds and have our lives in the background. We don't want to dehumanize ourselves in that process, so if family or life comes into the mix, don't feel the need to apologize. That's part of being alive: Take care of what you need to take care of, okay?

Freedom Dreaming in Difficult Dialogues

"Thanks for that, Eric," Jie offers. "Now let's turn to the conversation prompts we emailed earlier. We asked you to read excerpts from Robin Kelley's book and reflect on a series of questions about how we can connect his ideas to our work in DD. As we framed it in the email, freedom dreaming can be seen as *struggling for* something, a vision for the future, which might be contrasted with struggling against an oppressive reality. So, let's begin: How do each of you understand struggling against and/or struggling for?"

Elsabet unmutes, "Sorry, my background is kind of noisy. It's late here in Spain, but the street is still very packed with people! Can you hear me okay?"

"You're good," Jie responds, and others raise their thumbs.

Elsabet continues, "Okay, for me, struggling against means focusing on whatever the problem is. Like, if the problem is mass incarceration, which I often talk about, it is really the struggle against." She adds, "So while struggling against racism makes racism the focus, struggling for racial justice is bigger and requires a radical reimagining of what could be."

While Elsabet speaks, Leyla joins Zoom, waves at everyone, and unmutes themselves, "Hey y'all, how are you doing? I'm sorry I am late!"

Everyone waves back at Leyla. Eric updates Leyla and invites them to jump in any time they want. Leyla nods and jumps right in, "Struggle against often feels reactive. It can also be our attempt at reducing harm. When we struggle against, our attention will be focused on the most pressing issue and the other problems that are not as present will fade away in the background. So, struggle against often feels temporary because of how reactive it can feel."

After several more turns of folks sharing their thoughts on struggling against, Jie transitions us to discussing struggle for.

Borodine offers, "I would say, like Elsabet, that struggling for seems more radical. It requires more time, to consider what the end goal will be. And I think a lot of us get lost and even overwhelmed in struggling against, so we never get to the struggle for."

Eric begins to talk, nodding as he tries to write and speak at the same time, "Yeah, in addition to what Borodine mentioned, the 'struggle for' requires us to be more strategic, visionary. Like we are building something new because we are imagining a different reality that may feel utopian."

Elsabet agrees, "Yeah, we have all these obstacles and we want to get over them. But what are we going to get over it for? What are we reimagining and what do we want a better society to look like?"

There is a pause while everyone processes how struggling for can create new realities. Leyla moves the conversation by asking if we find ourselves struggling against or struggling for in our daily lives.

"I have more experiences of struggling *against*." Borodine begins, "But I wish I could struggle *for* a little more. I think struggling against is really tiring, especially for those who are doing that work."

"Doing that work?" Jie prods.

"I guess I mean, like," Borodine pauses a little before continuing, "I mean BIPOC folks at a predominantly white institution are always having to struggle against the subtle and sometimes not so subtle forms of racism."

"That resonates with me," Elsabet joins in, "I'm also a 'struggle against' person. I'm thinking of many conversations where I've named the problem, like with mass incarceration or whatever. And people are like, 'Okay, so what is a world without it? And I'm kind of stuck. Over time I've started to re-imagine more, but I still feel like I'm a 'struggle against' person."

"A 'struggle against' person?!" interjects Leyla. It is unclear whether this is a question or an exclamation. "It is kinda deep that we are talking about this as an identity."

Zabrina jumps in on the identity point, "I feel like we're socialized to struggle against because certain structures and powers in place want us to be stuck and not even think about the 'what ifs'. Like I remember being in a class and the professor asked, 'What if we didn't have police?' I don't think that ever occurred to me."

"Yeah!" Elsabet gets more animated, "Ruthie Gilmore, a prison abolitionist, argues it is not just imagining a world without police or prisons, but imagining a society where police and prisons are unnecessary. I don't think we are ever asked to do this type of imagining" (Kushner, 2019).

The conversation continued for a while with all of us feeling like we mostly struggle against and lamenting our inability to engage more in "freedom dreaming" (Kelley, 2002/2022). However, we had not really talked about these concepts in terms of DD. Eric pivots the conversation: "We haven't yet discussed how these concepts relate to our work in Difficult Dialogues. In DD, are we struggling against or for?"

Zabrina tentatively offers, "For me, I feel like DD is more about the struggle against. I see it as a space to get away from the "racial battle fatigue" (Smith, 2004; Smith et al., 2011). I feel like in most spaces on campus I am always struggling against racism."

Borodine adds, "I agree. DD is mostly about the struggle against. Or maybe," she pauses, "DD is a space I can go to learn and recharge myself for returning to the struggle against, which I think we've all said is the primary way we live, even the way we identify."

Elsabet offers, "Yeah, it is kind of like a gym space that gets you ready for the battle." Jie unmutes and turns her camera back on. She begins to speak as she repositions Aidan onto her shoulder to burp him, "What you are all saying rings true for me too. We modified DD to respond to calls to spend more time building community among the fellows. And, while important work, that was not what Eric and I had originally conceptualized."

That comment sits for a while. Finally, Chloe presses the "unmute" button. "Frankly speaking, if we never had this DD community, I wouldn't have felt hopeful. This space has provided a shell for me."

Elsabet asks, "Shell? Uh, what do you mean?" Chloe gathers her thoughts, and responds, "Hmmm, this shell is like a safe place. People trust each other. You don't fear your ideas will be criticized since everyone is open to new perspectives. DD is a safe community for us. And for me, the ability to create this community here, with people from all different backgrounds gives me hope."

Eric jumps in, "So Chloe, I really appreciate this comment, especially with the idea of 'hope.' I guess my question for you is whether you think having hope from the community is a form of freedom dreaming?"

Chloe, looking through her notes, adds, "I'm not quite sure, but I do think the hope from the DD community itself is a form of freedom dreaming. Just like I said earlier, although everyone is different, we listen and support each other."

After several seconds of silence, Zabrina echoes, "Adding to what Chloe just said, I think being in a community with People of Color gives me hope and energy. In previous schools, I was the only Person of Color, and holding the responsibility of educating my white peers and educators drained all my energy. Because of how I grew up, I need a community who will understand my experiences. Being in community with the DD fellows, Jie and Eric, I feel energized and a sense of hope because of what DD strives to accomplish. I think it's crucial to have spaces for folks of color, which is in itself a 'struggle for.' You need that community."

"I appreciate what Zabrina said," Borodine chimes in. "We really just need that sense of community and that community can be the foundation. By being in community, we can imagine a 'struggle for.' You might not realize it, but you're seeing an alternate reality where you can just be with People of Color and talk … and you're not afraid of how you're being perceived. And it's not only People of Color; we have white people in DD too. And the community is a source that helps us lean on each other and actually do the things that we want to do."

Chloe, excited about the conversation, interjects, "In my opinion, foundation is crucial when it comes to doing justice work, people building relationships with others—it is not just about the present, but also in the long run, for the future. We are creating a space in DD, which helps us imagine how other spaces might be. We are not just hiding from the racist world, we are beginning to build our vision for the world, just on a small scale with a small group of folks."

"Oh, I like that." Borodine then continues, "I think building community in these smaller spaces is where freedom dreaming can happen. It gives us space to feel free and see our dreams of the future by giving us a foundation. And when we can build these small worlds, it gives us hope to continue to fight."

Leyla's screen shows a heart emoji as Borodine finishes. Leyla then unmutes, "Yeah. When you're by yourself you can kind of cycle through the same problems and you can be limited in that effort, but when you share something with somebody else, hope increases."

Jie unmutes to add, "Wow. Everyone is helping me realize that freedom dreaming requires community, and even when you're struggling against racism, you can do it with a group of people, in a way that mirrors the world you're struggling for. We are creating spaces for ourselves, microcosms of love, hope, and support. We need to create examples of what we'd like on a small scale. I am really excited by this idea."

Borodine adds, "I mean just having people who can 'get you' is a taste of freedom."

There are lots of head nods and "mmm hmms" in response to the series of comments that has led up to this realization. While we're nearing the end of our meeting time, everyone seems more energized. The lament of being "struggle against" people seems to have faded, with the recognition that by being in the DD community, we are freedom dreaming, and embodying love, hope, and support.

Back on Campus: Centering Care and Relational Practices in Freedom Dreaming

A month later, the fall semester is about to begin. Jie and Eric feel a hum of excitement as the campus comes back to life. We meet up in a small conference room next to Jie's office on a Sunday afternoon. As the students walk in, hugs are exchanged by all. Jie and Eric place snacks in the middle of the conference table. Everyone grabs seats around the table, and we begin our check-ins. After the check-ins, Eric shifts everyone back to the previous conversation, "Last time, you all were raising powerful points that circled back to community—building community in DD as a form of freedom dreaming, being in community with one another, doing for each other. Jie and I want to probe this idea of community with y'all, since community is so often used that its meaning can be watered down. What does it mean when you say the community is the foundation?"

Chloe notes, "I think that community as a foundation provides so much that you're willing to sacrifice. In our last conversation, I woke up at 6:00 a.m. since I was in Hong Kong. I was texting my partner saying that I was tired before the meeting even started. Yet, after the session, I texted my partner saying, 'I can't go back to sleep; I'm just too energized after the meeting!' I feel like the community itself matters. And the community then motivates you to sacrifice for the group." She processes her thoughts, "I'm not sure if this is related to freedom dreaming—but sacrificing for each other, that entails something?" As Chloe wraps up her thoughts, she reaches for a can of seltzer.

Everyone in the room remains silent for a bit, processing Chloe's points. Most of us at this point are having some food for thought (literally and meta-phorically) when Elsabet responds to what Chloe said. "So, just to clarify my understanding of what you're saying, you are motivated to sacrifice because the collective provides a sense of support to continue the work?"

"Sort of..." Chloe says after taking a sip of her seltzer. "The community pro-vides the space to reimagine with people. It's an energizing environment where people can express their thoughts freely, build off one another, and create new knowledge. So, after I got off the call, I was just so excited and filled with hope. I sacrificed by waking up early for the Zoom call, but in the end, I felt so fulfilled."

Borodine nods, "Like being in a community allows you to do more power-ful self-care, even if you're sacrificing to be with the community."

Eric turns his body to look at Borodine: "I just want to emphasize what you just said. Basically, you seem to be saying that sacrifice is a form of self-care. That seems like a paradox, so help me by unpacking."

Borodine gives a gentle smile and shifts her glasses: "Yeah, I mean, it does sound contradictory, but in a way, by sacrificing something now, it could help you in the future. Or stated differently, by realizing that when you sacrifice for the community you are taking care of the community which, in turn, is taking care of you. So, your sacrifice is caring for yourself in a way too."

Jie jumps in, "Borodine raised the idea of future. So, is it the community we're in relationship to or are we in community with those who come behind us, that we don't even know yet?" She reaches for an oatmeal cookie and decides against it.

Eric teases Jie, "It's healthy because it has oatmeal." Jie rolls her eyes at Eric as he continues, "Like, are we doing Difficult Dialogues for us right in this moment or for all the Students of Color who come to our university after we graduate?"

Zabrina responds, "I think so. When I think about struggling for, I think about struggling for future generations in hopes that they don't have to experience what we've had to endure."

Borodine agrees: "Yeah, I think we are, because inherently when you are fighting for something, it's for you and for a community that you haven't met yet."

Elsabet offers a different view of sacrifice, "This conversation of sacrificing for the collective good—you can get lost in it. What if you sacrifice too much? I've been in a lot of advocacy groups where students are sacrificing a lot of their time and effort. And they're doing it for the greater good, but is it really self-care for them? Not really. And so, we have to be careful about that sacrifice and how far it could go for the individuals who are sacrificing themselves for the collective."

Chloe pushes back. "I agree, but maybe that is not the kind of collective that we are dreaming of and wanting to build? I have huge faith in this community. Like, let's say if I sacrifice a lot of myself. I believe that people here would say, 'Hey Chloe. I think you're doing too much.' I believe that this community is able to provide me with that care and sense of balance."

Jie says quietly, "The community takes care of you," as she writes this down. There is silence, but we are used to sitting with it, appreciating the care that we put into our words.

After a while, Leyla chimes in, "It is not just individuals sacrificing for the community; it is the community extending itself for the individual too. But if that is true, then the community cannot be some future community that we are not yet connected to. Going back to Elsabet's point, it is when there are relationships between the individual and others in the community that the community can look out for individuals and make sure that someone is not burning out. The energy and the self-care we get from the community is about relationships, so this doesn't seem to include some abstract future community."

"This talk about care and self-care and connection reminds me of something I heard on the Ezra Klein show when he interviewed Alison Gopnik (2023)," Eric says. "She said that 'We don't care for others because we love them: we love them because we care for them' (Gopnik, 2023, p. 61). What's important to me in this quote is that it is precisely through this sacrifice, this care for others, that love is developed. It is not the loving relationships that lead to the care and sacrifice, but the other way around. To me, then, building loving relationships requires these sacrificial acts of care. To me, then, the community cannot be some abstract group of people."

Leyla ponders aloud, "Yeah, it's also important to reclaim self-care. That commodified version of care is created by the fashion industry." They pause, "You will not feel relieved from the dis-ease of white supremacy with a lavish hot bath. It's a temporary solution to a long-lasting problem."

Jie says, "I'm trying to bring the threads together here—with hope, community, sacrifice, care, and freedom dreaming. I heard that there is hope in community, but not just in some abstract sense of community, but community grounded in authentic relationships. Without community—and more concretely, community based on relational practice—sacrifice and freedom dreaming aren't possible. I'm wondering if these connections are gendered for y'all? Because in Robin D.G. Kelley's (2002/2022) book, *Freedom Dreams*, the movements and the examples that he talks about, for me, feel very masculine. But as we said, freedom dreaming can be very small, intimate, and relational. Is that perhaps a feminist revisioning of freedom dreaming?" Her upward intonation suggests that she is still in the process of wondering.

"Hmm, is it the macro scale that makes it masculine, or the abstractness of the ideas and the absence of relational practice?" Eric asks, continuing, "It's worth connecting to Grace Lee Boggs and the importance of relationships for revolution (Boggs & Kurashige, 2012). She says you have to create community by beginning with the needs of the community and by creating caring, or maybe she says, loving relationships with one another."

Elsabet asks "Can we read something by Grace Lee Boggs?"

"To answer your question, Eric, about what makes freedom dreaming masculine," Leyla interjects, "I think it is the absence of relational practice. Maybe not absence. But the relational practice seems invisible, behind the scenes, almost taken-for-granted. Like the importance of eating together when you're in community."

Borodine adds, "I agree with what Jie said about it being gendered. In the history classes that I've taken, we've focused on, for example, women's groups and how they influence each other on a much smaller scale."

Elsabet nods and pauses to get her thoughts together, "I appreciate what you're saying Borodine. It reminds me of June Jordan's piece, and how she decides to end the 'Report from the Bahamas' (2003)." Jie and Eric had given everyone that essay to read before the last time they met. "Remember when June Jordan is on the plane and looking around, and everyone's drinking their beverages? After sharing that scene, she insists on the need to all be in relationship with one another, and how that could create meaningful change."

Many of us nod in agreement with Elsabet's thoughts. Jie says, "Ahhh. There is so much more we can explore here—but like always, y'all and this conversation have brought me to a new understanding of freedom dreaming, an understanding that centers relationships of care and love. That to me feels like our contribution."

We are now well past when we were scheduled to end. Scanning the room, Jie says, "I am conscious of time. Thank you all for making the time. Please remember to fill out both doodle polls, when we are going to regularly meet, and when to go apple picking."

"Yes, please do that today," Eric chimes in. "And not to sound cheesy, these have been such amazing conversations, and I feel so much more connected to you all."

"Ahh," Leyla says making her hands into the shape of a heart, "I am so glad I signed up for this, despite all the work! Ha!"

There are more "ahs" expressed. Elsabet rushes away because she is late for work. Others head out to dorms or meet-ups. Leyla and Chloe linger, talking as Jie and Eric straighten up the space, not wanting the conversation, or maybe the feeling of being in community, to end.

Conclusion: Group Reflections and Theoretical Insights

When we began the series of dialogues as a way to write this chapter, we had been wrestling with the tension between retreating inwards (as a mechanism of self-defense and self-care) and putting ourselves out there to engage a predominantly white campus in race dialogues. Through writing a critical co-constructed autoethnography, we probed our deeply-held beliefs and questions, and the stories and lived experiences behind them. We also came to interrogate the dichotomous either/or framework between racial justice work and care (self-and collective care), and between resistance against oppression and freedom dreaming. In writing this last section, we are also in dialogue with those who have given feedback to our chapter, making our group reflections and theoretical insights more multivocal and nuanced, expanding the "collective" to include those whom we think with and write to. These insights are:

- DD has to be a place of care and community for both the campus members who attend a Difficult Dialogues event and us, the fellows who facilitate the events—without such care work, dialogue about and for racial justice is not possible. And while we are still questioning how to center love, foster communities, and actualize our longing for deep connections across multiple lines of difference and power asymmetries, we recognize that we (as DD fellows) have to practice, with each other, what we want to see on and beyond campus. As adrienne maree brown (2017) notes, "[We] see our own lives and work and relationships as a front line, a first place we can practice justice, liberation, and alignment with each other and the planet" (p. 53). Within these smaller spaces, we can create, touch, and feel humanizing communities, which plant the seeds within us for larger-scale freedom dreaming.

- Care and community are often thought to be central to collective action. But writing this critical autoethnography, we have come to the idea that care and community work are *themselves* collective actions. This aligns with our theoretical framework of Black fugitivity and its insistence that intimacy, care work, and kin-making are fugitive practices of freedom dreaming (Gross-Wyrtzen & Moulton, 2023). This also resonates with what we have since read about infrapolitics, or the everyday "micro modes of resistance" (Scott, 1990, p. 183), that are transformative in their own right yet outside of organized social movements (see also Kelley, 1994).

- Freedom dreaming, as we have sought to engage with it here, engages the dialectics—the tensions and presumed contradictions between lived traumas and possible worlds, between self-care and collective care, between the structural and interpersonal, and between the mundane and radical. But working the dialectic, for us, has to start with the seemingly small, everyday relational practices.

Reference

Adams, T. E., Holman Jones, S., and Ellis, C. (2015). *Autoethnography*. Oxford University Press.

Boggs, G. L., & Kurashige, S. (2012). *The next American revolution: Sustainable activism for the twenty-first century*. University of California Press.

brown, a. m. (2017). *Emergent strategy: Shaping change, changing worlds*. AK Press.

Cann, C. N., & DeMeulenaere, E. J. (2012). Critical co-constructed autoethnography. *Cultural Studies Critical Methodologies, 12*(2), 146-158.

Cann, C., & DeMeulenaere, E. (2020). *The activist academic: Engaged scholarship for resistance, hope and social change*. Myers Education Press.

Freire, P. (1970). *Pedagogy of the oppressed*. Seabury Press.

Freire, P. (1998). *Pedagogy of freedom: Ethics, democracy, and civic courage*. Rowman & Littlefield Publishers Inc.

Garrett-Walker, W. L., Cann, C., & DeMeulenaere, E. (in press) Critical Autoethnography. In J. Salvo & J. Ulmer (Eds.), *Routledge Resources Online* (formerly: *Routledge Encyclopedia of Qualitative Methods*). Routledge.

Gopnik, A. (2023). Caregiving in philosophy, biology & political economy. *Daedalus, 152*(1), 58-69.

Gross-Wyrtzen, L., & Moulton, A. A. (2023). Toward 'Fugitivity as Method': An Introduction to the Special Issue. *ACME: An International Journal for Critical Geographies, 22*(5), 1258–1272. https://acme-journal.org/index.php/acme/article/view/2337

Harney, S., & Moten, F. (2013). *The undercommons: Fugitive planning and black study*. Minor Compositions.

Jordan, J. (2003). Report from the Bahamas, 1982. *Meridians: Feminism, race, transnationalism, 3*(2), 6-16.

Kelley, R. D. (1994). *Race rebels: Culture, politics, and the Black working class*. Free Press.

Kelley, R. D. (2018). Black study, Black struggle. *Ufahamu: A Journal of African Studies, 40*(2), 153-168.

Kelley, R. D. (2022). *Freedom dreams: The black radical imagination*. Beacon Press. (Original work published 2002)

Kushner, R. (2019 , April 17). Is prison necessary? Ruth Wilson Gilmore might change your mind. *The New York Times*.

Lewis, J. S. (2023). Fugitive Repair. *ACME: An International Journal for Critical Geographies, 22*(5), 1388–1397. https://acme-journal.org/index.php/acme/article/view/2376

Lorde, A. (1984) *Sister Outsider: Essays and Speeches*. Crossing Press.

Moten, F. (2003). *In the Break: The Aesthetics of the Black Radical Tradition* (NED-New edition). University of Minnesota Press. http://www.jstor.org/stable/10.5749/j.cttts6jk

Scott, J. C. (1990). *Domination and the arts of resistance: Hidden transcripts*. Yale University Press.

Smith, W. A. (2004). Black faculty coping with racial battle fatigue: The campus racial climate in a post-civil rights era. *A long way to go: Conversations about race by African American faculty and graduate students, 14*(5), 171-190.

Smith, W. A., Yosso, T. J., & Solórzano, D. G. (2011). Challenging racial battle fatigue on historically White campuses: A critical race examination of race-related stress. In R. D. Coates (Ed.), *Covert racism: Theories, institutions, and experiences* (pp. 211-237). Koninklijke Brill NV.

CHAPTER 5

Resisting Exclusion:
The Civic Engagement of a Female Muslim American Student Leader

Ma. Glenda Lopez Wui

Introduction

THE ATTACKS ON September 11, 2001, intensified the discrimination against and misconceptions about Muslims in the United States (Mohamed, 2021). These misconceptions include that Muslims are incapable of integrating into American society and hold beliefs that are against the American ideals of democracy (Read, 2015). Integration into American society is associated with engagement in civic issues in one's community (Putnam, 2000). Civic engagement is broadly defined as involvement in endeavors geared toward the common good (Adler & Goggin, 2005). Although American Muslims have been involved in civic endeavors, their contributions to society tend to be overlooked due to prejudices against them (Read, 2015). Another misconception is that Islam is antithetical to democracy, a system of governance that allows people's participation in issues concerning polity and egalitarianism, particularly where women are given the same opportunity as men to participate in governance and addressing community issues. Specifically, it is misconceived that Islam only allows women to deal with the affairs of the home and not of society (Sirin & Katsiaficas, 2011). This prejudice persists despite the increasing presence of Muslim women activists and politicians in American society (Farzan, 2022; Sahar, 2022).

This chapter presents a counternarrative to the misconception regarding the engagement of women Muslim Americans in community life by featuring the civic engagement of Mina (pseudonym), a female, Muslim American student leader based in a Southern city in the United States. Based on an in-depth interview I conducted with Mina, her story brings to light the civic engagement of a young Muslim student leader and how her religion helped nurture her civic engagement. This chapter also analyzes the role of Mina's social relations within her family and school in encouraging her civic engagement, towards drawing insights on how civic engagement can be enhanced among youth—especially the discriminated-against Muslims—given its positive impact on their well-being (Cureton & Aguinaldo, 2023; Schmidt et al., 2007). The succeeding part of the chapter discusses the related literature to situate the analysis for the study. First is the discussion on civic engagement, imagination, immigrant communities, religion, and women. Second is the role of social relationships, particularly in the contexts of family and school, in enhancing youth civic engagement. This will be followed by the presentation of the case study on Mina. Then, a discussion about the insights drawn from the study related to the topics of American Muslims, women, and youth civic engagement will conclude the chapter.

Civic Engagement, Imagination, Immigrant Communities, Religion, and Women

Civic engagement is regarded as an important indicator of an immigrant group's integration into American society (Putnam & Campbell, 2010). Civic engagement is considered a significant measure because it requires a dedicated and conscious effort that goes beyond partaking in and consuming American popular culture (Putnam & Campbell, 2010). Immigrants' participation in improving the economic, political, and social ways of life in their adopted country signals their connection with and integration into their new community.

Imagination and hope inspire civic action. In his study of movements for social justice in Africa and Third World nations, Kelley (2002) contended that people are drawn to the movements because of their imagination of a world that is better than their present reality. He argued that the imaginings are intertwined with the day-to-day struggles on the ground, as well as generated from a deep understanding of the oppression and the imperatives for new and relevant modes of analysis. Kelley (2002) added that rather than oppression, poverty, or misery, it is the hope of a better world that drives people to join social movements.

The work of Hawlina et al., (2020) is instructive in explaining how imagination can drive civic action. Hawlina et al., (2020) define imagination as "a process that enables distantiation from present circumstances to explore the past, the future, and alternate possibilities" (p. 31). Imagination provides the opportunity for individuals and groups to get away from the immutability of time and to unite around objectives that are generated from the processes of imaginings. Likewise, imagination is critical in the formation of civic action because it allows individuals to create and sustain the notion of the collective "Us" and the different "Others" (usually the perpetrators of injustice). Finally, Hawlina et al. wrote that cultural artifacts can serve as a critical tool in which imaginations can be articulated and shared. Artwork, novels, and films are cultural artifacts that can represent and objectify the imaginings of individuals and groups.

Among immigrant communities, religion can facilitate imagination and civic action (Levitt, 2008). Religious congregations are venues where immigrants find those that they share common identities with and develop social relationships (Stepick et al., 2009). Social relationships that are nurtured within the context of religious congregations give birth to civic activities benefitting communities. Being part of religious congregations with religious commitment influences civic engagement for the following reasons: (a) being part of a social group nurtures caring for the community; (b) religious spaces provide avenues for discussions of social issues; and (c) religion often promotes values that are consistent with being socially responsible (Crystal & DeBell, 2002). Being part of a religious community nurtures the imagining of a collective "Us" that facilitates caring for others, as well as being part of a group working for a cause. Religion also facilitates the imagining of social values (consistent with altruistic religious tenets) that should be pursued to realize a just and fair society. Among immigrant Muslims, a study found that their organized religiosity strongly predicted their civic engagement, thereby contravening the negative portrayal of Islam as the driver of radicalization and social disengagement (Vergani et al., 2017).

The connection between religiosity and civic engagement is also evident among immigrant youth. Studies show that those who are deeply involved in their religious communities also tend to be civically involved (Pachi & Barrett,

2014; Stepick et al., 2009). As to how gender is related to religiosity and civic engagement, research shows that women tend to be more religious and civically engaged than men (Bekkers & Wiepking, 2011). A more recent study by the Pew Research Center (2019) involving data from the United States and more than two dozen countries, further established the connection between religiosity and civic engagement. However, the data was not desegregated according to gender. In the case of immigrant women, particularly Latinas, they are active in civic activities even though they are religiously committed (Marquardt, 2005). Less is known about how religiosity plays out in the civic engagement of women as compared to men.

Regarding the immigrant Muslim community in the United States, Read (2015) found that religion was more associated with civic engagement among American Muslim men than their women counterparts. Read acknowledged, however, that recent studies on Muslim women's civic engagement are needed to better understand the religious and gender dynamics among the Muslim community. This is because of the varied interpretations of how Islam figures in women's community involvement. Traditional interpretations would restrict women only to the home and family, while progressive ones promote greater gender equality to address the socio-economic challenges of daily living (Read, 2015). This chapter aims to contribute to the call for a more recent and nuanced portrayal of female Muslim American civic engagement by examining the experiences of a female Muslim student leader.

Family and School in Youth Civic Engagement

Civic engagement brings various benefits to youth. Studies show that youth who are civically engaged are better emotionally, socially, and academically adjusted when compared to those who are not (Celio et al., 2011; Schmidt et al., 2007). Therefore, civic engagement is particularly helpful for Muslim youth, given their stressful lives due to their experiences of discrimination (Ahmed & Ezzeddine, 2009). This is more so in the case of Muslim women who experience greater instances of discrimination because of the more apparent cultural marker of their identity in their appearance via their hijab (head covering) (Rashid, 2017; Sirin & Katsiaficas, 2011).

Civic socialization usually begins in the family (Rossi et al., 2016; Youniss et al., 2002). Young people who are raised in homes with frequent political discussions and where adults volunteer are more likely to be involved in civic activities (Andolina et al., 2003; Kahne & Sporte, 2008; McIntosh et al., 2007; Wui & White, 2022). A study conducted by Kahne and Sporte (2008) showed that parents who discussed current events with their children helped enhance the children's civic commitment. When young people witness concern for current events and community in their homes, they are more likely to be committed to civic participation. Andolina et al. (2003) also wrote that youth raised in homes with regular political conversations become more involved in civic activities. By conversing about politics, families convey and educate their children about the importance of paying attention to issues in their community and the world around them and to take action, if needed.

School is another institution that critically contributes to youth civic engagement. Similar to family, young people spend much of their formative years in school, where they are socialized into values—including civic consciousness—which they could carry into adulthood (Zaff et al., 2008). Schools facilitate the development of civic engagement when they ensure the presence of an open classroom climate for the discussion of social issues, diligently teach civic content and skills, and stimulate a participative school culture where the opinions of students on school matters are welcome (Campbell, 2008; Kahne & Sporte, 2008; Torney-Purta, 2002).

The role of schools in enhancing civic engagement among Muslim students to improve their well-being becomes more important, given the challenges they encounter in their daily lives. Schools should be safe spaces for students to thrive and develop their civic engagement. However, it is oftentimes in schools where Muslim students experience hateful bullying from their peers who label them as "terrorists" and "violent" (Cureton & Aguinaldo, 2023, p.1). Also worrying are reports of teachers and staff participating in the bullying. A 2022 study conducted by the Institute for Social Policy and Understanding reported that 42% of Muslim families who experienced bullying said that the bully was a teacher or official at school (ISPU, 2023a). The same study also reported that half of the Muslim families with children in K-12 schools indicated that their child/children had been bullied in the last year because of their faith.

The story of Mina featured next narrates how her school contributed to her civic engagement. Mina's experience in high school enriches the discourse on school support for student civic engagement by bringing to light the culturally responsive practices of her school that nurtured her civic activities. Aligned with the framework of culturally relevant pedagogy (CRP), school staff learned about Mina's culture to support her civic activities (Ladson-Billings, 1995). CRP espouses that teachers should be aware of and learn about the cultural beliefs and practices of their diverse students to better support them in their learning.

The Story of Mina

I was acquainted with Mina when I was looking for participants to interview for my research on Asian American student leaders. I obtained her name from the list of presidents of student organizations in the directory of a university in an urban area of Southeast Texas. I contacted her and learned that she is of Pakistani lineage, which makes her an ideal respondent for my research. I wanted to include Muslim representation in my research, given my interest in understanding how Muslim youth leaders navigate American society given the discriminatory attitudes toward them. Mina's experiences as a female student leader are insightful because of the gender stereotype that Muslim women are discouraged by their culture to participate in socio-political affairs. After exchanging emails and text messages, we set an interview date to talk about her experiences as a student leader. Mina was a third-year B.S. biology student at that time.

Prior to the scheduled interview, I met with Mina to observe their interfaith project, where students put up tables at a building near the library entrance where anyone can stop by to ask members of the Muslim Student Association (MSA) for questions regarding Islam. I asked questions about how the Muslim community contains radicalism among their youth. For the interview, Mina and I talked for about an hour about how she became a student leader, the influences on her civic engagement (i.e., religion, family, teachers), her civic projects in high school and college, and her plans for the future. This chapter provides insights into how Mina's Muslim identity inspired her imaginings and civic action for her community.

Religious Identity and Civic Engagement

Mina founded the Muslim Student Association (MSA) in her high school when she was 16 years old. She said that Muslim students at her school were not proud of their identity and were uncomfortable identifying themselves as Muslims. They were also not friends with each other and did not do things together as Muslims. Hence, Muslim students at her school were unable to undertake projects that would showcase the Muslim culture. Mina said that because of the lack of unity, there were many misconceptions against Muslims that were left unaddressed. Mina draws from her religion, a unifying identity for her fellow Muslim schoolmates (Oppong, 2013), for them to unite and work together in educating their non-Muslim peers about their religion to efface discrimination.

MSA members conducted activities to improve understanding of the Muslim culture and religion at their school, like showcasing Muslim art. Mina narrated that she requested a non-Muslim teacher as faculty advisor for MSA because there were no Muslim teachers at her school during its founding. She helped expose the faculty advisor to Muslim culture to better understand the students' culture. Mina shares:

> In high school, actually I saw that … I moved from a really small town and then I moved to a place where there [were] a lot more Muslims and a lot more … people like me. But I saw that the people there weren't very proud of their identity and … Muslims weren't friends with each other. Nobody would be comfortable with saying "I'm Muslim." It was a very … different atmosphere from what I was used to when I was little when I lived in Philadelphia. I saw that problem and I decided to create the Muslim Student Association at my high school … I was 16 … So that's when I started that organization, and I really loved it because through that I was able to meet so many new Muslim people at my school. I didn't even know that they were there, and we all became really good friends. I think it was very important to not only us as a community to have that sense of community, but for other people in the school to gain … better insight on what Muslim is, who Muslims are, and what they're like, and what Islam really means, 'cause … (in) my high school, there's a lot of ignorance about Muslims just because the community wasn't

very strong. I was able to do a lot of activities that showed non-Muslims like, "okay, this is what Islam means and it's not what you think it is." So even teachers, I had to ask 'cause there was no Muslim teacher (during) my first year, so I had to ask a non-Muslim teacher [whom] I knew and ... she came to a lot of activities. She visited the mosque and she got a full tour and really liked it. I think I was able to change a lot of people's perspectives, about their (the Muslims') own religion and then non-Muslims on Islam.

After high school, Mina continued her engagement with issues concerning the Muslim community by becoming the president of the Muslim Student Association (MSA) in college. Mina already knew about the university-based MSA back in high school because they would often come to the campus for tournaments and activities. As she came from a small town where there were few Muslims at her high school, she was amazed that there were many Muslims in the university. After enrolling in the university, she started attending MSA meetings. Mina expressed:

When I got to my university, I was amazed because the Muslim population ... there's a lot of us. ... During high school we would have a tournament at the university every year, which was like ... all the MSAs in Texas. They would all come to the university and participate in a big tournament. Like different activities, art, writing, sports, everything ... In the university [there are] so many Muslims. ... Our MSA (in high school) was just like 10, 15 people. ... When I got here, I immediately got involved with them (MSA); I started going to meetings.

Mina said her being a Muslim Pakistani largely shaped her civic engagement. Her being a Muslim drew her in high school to MSA, where she spearheaded projects that helped others know Islam better. Likewise, her being a Pakistani drew her to the Kashmir conflict in college, and she was able to interact with those affected by the problem. The Kashmir conflict is a territorial issue involving India and Pakistan over the control of the Kashmir region, which resulted in human rights violations against the Muslim population and a humanitarian crisis in the area. Being aware of those who were victimized made her more empathetic and interested in working for those experiencing difficulties. Mina explained:

> My background pushes me to continue … I think if I was just born here and didn't have any issue (with my) background, I wouldn't really be able to see past my own demographic; I wouldn't be able to see … these issues right now [that] I'm in close contact with, that are happening in Pakistan. Or like that lady (who was in the MSA-organized Kashmir symposium) wouldn't have spoken to me if I wasn't Pakistani. So I think being in close contact with that culture and … with the people that are back there and suffering, then that … pushes me to work harder for a reason.

Family and School Support for Civic Engagement

Teaching Civic Values and Pride in One's Culture

Mina credited her parents for instilling her civic disposition. She said that her parents kept abreast of the news every day. Aside from the situation in the U.S., her parents also cared about events in their home country of Pakistan and other parts of the world. Mina said that talking to her father about what is happening around the world made her more concerned about social issues. She stated:

> My dad cares a lot about politics. Both of my parents, they watch news every day and they are involved in what's going on … even though they've been here for a long time. It's very easy to just turn off the TV and say, okay, now we live in the U.S.; it doesn't matter. … Some people might even see it negatively, like, "Oh, they should be more caring about U.S. politics." But they care so deeply about the issues in their country, and they're so involved with them. … My dad especially is always telling me about issues around the world. He really cares … I think just … having those conversations with him … made me care about what's going on.

Mina also shared that she was inspired by her parents to work for the Muslim community. She said that her parents have always been very proud of being Muslims. Mina said that it is sad that others are uncomfortable identifying themselves as Muslims because of their experiences of discrimination. Through MSA, Mina hoped that other people would learn about Islam and overcome their prejudices against it. When people are more accepting of Muslims, then Muslims are more likely to be comfortable in asserting their identity. As Mina put it:

> Growing up, my parents have always taught me to be very proud of, you know, "don't be afraid to say you're Muslim. ... Even nationality, don't be afraid to say." My parents are from Pakistan. ... They are very proud of my culture. My parents aren't the type to try to fit into society. They ... don't try to assimilate in a negative way. They like to keep all their culture and everything very close to them. So growing up, that was a very obvious thing for me, that I was really comfortable with that. So when I see other people (being) ... so uncomfortable with saying "I'm Muslim," it makes me sad.

School Support for Civic Activities

School helped nurture Mina's civic engagement. Her high school and college education provided her with avenues to pursue projects for MSA. She spearheaded several activities to gain support for MSA in her high school. MSA had monthly meetings where members talked about events where they could volunteer in the community or the mosque. MSA members volunteered with the Islamic Arts Festival every year, which happened in a mosque near their high school. Mina said that through this event, they were able to meet other Muslims in their community. Non-Muslims also came to see the artwork at the event. Mina shared:

> We did meetings. ... It'd be like every month. ... We talked about events in the community that we could volunteer at or about involvement in the mosque. We did ... the Islamic arts festival every year in November ... in a mosque close by. We would volunteer at that and invite all of our

teachers and friends to come to the festival. That's where my history teacher, the one who was my adviser ... that's where she came with her family, and she got a tour of the mosque. A lot of people from our organization ... were able to. I think from that, we were able to be exposed to a greater Muslim community. The Islamic arts festival was open to everybody. A lot of non-Muslims came. They were able to... see the beautiful art.

When people saw the beautiful Muslim art, Mina thought that they might think that Islam cannot be that bad if the art is beautiful. People also became curious and asked questions when they saw the artwork. Mina has been volunteering at the arts festival since she was in tenth or eleventh grade. She expressed:

> I think they were able to see like, okay, Islam can't be as bad as we think it is, if the art is so beautiful and ... it made them curious, [and] ask questions. Because of that, I've been involved with the Islamic arts festival for, like, ever since tenth or eleventh grade.

Mina said that they also hosted the film showing of *Kite Runner,* adapted from the book of Muslim writer Khaled Hosseini, for fund-raising and to educate people at her school about Muslims. Mina also organized Muslim students at her school to attend the MSA inter-school tournaments in the university. Mina described this experience

> We hosted a movie screening of... the Afghan-American author Khaled Hosseini ... on his book *The Kite Runner.* ... We hosted a movie screening of that for charity and we raised like $400, which was a big deal for us. ... We showed it in our school, so a lot of people came; we charged $3 or something per ticket. It's like, there's a movie about Muslims, so it exposed people to that. I think that was a good effort. Other than that, the biggest activity was probably the tournament at the university.

Mina shared that she would have wanted to propose Friday prayer sessions at her school, but was constrained by the fact that praying would happen during lesson hours. The venue for the prayers was also a problem. Besides, she said that some students were not even comfortable identifying themselves as Muslims, much more to excuse themselves from class to pray. Still, Mina thought that she should have pushed through with the proposal.

> [What] I wanted to establish … [but] never got a chance to was Friday prayer. . At the time, that was such a far stretch for people, because people weren't even comfortable with saying "I'm Muslim." To tell them to, you know, tell their teachers they have to go pray at this time would be like a whole [other] … really big steps. I wish I had done that in high school, but we weren't able to establish that 'cause it would be during class and we'd have to find a place to pray. That was something I wasn't able to do.

For the MSA in college, Mina talked about activities aimed at increasing awareness about the struggles of Muslims, such as the symposium on Kashmir. Mina said that her encounter with someone affected by the Kashmir issue increased her concern about those whose lives were impacted by the crisis.

> We (MSA) did an event about Kashmir to raise awareness for what's going on there. This was tricky because I would say MSA has never done anything, like, political. … We wanted to raise awareness for the humanitarian crisis about it. But… there were a lot of complexities to the issue. I talked to somebody after the event, and she said, "Kashmir is like, it hurts me. But if I just didn't care, … it wouldn't affect me; I could go on with my daily life." But I talked to her after the event, and she was crying. … [She] said her brother [has] been in jail for over three months and … [she doesn't] know if he's alive.

Aside from the Kashmir conflict, MSA conducted a symposium on Black Muslims who represent about a third of the American Muslim community (ISPU, 2023b). Black Muslims confront several challenges as they experience the same systemic racism faced by Black Americans, in addition to the religious discrimination experienced by Muslim Americans. The experiences of Black Muslims are also rendered less visible, given that Muslims are often racialized as Arab or South Asian (ISPU, 2023b). Mina said that learning about the difficulties faced by other Muslims motivated her to do more for her community.

> Because of the Kashmir event, we started doing more events like that. We're doing one called Refugee Panel. We have three refugees in our community who will talk about their experiences. ... Last semester there was a Black History Panel, so three Black community members came and talked about their experiences as Black Muslims, and that kind of stuff gives you inspiration. People from this background ... they've been through so much in life. ... Those activities definitely motivate me to do more.

Mina said that her dream of becoming a doctor relates to her aspiration of continuing her civic engagement, as she plans to practice her future profession in the service of others. Mina said she wanted to serve the medical needs of people in Pakistan or Muslim people in Asia, as doctors are lacking in those parts.

> My dream is to become a doctor. There's a lot of people suffering in countries like Pakistan and Muslim countries in Asia. ... Those countries lack professionals; ... that's why I want to go back there and help. ... I think it's sad that all the educated people from those countries end up leaving. They need more support.

Imagination Civic Engagement

Mina's Muslim identity propelled her imaginings and dream of social justice for her fellow Muslims. Her imaginings were accompanied by an appreciation of the struggles on the ground (Kelley, 2002) and the corresponding actions that need to be pursued to confront the challenges. This is related to what scholars argued about the nuances of social justice projects, such that they are shaped and driven by the perspectives and needs of the concerned communities (Tuck & Yang, 2018). She founded the Muslim Student Association in high school to unite her fellow Muslims and educate non-Muslims about Muslims' religion and culture to counter Islamophobia in her school and community. She continued her advocacy in college to raise awareness and to improve the plight of Muslims caught up in the Kashmir conflict and Black Muslims in the United States. She intends to continue serving the Muslim community through medical missions after her studies.

Mina's imaginings let her dream of a better reality for her fellow Muslims. Her imaginings allowed her to mobilize a collective "Us" (Hawlina et al., 2020) among fellow Muslims to raise awareness and act on improving their condition. Muslim cultural artifacts (e.g., artwork, films) were elements of the imaginings: Such were deployed to educate non-Muslims about the Islamic culture for better appreciation of the religion.

Conclusion

Imaginings inspire dreaming for social justice because they allow the exploration of realities that are better than the reality of the present. Mina's identity inspired her imaginings and civic engagement for the Muslim community. Her story brought to light important insights about female Muslim American civic engagement. First, Mina's religious identity helped nurture her civic engagement. This finding enriches the research on Muslim women's civic engagement where the relationship between religiosity and civic endeavor could be further examined (Read, 2015). Mina founded the Muslim Student Association (MSA) to unite her Muslim peers in high school so that they could take pride in their Muslim identity. Through the MSA, Mina and her fellow Muslim students undertook projects to educate their classmates about Islam to counter Islamophobia. Mina mobilized her religion as the unifying identity for her fellow Muslims, and utilized the Islamic culture to educate non-Muslims about the religion. In college, Mina continued advocating for discriminated-against Muslims, like those caught in the Kashmir conflict and Black American Muslims who experience both anti-Black racism and Islamophobia.

Second, Mina's civic consciousness was seeded within her family, who discussed social issues with her and taught her to be proud of her Muslim roots and identity. From her home, her school nurtured her civic engagement through the presence of non-Muslim teaching staff who learned about her culture and a high school that supported her civic activities in MSA. Mina's high school experience offers valuable lessons on how schools can be culturally responsive to nurture the civic engagement of diverse students. This is especially important as schools have been places where Muslim students experience bullying from peers (Cureton & Aguinaldo, 2023) and even teachers and school staff (ISPU, 2023a). Mina continued to find the nurturing environment in college that allowed her to pursue civic endeavors as president of the university-based Muslim Student Association. She plans to continue her civic activities as a medical doctor in Pakistan after completing her studies.

Muslim youth face challenges in integrating into American society because of ideological and institutional exclusion. Apart from family, schools play a pivotal role in youth's process of integration by providing a nurturing environment for their civic engagement. Encouraging Muslim youth's imaginings and dream of a better society inspire their participation in social justice projects. As Kelley (2002) argued, the imagining of a better reality is a more powerful driver to join movements for social justice than are experiences of oppression.

The current study has limitations that can inform future research on youth imaginings and civic engagement. As the chapter focused only on the experiences of one Muslim student leader, future research could extend the analysis to the civic activities of Muslim youth organizations and the experiences of their members. Further research can focus on the opinions of teachers in supporting the social justice projects of their minority students.

Reference

Adler, R. P., & Goggin. J. (2005). What do we mean by "civic engagement"?. *Journal of Transformative Education, 3*(3), 236-253. https://doi.org/10.1177/1541344605276792

Ahmed, S., & Ezzeddine, M. (2009). Challenges and opportunities facing American Muslim youth. *Journal of Muslim Mental Health, 4*(2), 159-174. https://doi.org/10.1080/15564900903245782

Andolina, M. W., Jenkins, K., Zukin, C., & Keeter, S. (2003). Habits from home, lessons from school: Influences on youth civic development. *PS: Political Science and Politics, 36*(2), 275–80.

Bekkers, R., & Wiepking, P. (2011). Who gives? A literature review of predictors of charitable giving part I: Religion, education, age, and socialization. *Voluntary Sector Review, 3,* 337-65.

Campbell, D. E. (2008). Voice in the classroom: How an open classroom climate fosters political engagement among adolescents. *Political Behavior, 30*(4), 437-454. https://doi.org/10.1007/s11109-008-9063-z

Celio, C. I., Durlak, J., & Dymnicki, A. (2011). A meta-analysis of the impact of service-learning on students. *Journal of Experiential Education, 34*(2), 164-181. https://doi.org/10.1177/105382591103400205

Crystal, D. S., & DeBell, M. (2002). Sources of civic orientation among American youth: Trust, religious valuation, and attributions of responsibility. *Political Psychology, 23,* 113-132. https://doi.org/10.1111/0162-895X.00273

Cureton, A., & Aguinaldo, E. (2023). Good Muslim, bad Muslim: Muslim refugee youths' identity development and civic engagement in school-based settings. *Youth & Society, 0*(0). https://doi.org/10.1177/0044118X231199125

Farzan, Y. (2022, November 26). Record number of Muslims elected in US midterms: "We should lean into who we are". *The Guardian.* https://www.theguardian.com /us-news/2022/nov/26/us-midterms-muslim-candidates-elected-politics

Hawlina, H., Pedersen, O. C., & Zittoun, T. (2020). Imagination and social movements. *Current Opinion in Psychology, 35,* 31-35. https://doi.org/10.1016/j. copsyc.2020.02.009

Institute for Social Policy and Understanding (ISPU). (2023a). *Islamaphobia is pervasive, systemic, and a threat to all: Understanding the prevalence, manifestations, and consequences of anti-Muslim bigotry.* https://www.ispu.org/institution-al-islamophobia/

Institute for Social Policy and Understanding (ISPU). (2023b). *Black Muslim experiences: Research and resources on Americans who are Black and Muslim.* https://www.ispu.org/black-muslims/

Kahne, J. E., & Sporte, S. E. (2008). Developing citizens: The impact of civic learning opportunities on students' commitment to civic participation. *American Educational Research Journal, 45*(3), 738-766. https://doi.org/10.3102/0002831208316951

Kelley, R. D. G. (2002). *Freedom dreams: The Black radical imagination.* Beacon Press.

Ladson-Billings, G. (1995). Toward a theory of culturally relevant pedagogy. *American Educational Research Journal, 32*(3), 465-491. https://doi.org/10.3102/00028312032003465

Levitt, P. (2008). Religion as a path to civic engagement. *Ethnic and Racial Studies, 31,* 766-91.

Marquardt, M. F. (2005). From shame to confidence: Gender, religious conversion, and civic engagement of Mexicans in the U.S. south. *Latin American Perspectives, 32*(1), 27-56. https://doi.org/10.1177/0094582X04271850

McIntosh, H., Hart, D., & Youniss, J. (2007). The influence of family political discussion on youth civic development: Which parent qualities matter?. *PS: Political Science & Politics, 40*(3), 495-499. https://doi.org/10.1017/S1049096507070758

Mohamed, B. (2021). *Muslims are a growing presence in U.S., but still face negative views from the Public.* Pew Research Center. https://www.pewresearch.org/short-reads/2021/09/01/muslims-are-a-growing-presence-in-u-s-but-still-face-negative-views-from-the-public/

Oppong, S. H. (2013). Religion and identity. *American International Journal of Contemporary Research, 3*(6), 10–16.

Pachi, D., & Barrett, M. (2014). Civic and political engagement among ethnic minority and immigrant youth. In R. Dimitrova, M. Bender, & F. van de Vijver (Eds.), *Global perspectives on well-being in immigrant families* (pp. 189-211). Springer.

Pew Research Center. (2019). *Religion's relationship to happiness, civic engagement and health around the world.* https://www.pewresearch.org/religion/2019/01/31/religions-relationship-to-happiness-civic-engagement-and-health-around-the-world/

Putnam, R. D. (2000). *Bowling alone.* Simon & Schuster.

Putnam, R. D., & Campbell, D. E. (2010). *American grace how religion unites and divides us.* Simon & Schuster.

Rashid, U. (2017). Muslim women in America: Challenges and politics of diversity within American Muslim community. *Journal of Muslim Minority Affairs, 37*(4), 481-495. https://doi.org/10.1080/13602004.2017.1405502

Read, J. G. (2015). Gender, religious identity, and civic engagement among Arab Muslims in the United States. *Sociology of Religion, 76*(1), 30-48. https://doi.org/10.1093/socrel/sru042

Rossi, G., Lenzi, M., Sharkey, J. D., Vieno, A., & Santinello, M. (2016). Factors associated with civic engagement in adolescence: The effects of neighborhood, school, family, and peer contexts. *Journal of Community Psychology, 44,* 1040-1058. https://doi.org/10.1002/jcop.21826

Sahar, N. (2022). Muslim women's activism in the USA: Politics of diverse resistance strategies. *Religions, 13,* 1023. https://doi.org/10.3390/rel13111023

Schmidt, J. A., Shumow, L., & Kackar, H. (2007). Adolescents' participation in service activities and its impact on academic, behavioral, and civic outcomes. *Journal of Youth and Adolescence, 36*(2), 127-140. https://doi.org/10.1007/s10964-006-9119-5

Sirin, S. R., & Katsiaficas, D. (2011). Religiosity, discrimination, and community engagement: Gendered pathways of Muslim American emerging adults. *Youth and Society, 43*(4), 1528–1546. https://doi.org/10.1177/0044118X10388218

Stepick, A., Rey, T., & Mahler, S. J. (Eds.) (2009). *Churches and charity in the immigrant city religion, immigration, and civic engagement in Miami.* Rutgers University Press.

Torney-Purta, J. (2002). The school's role in developing civic engagement: A study of adolescents in twenty-eight countries. *Applied Developmental Science, 6*(4), 203-212. https://doi.org/10.1207/S1532480XADS0604_7

Tuck, E., & Yang, K. W. (2018). *Toward what justice? Describing diverse dreams of justice in education.* Routledge.

Vergani, M., Johns, A., Lobo, M., & Mansouri, F. (2017). Examining Islamic religiosity and civic engagement in Melbourne. *Journal of Sociology, 53*(1), 63-78. https://doi.org/10.1177/1440783315621167

Wui, M. G. L, & White, C. (2022). *Civic engagement of Asian American student leaders.* Lexington Books.

Youniss, J., Bales, S., Christmas-Best, V., Diversi, M., McLaughlin, M., & Silbereisen, R. (2002). Youth civic engagement in the twenty-first century. *Journal of Research on Adolescence, 12*(1), 121–148. https://doi.org/10.1111/1532-7795.00027

Zaff, J. F., Malanchuk, O., & Eccles, J. S. (2008). Predicting positive citizenship from adolescence to young adulthood: The effects of a civic context. *Applied Developmental Science, 12*(1), 38-53. https://doi.org/10.1080/10888690801910567

CHAPTER 6

Championing Disruptive Dreaming Among Students:
A Collaborative Autoethnography of Adult Allies

Anna Mei Gubbins and Aubry Threlkeld

Introduction

Dreaming as a way of understanding radical possibility has roots in a range of radical social movements (i.e., Anzaldúa, 1987; hooks, 2005; King, 1963; Piepz-na-Samarsinha, 2021). Dreaming is often mistaken for inaction. Dr. Bernice King, at a recent gathering celebrating the 60th anniversary of the March on Washington at the National Center for Human and Civil Rights, stated that one of the most common misconceptions about her father, Rev. Dr. Martin Luther King, Jr., was that his dreams were somehow separate from his actions (King, 2023, personal correspondence). Dreaming, in particular radical dreaming, has been a part of every major social movement because through dreams we can discover possibilities where there seem like there are none. We came together to dream when we found ourselves working at a predominantly white-serving institution (PWI) that had not reckoned with its past and present. We saw that students, particularly BIPOC and 2SLGBTQIA+ (queer: two-spirited, lesbian, gay, bisexual, transgender, questioning/queer, intersex, asexual, + other iden-tities across sexual orientation and gender identity) students, felt under attack from the political and cultural wake of the Trump presidency and the desire for a complete dismantling of the diversity, equity, inclusion, and belonging (DEIB) project that higher education has engaged with for greater than 50 years.

Inspired by critical ideas emerging from social movements, including the American Civil Rights movement, Black feminism, and Queer power, we set out to become better adult allies supporting students doing social justice work at the educational institution at which we worked. We describe, through autoethnographic vignettes, our positionality at the institution, our commitment to this work, and our impact on this community over the course of one academic year. The italicized text represents our autoethnographic ligatures (moments of coming together) and vignettes (moments of reflecting apart): a style of writing we have used to demarcate our interdependence (i.e., Threlkeld & Pieplow, 2018). Academic text is represented throughout in unitalicized text. We have eschewed traditional academic chapter headers as much as possible to best represent our collective stories.

Context and Positionality Statements

Our collective stories are shaped by our individual and collective understanding of our positionalities. Anna Mei Gubbins positions herself as a Chinese-American, transracial adoptee from a middle-class family, raised in a Welcoming and Affirming (2SLGBTQIA+) American Baptist Church in New England in the late 1990s and early 2000s. Gubbins' passion for intercultural exchange led her to experiences living in Spain and Chile, but as a Spanish and English (but not Chinese) speaking woman, Gubbins continues to explore questions of authenticity and the gatekeeping of identity. Aubry Threlkeld positions themself as a queer, genderqueer, disabled, and Madqueer academic who is a white person of Romanichal descent. Their experiences of being racialized as white inform their approaches to racial justice work and enable them to dissect whiteness as dominant, hegemonic, and operating silently. They have variously been engaged in anti-racist practice for twenty years but had remained relatively silent in their work at this institution because they saw how the conservative administrative culture punished those who stuck out. We were both afraid and brave and needed the support of each other and the opportunity to care for those in our communities.

The institution where we worked, and our positions held while employed there, shaped our experience. It was a small private liberal arts college with a career orientation in the northeastern United States. The school was recently beginning to explicitly engage in DEIB efforts, and while there were new initiatives, it was still a conservative-leaning campus climate. There was often hesitation from the upper administration about structural and policy-level supports for racially marginalized and 2SLGBTQIA+ students. While the school continued to externally promote its commitment to supporting a diverse population, fewer than 11% of students identified as students of color and members of the 2SLGBTQIA+ community reported not feeling safe to be openly out on campus. Some students and staff left the institution explicitly because of this. While the two authors held roles that are traditionally siloed from each other due to the hierarchical structure of higher education, the small size of the institution, along with the smaller population of minoritized faculty and staff, afforded them the opportunity to collaborate. Gubbins was a new coordinator in the Diversity, Equity, Inclusion office, and Threlkeld was an academic leader on campus who had served the school for seven years. Throughout the year, both writers navigated differing understandings of the institution, their assigned roles within it, and the needs they saw emerge. They remained committed to dreaming a better future with the students during their remaining time with the institution.

Ligature 1: Fall Conference (Anna Mei)

My supervisor told me that for political reasons we should attend different sessions in the Faculty Fall Conference. I told her I was interested in the session: "Supporting Gender Creative and Gender Expansive Students." She said, "Yeah! That's Aubry. He's a good guy to know. We're collaborating on a project. He's ... he ... sometimes wears dresses and that sort of stuff. You'll like him."

Day of, I arrived early for the presentation and there was Aubry, standing at the podium, reviewing their slides for the presentation: chunky earrings, scarf, flowy black skirt—graceful, thoughtful, composed; and there I was, scurrying into the front row desk to see the screen and not be in the way of other people. I introduced myself, but quickly retreated to my seat when faculty members arrived. Aubry: "We're starting with a knowledge-based quiz because research shows we retain more when we have frequent low-stakes assessments along the way." Competition mode: activated. The questions were not particularly difficult: basic terminology, theory, and practical application, but I was still elated to earn first place. What made it even more delicious was when Aubry said: "I want to congratulate our first place winner, Anna Mei, who, if I'm not mistaken, got every single one of these questions correct." Dopamine rush.

Conceptual Frame

Our conceptual framework emerged from our conversations and context. We both worked at a small private liberal arts college in the northeastern United States that fit many of the characteristics of a predominantly white-serving institution (PWI): the student and faculty population, a majority of white, upper middle-class cis women. Our work together as adult allies emerged from our early conversations, where we discussed our collective values and interest in putting theory to practice. We discussed theories and methods like intersectionality as conceptualized by Black feminists (Bilge & Collins, 2016; Combahee River Collective, 1977; Crenshaw, 1989) and notions of allyship that recognized how allies can come from within and across diverse communities (Cumming-Potvin, 2023). We recognized the need to address multiple identities while decentering how whiteness constructed possibilities for dreaming among our students: "The major source of difficulty in our political work is that we are not just trying to fight oppression on one front or even two, but instead to address a whole range of oppressions. We do not have racial, sexual, heterosexual, or class privilege to rely upon, nor do we have even the minimal access to resources and power that groups who possess any one of these types of privilege have." (Combahee River Collective, 1977). We recognized that we cannot begin to do single-identity sociopolitical development when confronted with the reality of multi-issue resistance. Herein, our work began with our shared perspectives and appreciation for Black feminist epistemologies, which first recognize the experiences of anti-Blackness, racialization, and their co-construction with, and of, other identities.

Emerging work on student activism on college campuses has examined the sociopolitical development of Black women (Leath et al., 2022); Latina/o/x youth (Bennett et al., 2022); 2SLGBTQIA+ youth (Gandy-Guedes & Paceley, 2019); and women, broadly (Gulbrandsen & Walsh, 2012). Logan et al., (2017) argued that the early Trump years were not a significant impetus for Black student engagement in activism—presence on a PWI campus was enough motivation. Lewis and Barnes (2023), through a practice of queering, describe how administrators use covert choreopolicing to incorporate student activism into an organization's culture of inclusivity—in part, co-opting and diffusing their concerns. This motion, generally by administrators at PWIs, resonated with our experiences where DEIB discourses were being employed by our college—in our marketing and communications–but were not being adequately resourced, advanced, or critical. Some case studies suggest that movements and art exhibitions that centered race in the discussion of DEIB concerns were better able to meet the moment at PWIs (Phelps-Ward & Kenney, 2017; Reed and Lohnes, 2019).

Intersectionality has been used extensively to understand racially-minoritized student experiences. We contend that intersectionality, too, can help us understand how white students who may have marginalized identities do not show up as allies for their BIPOC peers. Across the institution, whiteness framed the possibilities of student experience (e.g., Duran et al., 2022). Therefore, racially marginalized students gravitated toward reconciling their non-whiteness with their belonging at the institution, and white students identified with other markers to differentiate themselves from each other. 2SLGBTQIA+ students who were racialized as white may not have seen racialization as part of their identity formation despite its importance, and BIPOC (Black, Indigenous, and People of Color) students may not have addressed the intersectionality among their identities because of the prevalent ways race impacted their experiences on campus. These minoritized students began to engage with social justice and advocacy organizations that aligned with their most salient identity: BIPOC students engaged most with the Racial Justice Club (RJC), even if they also identified as queer, and queer students of mixed ethnic background who were racialized as white engaged most with the school's Gay Straight Alliance (GSA). Throughout this year, we saw the ways that the PWI environment hindered the expansion of intersectional understanding of students' complex identities.

Though unaddressed and unacknowledged, whiteness bounded the possibilities of understanding multiple social identities and intersectionality generally, it also cultivated a prim and proper heteronormativity among the students, gendered interpersonal violence and abuse around dating, and ultimately influenced who was seen as "in" or "out." Our students' experiences could be easily understood through the matrix of heterosexuality described by Seal (2019) with respect to colleges and their forerunners of compulsory heterosexuality (Rich, 1980). Advertisements for the college lured students to a small campus in the northeast with the promise of wholesome activities, character building, and career preparation, each more so than the next reaffirming the need for a white, heterosexual, and gender-normative self-presentation for professionalism and career success. Perhaps, in our context, this is a manifestation of the neoliberal university after the Trump presidency, where radical attacks on the legitimacy and value of higher education silence formerly ambitious DEIB efforts.

Even the most diligent students who dare to dream about the impact they could have through advocacy work may face decision paralysis when deciding where to begin the attack against the structural violence of minoritized populations on campus, in our community, and in our world. The school asks our students to be leaders—to change community culture through inspiring programs that win over the hearts of their peers, colleagues, teachers, and perhaps most importantly, the donors, but it also asks that they do so without disrupting the status quo. The status quo was created by a society steeped in patriarchy, heteronormativity, ableism, white privilege, and capitalism, so how can we combat these inequitable structures while maintaining it? How do we, as employees within this system, support, and aid our students in navigating, disrupting, and dismantling it?

Ligature 2: Meeting Anna Mei (Aubry)

Our new provost (the fourth in as many years) asked that we, the administrators, write three goals that supported the college's strategic plan, and I couldn't wait to do more work around Diversity, Equity, Inclusion, and Belonging (DEIB). Roused by the murder of George Floyd in May of '20, the college created a position for a Vice President-Chief Diversity Officer (Fall '21), designated a "Center" for DEIB programming and initiatives (Fall '22), and hired a DEIB coordinator (Summer '22). These changes took years to implement, but I was impressed they happened at all, given the original message to the school's community when George Floyd was murdered: *"Do not protest. That is not what a civil community does."* Having worked at this PWI for some time, I knew the challenges of advancing DEIB, and I wanted to show my support. The Vice President wanted me to meet the new coordinator—I was told she was hard working and excited to join the team.

I met Anna Mei when I gave a presentation on supporting gender creative and expansive students. She was attentive, and she quickly and correctly answered the questions I posed to the group. After the session, I asked Anna Mei if she were willing to discuss events we could plan together. She lit up with glee, which was a refreshing change from my own perspective that had a "healthy" mix of critiques, generally. I knew students, faculty, and staff left because the environment was so conservative, and programming was not enough to shift culture, but when representation on campus was at an all-time low, we needed somewhere to start.

I experienced significant difficulty as I was socially transitioning as genderqueer. I didn't have many role models—and frankly got a lot of funny looks. Once, while presenting to a team of all-white, cisgender admissions officers, I had teal gel fingernails, and their stares chilled me to the bone. But then again students stopped me as I walked around campus and thanked me for "looking like them." It felt like the most earnest thing: to be an example.

I know the adage: *"Don't expect paradigm shifts from a reformist paradigm (like DEIB)."* But I wanted to do something. Thinking about the Rita Hester memorial I passed each day coming into the office, I dreamed of having a Transgender Day of Remembrance on campus because it was unconscionable that a whole college would continue to ignore gender non-conforming/non-binary/trans students. I hoped for the day where we would no longer treat racial justice as a danger to a healthy campus community. I yearned for a time and place where DEIB was no longer just a series of one-off events from a single-issue perspective. So I helped students and Anna Mei organize events. And I showed up.

Methods

Autoethnography has long been used as a method for understanding personal meaning making within a particular cultural context. Our collaborative autoethnographic work builds from Alexander's (2023) approach, which understands autoethnographic meaning making as a culture-centered qualitative research process that produces narrative that can function as a "curative for what ails us" (p. 826). Bolstering this culture-centered process has been our focus on working together to foster radical dreaming, such as has been modeled through collaborative autoethnographic writing (i.e., Holman Jones, 2015; Simmons and Williams, 2018). Bochner and Ellis' (2016) principles of evocative autoethnography became a set of guideposts: (a) Use a researcher's personal experience to describe and critique cultural beliefs, practices, and experiences; (b) Acknowledge and value the researcher's relationships with others; (c) Use deep and careful self-reflection … to name and interrogate the intersections between self and society, particular and general, personal and political; (d) Show people in the process of understanding and acting on that understanding; (e) Balance rigor while considering emotions, intellectual pursuits, methodological underpinnings, and creative writing; (f) Express concern for social justice (p. 62-107). The latter point here is expanded beyond a simple social justice framework to better mean what culture-centered work could be documented through our engagement with students and through the crystallization of that work through the writing of autoethnographic vignettes. We bolstered this latter methodological concern by considering Black feminist approaches to intersectionality, namely understanding how processes of racialization influenced the possibilities and stakes of assuming social identities and, therefore, what dreams could be dreamed.

To better understand our practice of taking up the mantle of adult allies, we engaged in regular reflective exercises where we would write narratives separately and then later share, discuss, and debate details. We expanded on details that related to the spirit of the story: supporting student identity development while confronting conformity pressure at a small PWI through modeling our own authentic truths, engaging in collaborative efforts, and consistently showing up for the students. As a research team, we examined our positionalities vis-à-vis intersectionality, racialized experiences, and adult allyship, and we used those mutual reflections to strengthen our collective writing, though not to sanitize it. We wrote both together and separately and edited each other's vignettes with permission.

Student Reactions and Student Organization Positionality

Our student leader allies had complex intersectional identities, which we considered throughout the process. In experiencing our support, these campus leaders engaged in DEIB work and began to deepen their own capacity for sharing their own stories, understanding the need for cross-identity allyship with each other even while their knowledge of gender diversity and racial and ethnic equity was burgeoning, and dreaming bigger by reaching out across campus.

We spoke extensively with the two undergraduate student leaders engaged in DEIB work with whom we partnered over the course of the year. With their permission, we share their words on the process of working with us, their adult allies, through event planning and participation. The names of the students below are pseudonyms.

Riley was the president of the student Gay-Straight Alliance. The organization's goal was to be a safe space for members of the 2SLGBTQIA+ community and their allies to come together and educate the greater college community about 2SLGBTQIA+ topics. This group existed in previous iterations, but due to large staff-support turnover, it had mostly gone dormant until Fall '22. Riley was a third-year student, and they had not actively engaged with previous versions of this group but wanted to take on a leadership role after witnessing the DEIB Department's commitment to supporting the organization. Riley identifies as a non-binary student with a mixed-race ethnic identity from the same northeast state in which the institution is located. While white-passing, Riley also began exploring the culture and language of their ethnic background during this school year.

> *Anna Mei ended up playing a very prominent role in my life. She helped me bring my ideas to life for Alliance and supported me as a college student and human being. … I also had the opportunity to work alongside Aubry. We collaborated on a presentation and conversation exploring gender expression to celebrate Trans Day of Visibility. … Aubry holds a wealth of knowledge about gender studies. I was a bit nervous going into the event, but Aubry's confidence in themself was uplifting and encouraging! … I truly loved working with both of them!*

Maryam was the president of the student organization Racial Justice (RJ). While this organization's title is technically nationally affiliated with a group that focuses on white allyship for BIPOC students, in the past two years at our institution, this group had become a safe space for mostly female-identifying students of color. The programs were designed to celebrate students of color, educate the wider college community about chosen issues different communities face, and build community. Maryam identifies as a third-year, female, Muslim (hijab-wearing) student of Middle Eastern descent from the same northeast state in which the institution is located.

> *Being involved in social justice work as a college student can get draining if you don't have the right support system. For myself, I've been involved in social justice in college since my freshman year, but it didn't really start to feel like social justice work until this past year. The rest of my peers in our organization and I were already planning on tackling the new school year head-on, determined to create some noise and make an impact on campus. We would not have been able to have as much of an impact as we did without support from staff members like Aubry and Anna Mei. Whatever we needed, they were there. ... I know for myself, Anna Mei and Aubry helped me to really come out of my shell more. They helped me to find my voice on this campus. ... Prior to this year, I never truly felt I had a place on campus. ... As a person of color in a PWI, juggling personal struggles, racial struggles, and academic struggles, it was and is never easy. Having that support system to go back to for help, or just to have someone to talk to, makes a world of difference, and I will forever be grateful for Anna Mei, who let me sit in her office for hours chatting away about life, and for Aubry who was immediately willing to help and support me and the organization I was a part of.*

Despite our institution's original inclination to give these students space to fail, to us, these testimonies from our student accomplices—our allies in defiant dreaming—serve as evidence that the supports we provided did not hinder their growth, but rather augmented it. The time spent having authentic discussions in which students could bring their whole selves and reflect upon their own experiences made them feel seen. With a strong sense of belonging created by this authentic engagement, these leaders gained confidence in their own power and knowledge and began to build on it to explore possibilities for potential programs. As adult allies who had more experiences with DEIB work, we advised our students, inspired them to explore different themes of their own choosing, and helped them intentionally shape their programming and engage their peers. Not only did we talk about these programs, but we also consistently attended them. We showed up, engaged fully, and gave students feedback after the events to make programming an iterative process. By being a consistent presence, we demonstrated our commitment to these students and their important DEIB work.

Vignette: An Evening Event with RJC (Racial Justice Club) (Anna Mei)

On a Monday evening, when most educational professionals are dragging their bags to their cars, Dr. Threlkeld arrived at the DEIB Center wearing red. Maryam, president of RJC, had gone to various administrators' offices to promote RJC's "Wear Red Day" campaign. She asked to hang red dresses to bring awareness to the atrocities committed against Missing and Murdered Indigenous Women (MMIW). Not only did Aubry approve of the art installation, they also agreed to host a documentary screening and discussion after the main event: dinner with a Native American ambassador.

Even though Aubry lived an hour away, there were only eight students attending, and the Native American ambassador and other DEIB staff had gone home. We chose to be there for the students—not just "be there" in the figurative, "I can talk during my designated office hours" way, but in a literal, "I am here holding space with you" way. By staying and, as the club's name implies, showing up, we created stronger bonds with our students.

The conversation after the documentary was real and vulnerable. We talked about what it would be like to not feel seen—to go missing and feel like no one in power cared. We talked about the hopelessness one can feel when advocating for racial justice, and wondering if anyone is paying attention. There was a break in the conversation, and Aubry brought forth an acknowledgement that moved our students: "I never thought this day would come. I had a sticker on my office door for MMIW years ago, but no one had taken up the cause. It seemed like no one cared. But there were red dresses across campus today, and that was you. So maybe we want to brainstorm other ways to get other people to come to these events, but from where

I am sitting, from knowing where this school was just a few years ago, I am amazed at what you have accomplished."

You could feel the tone of the room shift as the students made eye contact with one another and smiled. They felt validated and realized they should be proud of their efforts. The support and presence of these adult allies empowered them to continue to host events for the remainder of the school year, and just as we modeled the importance of presence, they began to show up for other organizations' events as well.

They created coalitions with the GSA (Gay Straight Alliance), various sports teams, and the community service department; and throughout the year, these groups supported one another. They uplifted each other's programs both on social media and more importantly, showed up for as many as possible. By showing up for vulnerable discussions, eating dinner, and wearing red, we become even stronger allies that inspire students to resist, repair, and rejoice.

Ligature 3: Campus Pride Month (Anna Mei)

On Friday April 28, we agreed to keep the rainbow curtain fringe across the doorway, the rainbow balloons taped to the tables, and our pride swag on display; however, when I enter the Center, the fringe has been ripped down. Only the blue painter's tape remains along the doorframe. When I ask about why it was taken down, my supervisor responded: "it's enough already with the pride stuff." Campus Pride Month has been over a whopping nine hours and two minutes, and it's already on to the next. We checked the box and that was sufficient.

It felt reminiscent of the entire year: we had a whole Center devoted to DEIB initiatives and programming. We had a Chief Diversity Officer. We did the DEI thing. The school felt like it was enough already. Although these steps were seemingly concrete and completed, they still felt performative without the policy changes, reflective empathy, and continued commitment to show up for the people who were marginalized by the professional and social culture on campus.

Yes, it's true, we already did a lot for Pride Month, but more than this month, I'm proud of how this group came together at any size: five students folding origami hearts, 11 students discussing volunteering with the local queer youth center, and 500 students learning about the history of drag performance while playing BINGO hosted by drag queens.

My heart grew three sizes when 14 students came to learn about gender identity with Aubry. I was inspired by the time and effort Riley invested in promoting the program, understanding the material covered, and sharing vulnerably with the group. The participants reviewed the program favorably, saying they got a lot out of it, and wishing other people would come to learn more. Aubry said that Riley was "a rock star who spoke with such poise and eloquence," and that was what brought tears to my eyes.

Aubry helped me recognize the immense progress this group, and specifically Riley, made. They volunteered for the position when no one else had the capacity, and within six months, they were creating collaborative educational presentations and speaking in front of a group. They found their confidence in their dedication to advocating for and educating others about the 2SLGBTQIA+ community. I was humbled by the way that they trusted me, a new-to-the-institution coordinator, as their adult ally. We co-constructed this new iteration of the GSA over the year through consistent meetings that demonstrated a commitment to furthering advocacy, education, and support.

There was a lot to be proud of on April 28. Sixty-three community members and allies marched across campus handing out rainbow flags to anyone who walked by—telling them that they are loved and that they belonged. The rain held off, and even though the sun was not brightly shining, the water droplets from the fountain created a mist of mini rainbows. Everyone marched to the Center for a collaborative love-language themed party that took months to plan; but, by May 1, at 9:01am, it was enough already. But it wasn't enough. It is never enough.

There were 589 anti-trans bills proposed across the country in the year 2023 alone (Trans Legislation Tracker, 2024). There is only one state that has not proposed an anti-trans bill, and no, it is not our "woke" northeastern state: it's Delaware. And even though a "Queer Committee" was formed to support the 2SLGBTQIA+ community on our campus, when this group made recommendations, the school always found reasons to delay responding to their requests. A survey and needs report of gender inclusive bathrooms was completed in 2022 and revisited by GSA students this year, but there still weren't gender inclusive restrooms in every building on campus, and even though there were multiple students in need of support, there was no formalized policy for how to help trans students with name changes on campus. I advocate for them with three different departments, only to have limited success. Our policies were failing our students, and there was little more I could do besides send a fourth email with the subject line: "Name Change, Update?"

So, at 9:02 a.m., I followed instructions and took down the pride balloons. Then I taped them to my office wall. I kept the pennants that say "Love." I MacGyvered from rainbow flags, twine, and a straw. I hung them on my office door facing outward because there will never be enough pride. I was proud in April, and the students needed to know that I'm still proud in May, and I will still be proud year-round.

Conclusion

Even though both the RJC (Racial Justice Club) and the GSA (Gay Straight Alliance) were social-identity based, social-justice focused, student-led organizations whose missions to support minoritized students on campus made them targets for tokenization by the administration, they were considered student clubs and thus were subjected to oversight by the student activities department. This department valued students' autonomy, giving them minimal oversight to develop their own pathways. They justified this more laissez-faire approach by highlighting the importance of students learning accountability for their actions and from their mistakes. However, by applying a hands-off approach to all organizations with the expectation of potential failure, this department did not acknowledge that potential failures from RJ and the GSA, whose goals are to be spaces for members of marginalized communities, had more significant repercussions.

There is an ever-oscillating quest to find balance between challenging students to develop into independent learners and creating scaffolding that supports students' ability to thrive. In textbooks outlining student development theory for graduate-level professionals, psychology professor, Dr. Nevitt Sanford's theory of Challenge and Support (1967) is consistently raised. This theory asserts there is an optimal balance of providing challenge and support to a student to maximize their growth: if a student is neither challenged nor supported, they are likely to disengage from the activity; if there is too much support and too little challenge, the student's progress may become stagnant as they find the experience tedious; but if there is too little support and too much challenge, the student could become overwhelmed and retreat into their own stress rather than engage with the material (Patton et al., 2016).

By treating all students at the PWI with an equal level of challenge while not accounting for the additional challenges RJ and the GSA faced as groups supporting minoritized students and taking on discussions of human rights violations and dehumanization of people with whom they shared an identity, the school was not providing equitable treatment, so we decided to provide additional supports for these organizations. We consistently asked ourselves, how can we, as adult allies, create equitable systems for our students? How can we most effectively encourage, support, motivate, and uplift these students and their dreams that disrupt our current hellscape? Throughout the year, we took on this challenge by modeling authenticity, encouraging collaboration and co-alition building, and consistently showing up for all our students.

A year-long effort to support students collectively resulted in mutual bene-fits. Our students and the groups they led hosted a record number of events, felt more powerful, and ultimately reported feeling like they belonged. Despite our temporary successes, none of us felt like the work was done, nor that we could continue at this level forever. It was ultimately unsustainable and undervalued at the institution. While both writers have since left for new professional lives, we have formed a lifelong connection across age, gender, sexuality, and race and ethnicity. We accomplished this by proudly being our authentic selves, showing up, building trusting relationships, listening with empathy and humil-ity, encouraging collaboration, and occasionally giving advice to help student leaders achieve their goals. As Kezar (2010) noted, we decided to partner with our students to provide clear support from within the institution, and as ref-erenced in Lange et al. (2022), we fulfilled the commonly identified supports college activists desired: listening and validating oppression, showing up, and providing resources.

Throughout our collaborative writing process, we recognized the ways in which we felt the student leaders had grown in confidence around their identi-ties. Future research could monitor these relationships in practice and examine how identities emerge and become more complex, as well as how intersectional campus organizing could contribute to deeper and broader relationships for all.

Postlude: Teaching Maia Kobabe's Gender Queer (Aubry)

I co-taught my last class before I realized it. We read and discussed Maia Ko-babe's (2019) Gender Queer, the most banned book in the United States, in an English seminar. Many of the students were visibly uncomfortable with the topics brought out in the text: gender confusion and queering, non-binaristic thinking, multiple processes of coming out, xenopronouns, and non-binary and trans healthcare. Some chose to express how reading it was against their religious views, and so they were given an alternate assignment by the faculty lead. While teaching, I shared some of my experiences with being genderqueer and coming out to myself nearly 20 years earlier. I discussed how hard it was to live when political rhetoric vilified my very existence. To our collective surprise, my co-teacher even came out as bisexual to share some of her experiences: she never felt comfortable telling anyone on campus, and she had been teaching there for more than 20 years. Two students from the class came to my office and thanked me for being willing to discuss asexuality and gender creativity. They reiterated how hard it was for them to come out at our college and why this class was important. So why didn't I feel better?

Anna Mei accepted another job continuing DEIB work. The climate at school made working there untenable. Our allied students were going home for the summer. And the silent treatment I was getting from other administrators, including former friends, was palpable. I started to have anxiety attacks just going to work. I couldn't sleep, and I had gained significant weight. My social worker told me to quit. I saw in The Chronicle of Higher Education the harrowing stories of lifelong administrators dying in office. I realized then and perhaps permanently how much I suffered—how much we had suffered. I knew to keep doing this work, I would need to move on.

Reference

Alexander, B. K. (2023). Onboarding, Orientation, and Mentoring as Culture-Crafting Processes: A Rac(e)y Autoethnography of Resistance in Higher Education Administration. *Qualitative Inquiry, 29*(7), 825-839. https://doi-org.ezp-prod1.hul.harvard.edu/10.1177/10778004221144072

Anzaldúa, G. (1987). *Borderlands/La frontera*. Aunt Lute Books.

Bennett, C. B., Ramos, D., & Wyatt, R. (2022). Latinx youth's funds of knowledge: Empowering activist identities in a Nuevo South College Access Program. *Journal of Hispanic Higher Education, 21*(3), 282–296. https://doi.org/10.1177/1538192720963717

Bilge, S., & Collins, P. H. (2016) *Intersectionality*. Polity Press.

Bochner, A. P., & Ellis, C. (2016). *Evocative autoethnography: Writing lives and telling stories*. Routledge.

Combahee River Collective (1977). *The Combahee River collective statement*. [Web Archive]. Retrieved from the Library of Congress, https://www.loc.gov/item/lcwaN0028151/

Crenshaw, K. (1989) Demarginalizing the intersection of race and sex: A Black Feminist critique of antidiscrimination doctrine, feminist theory and antiracist politics. *University of Chicago Legal Forum*. (1989)1, Article 8. https://chicagounbound.uchicago.edu/uclf/vol1989/iss1/8

Cumming-Potvin, W. M. (2023). *LGBTQI+ allies in education, advocacy, activism, and participatory collaborative research*. Routledge.

Duran, A., Foste, Z., Garcia, C. E., & Snipes, J. T. (2022). How campus space becomes white place: Advancing a spatial analysis of whiteness in higher education. *Journal of College Student Development, 63*(6), 611–625. https://doi.org/10.1353/csd.2022.0051

Gandy-Guedes, M. E., & Paceley, M. S. (2019). Activism in southwestern queer and trans young adults after the Marriage Equality Era. *Affilia, 34*(4), 439–460. https://doi.org/10.1177/0886109919857699

Gulbrandsen, C. L., & Walsh, C. A. (2012). It starts with me: Women mediate power within feminist activism. *Affilia, 27*(3), 275–288. https://doi.org/10.1177/0886109912452640

Holman Jones, S. (2015). The dreamer, the dreaming, the dream. *Departures in Critical Qualitative Research, 4*(3), 1–4. https://doi.org/10.1525/dcqr.2015.4.3.1

hooks, bell. (2005). *Sisters of the yam: Black women and self-recovery* (Classics ed.). South End Press.

Kezar, A. (2010). Faculty and staff partnering with student activists: Unexplored terrains of interaction and development. *Journal of College Student Development, 51*(5), 451–480. https://doi-org.ezp-prod1.hul.harvard.edu/10.1353/csd.2010.0001

King, M. L. (1963, August 28). *I Have a Dream*. [Speech audio recording]. https://www.peptalkindia.com/wp-content/uploads/woocommerce_uploads/2018/03/Master_the_art_of_public_speaking-gbwlby.pdf#page=30

Kobabe, M. (2019). *Gender queer: A memoir*. Oni Press.

Lange, A. C., Quaye, S. J., Linder, C., & Evans, M. E. (2022). Relationships between institutional agents and student activists. *Peabody Journal of Education, 97*(5), 616-630. https://doi.org/10.1080/0161956X.2022.2125761

Leath, S., Ball, P., Mims, L., Butler-Barnes, S., & Quiles, T. (2022). "They need to hear our voices": A multidimensional framework of Black college women's sociopolitical development and activism. *Journal of Black Psychology, 48*(3–4), 392–427. https://doi.org/10.1177/00957984211016943

Lewis, A. F., & Barnes, K. (2023). "Racism lives here" In M. Zebracki & Z.Z. McNeill (Eds.), *Politics as public art: The aesthetics of political organizing and social movements* (1st ed.) (pp. 96–115). Routledge. https://doi.org/10.4324/9781003231141-11

Logan, G., Lightfoot, B. A., & Contreras, A. (2017). Black and brown millennial activism on a PWI campus in the era of Trump. *The Journal of Negro Education, 86*(3), 252–268. https://doi.org/10.7709/jnegroeducation.86.3.0252

Patton. L. D., Renn. K. A., Guido. F. M., & Quaye S. J. (2016). *Student development in college: Theory, research, and practice.* (3rd ed.). Wiley.

Phelps-Ward, R., & Kenney, J. M. (2017). *No Struggle, no progress: Examining Black faculty/staff experiences with campus activism and belonging.* [Paper]. Annual Meeting of the American Educational Research Association, San Antonio, TX. https://eric.ed.gov/?id=ED605009

Piepzna-Samarasinha, L.L. (2021). *Care work: Dreaming disability justice.* Arsenal Pulp Press.

Reed, R., & Lohnes, J. (2019). Tripping the Black fantastic at a PWI: Or how Afrofuturist exhibitions in an academic library changed everything. *Alexandria* 29(1-2), 116–129. https://doi.org/10.1177/0955749019876383

Rich, A. (1980). Compulsory heterosexuality and lesbian existence. *Signs,* 5(4), 631. http://search.proquest.com.ezp-prod1.hul.harvard.edu/scholarly-journals/compulsory-heterosexuality-lesbian-existence/docview/1300107822/se-2

Seal, M. (2019). *The interruption of heteronormativity in higher education: Critical queer pedagogies* (1st ed.). Palgrave Macmillan. https://doi.org/10.1007/978-3-030-19089-7

Simmons, K. L., & Williams, K. N. (2018). I was dreaming when I wrote this. *Social Text,* 36(2), 145–164. https://doi.org/10.1215/01642472-4362409

Threlkeld, A., & Pieplow, S. (2018). Method to our madness: Teaching across mental disability. In M. Jeffress (Ed.), *International perspectives on teaching with a disability* (pp. 172–187). Routledge.

Trans Legislation Tracker. (2024, January 2). *2023: Anti-Trans Bills: Trans legislation tracker.* https://translegislation.com/

CHAPTER 7

"We Don't See That in Our History Books…"
Dialectic Conversations on Designing for Collective Social Dreaming in History Education

Ava Jackson and Corey Winchester

Introduction

THIS CHAPTER IS a dialogue between two authors, Ava and Corey, also re-searchers, educators, activists, philosophers, and friends, who delve into their shared exploration of learning and identity development in a critical history high school class. We respond to a current moment of possibility in the field and broader society by re-imagining history education as a site of educational justice, resistance, and liberation. We build on work challenging preconceived notions of the disciplines (Warren et al., 2020) to explore the political, ethical, and intellectual possibility of critical history education (Santiago, 2019) in supporting young people as historical and political agents of change in and out of the classroom (Gutiérrez et al., 2019).

Inspired by hooks (1994) and Boggs and Kurashige (2011), we present our theorizations and imaginings as *dialectical conversations* to retain the conceptual and political nuance often obscured in research publishing and as a method-ological contribution in taking seriously dialogicality (Bakhtin, 1981), not just as a political practice, but a research commitment. From this commitment, as learning scientists, we seek to understand the ways that dialectical conversations, defined as the seeking and iterating of individual and collective truths grounded in interrogating and questioning data, systems, structures, thinking, and practices for an evolution of theory towards justice, have informed our learning as researchers. We will explore this idea further, as it is the basis of our conceptual framework from which we explicate not only our learning as researchers, but also how we understand historical thinking as social dreaming in history education for young people. Thus, we explore three questions:

1. If and how do transcending binaries of teacher-student (Vossoughi et al., 2021) and normative boundaries of school disciplines help us explore liberatory education as a collective prefiguration (Griffin & Cole, 1984) of the world as it could be?

2. If and how do young people use historical thinking as a practice of social dreaming (Gutiérrez, 2008)?

3. How did our use of dialectical conversations help us explore these questions of teaching and learning in a liberatory education classroom?

We explore these questions in the context of a critical history high school class taught by Corey. We are uniquely positioned to engage dialectically about our research site, as Ava, then a Ph.D. candidate in Learning Sciences, facilitated co-designed research (Erickson, 2006) in Corey's classroom. In the years since the research was conducted, Corey became a Ph.D. student in Learning Sciences, as well, presenting an opportunity in this book chapter to theorize further with Ava in the spirit of bell hooks (1994), who engaged in a playful dialogue with herself and her writing voice, inspired by Freire's (1970) attunement to dialectics in *Pedagogy of the Oppressed* as well as Boggs & Kurashige, (2011) use of dialectics as a philosopher, activist, and community organizer.

We begin by sharing our respective stories, offering personal narratives about how we as individuals came to this work and partnership. We then offer an overview of our conceptual framework and our corresponding methodology for exploring questions of teaching and learning in liberatory education. For the rest of the chapter, we share a re-telling of our dialectical conversations describing the pedagogical design of Corey's class and examples of historical thinking as experienced by students. Our narrative focuses on the importance of relational collectivity in the design and mediation of teacher-student relationships, the conceptual centrality of historical thinking in developing student historical and political agency, and the methodological possibilities gathered from a collaborative, dialectic analysis of a learning environment.

Corey's Story

I was surprised to find the first email communication between Ava and me in my district inbox after all these years, with a subject line reading, "Meeting to talk about Critical Pedagogy?" sent on a cold January day in 2018. Little did I know how life-changing this moment would be for me, both personally and professionally. This introduction profoundly brought us into conversation with one another, centering our lived experiences on how we individually and collectively work towards enacting versions of educational justice and our proleptic orientations for our work as educators. As a Queer, Black, cis-male identifying high school history and social science educator who is also a first-generation college graduate, I have spent over a decade refining both the art and science of my teaching such that my students and I could collectively walk away with a better sense of who we are and who we are in relation to one another. That sensemaking, which inspired my path into teaching, also carried significant social, political, and cultural implications, some of which I made explicit in my teaching, like sharing my own personal story with my students as to why I became a teacher, while others were implied in practice, like with my selection of written and visual texts by authors of color to explore in my classroom. In my service as a classroom teacher, I did not always have the language to understand how I was building capacity for students to engage in their sensemaking, but Ava's research as a learning scientist provided new and emergent language to see and better understand the sensemaking that was occurring in my classroom for both myself and the students in the space, one that was rooted in critical pedagogical practice.

Ava's Story

I entered graduate school wanting to explore the impact of critical pedagogies on student learning and identity development. Having gone straight from my undergraduate studies to a Ph.D. graduate program, my professional experience in K-12 education was limited as a researcher and non-existent as a teacher. Rather, it was my experiences as a Black woman navigating the peripheries of upper-class, white suburban educational and social contexts while contending with my family's own financial insecurity that motivated my scholarship. I experienced how schooling can reify oppression within systems of racism, classism, and sexism; I also experienced how schooling can be life-giving and offer radically loving experiences of community building and dreaming. It was in these contradictory moments that I saw the potential of education not just as a project for creating a liberatory future but a proleptic experience of liberatory futures, now. As a first-generation college student, I committed my undergraduate and graduate schooling to learning how to see, analyze, and study these moments of educational dignity to challenge and reimagine teaching and learning as revolutionary practices of world making. It was through these experiences that I also learned the importance of doing this work with others; the entirety of my research experience is characterized by collaborative partnerships grounded in the values of Participatory Design Research (Bang & Vossoughi, 2016). Just as I study teaching and learning as processes of liberatory change, I do the same as I engage in research.

So, when I think back on my partnership with Corey, I remember realizing very quickly how incredible he was; he was a state- and nationally-recognized teacher, unwavering in his commitment to teaching as a political practice. I knew there was so much I (and educators, researchers, and theorists) could learn from his practice. When we first started to chat about our respective research interests and questions, I noticed how his perspectives and experiences as a teacher expanded and nuanced my questions on critical pedagogies and student history learning. He helped me understand where and how our developing concepts and ideas can be most helpful for teachers and students. These early conversations set a precedent for our partnership to be a relational experience of continual growth, care, and world-building—a precedent with significant consequences for our study of liberatory education.

Conceptual Framework

At this point, we as authors will use both the third person and a collective "we" as we story our shared research. Collectivity is foundational to the conceptual framing we take up in sharing this work, building on what we refer to as dialectical conversations, collective relationality, and historical thinking as social dreaming. Together, these ideas support our three research questions in how we seek to understand reimagined and fluid understandings of teacher and student relations in exploring liberatory education beyond normative disciplinary boundaries (RQ1), how young people use historical thinking as a practice of social dreaming (RQ2), and how dialectical conversations as a methodological practice expand new frontiers in how we understand teaching and learning through justice-oriented approaches (RQ3).

Dialectical Conversations

Inspired directly by Boggs' use of dialectics (Boggs & Kurashige, 2011), specifically in the ways that she used conversations towards the end of her life as a form of activism to evolve and expand the revolutionary and liberatory thinking of those who had chosen to engage in dialogue with her, we define dialectical conversations as the seeking and iterating of individual and collective truths, grounded in interrogating and questioning data, systems, structures, thinking, and practices for an evolution of theory towards justice. Boggs' understanding of dialectics was mainly informed by her philosophical studies of Hegelian dialectics, which also informed early critical theoreticians like Karl Marx and Federick Engels, individuals whose emergent theories primarily challenged Eurocentric systems of capitalism and classism (Boggs & Kurashige, 2011).

Boggsian dialectical approaches (Boggs, 1978; Boggs et al., 2011) are best experienced when two or more parties choose to engage consensually in dialogue with one another's ideas, histories, and understandings, especially when they are complex and/or contradictory, such that those parties work through struggle to find new meaning and grounding in their theories of change towards justice. This can look like the use of questions in dialogue like, "I understand what you're saying, but I am confused. Can you tell me more about 'X'?" or "I really vibe with these ideas and I'm wondering if you considered 'X'?". Boggs' theories of changemaking have informed theories of change like Kelley's (2002) freedom dreaming and brown's (2017) emergent strategies. As Boggsian dialectical approaches enjoyed space in Corey's pedagogical practice as an educator, we decided to explore the ways in which dialectical conversations about the data Ava collected in Corey's class could be generatively revisited as we both seek to understand new dimensions of teaching and learning towards liberatory and just futures.

Collective Relationalities of Learning

As collective dialectics shape our methodological approaches to research, so do they shape our theoretical orientations of teaching and learning. Inspired by critical sociocultural theories of learning, we understand learning as an interactive, interconnected, interrelational phenomenon situated in time and context (Esmonde & Booker, 2017). Within frameworks of collective relationality, conceptual emphasis is placed on the relational processes mediating educational experiences as experienced beyond the individual. In learning environments that are designed to support collective relationalities, learning is often characterized by a pedagogical ethos of joint-activity (Vossoughi et al., 2021) as experienced across multi-modal (discursive and embodied) and moment-to-moment interactions. In other words, collective relationalities are designed in the ways teachers and students learn to speak, think, and be with one another as collaborative thought partners within and beyond the classroom space. By incorporating collective relationalities into our conceptual framework, we aim to explore teaching and learning as holistic, interactional processes of knowledge-building through intersubjectivity that can be dignifying and affirming to young people (Espinoza et al., 2020; Jackson, 2021).

Historical Thinking as Social Dreaming

Lastly, our orientations to dialectical conversations and collective relationalities require us to challenge preconceived notions of disciplinary education and normative assumptions of knowledge production and action (Bang et al., 2012; Shotter, 2006a). This challenge manifests in our engagement with expansive disciplinary learning, which grounds "forms of onto-epistemic heterogeneity in ideas and practices that disallow conceptual flattening and colonial enclosure (e.g., heterogeneity as 'multiculturalism')" and "entails opening ourselves to living more ethically and politically responsive relations" (Warren et al., 2020, pg. 279). In history education specifically, we incorporate an expansive disciplinary approach in our analysis of historical thinking, not as narrowly constrained to conceptual practices or tools but as personally meaningful, politically interrogative, and ethically constructive. Within an expansive disciplinary orientation to history education, historical thinking is taken up as an onto-epistemology of seeing the world as it was, as it is, and as it could be. In other words, historical thinking functions as a practice of social dreaming, the collective imagination of more just worlds (Gutiérrez, 2008).

Our understanding of social dreaming also builds on ideas expressed in Espinoza's (2008) work exploring humanizing social relations in learning environments, conceptualizations of freedom dreaming in and across social movements (Kelley, 2002), and the intersections of social movement building as learning, articulated in teaching and learning frameworks like abolitionist teaching (Love, 2019), urgent pedagogies (Muhammad 2020; 2023) and speculative pedagogies (Garcia & Mirra, 2023). With this conceptual framework of dialectical conversations, collective relationalities, and historical thinking as social dreaming, we offer our explorations into the rich forms of teaching and learning experienced in a liberatory-oriented history classroom.

Research Project and Methodology

Ava's dissertation study conducted several years ago in one of Corey's 11th grade U.S. history classes at a high school in a Midwest suburb outside of Chicago, IL, serves as the foundation for this dialectical conversation. Scheduled for the last period of the school day, 15 of the 23 enrolled students participated in the project. The racial/ethnic and gender demographics of participating students (as self-identified in surveys) is as follows: 7 Black, 5 white, 1 Asian/Asian American/Japanese American, 1 Latina, 1 Hispanic, 1 Bi-Racial/Black; 7 women, 8 men. The classroom itself was covered in different posters and artifacts from various political leaders and visionaries, marking the different ideological influences on Corey's pedagogy and activism (see Figure 7.1). Organized in small groups of four or five, students would sit at their assigned tables and participate in a variety of planned activities: small- and whole-group discussions, interactive readings of texts, individual and group projects, watching videos, or listening to presentations. While the planned activities varied day-by-day depending on topic and content, Corey's classroom was a space for students to relax and engage in conversations (formal and informal), creating an inviting environment for self-reflection and questioning.

Figure 7.1 *Corey's U.S. history class.*

Note. These two pictures are screenshots from video recordings of Corey teaching the U.S. history class.

Ava visited Corey's classroom around three times a week to collect a variety of qualitative data sources (jottings, field notes, student artifacts, video recordings, interviews, surveys) to capture the interactional dimensions of Corey's pedagogy and the emergent forms of student history learning and identity development. Through Ava's study, she argued that Corey's pedagogy, characterized by a commitment to co-thinking, created the conditions for students' development of relational, critical social analytic, and history knowledge-building practices (Jackson, 2021). Recently, we had the opportunity to engage in a meta-analysis of Ava's data which was collected in Corey's classroom through dialectical conversations. With Corey now training as a learning scientist, we have the opportunity to revisit hotspots (Jorden & Henderson, 1995) from Ava's dissertation study with new lenses for seeing the types of student learning that occurred in his class several years ago.

Given our evolving methodological practice (see Figure 7.2) embodied in a Third Space (Gutiérrez & Vossoughi, 2010), collaborative, axiologically-driven (Bang et al., 2016), codesigned research-practitioner partnership, and in the spirit of Boggsian dialectics (Boggs, 1978; Boggs & Kurashige, 2011), in this chapter, we seek to synthesize our understanding of what the teaching and learning of history looked like in a classroom that employed critical pedagogies, exploring how young people engage in historical thinking. We do this by storying a learning environment that transcended binaries of teacher-student relationships (Vossoughi et al., 2021) and normative boundaries of school disciplines in ways that helped us explore liberatory education as a collective prefiguration (Griffin & Cole, 1984) of the world as it could be, conditions that made social dreaming a practice through using historical thinking as an interwoven intellectual, political, ethical, relational, and academic agentic practice.

Figure 7.2 *An evolution of methodological practice.*

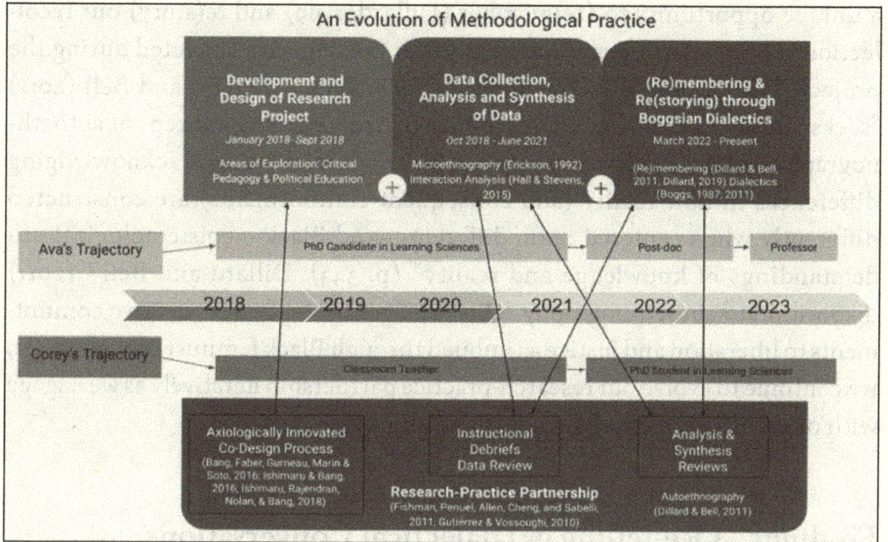

Note. Figure 7.2 shows the relationships of three aspects across time that have informed the methodological practice employed in this chapter: (a) Ava's and Corey's trajectories as educators and researchers, (b) the evolution of the designed research project, its data collection, analysis, review, and meta-analysis through (re)membering (Dillard & Bell, 2011) and Boggsian dialectics, and (c) the evolution of Ava and Corey's relationship within a dynamic research-practice partnership. The vertical lines across the life course of the project, connecting evolutions of (b) and (c) as mentioned in the previous line, represent the ways Ava & Corey mediated understanding about their work across time. We now have language to name those mediations as dialectical conversations that happened across time. This paper is mainly a manifestation of the last vertical line in the figure.

With the context of how we have come into this work provided here, we describe our methodological practice as evolving for several reasons: First, our positional trajectories in relation to this research project have shifted over the years. Ava moved from being a Ph.D. student in Learning Sciences to being a professor, and through that process, has continued to explore data from her doctoral studies. Corey moved from being a classroom teacher, whose classroom was the site of this research, to becoming a Ph.D. student in Learning Sciences. Given our evolving epistemological understandings as emerging learning scientists, this chapter offers a more nuanced understanding of phenomena for what Ava argued in her dissertation as the types of "pedagogical dispositions and relational attunement necessary for implementing critical pedagogies that support expansive forms of disciplinary learning" (Jackson, 2021, pg. 3).

Second, with our positional trajectories and our shared interests, we had a unique opportunity to (re)member (Dillard, 2019) and re(story) our recollections of the learning environment given the data Ava collected during the project. This notion of (re)membering according to Dillard and Bell (2011) "seeks a more critical and complex engagement with the concept of autoethnography, drawing upon transnational Black feminist thought, acknowledging differences in how reality (and consequent commitments) are constructed differently when centered upon different—and Black—epistemological understandings of knowledge and reality" (p. 343). Dillard and Bell's (2011) disposition to autoethnography acknowledges both of our collective commitments to liberation and justice as imbued through Black feminist thought. Last, we continue to evolve our research-practice partnership iteratively as we engage with one another in debriefing data and analysis.

Findings: A Re-telling of Dialectical Conversations

Thus far, we have provided the stories of our individual and collective pedagogical, political, and axiological values that characterize our teaching, research, and activism. As research and pedagogical collaborators grounded in a shared onto-epistemology characterized by collectivism, dialogism, and proleptic social change, we initially began exploration of the data by asking: How did these values shape how learning was seen and experienced in Corey's class? How did our values create the conditions for particular kinds of historical learning, and how do our perspectives help us see these forms of learning? Our dialectical conversations re-narrating our experiences from class became consequential in seeing how students learned to think and be with each other. As we sought to explore the data dialectically, those initial questions helped us to frame this chapter's research questions to understand reimagined and fluid understandings of teacher and student relations in exploring liberatory educations (RQ1) and how young people use historical thinking as a practice of social dreaming (RQ2).

Based on individual and collective analyses grounded in micro-ethnographic, interactional, and discourse analyses, we illuminated the meaningful ways students engage in history as a collective and complex process of critical reflexivity and imagination (Jackson, 2021). Our initial intention for this chapter was to share some of these insights by revisiting the data and talking through how we saw student learning as consequential to the critical history pedagogy enacted by Corey. However, after once again talking through our respective narratives of our classroom experience and exploring individual moments across the school year through a collective inquiry, our dialectical conversations revealed something new about students' historical learning. The forms of historical thinking students took up were not just a means to enact social dreaming but were practices of social dreaming in and of themselves. This is not a superficial distinction in semantics; often, history and other academic disciplines are treated as separate from critical social analysis and political education, with the goal of critical pedagogies often discussed as "add-ons" to normative curricula. While the intentions of this rhetoric and educational movement may be genuine in the creation of liberatory educational experiences, these initiatives run the risk of superficially integrating the core values of critical pedagogies as supplemental or secondary to the primary disciplinary curricula, reaffirming the belief that the discipline and critical social analysis and political education are separate domains.

This was not what we experienced nor saw in our dialogic analysis of the data. Rather, Corey's pedagogical design, characterized by collectivity, dialogue, and heterogeneity, invited students to build a conception of history not as "settled" and overly informed by Western onto-epistemologies, but instead as an iterative, expansive, and onto-epistemologically heterogeneous discipline. Situated within this disciplinary perspective, students experienced historical thinking not as a school-based practice but as a third way (Vossoughi et al., 2021) of being with one another to engage in social dreaming and liberatory praxis. We demonstrate these findings by first showing how the pedagogical design of collective relationalities worked to challenge teacher-student binaries, how this design created the conditions for students to engage collective inquiries of historical thinking, and how these experiences of historical thinking reflected practices of social dreaming. By framing our findings within our dialectical conversations, we hope to exemplify the theorizing we have accomplished as researchers in response to RQ3.

Collective Relationality: Beyond the "Teacher" and "Student" Binary

To begin, we want to share our reflections from one of the selected hotspots, a particular class early in the school year. Corey began class with a discussion on current events. Although this was not the first time Corey initiated students to discuss questions, thoughts, and tensions around current events, students seemed somewhat reluctant to take up these discussions lately, often letting the time slip by in silence until Corey either shared something himself or he moved on with the day's activities. On this day though, Corey addressed the apparent reluctance of students in having these discussions. We recounted this interaction in our conversations:

> *Ava:* So that was the day when you were trying to get students to talk about some kind of current event, and no one was really getting into it. And you pushed, saying "we're gonna have these conversations—we need to have this conversation.' You asked students: 'Are you comfortable having these conversations?" And one of the students, Laquantre, said "I don't think we're like really wanting these conversations, because maybe it's not the right space to have it. Because some people may be nervous to speak and that emotions get high and tempers flare." In response, you made an important point [that] the class is actually not a safe-space in the sense that students can say anything and there would be no repercussions. Rather, your class was a place where we can grow and figure out how to do this together.
>
> I think that's really important, because a lot of teachers often assume that you can have these conversations without talking to students about whether they're comfortable having them or not. What I really loved about this, too, is how you openly talk about these tensions. Like, "yeah, that this is a space where you'll be having these conversations, that they're going to happen one way or another, and it's okay to be scared."
>
> *Corey:* You know, for the young folks in that moment, there's a realization that the history that we're talking about isn't transactional like how school often feels like—we have a responsibility. There's an ethical

responsibility, there are relational responsibilities, and there's political responsibility, but teachers have been discouraged from talking about it. **I feel like I was building political agency in myself, and also with the students.** I was having conversations about things that I know weren't being had in the other spaces and classes that students navigate during the day. I know this because students would tell me, "We don't talk about this in other classes; we only talked about this here." I know this is important. I've also come to understand the way that folks understand their relationship to other people, and how their actions are actually going to impact folks that aren't proximate to [their] world. **As I reflected on being far away from my family, I would ask myself: How am I building a level of understanding agency or cultivating that agency within them?** To continue to make good decisions or to decide to make the decisions? Because that's going to impact people that I love; that's going to impact me, here. So that always felt very different.

Here, we want to highlight a profound reflection on Corey's teaching and intention, and why he explicitly confronted student hesitancy in having challenging political conversations in class. Specifically, he pronounced the importance these discussions have for both students *and himself.* While engaging in activities like discussing current events is often artificially created by the teacher in the service of students to support their analytic practices or development of a historicized sense of time, Corey saw his learning as equally implicated in these discussions, channeling a sense of urgency in creating these pedagogical opportunities for conversation. His sense of urgency was further emphasized by recognizing the essential role history education has in supporting students in building ethical relationalities to each other and their sense of selves in the world ("I would ask myself: How am I building a level of understanding agency or cultivating that agency within them?").

To Corey, designing moments for collective reflection on current events was not a supplemental activity to further support student practice of history practices, but a necessary opportunity to explore *with* students the sociopolitical tensions as enactments of oppressive systems. To do this meant engaging in thinking with students, not for students. This move beyond the teacher-student dichotomy towards more collective relational processes of learning was explored again as we shifted our focus to the middle of the school year, reflecting on how the current events conversation and other pedagogical moves towards cultivating collective relationalities became directly implicated in students' historical inquiry:

> *Ava*: And I can imagine, especially being early in the year, Bolaji (one of the students in class) just wasn't used to having these conversations and being taken seriously. I think that really underlays the shifts for a lot of students—they started to really believe that you were taking them seriously, and they should take each other seriously. That doesn't happen a lot for young people. Moving forward to the winter, we saw many of these shifts during the unit on American Imperialism, U.S.-Mexico relations, the collective reading of *Borderlands* by Gloria Anzaldúa, and a discussion on the Arizona Ethnic Studies Ban. Hearing you narrate your reasoning for bringing these topics together, I could feel how personal it was to you. You took the time to discuss why it's important for you to talk about the role of racism and U.S. history—because there are those who can't say that without being fired, arrested, or worse.

That really hit home for students, especially for Bolaji. When he asked you why Anzaldúa would teach Chicana studies if she could get in trouble, his question was dismissed as disingenuous or obvious by the other students. But you revoiced the question to the broader class, giving it legitimacy: Why would she teach this? Students, including Bolaji, started talking about how it was important to her, like teaching U.S. history is for you, and the ways she was engaging in political change by choosing to teach Chicana studies. You elevating it worked to affirm his role in this learning community, positioning his questions and ideas as valuable and necessary as the kinds of thinking you all were trying to do in the moment. While students initially dismissed his question, you demonstrated the importance of taking each other's ideas and questions seriously. Bolaji's question wasn't simple; rather, it helped unveil how the personal was historical and political—how the personal realities Anzaldúa navigated were directly linked to the broader political context of the Americas, as further shaped by the histories of the different communities she navigated and embodied. That realization was made alongside your own narrative of how your teaching U.S. history was also personal, political, and historical.

Your narrative, your story modeled the political and ethical importance of engaging history, but also the ways your personal experiences and perspectives are consequential to historical thinking (and to engage historical thinking requires confronting the personal and political). Once again, you positioned yourself as not just a normative teacher in the space, but a teacher who was collectively learning and thinking with students.

Before sharing Corey's response to Ava's reflection, we want to highlight the importance of this revelation: Corey's revoicing of Bolaji's dismissed question pedagogically worked to model to students the importance of collective relationality for historical thinking. Although the question was initially received as obvious and perhaps disingenuous, Corey's invitation to engage the question and the resulting conversation illuminated how what appeared to be a simple question on Anzaldúa's personal choices and experiences actually unveiled the intersecting connections between historical context and political systems as grounded within Anzaldúa's stories, as the intersection of macro-systems are constantly invoked and re-made in the moment-to-moment interactions and experiences of individuals. While Corey could have explicitly told students to not dismiss Bolaji's question, his approach to revoicing and authentic inquiry into the question worked to position himself alongside students as necessary thought-partners, giving students an opportunity *to actually feel* what it means to engage in historical inquiry as co-thinkers. This disruption of teacher-student binaries was a central characteristic of Corey's pedagogy, and in our dialectical conversation we explored how this pedagogical design created the conditions for students to experience collective inquiry within historical thinking.

Collective Inquiry for Historical Thinking

In Corey's response, he reflected on how he came to see Bolaji's question and the collective response in class to it as historical thinking:

Corey: I know that what we are talking about is in relation to students and them participating beyond the classroom, but if teachers aren't or choose not to bring their full selves, it makes me wonder about how young people will feel agentic. I appreciate having language to see differently. Young folks are still trying to figure out what's the right language for how to talk about these ideas. I want them to feel like you can take a risk, you can have a half-baked idea, which happened so much in that class. **And I also think I got to support the evolution of what it means to think and theorize in a way that is leaning towards more nuanced learning.**

Another example is Taylor (another student from class)—she would often say things that I felt didn't reflect how she was actually thinking about things. So I would work with her to try to unpack what she's really getting, helping offer language to better reflect her ideas. There [are] a couple of classes where I can remember doing that and supporting folks with trying to get more deeply at what they wanted to say. **Yeah, doing this takes them seriously. It honors them as theorists, thinkers, and people that I'm trying to learn from.**

I would think sometimes: you know what, I got to sit and listen. Sometimes they would say things and I would think "this [doesn't] feel right to me … but it's important for me to hear folks out," and they would further explain and help me understand what they were trying to say. That is a really important ethical and political relational consideration. I'm glad that Taylor was able to talk about that in her interviews.

For Corey, a central facet of supporting students to engage in the historical thinking explored by Ava in the Anzaldúa example was supporting students to view their own thinking and that of others as incomplete yet necessary resources for historical thinking. Similar to how historians often characterize historical evidence and narratives as subjective artifacts situated in time and space, a person's ideas, perspectives, and experiences also function as historical evidence—helping to explicate, nuance, substantiate, and complicate moments in time that will never offer an objective picture of an event but more authentically reveal how realities as experienced and understood are multifaceted and shaped by political, ethical, and cultural considerations and values. Corey narrated this belief by describing how he worked to get students to see each other as necessary co-thinkers for understanding the world as it was, is, and could be.

This process of understanding or theorizing, as he characterizes it, is the historical thinking he validated and modeled in class. While his descriptions of how he worked with Taylor to help her build language to explain ideas could (and should) be viewed as good teaching practice, Corey makes clear that was not the only reason he did this: "doing this takes them seriously … as theorists, thinkers, and people that I'm trying to learn from." For Corey, pedagogically supporting students in developing a practice of historical thinking as a collective act of social dreaming was imperative not just because he was a teacher, but because he and his students were agents of social change. He approached his students first and foremost as people to build new worlds with; thus, supporting students in developing conceptual practices and dispositions in theorizing and analysis also supported his development in theorizing and analysis. His seriousness about collective learning and action was felt by students; as Corey mentioned, many students (including Taylor) reflected on the meaningful impact of Corey taking them seriously even as they worked through their ideas and refined their language. In Ava's interview with Taylor at the end of the school year, she reflected on the importance of her classmates taking up the relational practice of taking each other seriously in their historical thinking:

So it's like, you might say something one way, but then we all get to the same conclusion. [For example], I take a long time to get to my point across sometimes because it's like my brain is really faster than like my mouth. So by the time I get there, I circled all the way back around the world. [But] the people in this class really help you get there. You might say like, "Oh, the Civil Rights Movement was in 1892," and everyone is like, "No, what? No." And then you're like, "Oh no, I meant blah blah blah." And then they are like, "Okay, you're good." You all start to have this assumption that even if someone said something that didn't sound right, you always assume that they had good intentions or something's there. There's a reason why they're saying something, and it was kind of like you all try to help each other to get to that point. It's like, "I know you're trying say something; it's not coming out right. So where are you coming from, [and] how can I help you get there?"

Taylor's description demonstrates the consequential impact of collective relationality on how students came to experience and take up their historical thinking in class. In particular, we want to build on Taylor's closing sentiment of how she and her classmates approached their historical thinking as a means "to try and help each other" in building collective understanding.

A Turn Towards Social Dreaming

Throughout our dialectical conversations, we explored how Corey frequently involved and modeled relational practices to foster an approach to history and historical thinking that was a practice of social dreaming. While much of this conversation has looked at examples of embedded connectedness of the class engaging historical thinking as a personal, political, and historical process, we haven't spoken much about the "dreaming" aspect of this practice. How were these moments of historical thinking enactments of social dreaming? While Ava explores other examples of future-making and imagination in students' history learning (Jackson, 2021), we want to spend time on how the collective relationality, foundational to these experiences of historical thinking, reflected proleptic moments of students engaging alternative models of education and society more broadly.

> *Corey:* I think my concern is like, what does it look like for young people who have to cultivate that desire to engage? To challenge the question? One of the things that I realized about this conversation that I think is going to be important to write about and continue iterating on is this idea of the moments that are political, our micro moments—**how folks are choosing to be in relationship with one another and how folks are choosing to understand and give grace to themselves.** They are the ways folks are understanding the capacity that they have to speak, to use their voice. These aren't big, grandiose things—**but are just as important in creating liberatory worlds.**

> *Ava:* Yes, seeing the ways that these students engaged with historical thinking was very different from how I used to think about it. **I still think so much about interviews with students about the excitement**

and joy and pride that they have carrying forward some of this stuff to other spaces and feeling like they are helping lead the learning of other people. Even if they don't really remember the history content, I think it's so much more exciting and beautiful.

What if we taught history with the goal of having people think and approach it like Taylor and Savannah (another student from class)? We taught students to really want to listen, to understand, push and share, and be confident in their thinking and opinions, while also wanting to learn and grow with others. I think that's what gets me most excited when I look at this data and reread the conversations that students have with each other. For me, it reflects a deep understanding that like, if you truly want to explore these questions about history, about the world, **we can't do it alone.** But to do this with others does require a sense of care, of critical reflection.

So we get moments like Roxana shifting their perspective on Bolaji. Students didn't care for each other just for the sake of caring. They cared for each other because they wanted to do this together. There's something about that, that emphasis that is completely missing in history. **Anyone could do the modeling or like anyone could do the historical argumentation, historical analysis, but what's that layer below that, that shapes the ways we think about history as an experience of social change?** What kind of analysis actually becomes the analysis we want versus the one that reproduces the very harms students are fighting against? I think that's … that's the layer that's like, honestly, the hardest to name. But also, that's what we saw happening in this class.

Historical thinking was an experience in which students learned to be with one another as changemakers and dreamers. Under Corey's pedagogical guidance, they learned to view each other as essential thought partners for understanding the world. This recognition was consequential to how they engaged as historians. Students recognized the responsibility of seeking and incorporating others into historical inquiry as an intellectual practice and as a commitment toward respect and empathy. We see this in how Taylor recounts her experiences of being valued and affirmed by her peers and in the ways students carried forward this process of historical thinking beyond the classroom space, "carrying forward some of this stuff to other spaces and feeling like they are helping lead the learning of other people." To students, engaging in historical thinking as a collective process of critically reflecting and understanding the world as it was, is, and could be, furthered their understanding of the multiple realities of existing in oppressive systems. This, in turn, became the inspirational foci for imagining new worlds while enacting these new ways of being in the immediate.

As students recognized the complexity of lived experiences historically and personally, they experienced alternative models of relationality and collective inquiry as a means of liberation, embodying new ways of being and habits of mind that were reflected in their social dreaming. Ava explores the dialogic relationship between these collective relationalities with students' complex and imaginative historical thinking in other works (Jackson, 2021).

We want to conclude with a discussion of our findings and the resulting implications of designing for history learning in ways that elevate "the ways we think about history as an experience of social change."

Discussion and Implications

As research collaborators, we have spent the past several years exploring a fundamental question: how do we design educationally-just and liberatory learning environments? We have approached this question as teachers, designers, researchers, learning scientists, activists, and friends. While each of these roles emphasized different aspects of this question in our work, our dialectical conversations helped us see how integral these roles are to our individual and collaborative experience, studying, teaching, and learning.

The amalgamation of our social roles across time, and the experiences these roles carried, helped us see, during our dialectical conversations and our synthesis of these conversations, how students' engagement in historical thinking as a practice of social dreaming mirrored our experiences of learning to be with and think together as consequential to seeing and designing for learning. The values and ideological commitments that brought us together in collaborative design, teaching, and research provided the onto-epistemological conditions for students to build new understandings of history as a discipline and as a way of engaging the world. These conditions were characterized by a pedagogical design that challenged teacher-student dichotomies and treated the history discipline as an expansive, intersubjective collective project of knowledge-building and imagining.

Corey's pedagogical design was one that foregrounded relationality as foundational to liberatory education. By intentionally cultivating a learning environment that invited students into a collective ethic, characterized by pedagogical practices Corey cultivated in non-class-based learning environments (Winchester, 2018), Corey designed proleptic educational experiences in which students explored what it meant to be in a dignifying learning community. While the relational process was foundational to the creation of this learning context, it was not separate from the history content or critical analysis: For Corey, to engage in history meant engaging in critical analysis of the past, present, and future with others. To teach history necessitates teaching an experience of liberation—an experience we saw in the ways students learned to value each other as intellectual and political collaborators, as explored with Corey helping students see the legitimacy of Bolaji's participation in the collective inquiry and Taylor building a new relationship with her thinking. This experience of liberation seemed to be a proleptic necessity for creating the conditions for students to see themselves and each other not just as peers or friends but as intellectual and political comrades for understanding the world as it was, is, and can be.

Our dialectical conversations offer insight for educational designers and educators to explore not only a few dimensions of what experiences of liberation can look, sound, and feel like for teachers and students alike, but also how the creation of these experiences goes beyond any specific pedagogical practices or curricular tool but requires a fundamental engagement with "history as an experience of social change"—an engagement taken up by students because of Corey's principled engagement with collectivity, reflexivity, and social dreaming in the relational dimensions of his pedagogy.

Conclusion

In this chapter, we offered an initial exploration into the generative potential of dialectical conversations for exploring the collective potential of history learning for supporting social dreaming within liberatory educational contexts. As a theoretical offering and methodological intervention, we offer our analytic narrative as a contribution to this editorial series exploring the cultivation of youth dreaming and political action. With a specific exploration of a formal history classroom, we demonstrated the potential of historical thinking as a practice of social dreaming and the pedagogical conditions that can inspire students into the collective relationalities that lead to liberatory world-making. However, it was through our dialectical conversations that we were able to see such insights, reminding us that just as teaching and learning are collective processes of political possibility, so is the study and design of these educational processes. We hope this chapter exemplifies the intellectual and political potential of these methods for supporting the design, study, and teaching of justice-oriented history education as a practice of social dreaming.

Reference

Anzaldúa, G. (2007). *Borderlands/La Frontera: The new mestiza* (3rd ed). Aunt Lute Books.

Bakhtin, M. M. (1981). *The dialogic imagination: Four essays.* University of Texas Press.

Bang, M., Faber, L., Gurneau, J., Marin, A., & Soto, C. (2016). Community-based design research: Learning across generations and strategic transformations of institutional relations toward axiological innovations. *Mind, Culture, and Activity, 23*(1), 28-41.

Bang, M., & Vossoughi, S. (2016). Participatory design research and educational justice: Studying learning and relations within social change making. *Cognition and Instruction, 34*(3), 173–193. https://doi.org/10.1080/07370008.2016.1181879

Bang, M., Warren, B., Rosebery, A. S., & Medin, D. (2012). Desettling expectations in science education. *Human Development, 55*(5-6), 302-318.

Boggs. (1978). *Conversations in Maine: Exploring our nation's future* (1st ed.). South End Press.

Boggs, & Kurashige, S. (2011). *The next American revolution: Sustainable activism for the twenty-first century.* University of California Press.

brown, a.m. (2017). *Emergent strategy: Shaping change, changing worlds*. AK Press.

Dillard, C. (2019). You are because I am: Toward new covenants of equity and diversity in teacher education. *Educational Studies, 55*(2), 121–138. https://doi.org/10.1080/00131946.2018.1523791

Dillard C., & Bell, C. (2011). Chapter twenty-one: Endarkened feminism and sacred praxis: Troubling (auto) ethnography through critical engagements with African Indigenous knowledges. *Counterpoints, 379,* 337–349.

Erickson, F. (2006). Studying side by side: Collaborative action ethnography in educational research. In G. Spindler & L. Hammond (Eds.), *Innovations in Educational Ethnography: Theories, Methods, and Results* (1st ed.), (p. 23). Psychology Press.

Esmonde, I., & Booker, A. (2017). *Power and privilege in the learning sciences: Critical and sociocultural theories of learning*. Routledge.

Espinoza, M. L. (2008). *Humanization and social dreaming: A case study of changing social relations in a summer migrant educational program*. (Publication No. 3302577) [Doctoral dissertation, University of California, Los Angeles]. ProQuest Dissertations Publishing.

Espinoza, M. L., Vossoughi, S., Rose, M., & Poza, L. E. (2020). Matters of participation: Notes on the study of dignity and learning. *Mind, Culture, and Activity, 27*(4), 325-347.

Freire, P. (1970). *Pedagogy of the oppressed*. Penguin Classics.

Garcia, A., & Mirra, N. (2023). *Speculative pedagogies: Designing equitable educational futures*. Teachers College Press.

Griffin, P., & Cole, M. (1984). Current activity for the future: The Zo-ped. *New Directions for Child and Adolescent Development, 1984*(23), 45–64. https://doi.org/10.1002/cd.23219842306

Gutiérrez, K. D. (2008). Developing a sociocritical literacy in the Third Space. *Reading Research Quarterly, 43*(2), 148–164. https://doi.org/10.1598/RRQ.43.2.3

Gutiérrez, K. D., Becker, B. L. C., Espinoza, M. L., Cortes, K. L., Cortez, A., Lizárraga, J. R., Rivero, E., Villegas, K., & Yin, P. (2019). Youth as historical actors in the production of possible futures. *Mind, Culture, and Activity, 26*(4), 291–308. https://doi.org/10.1080/10749039.2019.1652327

Gutiérrez, K. D., & Vossoughi, S. (2010). Lifting off the ground to return anew: Mediated praxis, transformative learning, and social design experiments. *Journal of Teacher Education, 61*(1-2), 100-117.

hooks, b. (1994). *Teaching to transgress: Education as the practice of freedom*. Routledge

Jackson, A. (2021). Critical history education: A case-study of design, learning, and identity in a high school history class (Publication No. 28769966). [Doctoral dissertation, Northwestern University]. ProQuest Dissertations & Theses Global.

Jordan, B., & Henderson, A. (1995). Interaction analysis: Foundations and practice. *The Journal of the Learning Sciences, 4*(1), 39–103. https://doi.org/10.1207/s15327809jls0401_2

Kelley, R. D. G. (2002). *Freedom dreams: The Black radical imagination.* Beacon Press.

Love, B. L. (2019). *We want to do more than survive: Abolitionist teaching and the pursuit of educational freedom.* Beacon Press.

Muhammad, G. (2020). *Cultivating genius: An equity framework for culturally and historically responsive literacy.* Scholastic.

Muhammad, G. (2023). *Unearthing joy: A guide to culturally and historically responsive teaching and learning.* Scholastic Inc.

Penuel, W. R., Fishman, B. J., Haugan Cheng, B., & Sabelli, N. (2011). Organizing research and development at the intersection of learning, implementation, and design. *Educational Researcher, 40*(7), 331-337. https://doi.org/10.3102/0013189X11421826

Shotter, J. (2006a). Understanding process from within: An argument for 'withness'-thinking. *Organization Studies, 27*(4), 585–604.

Santiago, M. (2019). Historical inquiry to challenge the narrative of racial progress. *Cognition and Instruction, 37*(1), 93–117. https://doi.org/10.1080/07370008.2018.1539734

Vossoughi, S., Davis, N. R., Jackson, A., Echevarria, R., Muñoz, A., & Escudé, M. (2021). Beyond the binary of adult versus child centered learning: Pedagogies of joint activity in the context of making. *Cognition and Instruction, 39*(3), 211-241. https://doi.org/10.1080/07370008.2020.1860052

Warren, B., Vossoughi, S., Rosebery, A. S., Bang, M., & Taylor, E. V. (2020). Multiple ways of knowing: Re-imagining disciplinary learning. In N. S. Nasir, C. D. Lee, R. Pea, & M. M. de Royston (Eds.), *Handbook of the Cultural Foundations of Learning* (pp. 277-294). Routledge.

Winchester, C. (2018). Engaging with critical leadership development with high school students. In J. Dugan (Ed.), *New Directions for Student Leadership.* Jossey-Bass.

CHAPTER 8

Dreaming Otherwise:
Creative Policy Negotiation and Creating Communities of Recognition for Multilingual Immigrant Youth

Reva Jaffe-Walter and Kathleen Rucker

Introduction

PUBLIC SCHOOLS ARE located in the interzone between policy and child – situated between the dreams of politicians and the dreams of children and families. School leaders have to develop a clear understanding of their school's vision in order to navigate these dreamscapes and maintain course in a sea of shifting external demands. In this chapter, we focus on the role of school leaders as they work to "craft coherence" between external policy mandates and stakeholders, and messaging and shaping the course of mandates within the internal communities of their schools (Honig & Hatch, 2004; Jaffe-Walter, 2008; Spillane et al., 2002). Reflecting on different instances of creative policy negotiation within Internationals Network for Public Schools (INPS) sites, we explore the possibilities for leaders and educators in other schools serving immigrant youth who are English Learners (ELs). We consider the following questions:

- How have generations of leaders within the INPS network learned and passed down commitments to creative policy negotiation?

- What solidarities and relationships make this work possible, and what factors limit it?

In doing so, we argue that resistance to dehumanizing policies should be a core competency of all leaders and teachers serving minoritized communities. Much has been written related to the so-called unintended consequences of nationalist and high-stakes policy regimes for schools serving youth of color and immigrant youth, including the increased dropout and pushout of these students and the narrowing of curriculum (Menken, 2006). This chapter shares qualitative case study research and insights from high schools exclusively serving multilingual immigrant youth and considers how school leaders actively negotiate and resist policies that are incoherent with the values of their school communities. As an educational anthropologist who has studied schools that are sites of possibility for immigrant youth and as a school principal of an international school serving these students, we provide examples of solidarity in which school leaders have come together to resist incoherent policies and to engage in "creative compliance" (Jaffe-Walter, 2008. p.2059; Weis & Fine, 2004).

Methods

This chapter draws on data from two larger ethnographic studies of the schools within Internationals Network of Public Schools (INPS)—a network of high schools that serve newcomer English Learners (ELs) and focuses on one school which was a site in both studies. This research sought to understand the structures and practices that lead to the school's reputation as a site of possibility for recently arrived immigrant youth. The Internationals Network exclusively serves recently arrived immigrant students who come from 119 countries and speak 90 different languages. Over 90% are considered low-income, and many are undocumented. Within the school site discussed in this chapter, Reva worked with a research team to interview both principals and assistant principals, teachers, and students, including Kathleen, the school leader. This paper draws on interviews with school leaders and teachers and professional meeting observations to gain an understanding of how leaders navigated policy mandates and positioned teachers' professional knowledge.

Field notes, interviews, and focus group transcripts, as well as observation notes, were coded and analyzed to explore how leaders negotiated external policy mandates, the professional culture, and authority and autonomy in schoolwide decision-making and processes. For the purpose of this chapter, Reva and Kathleen analyzed data from Reva's ethnographic research alongside Kathleen's personal reflections on her experiences as the school leader and processes of navigating external mandates. Shifting her position from participant to co-author created a unique opportunity to think together about the critical dimensions of policy negotiation. Thus, this chapter departs from earlier work that positioned one author as participant to democratize processes of educational knowledge production, allowing participants and researchers to engage in processes of educational dreaming and resistance that interrogate top-down educational structures (Batallan et al., 2017).

Literature Review

Our work conceives of policy negotiation as a process involving creative and ongoing interactions among districts, schools, teachers, and students. That is, we consider how policies are "peopled" by actors who adapt, adopt, and resist them (Lipsky, 2010; Nielsen, 2011; Sutton & Levinson, 2001). Following Ball (1993) and Shore et al. (2011), we consider how collections of related policies constitute policy ensembles or policy worlds that produce "regimes of truth" (Foucault, 1977, p. 30)—defining "problems" in ways that describe particular solutions or logics for thinking about policy enactment, often driven by the educational dreams of actors who have no knowledge of the inside worlds of schools. However, we also recognize that leaders' sense of what is possible in schools is mediated by a constant barrage of politically motivated directives. Reacting to daily pressures and predetermined funding streams often leaves little space for negotiation and imagination (Virella, 2024). However, this case reveals how leaders within a network have supported one another over time and have been encultured to dream otherwise, collectively identifying ways to address mandates in ways that protect the core values of the schools.

As immigrant students and their families are increasingly under siege amid discourses of xenophobia and non-belonging (Costello, 2016), there has been increasing attention to how school leaders can foster political empowerment and civic engagement among immigrant youth and their families (Burkett & Hayes, 2018; Crawford, 2017; Hamann & Mitchell-McCollough, 2020; Jaffe-Walter, 2019; Liou, 2016; Miranda, 2017). A number of scholars have documented how leaders of immigrant-serving schools have advocated for undocumented students and offered "sanctuary schooling"(Miranda, 2017, p. 1) designed to buffer anti-immigrant policies and discourses (Bajaj et al., 2022; Crawford, 2017;). Similarly, Bernstein et al. (2020) document how school leaders in Arizona dreamed otherwise, resisting state language policies that marginalized English Language Learner (ELL) students, barring access to rich bilingual instruction. In addition to immigration policies, leaders play an important role in negotiating accountability policies and shaping how they influence teachers' work with immigrant multilingual learners (Palmer & Rangel, 2011).

Many studies have documented the unintended negative effects of accountability policies, which have been shown to include curriculum degradation (Palmer & Rangel, 2011), increased tracking, drop-out and push-out rates (Berliner, 2011; Darling-Hammond & Cook-Harvey, 2018; Martin, 2016; Menken, 2006; Sunderman et al., 2005; Umansky, 2016; Callahan, 2005), and increased tracking. The challenge of preparing newly arrived multilingual learners for high-stakes exams that are not developmentally appropriate is overwhelming for teachers and draws valuable resources and energy away from the creation of responsive teaching and learning (Hakuta, 2011; Gichiru, 2014; Martin, 2016). Teachers of immigrant English Language Learners face not just increased test pressures, but also a greater likelihood of isolation within school professional networks (Harper et al., 2008; Liggett, 2010; Hamann & Reeves, 2013) and without ongoing support to sustain reform efforts. Gichiru's (2014) study of teachers working with recently arrived Somali students, amid accountability pressures, were more likely to experience isolation and marginalization and were less likely to engage in productive collaboration with peers (Brooks et al., 2010).

Leaders play a critical role in shaping how external policy mandates are negotiated within schools and inform teachers' abilities to serve immigrant EL students. Martin's (2016) study of accountability policy and English Learners shows not only how policy pressures led to tracking and push-out for EL students but also resulted in the marginalization of their teachers. However, there are also examples of school leaders who resist accountability pressures and the stigmatization of EL students in the ways that they navigate policy mandates (Bonanno et al., 2020). In addition, Jaffe-Walter (2008) illustrates how leaders in schools serving recently arrived immigrant students who are ELs navigated incoherent accountability policies to reduce teacher anxiety and support teachers in developing rich interdisciplinary project-based curricula.

These studies underscore the central role school leaders play in mediating policy mandates in ways that influence immigrant multilingual students' access to educational resources (Palmer & Rangel, 2011). Within the Internationals Network for Public Schools (INPS), leaders have historically approached new policy mandates and initiatives from a critical perspective, considering how they will be taken up by teachers and young people within the ecosystems of schools. While all leaders are continually navigating policy mandates, given how education policies have disproportionately affected schools serving marginalized students such as non-native speakers of English, we argue that negotiating policy is a critical dimension of socially-just leadership for schools serving multilingual immigrant students (Jaffe-Walter & Villavicencio, 2023; Turner, 2020).

A History of Resisting Incoherent Policies to Enact Responsive Education for Immigrant Youth

Historically, resistance to incoherent policy mandates has been a core value within the INPS. In the early days of the first of the network's schools, which was established in 1985, school leaders brought educators together to collectively consider how the school might better serve the needs of its immigrant students. After a period of intensive observation and discussion, they decided to change the structure of the school by establishing extended class periods for project-based work, heterogeneous student groupings, dedicated time in the school week for teacher collaboration, and a democratic governance structure. To implement these new structures that were not aligned with the logic of external policies around staffing, scheduling, and financing, school leaders engaged in extensive negotiations with the union, the Board of Education, and the state (Schmerler, 2002).

In 2005, when they recognized that the statewide high-stakes Regents exams were not aligned with the needs of their recently arrived ELs and created pressures that challenged internal commitments to project-based curriculum, INPS leaders joined forces with the New York State Performance Standards Consortium, a collaborative of like-minded schools, and negotiated a waiver that now replaces four of five statewide Regents exams with performance-based assessments. Using a democratic process, teachers and leaders from three international schools came together to create and refine assessments that extended their instructional model, offering opportunities for youth to demonstrate their knowledge in presentations to teachers, fellow students, and community members who all contributed to the evaluation process. Even today, twenty years later, teachers in INPS schools are still aware of the stifling nature of high-stakes test pressures and the ways that the waiver has allowed them to create curricula that is more responsive to the needs of their immigrant EL students. As one teacher from the school shares:

> Yeah, 'cause I think it's the waiver that encourages openness, creativity, and teachers don't have to be burdened with test prep. If teachers have come from Regents schools … you've gotta deprogram all of that, it gets so deep in their brain and into their practice. It is very powerful, because they see it as authority. They see it as, "this is the prescribed curriculum." Even if we can critically reflect on that, from many different angles, we should be able to work through that assumption and shift it around. Still, I feel like it hangs onto people.

This teacher reflects on how test pressures limit the development of responsive curricula for her EL students and shares how the network's creative negotiation of policy has created space for thinking otherwise. Rather than presuming that high-stakes tests were non-negotiable and then making compromises in their instructional practices, leaders and teachers within the schools fought for more responsive modes of assessment that now are held up as an example in the state and nation as best practice for EL assessment.

In addition to creatively negotiating policies related to instruction and assessment, leaders within the network have re-imagined teacher evaluation policies to reflect their commitments to shared leadership. In 2020, Kathleen found that the citywide teacher evaluation system, drawing on the work of Charlotte Danielson, was not coherent with her school's approach to teacher-learning focused on teacher collaboration and inquiry work. Responding to teachers' anxieties about individual evaluations, the faculty worked to create an inquiry process that was more team-based. In one planning meeting, the instructional coach shared:

> I'm very concerned that the evaluation process could constrict the conversation: Maybe we should all use this time to reflect here about what I got here that could influence my practice next year. Like not just the person who is presenting but everyone could reflect on what they learned from the evaluation and how that will change what we will do next year. That way, it's all of us building something together.

Together, the faculty shifted the teacher evaluation process from one focused on individual teachers to one that emphasized community learning through team-based research topics designed to address emerging problems of practice. Teachers identified topics, gathered data reflecting on their students' experiences, and then shared their learnings with the rest of the school community (see Jaffe-Walter & Villavicencio, 2023 for more detail).

Sharing Power and Policy Negotiation: A Leader's Perspective

It is easy for a school leader to lose their way in the deluge of contradictory demands, including "accelerate learning" while teaching students "basic literacy and numeracy" … or to fast-track students for the world of work when we know that many of these jobs we are tasked to prepare them for will be obsolete in a few years. Formulating a strong sense of purpose as a school community is essential and requires that school leaders constantly interrogate their assumptions alongside colleague–assumptions about who their students are, assumptions about how/what students should learn, assumptions about how to assess learning, and assumptions about families and our society. One's clarity as a school leader comes from the strength of this interrogation–not just blindly accepting a set of beliefs but truly shaping these beliefs as you work with young people and families. This may sound like unstable terrain for a school because it means that systems and structures will be shifting, but when done *in* community, not *to* community, the changes can be long-lasting; when they take root, they will endure. One strategy I have found useful is to spend time as a faculty deconstructing our core values, examining the origin of those core values and how they are embodied by our school systems, structures, and practices. For example, one of our core values, which we collectively surfaced in our faculty discussions, was *shared power*. Collectively, we deconstructed/reconstructed what shared power means on the individual and school levels, asking ourselves what we are moving away from and what we are moving towards, explicitly stating what shared power looks like in a classroom and explaining why it is important.

Each year, school leaders are asked to respond to mandates from all levels (federal, state, and city), and there is a moment of interpretation when you have the agency to consider ways to meet those mandates. As a school leader for newcomer multilingual learners, I consider all mandates through the lens of our school's core values, history, and philosophy. When non-alignment occurs, rather than adjusting my school practices to meet the needs of the policy, I try to be strategic and consider how existing effective practices can be reframed to meet the needs of the policymakers.

As a leader, I believe a policy should adapt to the needs of a school, and not the other way around. For example, literacy is a rallying cry in this post-pandemic moment and has led to a resurgence of standardized corporate-backed reforms and structures promising to "get students on track." As I contemplated how we would approach this as a school community, I started with our shared values of inquiry, autonomy, and shared power and saw immediately that there was no pre-packaged external program that would work for our students. We had to build from within, understand our students' unique needs, understand the strengths and abilities of our teachers, consider the world our students would be stepping into in a few years, and that is where our literacy work would find traction. We began working with a literacy coach who helped us to understand some latent issues that we had not explored, including the fact that many of the sounds that are common in English do not exist in the languages of our newly arrived multilingual learners. Students needed explicit practice with these sounds, starting with their strengths, their native languages, looking for sound patterns in English, and bridging from what students know to build up their literacy.

We recognized that standardized assessments failed to elucidate the complexity of what our students were experiencing when they struggled to decode a word. Engaging teachers and students in this inquiry process fostered a collective curiosity about language acquisition and strengthened relationships within our community. As a leader, my work is to empower and support teachers who understand the nuances of their students' lives and learning processes. When facing new policy mandates, I always ask these questions: Who stands to profit from this policy? How does this policy sit within our school values, history, and philosophy? Where are the opportunities to broaden the policy to meet the needs of our students? What are the longer-term implications of this policy (especially regarding technology, data collection, and surveillance)? Does this policy empower or disempower our staff, students, and families?

Creating a Culture of Critical Policy Literacy and Teacher Empowerment

Our research finds that creative policy negotiation is not only taken up by leaders but is a stance taken up by all members of the community. In the democratic committee structure of the school, teachers are shapers of school policy and support the work to re-imagine external policy mandates (like the Regents exams and teacher evaluation), and also internal school policies like discipline policies, grading, and professional development. One teacher from the school described how decisions were made top-down in her former school. She then described how the culture of our school, her new school, was very different, given the expectations of teachers to be involved in making schoolwide decisions:

> We do have a lot of over-achievers, but in a good way. People who are, like, "I'm gonna just try this. I'll draft it, and you can change it if you want to." People feel like they can talk about it, or that we talk about it as a team. Or we bring it up with our UFT rep.

Hiring in these schools also focused on teachers' willingness to engage deeply with peers in reflection related to their own practice and an orientation towards understanding the needs of ELLs.

The structure of INPS schools relies on the local knowledge of teachers who have the greatest understanding of the complex needs of their recently arrived immigrant students and, as such, can help ensure that school policies and practices are supporting students' development. Teachers meet twice weekly on grade-level teams to develop project-based interdisciplinary curricula. In addition, all teachers have the option of participating in committees where school-wide policies are created, and they receive monetary compensation for this additional work. The most important of these is the Teaching and Learning Committee, which has representatives from each teacher team and is focused on creating responsive teaching and learning systems and structures, and supporting reflective dialogue among teachers. Other committees include the Competency Based Education Committee focused on grading policy, the Restorative Justice Committee which is dedicated to school discipline policy, a Hiring Committee which makes hiring recommendations for new teachers and staff members, and the Consultation Committee which gives the leadership team feedback on school climate and culture. These democratic school structures that position teachers as shapers of schoolwide policies and practices have contributed to teacher empowerment and growth and collective responsibility for their immigrant EL students (Ingersoll et al., 2018; Jaffe-Walter, 2018; Jaffe-Walter & Miranda, 2020).

Implications

In this chapter, we theorize that creative policy negotiation has been a core commitment within INPS schools and is an important element of creative responsive schools for immigrant EL students. First, the examples we present illuminate how resisting top-down incoherent mandates like high-stakes standardized tests and teacher evaluation paradigms create space for dreaming of more humanizing schools and practices that center the needs of youth and the teachers who serve them. We show how leaders within INPS schools have adopted a more critical stance towards external policy mandates, carefully calculating whether external policy mandates are aligned with the needs of their community.

Second, we acknowledge how, in some ways, INPS leaders have support and alliances that enable resistance to incoherent mandates that other schools may lack. Commitments to creative policy negotiation within the network are reinforced in monthly leader meetings where leaders collectively brainstorm about how to contend with new mandates and ever-changing district priorities.

In addition, many of the current generation of INPS leaders were formerly teachers, paraprofessionals, or even alumni of the schools and were "culture carriers" (Jaffe-Walter, 2008, p. 2047), strengthening core commitments to critical policy negotiation and empowering teachers over generations of scaling up the school design. Further, these leaders build on strategic relationships with district leaders and other stakeholders, like the New York State Performance Coalitions.

This raises questions about the kinds of structural supports required for this work and the possibilities of alliances that make envisioning more responsive policies possible. Many of the schools serving immigrant and multilingual students are labeled as "underperforming" and as such have higher turnover of leaders and teachers which complicates the formation of these sustaining networks and alliances. We also recognize the inherent risks involved in actively resisting policies as lone leaders without strategic alliances, working in schools that are under public scrutiny. We have witnessed situations in which leaders have fought incoherent policies and advocated for their students in ways that led to their dismissal.

Third, our analysis contributes to the literature on creative policy negotiation by not only focusing on the outward facing work of school leaders who resist incoherent policies like exclusionary immigration policies and state language policies, but also examining the ways creative policy negotiation happens on multiple levels within school communities: between leaders, other administrators, and teachers, and in the classroom between students and teachers (Bernstein et al., 2020; Crawford, 2017). This work involves a day-to-day vigilance in relation to how external policy mandates can play out within the ecologies of schools and classrooms: for example, in the moment in which the instructional coach recognized the escalation of teachers' fears of individual scrutiny in relation to classroom observations and her intervention, which created a shift towards community learning and collective responsibility. Our findings reveal how creative policy negotiation is taken up in myriad interactions in schools, in participation in schoolwide decision-making, and ongoing inquiry work related to building more responsive modes of teaching and learning and fostering belonging for immigrant students. Thinking otherwise and dreaming of more humanizing schools for immigrant EL students is not just about resisting incoherent policies, it involves fine-tuning practices and deepening relationships between teachers and students. While in many schools, leaders and teachers are passive in the face of substandard educational opportunities or policies that have so-called unintended consequences for immigrant EL students, the culture and structures at the school which has been in focus in this chapter, empowers teachers to actively innovate and dream up more responsive practices and forms of teaching and learning.

Conclusion—Kathleen on Making Space for Resistance and Imagining Possibility

In closing, we hope this chapter can open dialogues about how we might forward dreams of schools that center the knowledge and experiences of their students and educators. However, while we offer up these examples of collective dreaming, we also acknowledge how, as Kelley (2002) argues, "the conditions of daily life, of everyday oppressions of survival, not to mention the temporary pleasures accessible to most of us, render our imagination inert. We are constantly putting out fires, responding to emergencies, finding temporary refuge, all of which make it difficult to see anything other than the present" (p. 11). Thus, we explore the conditions and historical memories of resistance that make policy dreaming possible.

We can hold our community close, know them, love them, and nurture them; show them that maybe just for this brief moment of time, this is what it means to be part of a democratic society - a world within a world - where they are seen and heard. When school leaders make educational dreaming a norm in schools as we have described, this ethos permeates all layers, inspiring teachers to create relevant and engaging curricula and likewise, invigorating students to be active learners within and outside the classroom. It is the responsibility of the school leader, in tandem with teacher teams, to have the courage and confidence to set the conditions for this dreaming. In most schools, we are overwhelmed with the number of additional mandates and requirements, so this often means taking a subtractive stance, collapsing requirements so as to creatively comply and still make space for dreaming. Working with new immigrant students, the urgency is real. We have such a unique opportunity, as our students generally arrive with a strong sense of possibility upon entering this new country. We have a brief window to assure them that they matter through a culturally responsive curriculum that validates their language, lived experiences, and dreams; where discussions and dialogue are possible; where ambiguity is tolerated and uncertainty is allowed; and where complexity is not hollowed out or reduced to a binary. For the brief time that our students are in our presence, this part is not a dream, but very much a reality ... a reference point that students will carry forward.

Additionally, it is notable that at a time when teacher turnover has hit new highs in the U.S., INPS schools maintain remarkably high teacher retention rates. Our attention to nurturing adult creativity and autonomy undoubtedly contributes to this success. So, educational dreaming is critical for the material benefits in the day-to-day functioning of the school (teacher attendance, morale, and retention), as well as the contribution to the overall deeper purpose of the school community—we are not just here to replicate what exists, but to imagine and build a better future.

Reference

Bajaj, M., Walsh, D., Bartlett, L., & Martínez, G. (2022). *Humanizing education for immigrant and refugee youth: 20 strategies for the classroom and beyond.* Teachers College Press.

Ball S. J. (1993). What is policy? Texts, trajectories and toolboxes. *Discourse: Studies in the Cultural Politics of Education, 13*(2), 10–17. https://doi.org/10.1080/0159630930130203

Batallan, G., Dente, L., & Ritta, L., (2017) Anthropology, participation, and the democratization of knowledge: Participatory research using video with youth living in extreme poverty. *International Journal of Qualitative Studies in Education, 30*(5), 464-473, DOI: 10.1080/09518398.2017.1303214.

Berliner, D. (2011). Rational responses to high stakes testing: The case of curriculum narrowing and the harm that follows. *Cambridge Journal of Education, 41*(3), 287–302.

Bernstein, K. A., Katznelson, N., Amezcua, A., Mohamed, S., & Alvarado, S. L. (2020). Equity/social justice, instrumentalism/neoliberalism: Dueling discourses of dual language in principals' talk about their programs. *TESOL Quarterly, 54*(3), 652-684. https://doi.org/10.1002/tesq.582

Bonanno, S. L., Ynostroza, A., & Alejandre, E. (2020). Standardized testing and mariachi: Dilemmas of a culturally sustaining dual-language principal. In E. R.

Crawford & L. M. Dorner (Eds.), *Educational leadership of immigrants* (pp. 58–70). Routledge.

Brooks, K., Adams, S. R., & Morita-Mullaney, T. (2010). Creating inclusive learning communities for ELL students: Transforming school principals' perspectives. *Theory Into Practice, 49*(2), 145–151.

Burkett, J., & Hayes, S. (2018). Campus administrators' responses to Donald Trump's immigration policy: Leadership during times of uncertainty. *International Journal of Educational Leadership and Management, 6*(2), 98–125.

Callahan, R. M. (2005). Tracking and high school English learners: Limiting opportunity to learn. *American Educational Research Journal, 42*(2), 305–328.

Costello, M. (2016). *The Trump effect: The impact of the presidential campaign on our nation's schools.* Southern Poverty Law Center.

Crawford E. R. (2017). The ethic of community and incorporating undocumented immigrant concerns into ethical school leadership. *Educational Administration Quarterly, 53*(2), 147–179. https://doi.org/10.1177/0013161X16687005

Darling-Hammond, L., & Cook-Harvey, C. M. (2018). *Educating the whole child: Improving school climate to support student success.* Learning Policy Institute Palo.

Foucault M. (1977). *Discipline and punish: The birth of the prison.* Pantheon Books.

Gichiru, W. (2014). Struggles of finding culturally relevant literacy practices for Somali students: Teachers' perspectives. *New England Reading Association Journal, 49*(2), 67.

Hakuta, K. (2011). Educating language minority students and affirming their equal rights: Research and practical perspectives. *Educational Researcher, 40*(4), 163–174.

Hamann, E. T., & Mitchell-McCollough, J. (2020). The paradoxical implications of deported American students. In E. R. Crawford & L. M. Dorner (Eds.), *Educational leadership of immigrants: Case studies in times of change* (pp. 88-95). Routledge.

Hamann, E. T., & Reeves, J. (2013). Interrupting the professional schism that allows less successful educational practices with ELLs to persist. *Theory Into Practice, 52*(2), 81–88.

Harper, C. A., de Jong, E., & Platt, E. (2008). Marginalizing English as a second language teacher expertise: The exclusionary consequence of No Child Left Behind. *Language Policy, 7*(3), 267–284.

Honig M. I., & Hatch T. C. (2004). Crafting coherence: How schools strategically manage multiple, external demands. *Educational Researcher, 33*(8), 16–30.

Ingersoll, R. M., Sirinides, P., & Dougherty, P. (2018). Leadership matters: Teachers' roles in school decision making and school performance. *American Educator, 42*(1), 13.

Jaffe-Walter R. (2008). Negotiating mandates and memory: Inside a small schools network for immigrant youth. *Teachers College Record, 110*(9), 2040–2066.

Jaffe-Walter, R. (2018). Leading in the context of immigration: Cultivating collective responsibility for recently arrived immigrant students. *Theory Into Practice, 57*(2), 147-153.

Jaffe-Walter, R. (2019). Ideal liberal subjects and Muslim "Others": Liberal nationalism and the racialization of Muslim youth in a progressive Danish school. *Race Ethnicity and Education, 22*(2), 285-300. https://doi.org/10.1080/13613324.2018.1468744

Jaffe-Walter, R., & Miranda, C. P. (2020). Segregation or sanctuary?: Examining the educational possibilities of counterpublics for immigrant English learners. *Leadership and Policy in Schools, 19*(1), 104–122.

Jaffe-Walter, R., & Villavicencio, A. (2023). Leaders' negotiation of teacher evaluation policy in immigrant-serving schools. *Educational Policy, 37*(2), 359–392. https://doi.org/10.1177/08959048211015

Kelley, R. D. G. (2002). *Freedom dreams: The Black radical imagination*. Beacon Press.

Liggett, T. (2010). "A little bit marginalized": The structural marginalization of English language teachers in urban and rural public schools. *Teaching Education, 21*(3), 217–232.

Liou, D. D. (2016). Fostering college-going expectations of immigrant students through sympathetic touch of school leadership. *Multicultural Perspectives, 18*(2), 82–90. https://doi.org/10.1080/15210960.2016.1155152

Lipsky M. (2010). *Street-level bureaucracy: Dilemmas of the individual in public service*. Russell Sage Foundation.

Martin, P. C. (2016). Test-based education for students with disabilities and English language learners: The impact of assessment pressures on educational planning. *Teachers College Record, 118*(14), n14.

Menken. K. (2006). Teaching to the test: How No Child Left Behind impacts language policy, curriculum, and instruction for English language learners. *Bilingual Research Journal, 30*(2), 521-546. https://doi.org/10.1080/15235882.2006.10162888

Miranda, C. P. (2017). Checks, balances, and resistance: The impact of anti-immigrant federal administration on a school for immigrant teenagers. *Anthropology & Education Quarterly, 48*(4), 376-385. https://doi.org/10.1111/aeq.12215

Nielsen G. B. (2011). Peopling policy: On conflicting subjectivities of fee-paying students. In C. Shore, S. Wright, & D. Però (Eds.), *Policy worlds. Anthropology and the analysis of contemporary power* (pp. 68–85). Berghahn Books.

Palmer D., & Rangel V. (2011). High stakes accountability and policy implementation: Teacher decision making in bilingual classrooms in Texas. *Educational Policy, 25*(4), 614–647. https://doi.org/10.1177/0895904810374848

Schmerler, G. (2002). One man's continuing war against recentralization: A long struggle for school autonomy. *Phi Delta Kappan, 83*(5), 370-374.

Shore C., Wright S., & Però D. (Eds.). (2011). *Policy worlds: Anthropology and the analysis of contemporary power* (Vol. 14). Berghahn Books.

Spillane J. P., Diamond J. B., Burch P., Hallett T., Jita L., Zoltners J. (2002). Managing in the middle: School leaders and the enactment of accountability policy. *Educational Policy, 16*(1), 731–762.

Sunderman, G. L., Kim, J. S., & Orfield, G. (2005). *NCLB meets school realities: Lessons from the field*. Corwin Press.

Sutton M., & Levinson B. (2001). *Policy as practice: Toward a comparative sociocultural analysis of educational policy* (Vol. 1). Greenwood Publishing Group.

Turner, E. O. (2020). *Suddenly diverse: How school districts manage race and inequality*. University of Chicago Press.

Umansky, I. M. (2016). Leveled and exclusionary tracking: English learners' access to academic content in middle school. *American Educational Research Journal, 53*(6), 1792–1833.

Virella, P. M. (2024). Cultivating critical hope while leading during crisis: A qualitative cross-comparative analysis. *American Journal of Education, 130*(2).

Weis, L., & Fine, M. (2004). *Working method: Research and social justice*. Routledge.

CHAPTER 9

Dreamweaving Youth Expressions Through Multimedia Methodologies:
"The Words That They Were Never Told and Were Wishing To Hear"

Jorge F. Rodriguez, PhD, Bernadine Cortina, and Jessica Tonai

THE FOLLOWING CHAPTER explores conceptually and theoretically the dreaming and stories of two youth, that we will call, Briana and Karla, who dared to embody their stories as artistic expressions in collaboration with the Santa Ana Youth Media Project's (SAYMP) Dreamweaving initiative. The youth stories being shared and documented via media emphasize the power youth possess when they are encouraged and nurtured within their dreaming. This chapter acknowledges the insights and strengths of youth as imaginative, innovative, and non-conforming to expectations of dominant society. What is evident throughout this chapter is that youth can engage growth and self-development as they embody their artistic dreaming into reality. The youth within this chapter had the courage to dream radically by sharing their stories as meaningful artistic expressions defying expected and normative youth behavior. They created thematic video poems, song lyrics, and music videos, and worked with college students to manifest their art in transformative and fulfilling ways. What is powerful about these youth testimonies and collaborations is that the youth of this project flourished when they were nourished, supported, and motivated to be genuine with who they are. Youth have the self-determination and courage to speak truth to power in ways that are honest and uncompromised.

We hope that the conceptual analysis this chapter explores can speak to other community organizers and educators as to the value of a truly community- and youth-led initiative. This chapter will work through the writings of Margerie Evasco as we conceptualize their proposed insight of "Dreamweaving;" La Velle Ridley and their conception of "Imagining Otherly;" D.G. Kelly and their provocative contribution of "Freedom Dreams;" Audre Lorde's offering of "Transformation of Silence into Language and Action;" and Merlinda Bobis's "Salba Istorya/ Salba Buhay" ("Save Stories/ Save Lives"), (Evasco, 1987b; Ridley, 2019; Kelley, 2022; Lorde, 2007/1984; Bobis, 2017).

Review of such literature is embedded and tailored throughout the chapter, specifically addressing how the SAYMP Dreamweaving initiative has been immensely influenced and has applied such literature in practice. The Dreamweaving initiative has chosen to develop a community-and youth-led initiative that can amplify youth and community stories in ways that are accessible and translatable to other youth and communities engaging with our media. We take the lead of our youth, as very few community and educational spaces create the space for youth and community to amplify youth voices and/or encourage youth dreaming.

The media projects being discussed within this chapter, specifically Briana's and Karla's videos, can be viewed within the Santa Ana Youth Media Project (2019) website, https://www.saymediaproject.org/. Our project's website acts as a cornerstone for all the projects being realized in collaboration with our youth. Please feel free to explore our content videos and video essays of youth expressions and testimony within the context of Santa Ana and the larger Orange County.

Vignette: October 2022, Orange County Film Fiesta, Santa Ana, CA

The room was dimly lit by the documentary playing on the screen. As we walked into the room a couple minutes late, we tried to move in as quietly as possible. In the light of the screen, our eyes caught the table full of snacks and refreshments in the corner and the colorful decorations on the walls with the "OC Film Fiesta" sign. Although the room was dim and people were drawn to the documentary, there was still a silent hum of lively energy in the air.

High school senior, Briana, sat in the row in front of us with her two younger siblings. Seeing that we had entered the room, she turned to wave and broke into a big smile. We noticed that her young sister was holding a bouquet of flowers Briana's siblings must have gotten for her. When the documentary ended, we heard a familiar piano melody as the opening scene to "home: un lugar para todos" started to play. We looked excitedly around at each other. Once Briana's siblings saw her name on the big screen, they started to get loud in all their excitement, and Briana laughed a bit as she tried to quiet them down. As we snuck a peek at Briana's expression, we caught how her face lit up with surprise, awe, and joy at seeing herself and her story on the screen. Her eyes would also flit around the room, trying to see other people's expressions.

When the lights came on for a Q&A session, Briana walked with us to the front of the room where audience members immediately gave affirming comments and remarks on her story and asked her questions. She was taken aback at first by the energy, then started chatting away and responding to questions. As questions were being addressed to the rest of the film team, we would sometimes catch her silently looking around the room again and taking a deep breath as if really taking in how people had witnessed her art and had wanted to know more. In the light of the intimate room filled with other storytellers and community members, she seemed to be reveling, with a quiet and full joy, at the meaning of her story finally being witnessed and celebrated. After the screenings had finished, we walked with Briana outside to the little photo booth area that the OC Film Fiesta organizers had set up. Holding the bouquet of flowers her siblings had handed to her, we were laughing fondly together as we took a bunch of pictures of her and a couple of all of us together as a group. The memory of her joy that day and the warmth it gave us remains the most vibrant part of this memory that we hold onto still.

That afternoon was special and significant for all of us and is a memory we will always hold dear. Nonetheless, Briana also carried some tension internally that night, negotiating family commitments and responsibilities with her accomplishments. The Film Fiesta was scheduled at the same time as some of her family events, so Briana's presence at the Film Fiesta with her siblings demonstrated determination in significant ways. Briana's dilemmas at the event are not unusual among youth of her age, though given the social context of youth and families within the city of Santa Ana, we were able to appreciate the strength and commitment Briana showed in attending the Film Fiesta.

Santa Ana is a low-income, immigrant city where 76% of the city's population is of Latina/o/x descent (U.S. Census, 2022). Families within the city of Santa Ana struggle to get by economically, often holding two or three jobs to make ends meet (Russo & Guerrero, 2017). It is very common for multiple families to rent households intended for a single family–oftentimes sharing the house rooms, living rooms, and garages to keep the cost of living low (Gonzalez & Sarmiento, 2017). The multi-family living arrangements are necessary and often the only resource toward surviving economically within Orange County's high renting market. Santa Ana is the 13th largest city in the state of California, classified as one of the most densely populated cities with over 10,000 residents per square mile. Notably, Santa Ana is also one of the youngest cities in the nation where over 25% of the city's population is 18 years of age and younger (U.S. Census, 2022).

This information characterizes Santa Ana as a unique and complex environment at the intersection of class and race dynamics rooted within the context of the larger Orange County. Santa Ana is in the heart of Orange County, a historically conservative and affluent county housing some of the wealthiest cities in the nation (Arellano, 2008; Lewinnek et al., 2022). Orange County is home to Disneyland, Huntington Beach (Surf City USA), Newport Beach, and Dana Point. These cities are some of the most affluent areas with much of their populations being white and of upper-middle to upper-class residencies. Orange County is the backdrop for Hollywood reality TV shows. These shows represent the over-essentialist narratives filling Orange County's mainstream identity (Brooks & Hebert, 2006; Arellano, 2008; Lewinnek et al., 2022).

Given the striking contrast between the low-income and immigrant communities within Santa Ana and the larger Orange County environment, youth navigate racial, ethnic, and class-based struggles that pigeonhole their identity in stereotypical and demeaning ways. Santa Ana has a long history of deficit-based perspectives that engulf how youth and families are perceived; a plethora of stories can be gathered describing the racial and ethnic disparities that youth and families experience within Santa Ana (Carroll, 2016; Lacayo, 2016). The city's budgeting, for example, has historically favored the police department, and within the 2017-2018 fiscal year, the City of Santa Ana allocated more than 53% of its budget to "public safety," which also encompassed any youth-based programming. Within the 2017-2018 budget projection, the City of Santa Ana proposed to spend 19.5 million dollars on policing and approaches that criminalize youth, and 15.3 million allocated toward "positive youth development" (Russo & Guerrero, 2017, p. 3).

The city's proposed vision for "positive youth development" however has embodied a deficit approach to how youth should engage and behave within the city (Russo & Guerrero, 2017, p. 3). Youth within the city are perceived to be bad, poor, gang-affiliated, unruly, and are prescribed top-down, discipline-based programming embedded in meritocratic lenses for what Santa Ana authorities perceive an ideal young citizen should resemble (Ladson-Billings, 2006; Pho, 2020; Pho, 2023: Russo & Guerrero, 2017). The city of Santa Ana positions the police officer and its department as ideal role models for how youth should behave. Nevertheless, youth tend to see through this positioning and often resist city-sponsored programming. The youth of Santa Ana are brilliant, resilient, and transformative; they are aware of their positionalities yet love and push their city for more holistic youth spaces and perspectives on youth culture (Gonzalez, 2023; Russo & Guerrero, 2017). The youth of Santa Ana are known to have some of the most active and thriving underground punk and skating scenes; nonetheless, these activities tend to be criminalized (Taylor, 2023). Skateparks within Santa Ana are a relatively new concept, and youth-friendly public performance venues are non-existent. The city of Santa Ana does not have youth-led centers that appeal to youth development other than ones that are meritocratic and deficit-based (Gonzalez, 2023).

What is evidently powerful to witness is that even though such inequalities exist, youth are still able to embody their dreams in expressive and determinant ways (Rodriguez et al., 2020). The youth of Santa Ana are powerful and keen in understanding their positionality. They are aware of the dominant narratives surrounding their experiences, and regardless of the odds stacked against them, they can create, dream, and transform their social conditions expressively (Rodriguez, Reed, & Garcia, 2020).

Given this context of youth in Santa Ana, the Santa Ana Youth Media Project understands the importance of capturing youth expressions, desires, and narratives through digital media. The Santa Ana Youth Media Project understands the power that emanates from youth and proposes to document youth dreams and their stories in ways that others can see. The Santa Ana Youth Media Project believes in the possibility of radical hope and the embodiment of youth dreaming.

Methods

We created two separate video projects: first, one with Briana, and a year later, one with Karla, both high school seniors from Santa Ana. Our process was centered around honoring their stories by allowing their projects to be youth-led, aiming to reduce harm, and centering a relational rapport which focused on establishing trust and collaboration. Our team consisted of three leading individuals: a local Santa Ana-grown resident and faculty; an Orange County-grown university student; and a student from the same California university who was raised outside of the Orange County context, but was no less committed to the stories being documented within our initiative. The Dreamweaving project later incorporated a university student film crew that helped develop the music video for Karla; as a result of that experience, this crew has committed to joining the Santa Ana Youth Media Project's Dreamweaving Initiative in all future projects. This chapter, however, will focus on the positionalities and developments created by Founder and Director of the Santa Ana Youth Media project, Dr. Jorge F. Rodriguez, and Founders of the Dreamweaving Initiative at a local California university, Bernadine Cortina and Jessica Tonai.

The Santa Ana Youth Media Project is a community-engaged project that is centered around the context of community and youth development. Its purpose is to amplify youth and community testimony by establishing a media outlet that can amplify youth voices and center equity and justice within its projects. The university connected with this project is centered geographically within the center of Orange County, and its proximity to the Santa Ana community is only about a three-to-four mile difference. The Santa Ana Youth Media Project was proposed as a collaborative that would unite university students with Santa Ana and Orange County community organizers, youth, and residents. Dr. Jorge F. Rodriguez was born, raised, and is still a resident within Santa Ana; he is a first-generation college graduate male of Mexican decent whose family migrated to the U.S. in the late '70s. Jorge is acutely aware of the contextual struggles youth experience as they navigate mainstream educational paradigms of success, meritocratic idealism, and culturally insensitive curriculum. Jorge's experiences of being raised within the Santa Ana context emulate the youth and community's struggles of poverty, anti-immigrant sentiments, racism, and lack of educational resources. As a faculty member and educator, he is now committed to creating spaces within Orange County where youth and community can be seen and experienced as beautiful and significant contributors (Acosta & Mir, 2012). The following positionality statements from our collective authors contextualize who we are and why we are committed to this work.

My name is Jessica Tonai, and I was born and raised in Orange County and am currently a music education student at a California university. Because I am hoping to work in K-12 schools in Orange County, I feel a responsibility to examine the flaws in our public education system and to help counteract them. I wish to bring to the educational system, and this project, a kind of creativity that I believe is missing from public schools. In my experience, schools often stifle creativity by "teaching to the test" and having mostly teacher-centered learning. I hope that our Dreamweaving projects can center the students' wealth of knowledge, and offer an opportunity for them to take on a creative leadership role to share their stories within their communities and schools, where they spent most of their time. I grew up in Orange County, though acknowledge that my experience differs from the experiences of many Santa Ana youth. My experience is centered within a middle-class family in a more affluent South Orange County area. Because of this context, I approach this project by prioritizing high school youth as experts in their own experience. I hope to be in collaboration with youth of Santa Ana while sharing each other's context, while learning and appreciating the social constructions of difference being explored.

My name is Bernadine Cortina, and I am currently an English literature student at the same California university that Jessica attends. I hope to be able to help further literary possibilities in the Philippines by taking all that I have learned in my time here and starting a career in publishing there at some point. I felt personally drawn to the project because of my passion for storytelling and my own migration experience. I was born in the Philippines and lived there for 16 years before moving to California with just my mom and my younger sibling. Since coming to California, I faced so many painful absences. I stopped seeing my language, my heritage, and myself in stories and in my education here. I also carried the pains of having been discouraged from speaking up or finding value in my lived experience as a young girl of color throughout the education system and in family spaces. It was very transformative for me to have a professor in college, Professor Sarah Rafael Garcia, be the first to tell me that I was a writer. Through her and through finding Pinay literature, it began to cultivate bravery within me around my own creativity, and just as others have done for me, I hoped to be able to encourage other young storytellers to take up space and share their own stories. For me, this involves mindfulness and care around the areas of difference I hold from the Santa Ana youth we work with, as someone who comes from the outside and who does not intimately know the Santa Ana or Orange County context, and who comes from a family that was affluent in the Philippines and had the class resources to migrate and support my education in a private university. Like Jess, I dream of *co-creating* a space for storytelling, where the youth are the ones leading in their storytelling and visioning as they are the loving experts on their communities and their lived experiences.

Our projects begin with our collective and individual stories. We recognize that the telling of our stories is primarily in building relationships with each other as a team and in collaboration with the youth and community. A significant part of our methodology also centers the use of critical media literacy. We conceptualize the use of media as a third language, or a third form of communication, that can bring to life sentiments, frustrations, and unspoken feelings that can be difficult to communicate. We also acknowledge that youth are masters for creating media and forms of communication that are far more advanced and nuanced than we like to credit. The Santa Ana Youth Media Project understands that the use of media and its intersection with testimony and storytelling develop a bridge towards meeting youth and their interest with the exploration of their worlds. Critical media literacy gives our projects the guidelines and parameters toward interpreting and creating the unknown stories important to our society (Kellner & Share, 2005; Cerecer et al., 2013). Critical media literacy further allows our project to create and document our own stories through a critical lens. Given the mass number of media being produced within mainstream venues such as Hollywood, social media, and commercialization, critical media literacy gives our project the ability to interpret our social realities in contrast and counter to dominance. When youth and community within Santa Ana speak reflectively and genuinely about their experiences, they speak truth to power in ways that mainstream media avoid. Critical media literacy is a vital tool towards documenting and amplifying youth and community voice (Kellner & Share, 2005; Cerecer et. al., 2013).

The Santa Ana Youth Media Project worked with a local high school to identify students who might be willing to participate within our Dreamweaving project. After working with a local teacher, two students were identified, and these students were presented with our project. Following their receipt of a Critical media literacy framework and signing of personal release documents, Briana and Karla were invited to act as directors on their videos and come up with the theme of their project, choose the media they wanted to use, and make any other creative decisions necessary. At each meeting, we had consistent conversations with the students about the importance of their lived experiences and how we could portray those in the project with honesty, and reminded them that this was *their* project, and we were all there to facilitate its creation.

We met with these students two to three times a month. The first few meetings with Karla were conducted in places familiar and comfortable to her. First, in her high school teacher's classroom with her teacher present, and then at a restaurant across the street from her school. All our meetings with Briana were online due to COVID-19 concerns, and our first meeting with her also included her high school teacher. When asking any personal questions to inform the projects, we emphasized that they should only share what they were comfortable sharing with us. We also used the method of communication the students informed us they would be most comfortable using for updates in between meetings. The Santa Ana Youth Media Project was sensitive to the needs of the students and developed the project at their pace. From initial content development with the young directors to the production of their videos, each Santa Ana Youth Media project usually takes anywhere from six months to a year. Our pace is intentional as we center process and are aware of all the commitments each participant balances.

Youth Testimony—"Briana's" mandate:

In the spring of 2022, we university seniors, Bernadine and Jess, happened to be looking to work with local high school students for a project in our Music Education and Social Justice class. We reached out to Professor Rodriguez to see if he had any connections with teachers at schools in Santa Ana, as we had wanted to create a semester project with high school students that defied traditional approaches to arts education. Through Dr. Rodriguez's connection with a teacher at a local high school, we got in contact with Briana, whom we immediately recognized as an exceptional poet who was interested in sharing her work with us.

Our first meeting with her was on a Zoom call through her high school teacher who identified and reached out to students who might be interested in the project. After only a bit of prompting from her teacher, Briana decided to share two poems with us that were vulnerable and loving, about how she sees the women in her community. We ended up working with her on her art form, poetry, and we proposed she write about a topic of her choosing. She wrote several drafts of poems over the next few weeks.

As we were brainstorming themes for the poem, together we settled on the concept of home, inspired by then, OC youth poet laureate Tina Mai's community poem prompt (Mai, 2022). We facilitated the creation of a poetry video that was multimodal, combining Briana's interests and love for both poetry and music. Bernadine, who is a writer, workshopped Briana's poem with her for the remainder of the semester. We sent drafts and feedback for the poem back and forth for a few weeks. When the poem was finalized, we asked Briana to send a voice recording of it along with photos and videos. On her phone, she already had photos of places in the city she would pass every day on her way to and from school. Using all these materials, Jess edited the video at the end of the semester. Once it was finished, we sent the full video to Briana over email, who was overjoyed to see how it all came together. She also shared a keen interest in looking for spaces to share her work because, as she wrote to us, "it can be helpful to show others the words that they were never told … [words they] were wishing to hear," which is something that continually guides our work. The following poem by Briana became the focal point for the video discussed in this chapter.

Home: un lugar para todos

Not only a place
But a community
That is full of history
Emotions
And pain
Where we together act as
a family,
protecting it
Saving it
Knowing and remembering
That even if there's a war going on
we can still smile and get along
Because this is family
Where even as you walk down the street
You can smell food
that your mom and dad
Would make when you were a child
Or when your birthday would come along
And families would gather together
eating
Talking
And laughing
Home
That is what Santa Ana feels like
Feeling safe
Without worries
Because no matter what happens
These people
your family
Your home

will always have your back
Because we are equal
Brilliant
And successful
And when an obstacle gets in the way
We fight back
Knowing that we are strong and hardworking
Like the sun and the moon
Feeling
seeing
And hearing what others do
The pain
The happiness
And cheers of a happy family
Knowing too that this doesn't only happen in Santa Ana
But the whole world too
We are one
Because we will always have each other's back
So don't forget that
No matter the cause
if you feel left out
Just know that we love you
Because this is
My world
Your world
And our home

Briana's poem is one that speaks about her city with so much love, while it also acknowledges the realities within Santa Ana and speaks back against the ways the city is viewed. Here, she puts forward her imagining of the city and the people there as her home—words she wanted those in her community to also hear.

The space that would become a home for her work and other stories like hers would be the Santa Ana Youth Media Project. After sharing Briana's video and testimony with Dr. Rodriguez, we brainstormed how to make a sustainable space for youth storytelling. When we were thinking of our mission and what to call the project, we decided to name our initiative, "Community Dreamweavers."

Dreamweavers Project

In this section, we share with you the voices and literature around dreaming that have formed the foundations of our work, and that begins with Filipina poet Marjorie Evasco. The term "dreamweavers" is taken from Marjorie Evasco's (1987) essay, "Other Voice: Response to Anzaldúa." Evasco lovingly uses this term to name her Pinay elders (Nanay Tinay, Manding Marintay, Insi Lolang, and Nanay Isin) who were weavers of *tikog* and *romblon* mats that they sold to pay for their brothers' education and meet their family's needs. In order to weave and sell enough, they never got to go to school. Evasco wonders about her Pinay elders' "subterfuge poetry" as they wove their hopes, dreams, and frustrations into these colorful mats and patterns (Evasco, 1987 p. 4). Like Manang [older sister] Evasco, we refuse to be engaged in erasure. We honor her dreamweavers and all the dreamweaving that happens in our communities as we believe that our art and our dreaming are often a part of our day-to-day activities, even, and especially, the things we do not always consider to be noteworthy or a form of art. Similarly, youth are not often given a place or time to express their dreams, so those dreams are woven into their everyday activities and things they do for fun. Some students spend their free time writing, dancing, or singing, which are more traditionally recognized forms of art and expression, while others skateboard, make TikToks, or love creating graffiti art. We perceive all these expressions to be "dreamweaving" that supports and prepares youth to navigate oppressive systems that often push youth toward erasure and marginalization. We honor Evasco's dreamweavers and, in parallel reflection, acknowledge all the dreamweaving that happens in our communities.

We came to Evasco's work through collaborator Bernadine Cortina, a Filipina poet, as she strove to find the words she needed to hear. When we started creating the framework for the Dreamweavers Project, Briana's example recalled the women in Evasco's family that she so dearly loved. Laying on one of her Nanay Tinay's colorful mats, Evasco thought about the verbs that were hidden in the strands that formed the mats, blankets, and robes these women wove (Evasco, 1987). She imagined in her Nanay Tinay's weaving her hands embedding the night's long silence as she imagined possibilities, rearranged configurations, and dreamed designs that had not yet been imagined (Evasco, 1987). Very powerfully, Evasco reflects in this letter to Gloria Anzaldúa that, in a world where lives are circumscribed, when tongues are tied or cut, and our visions and dreams cannot be translated into the larger world, it is our hands that transform the materials we work with into testaments of how we dream, and that art holds covert legacies that reveal how workdays were made bearable by "transforming our ways of living with our ways of creating" (Evasco, 1987, p. iv). Just as Evasco sees subterfuge poetry in the hands of the women in her life, so too do we see it in Santa Ana's youth and in their diverse ways of expressing and creating.

Yet, it is a challenge too, as Evasco warns us of the mounting forces that exhaust many creative women, especially poor women, whose skills are labeled as "non-productive" because they are perceived as only cleaning other people's houses, washing other people's clothes, or minding other people's children (Evasco, 1987). This limiting language and the hostile gaze that labels women's and youth's forms of dreaming as "non-productive" creates the conditions for these poetics to be minimized, erased, and even lost.

There is a necessity to find space for and to urgently learn how to read and hold all forms of this subterfuge poetry. We argue that dreamweaving is a manifestation of Robin D.G. Kelley's idea of freedom dreams. In *Freedom Dreams*, Kelley (2022) looks at Black social movements where he unearths what he calls "poetry that dreams of a new world" (p. 10). In his work, he speaks profusely about the importance of these imaginations of freedom in the ongoing struggle for liberation. Like Evasco's concept of dreamweavers, Kelley (2022) envisions freedom dreams "in the poetics of struggle and lived experience, in the utterances of ordinary folk, in the cultural products of social movements, in the reflections of activists" (p. 10) where different cognitive maps of the future, of the world not yet born can be discovered. He emphasizes that this work of dreaming is one that earlier generations have also done, and that these dreams of freedom and the space to imagine are necessary to bring about liberation in a way that all the protests and demonstrations in the world cannot do without.

In conversation with Evasco's work with dreamweaving, we are recognizing that the poetry of freedom dreams exists all around us and in the life-affirming and life-sustaining acts of artistic creation we engage with in our daily lives. Just as Evasco's loved ones showed her, as they wove their dreams into these colorful mats, the act of dreamweaving is one of creation: making the imagined real. Kelley (2022) also meaningfully poses the question: "What are today's young activists dreaming about? We know what they are fighting against, but what are they fighting for?" (p. 8). We find our work with young dreamweavers offers a response.

In La Velle Ridley's (2019) article, "Imagining Otherly: Performing Possible Black Trans Futures" in *Tangerine*, she theorizes the framework of "imagining otherly" to articulate how the act of imagination "functions as both a survival tactic and epistemological framework for addressing the possibilities that lie in moving beyond the polarizing ways of engaging with power: to resist or comply" (p. 482). We engage with Ridley's perspective on imagination as generative for creating possibilities beyond resistance and compliance as we look to our youth's work and recognize in them these other possibilities they speak to and create. For example, in Briana's work, using photos and images of Santa Ana that she took herself on her way to school or on the way home, with language that centers her hopes and the people she loves, she emulates how youth are moving beyond resisting to create counter-stories. The imaginings of the city as home in her poem created a different, contradictory narrative where the limitations against youth do not exist. Her Santa Ana is joyful, free, loving, resilient, and supported. Her vision, while acknowledging and holding the difficulties of her city, emphasizes her city as an experience of home and offers a reprieve, a space for breath, and a vision of freedom in the now that also pushes back against the delegitimization and devaluation of youth experiences that she has faced.

We are also considering literature that guides our perspectives on the power of storytelling. Here we turn to Audre Lorde (1984/2007) and her essay, "The Transformation of Silence into Language and Action." Reflecting on her experience with breast cancer and her own mortality, she speaks to the urgencies of breaking silence: "my silences had not protected me. They will not protect you" (p. 41). She also speaks to how the act of breaking silence then connects her more deeply to community as she emphasizes how it is silence and not difference that separates us from one another. Her work with transforming silence into language and action is something we see reflected within the Dreamweavers project—as youth break their own silences, and we bear witness to how that is able to transform so much for them and bring them into closer relationship with the communities they love.

Lastly, we reflect on storytelling itself through Dr. Merlinda Bobis's (2020) lecture "Isalba Storya, Isalba Buhay: Following the Water." In her work, she puts forward the idea that we save stories, and enact them to save lives. The storytelling of our youth points us to the changes they want to see and the world they want to make through their storytelling and imaginative praxis.

Our dreamweavers deeply remind us that, as Kelley (2002) states, the catalyst for social movement is not misery, poverty, or oppression but instead radical hope. For us, we find it here with our youth's acts of dreamweaving—of imagining, creating, *and* remaking a world different from the one they inherit.

"Karla's" Story

Karla's dream was to not feel alone, though she found hope in the melody and the song she composed for the project. High school senior and songwriter, Karla was the first student we got to work with on the Dreamweavers project after it was established. We sent out an application to students at the same school in which Briana attended and asked what stories they wanted to share. Karla submitted song lyrics to us about feeling alone while growing up when she couldn't have her loved ones around as much as she needed them. Like Briana, Karla also chose to focus on the theme of "home" and wanted to tell the story of how, since she moved frequently, "home" to her was never tied to a physical place but to the people who were most important to her. This is a shared experience of multiple youth growing up in Santa Ana who are not able to stay in long-term living situations, and who may not have support from family members at times when those family members need to be out working late or working multiple jobs to support the family. She described her feelings of loneliness in the lyrics below:

Home

Where did you go?
It's cold without you home
I miss your hugs
And the times it was only us

Reminiscing the good times
Overlooking the bad times
Oh, where did you go?

You made anyplace feel like home
You made sure I was always warm
But one day, you walked out the door
And now I need you home
(Y ahora te quiero conmigo)
I feel so alone
(Cause we come from a place where we don't feel safe)
And now I need you home
(Without you by my side, holding me tight-es todo que te pido)
I feel so alone

If you knew how much I needed you
Would you have walked out the door?
Or would you have turned around
To hug me
And told me you love me
And welcomed me home?

Karla's poem is one that voices her longing for home and ends with her imagining her loved one returning home to her. While her poem does not materially change the conditions that make it necessary for her family to work away from her, it is a powerful and meaningful voicing of the impact on Karla and what she wishes for instead. Her experience deeply reminds us of Kelley's (2022) words as he wrote, "It is a testament to the legacies of oppression that opposition is so frequently contained, or that efforts to find 'free spaces' for articulating or even realizing our dreams are so rare or marginalized" (p. 10). Karla and other youth may not see a path forward to making their specific dreams into a reality, but just being given a space to name their grief and to recognize that their dreams and longings are powerful further plants the seed of imagining new radical futures. The act of performing her dream as well–of giving voice to it, of creating an embodiment that names her personal grief and articulates a wish she wanted while also being a direct part of a music video's creation, from the visuals to the narrative structure and musical video style, creates youth representation for themselves in music and songs. We are reminded of Ridley's (2019) sentiment that echoes Audre Lorde—that performance is not a luxury either (p. 487). Karla has more deeply opened up a process of becoming, where there is both learning and meaningful unlearning that takes place.

Being connected to the university proved to be extremely valuable to Karla's project. The university has a well-established film program, so we were able to connect with film students who have access to professional equipment for Karla's project, to create a high-quality music video. Over the course of the 2023 spring semester, Karla worked with Jess on a song using the lyrics she submitted and met with the film students to solidify the narrative she wanted to see in the music video. Karla really stepped into the freedom she was given on this project and, with each meeting, gained more confidence in taking on a directive role among folks who were all older than she was. The project continued into the summer, where we filmed at different university students' houses and got to see components of Karla's story and the dreams she had for the music video coming to life. A set full of moving boxes depicted the transitory home she spoke of, and shots set in "Karla's room" showed us her songwriting process and how the experience of being home alone with her thoughts often led her to create.

During this process, Karla expressed to us that she was beginning to understand the struggles of her family and friends in a new light and did not feel the same way she did when she wrote the song lyrics. The lyrics initially came from a place of longing for them to do more for her, but she later came to see the context behind why the people in her life could not always be there for her.

She started to empathize with them more. Karla was planning on going away for college that fall, so working on this song was especially meaningful for her to be able to look back on her past relationship with her mom as she learns how to sustain a relationship of continued connectedness with her when leaving home. This new outlook on her family and friends is evidence that she was able to create a new world for herself through this art. She engaged in radical imagination through the exploration of her own feelings in songwriting to process complex dynamics with her family and friends and look towards how she wants to sustain those relationships in the future.

Conclusion

The Dreamweaving project has afforded us an opportunity to be reflective and intentional in the work being developed with youth of Santa Ana. As our small project grows, we are increasingly aware of the potential youth have towards transforming their communities collaboratively. Our Santa Ana Youth Media Project's Dreamweaving initiative has come up with four pedagogical insights that have arisen from the praxis being exercised within our youth work. These concluding and preliminary insights were developed in the process of collaboration with the youth being highlighted within this chapter. Specifically, these pedagogical insights have been developed through a lens of critical reflection, observation, and dialogue. These insights are based in practice and speak toward the values and parameters that guide our work within an equitable approach. As students, community organizers, and academics, we would like to emphasize the importance of community and youth-led initiatives toward storytelling and speaking truth to power. Flexibility and community-guided initiatives are at the core of our pedagogical approach when amplifying youth and community voice. We hope that the following concluding pedagogical insights regarding our work being developed may serve as a transformative process for all community and youth-led initiatives.

1. Recognize inheritances:
   Youth storytelling is healing, and voicing out is powerful. Storytelling is for ourselves and for our communities, but in order to create authentic

spaces for storytelling, we encourage questioning inherited dreams to act more intentionally from an awareness of our many inheritances. For youth and for educators, making the distinction between inherited dreams and dreams we self-determine is crucial for creating spaces centered on transformative storytelling. Within the project, we came upon this insight through dialogue with our youth, as they shared how being given the space to lead with their dreaming was a new process for them. It brought up conversations around dreams that are inherited from family and the school system and how other possibilities outside of these inheritances are not given as much space to exist. When we are in dialogue with our youth around dreaming, we listen for inheritances and offer a space to imagine differently - other wants, needs, hopes, and wishes are present but may not have been articulated yet.

2. Use media as a tool for youth self-transformation:
    Media can serve a purpose of cultivating opportunities for youth to move beyond imposed silence. The creation of youth-led media can cultivate capacity to dream, and in some cases realize such dreams. The creation and interpretation of media can act as a third form of communicating, and youth are able to explore and share experiences, insights, realities, and reflections through the compositions of images, stories, art, music, and film. When working on Karla's music video, it was powerful to see how Karla drew out images that resonated with her song lyrics in collaboration with our team. Karla was able to voice out scenes and imagery that emphasize her own stories and tensions being experienced. As Karla spoke of the feelings she felt within her song, she was able to channel such feelings into a video shoot that allowed for her story to be told in creative ways. Her music video included a childhood bedroom, family pictures, and personal notes, highlighting the lyrics on the wall. To place Karla in a memory within her lyrics physically being demonstrated throughout her video was powerful to visualize and experience. Media has the ability to speak in tones that communicate beyond words.

3. Share and amplify youth stories:
    While the act of creating a story is powerful in itself, stories are never created or told in isolation. Community can bear meaningful witness

to these stories. Create spaces for these stories to be heard and shared. We've been witness to how mutual recognition and affirmation can happen in the space as these stories met unspoken needs - words were heard that needed to be heard and stories that needed to be told were told. Sharing youth stories breaks silences, amplifies the impact of their narratives, and allows their stories to do their work in the world. This insight was directly inspired by Briana's mandate as she asked, after the creation of her poem, to also find a space to share it. She was thinking then about how these are words that others may also need to hear. It was her insight that led to the very creation of the project, which is about creating and amplifying youth stories.

4. Recognize the impact of youth stories:
   Expression through media helps youth visualize the world they want to see, an important first step in eventually shaping their futures. For example, Briana visualizes a world in her poem where her community was interconnected with others around the world, with everyone supporting one another. Her words work to shift viewers' understanding of Santa Ana away from a deficit-based perspective by expressing the supportive and loving nature of her city, and seeking to connect her community with those outside it by highlighting similarities.

We hope these pedagogical insights will be helpful as a starting point towards developing community-led initiatives within your context. These offerings intend to center youth and community context at the core of all our work. Common practice amongst our collective is the development of constant reflection and dialogue with all collaborators of our project. To be constantly reflective with the relationships, initiatives, and intentions of our work is vital in developing an equitable project. The reflections below can serve as an example of how we embody such critical reflections.

Reflections

There is a special opportunity for youth-to-youth connection in this process. As college students, Bernadine and Jess bonded with the high school students over the trials that educational institutions put us through and could share our experiences on how to navigate that world. We know that spaces for youth to tell their stories freely are not always existent in schools, in communities, or at home, an absence we both knew personally well. Looking back now, perhaps this project was also growing from a need we hadn't articulated yet – the need for space for storytelling and expression that we also wish we had.

Thinking about how bearing witness to our dreamweavers also gave us radical hope, we think of how Kelley (2022) reminds us that a revolution does not come from a chain of clever maneuvers and tactics but is instead a process that can and must transform us. As fellow youth in this project, we have also been meaningfully changed in participating and bearing witness to these stories and these loving acts of creation. It was healing to both of us to witness these youth take up space and come to their voice earlier than we had. Within documenting our Dreamweaver project for this chapter, we also asked Dr. Rodriguez, our professor and collaborator, to express the impact of dreamweaving and the Santa Ana Youth Media Project. His response was:

As an educator, I believe in the power of dreaming; I hold sacred the radical possibility of creating. My mother taught me the importance of radical hope and dreaming, to imagine beyond what is perceived as possible, a way to start a process of fulfilling for ourselves a new reality. My mother spoke into existence dreams that felt unattainable, yet somehow over-exceeded the limitations of her imagination. To think of our family's immigration story, the poverty experienced, the navigating of school deficit systems, learning and   navigating a different language, enduring the negative impacts of patriarchy, leaving her mother and not being able to see her because of un-documentation; all these struggles were a part of our family's story. Nevertheless, her dream set into motion unwavering hope that gave us, her children, determination, and resilience. When I began the Santa Ana Youth Media Project it started as a dream to create a media platform that youth could own, develop, and create given to their needs, expressions, and transformations. To see this dream unfold in transformative ways together with my students is enacting change in ways I never imagined.

Finally, embodying the way that Evasco names herself as a daughter of silenced women and seeing how her framework of dreamweaving came out of love and her desire to be able to read and break silences, we have been able to see how her vision of freedom has also allowed us, in some way, to end the silence and erasure around forms of youth dreamweaving and storytelling in Santa Ana. To make space for these stories now extends this work beyond our imaginations. We see all of what has grown since we started this endeavor in us, in the youth we've worked with, and in all the community that has witnessed, been loved, and been changed by the stories spoken here. We recognize how we are a meaningful part of a vast ecology of dreaming and storytelling where each story weaves into and affects another person's story. It really is as Octavia Butler (1993) says: "All that you touch, you change. All that you change changes you" (p. 13). Dreamweaving truly is happening all around us, not only in practice but also in its impacts.

Reference

Acosta, C., & Mir, A. (2012). Empowering young people to be critical thinkers: The Mexican American studies program in Tucson. *Voices in Urban Education*, 34(1).

Arellano, G. (2008). *Orange County: A personal history.* Simon and Schuster.

Bobis, M. (2017). Salba istorya/Salba buhay: Save story/Save lives: Collaborative storying in the wake of typhoons. In A. Collett, R. McDougall, & S. Thomas (Eds.), *Tracking the literature of tropical weather: Typhoons, hurricanes, and cyclones* (pp. 151-176). Palgrave Macmillan Ltd.

Brooks, D. E., & Hébert, L. P. (2006). Gender, race, and media representation. *Handbook of Gender and Communication*, 16, 297-317. https://www.focusintl.com/GD142-%20Gender,%20Race%20and%20Media%20Representation.pdf

Butler, O. E. (1993). *Parable of the sower.* Grand Central Publishing.

Carroll, R. (2016). *"They just don't fit in": UCLA study links racism and segregation in Orange County.* The Guardian. https://www.theguardian.com/us-news/2016/sep/19/ucla-study-racism-segregation-orange-county.

Cerecer, D. A. Q., Cahill, C., & Bradley, M. (2013). Toward a critical youth policy praxis: Critical youth studies and participatory action research. *Theory Into Practice*, 52(3), 216–223. http://www.jstor.org/stable/43893886

Evasco, M. E. (1987). *Dreamweavers: Selected poems 1976-1986 won the 1987.* Book Development Association (BDA) Gintong Aklat award for literary work category. https://animorepository.dlsu.edu.ph/events_diary/444

Evasco, M. E. (1987a). The Other Voice: Reply to Anzaldúa. In M. Evasco (Ed.), *Dreamweavers: Selected Poems 1976–1986.* Aria Edition, Inc. "Dreamweavers." Dreamweavers: Selected Poems 1976–1986. Aria Edition, Inc., 1987.

Gonzalez, E., & Sarmiento, C. (2017). *The gentrification of Santa Ana: From origin to resistance.* PBSSoCal. https://www.kcet.org/shows/city-rising/the-gentrification-of-santa-ana-from-origin-to-resistance

González L. Y. (2023): *Santa Ana City Council must include a youth center in this year's budget.* Voice of OC. https://voiceofoc.org/2023/05/gonzalez-santa-ana-city-council-must-include-a-youth-center-in-this-years-budget/

Kelley, R. D. G. (2002). *Freedom dreams: The Black radical imagination.* Beacon Press.

Kellner, D., & Share, J. (2005). Toward critical media literacy: Core concepts, debates, organizations, and policy. *Discourse: Studies in the Cultural Politics of Education, 26*(3), 369-386.

Lacayo, C. (2016). Latinos need to stay in their place: Differential segregation in a multi-ethnic suburb. *Societies, 6*(3), 25. http://dx.doi.org/10.3390/soc6030025.

Ladson-Billings, G. (2006). It's not the culture of poverty, it's the poverty of culture. *Anthropology and Education Quarterly, 37*(2), 104-109. https://navejar.com/handouts/Other/Its_Not_the_Culture_Of_Poverty.pdf

Lewinnek, E., Arellano, G., & Dang, T. (2022). *A people's guide to Orange County.* University of California Press. https://doi.org/10.1525/9780520971554

Lorde, A. (2007). *Sister outsider: Essays and speeches /by Audre* Crossing Press. (Original work published 1984).

Mai, T. (2022, April 8). *OC Youth Poet Laureate Curating a Community Poem For & By Youth.* Off the Page Series. https://www.libromobile.com/post/oc-youth-poet-laureate-curating-a-community-poem-for-by-youth

Pho, B. (2020). *Santa Ana's youth go profane in public comment to get noticed by City Council.* Voice of OC. https://voiceofoc.org/2020/07/santa-anas-youth-go-profane-in-public-comment-to-get-noticed-by-city-council/

Pho, B. (2023). *Santa Ana leaders look at balancing their city budget while staring down a financial cliff.* Voice of OC. https://voiceofoc.org/2023/05/santa-ana-leaders-look-at-balancing-their-city-budget-while-staring-down-a-financial-cliff/

Project Virkurso. (2020, June 2). *Merlinda Bobis on Philippine literature/creative writing | Project Virkurso Lecture Series* [Video]. YouTube. https://www.youtube.com/watch?v=oQpuSfIHo-I

Ridley, L. (2019). Imagining otherly: Performing possible Black trans futures in *Tangerine. TSQ: Transgender Studies Quarterly, 6*(4), 481-490.

Rodriguez, J. F., Reed, C., Garcia, K., (2020). "It was time for us to take a stand": An Ethnic Studies Classroom and the Power of Youth Voice L., Hogg, *Pedagogies of With-ness: Students, Teachers, Voice, and Agency* (Ch. 6).

Russo, M., & Guerrero, J. (2017). *Status of youth investment in Santa Ana, Prepared by the Advancement Project.* Scribd. https://www.scribd.com/document/343212491/Status-of-Youth-Investment-in-Santa-Ana

Santa Ana Youth Media Project. (2019). *Santa Ana youth: Perspectives of their City.* https://www.saymediaproject.org/project-19

Taylor, E. (2023). *Skating across Orange County*. Voice of OC. https://voiceofoc.org/2023/10/skating-across-orange-county/

U.S. Census Bureau. (2022). *QuickFacts: Santa Ana city, California*. https://www.census.gov/quickfacts/fact/table/santaanacitycalifornia/PST045222

CHAPTER 10

Questioning with Love:
Developing Racial Literacy to Disrupt Racism

Simona Goldin, Danita Mason-Hogans, Justin Clyburn, and Shelby Freeman

Introduction

AMID VIOLENT ATTACKS on truth-telling, we seek to understand how students develop racial literacy and how they learn about systemic racism and name assets that are often erased or unacknowledged in historically marginalized communities. We are a group of undergraduates who took part in this work during our first semester of college alongside our community- and university-based teachers, who join us as authors here. Together we ask: "What is good here?" (Lawrence-Lightfoot & Davis, 2002), grounded in the knowledge that racism is endemic and that communities, including our university community, have important assets and capitals.

We detail how theory can be used to understand the world we inherit and to (re)imagine a more racially just world. Love (2019) writes that theory is a North Star, guiding the way and helping "to explain to us how the world works, who the world denies, and how structures uphold oppression" (p. 146). We use theory to learn about generations of oppression and violence in our local community, with and from Black generational community members who trace their lineage in this place across multiple generations. Using critical race theory as a frame, we leverage community cultural wealth (Yosso, 2005), naming assets and interrogating deficit frames (Goldin et al., 2021). We focus our analysis here on the following research questions:

1. What learning supports and resources enable young people to see, name, and disrupt systemic racism that is, as Tatum (2007) wrote, like a smog that "always, day in and day out, we are breathing in" (p. 86).

2. How do we as undergraduate students learn about racism in the pursuit of justice and develop racial literacy?

Our analyses feature our trajectories of learning and unlearning, tracing the ideas we came with, and how we challenged these ideas and worked towards more racially just understandings.

Who are We, and Where are We?

This study took place at our public university, an institution which has a storied and violent past that continues to inform and construct the present. The university was built with the forced labor of enslaved peoples, and the town it is in boasts beautiful stone walls everywhere, built by chained hands. The university also has a segregated cemetery on campus, where many white elites and their "help" are buried on opposing sides. In the 1990s, the segregated, Black-only side, was used as a parking lot for sporting events, desecrating the sacred space Reclaiming, 2018. More recently, in 2018, the university came under fire for its "Silent Sam" statue representing students who served on the confederate side of the Civil War. The statue was placed centrally on campus, and the opening speech was given by a known high-level KKK member when it was unveiled in 1913 (Calfas, 2018). The research team came together after the course, Education in a Multicultural Society, had concluded. Each of the research team members had engaged in the course in different ways—as students, guest speaker, and professor—and all shared a hunger to better understand the impact of our work, learning together.

Danita Mason-Hogans is an oral historian, memory worker, and native of North Carolina, from a family of seven generations of *movement people*. She uses oral histories to advocate for policy change and works at another local university in partnership with veterans of the Student Nonviolent Coordinating Committee (SNCC) and today's activists to center equity when documenting national and local movement history. Her TED talk provides an explanation of the critical oral history methodology which she helped to adapt.

Justin Clyburn is an African American student, also from North Carolina, and is a current university sophomore. As a child, Justin's parents never shied away from telling Justin that society would look at him differently because of the color of his skin. Justin realized he could not be naive thinking that discrimination did not exist on his campus. Therefore, Justin began to view his new surroundings through more of a critical lens to investigate how some circumstances enable discrimination to be unnoticed. Justin both critically analyzed his new southern university home while still embracing the positive aspects of the school which he loved so much as a new student.

Shelby Freeman is also a North Carolina native, born and raised in the same town she moved back to after serving in Boston with City Year Ameri-Corps for a year. In Boston, Shelby worked in a Title I school with an entirely non-white population of students within Boston Public Schools' school system. Shelby is a white woman coming from a wealthy family, something which has led to many intrinsic biases she has worked to address throughout this work. Her childhood home, built in 1905, borders a district which was historically segregated. This especially highlighted the persistent racism present within the community in which she grew up. Shelby came to class with both local influences and an impactful experience with the education system.

Simona Goldin taught the first-year seminar, Education in a Multicultural Society, that Justin and Shelby participated in during their first year. Having just moved from the Midwest, this was the first semester that Simona taught at a southern school, and she brought real curiosity to what this work could or would look like. She is a white, Jewish mother, whose work attends to race and racism in U.S. public schools. Her scholarship is grounded in the understanding that brilliance is equally distributed, but opportunity is not.

Learning About Race and Racism in U.S. Public Schools: Course Resources and Assignments

This course was a "first semester seminar" that brought together 24 first-year undergraduates from across the university to learn about education in a multicultural society. The class was grounded in the knowledge that (a) racism is endemic, (b) historical racial injustice is not just historic but is contemporaneous, and (c) communities, including the university's community, have deep and important assets, or capitals. As we set about "tangling with race and racism in U.S. public schools" (Goldin et al., 2021), we drew upon resources, including theoretical frames, a guest lecture with Ms. Mason-Hogans, and an opportunity to examine and learn from primary source ephemera from a segregated high school that was local to the university (see Table 10.1). Students were supported to analyze these ephemera, looking for evidence of thriving and joy at the high school. In order to do this, they (a) drew from Lawrence-Lightfoot's work on portraiture, in which she argues that "the researcher who asks first 'what is good here?' is likely to absorb a very different reality than the one who is on a mission to discover the sources of failure" (Lawrence-Lightfoot & Davis, 2002), and (b) used the lens of community cultural wealth.

Table 10.1 *Course Resources to Support Tangling With Race and Racism in U.S. Public Schools.*

Theoretical Frames	Learning more from Danita Mason-Hogans: Generational Chapel Hillian & civil rights historian	Primary source research: Joy and thriving at Lincoln HS (LHS), Chapel Hill (CH) history in the now
Studied asset/deficit frames together, practicing, naming and disrupting deficit frames	Ms. Mason-Hogans taught us about CH Black generational history, and the ways in which that history is entwined with our university's history.	The class took a field trip to the library to study a set of ephemera from one local high school, looking at them as artifacts that represent everyday ways of being. Each of the ephemera includes photographs, HS newspaper entries, and oral histories. All of these ephemera were produced by the high school's students, faculty, and community.
Learned about CCWM (Yosso, 2005), practiced using this as a way to "see" capital in video and textual artifacts	**** See Ms. Mason-Hogans' testimony below*	
Learned about Lawrence-Lightfoot's work and how to ask: "what is good here" in research and practice		Students were supported to analyze and learn from these ephemera using the lens of CCWM. Students were also asked to look for evidence of thriving and joy at the local high school.

Along the way, we practiced listening and seeing, learning and unlearning. Our work was interactive, drawing upon each other's sensemaking and class resources. These frames were our touchstones as we welcomed Ms. Mason-Hogans, a seventh-generation Black Chapel Hillian, and two members of the Chapel Hill Nine, Mr. Mason and Mr. Merritt, to our class. It helped us understand *Brown v. Board* with more nuance, and why Mr. Mason said of *Brown*: "We got what we wanted, but we lost what we had." In understanding, we continued to dream about how we (re)write history in more truthful ways and dream change into being.

I carry my ancestors with me wherever I go. The ancestors who instruct me, whose footprints I follow, and whose path I try to go forward together with Students. … I'm from CH, from seven generations on both sides of my family, and I come from people who were laborers for this university since the university's inception.

I descended from the Thomas A. Mason plantation, with Mason being one of the founders who donated land to establish the university and the town that surrounds it. Thomas A. Mason's plantation was so large that it encompassed three counties. It was a huge plantation and is still standing today. Although he is credited for being one of the founders of this university, he and other white founders did not fund the university alone. [It] was funded and built with Black escheated bodies on stolen native land, so families like mine were unwilling economic founders too. The ancestors in my family go back to the native people, and on the plantation from time to time you can find little arrowheads or artifacts that indicate that we were there. Before the colonists came, there were native people on that soil. The trees talk to me sometimes when I travel to the plantation, and they tell the stories of my ancestors. Some of them labored by gathering water from the well to wash with and cook. Some hauled wood to warm houses and purify water. Some provided transportation by horse and buggy to and from the university. But a vast majority of the people that I descend from were farmers. We were pig farmers, and we had corn, and we had crops that helped to cultivate nutrition for the community and for the university. Black people in this town laid the foundation literally for the university, so, I'm very proud to descend from this family, that with their brilliance, creativity, and hard, uncompensated labor, built and sustained our nation's first public university.

Figure 10.1 *Histories Overlooked: Sophia's Reflections and Responses to Ms. Mason-Hogans' Talk.*

Sophia's reflection on how the university was built by people who were enslaved.
"The Battle House. The Battle Hall. All these buildings have a name on them. The streets are named for slave-holding families. But you can't even find the names of the people who built this place."
Sophia's uncovering of how a place she treasures is connected to historical abuse and mistreatment that has been overlooked and forgotten.
"My perspective and the single story of this house have been challenged by a complete contrast: where I saw a foundation of the generosity of grace, there is also a foundation of greed and abuse. Where I experience truth-seeking critical discussions over the modern interpretation of scripture, is a place where the same texts were abused for many years."

It's important for people who are associated with the university and have inherited the fruits of this free labor to know about the community that surrounds the university and are still here laboring for and living under the grandeur of [this school's] reputation. When a person typically thinks about [this school], the conditions of its creation do not typically come to mind. The university often is known for its great wealth. It [has] a huge endowment. It's also very aptly known for the medical research that it has conducted over the years. It's known for university expansion. I'm 56 years old now, and I have never known a point in my life where the university was not expanding. There's always a new building. There's always new construction going on at the university. Also, because so many professors and people who are connected with the university place a lot of children in our local education system, the local town and city schools are at the top of many people's lists of great school systems. My mother used to work at the Admissions office, … starting in 1969. The students that went to [the local public schools] even had special consideration because the school system was supposed to be so good for the students.

Of course, people know about [our] football and basketball. They know about the sports, and [we] local people are very proud to be from [this town], and we wear sweatshirts and t-shirts and go to the games to mark our pride in our hometown. When we were coming up, most of the young men that I went to school with, my brother and my cousins, would go to the games and sell sodas and other snacks on the game weekends. This tradition goes all the way back to even my father, who started when he was three years old. My grandfather would put a little bow tie on him, and he would go and serve at the fraternity houses.

Figure 10.2 *Continued and Growing Pride in the University: Students' Reflections and Responses to Ms. Mason-Hogans' Talk.*

<table>
<tr><td>University pride, shared across generations.

"It once was carted over to the street every Saturday home football game, southern tailgating tradition ingrained in my lifestyle as I tried to swindle college students walking by into paying $4 for a blue solo cup of Country Crock powder mix lemonade. My father talks about work, he asks about school, after all, he is a [institution] alumni and likes to see how the university has changed." Shelby</td></tr>
<tr><td>University pride of place.

"The flood of [institution] blue in one of the busiest areas on campus is a vivid reminder of the widespread feeling of pride people feel regarding this university and the community which it has built." Evelyn</td></tr>
<tr><td>The joy that the university instills in its students that is never forgotten.

"Living here, with the history and views and people, has allowed for me, or so I think, to have the best experience at [university] a freshman could ask for." Mackenzie</td></tr>
</table>

So, my family, for generations, has had a really unique view of [this university:] The view from the servant quarters. The perspective is different from the narrative that a lot of people talk about when they talk about [this school]. … The wonderful time that they spent [here], whether it was four or forty years, was made possible by a community largely invisible to them, with a vastly different perspective of the university.

What is not known as widely is that, yes, [this institution] has a billion-dollar endowment. But the university was established unlike a lot of universities, with escheated labor. An escheat is when somebody passes away, and there are no heirs to the property, and their property then is given to the state. And my ancestors, Black people, were considered property. So not only were Black people the laborers who sustained the university, the laborers who built the university; we were also the physical and financial foundation of this great university through our role as escheated property and the unpaid labor force of construction workers, housekeepers, cooks, transportation providers, and farmers. So yes, [this school] has wealth. Our perspective is that that wealth came at a cost to Black people.

Figure 10.3 *Investigating Shared and Unequal Histories: Students' Reflections and Responses to Ms. Mason-Hogans' Talk.*

<table>
<tr><td>

Reflecting on the African Americans who built the university, and who was to reap the benefits of the university.

"I left the arboretum curious: Who was a part of the skillful construction efforts? What efforts did they go through so … [the] arboretum could be built? This little grotto masks the resilience and labor of the minority community and of activists who advocated for educational equity in [town]. It stands clear that the university was not built for people of color." Saira

</td></tr>
<tr><td>

Investigating university spaces and illustrating the drastic difference in respect and honor for white and African American people.

"As I pass the white area, I am intrigued by the historical architecture of the intricate headstones as they commemorate and celebrate prominent old white members of the Chapel Hill community. In contrast, as I near the African American area of the cemetery, the only emotions I am greeted with are an air of sadness and shame." Yara

</td></tr>
</table>

Medical research is something that [this university] is known for. The question for us local, generational Black people is: who do you think that research was visited upon? Eugenics was practiced here, and on local Black people. Because we were in such close proximity to the university, we were the very first victims of this medical research. And I would argue and contend that [that] medical research still goes on today.

University expansion was also at a cost for us local Black folks. I can't tell you how many times the local Black community was displaced and moved around, and many of us, including myself, who are from this area, cannot afford to live here in [town] anymore. The heavy cost of this disruption, in my case, [is] a tear in the legacy of seven generations of people who have lived [here].

Figure 10.4 *Investigating Familial and Communal Entanglements: Students' Reflections and Responses to Ms. Mason-Hogans' Talk.*

Reflecting on the wealth gap, gentrification, and pushing historical communities out of neighborhoods.

"I had some experiences with [the elementary school] area where Danita grew up. My home borders that district, my younger sisters got redistricted to attend new … elementary when it was built in the 2010s. This caused discussion in our home about how it would 'lower property value' for the house." Shelby

The local education system is highlighted and heralded all over the country. What people don't talk about is that [the local public school system] has the second largest achievement and opportunity gap in the nation. We have the greatest wealth gap in the state. So, there are a lot of things that the university is known for that our family did not benefit from. What we do have, however, are seven generations of memories. They are parallel memories to the University, and we hold these memories along with our [local] pride.

We hold memories of people like my ancestor, Sally Mason, who had the words written on her tombstone: "our black mammy." Her reward for being such a good servant to the Thomas A. Mason clan was to be buried inside the gate with the white Mason family, and outside of the area with her children—to be buried with the white family so that she could serve them once she got to heaven. This was a normative practice [here]. So, we don't talk about that type of history. We don't talk about how difficult it was to get a job and obtain land after the Civil War, how some of our ancestors literally had to live in the woods. Some of us had to live in the woods in order to survive, and developed all kinds of diseases of malnutrition, such as rickets and pellagra, because we did not have a lot of food to eat. Some of the stories that are also passed down in our family come from great [my] grandfather who spoke of his father who was enslaved, and shared how the slave master would put hog grease on the faces of the enslaved folks so that he could make it seem to his white peers that he was feeding [the] enslaved people, and he was not.

Figure 10.5 *Learning About Segregated Cemeteries on Campus: Students' Reflections and Responses to Ms. Mason-Hogans' Talk.*

"A new level of shame plagues me as I reflect on the University's inequitable history with the cemetery. In the past, during a [football] game, desperate and disrespectful visitors parked on the African American section of the graveyard with no regard for the bodies that lay beneath their tires." Yara
"Excited conversation creates a festive air in contrast to the eerie cemetery atmosphere; however, no amount of progress and joy could eraste the segregated history that lies within the ... cemetery." Yara

We talk about New Deal legislation which meant so much to growth and expansion of the University. But not for somebody like my grandfather, a WWII vet; yet, he and others like him, were largely locked out of many of the benefits of the GI Bill programs and other grants that helped to expand this University.

Figure 10.6 *Coming to Question: Students' Reflections and Responses to Ms. Mason-Hogans' Talk.*

"At one point, she (Danita Mason-Hogans) talked about the last name Battle, and how it originated from a prominent family in [town] ... I wondered if this Kemp P. Battle had anything to do with the beautiful Battle House which I had come to love over the past month." Sophia
Questions whether histories of racism discourage students of color from applying to the university. "I wondered to myself, why is it that more people of color are not interested in attending the university." Justin

And throughout it all, the memories that we hold are also the astonishing beauty that comes from this community—the strong sense of family, kinship, cooperation, help, and unity that is also our hallmark. I think right now, we're in such a polarized time, and it's important to look back in the ways that we worked together collectively to solve issues and problems and behold the many points of pride, brilliance, and resilience that come with being a local Black community member. We hold those memories, too, close to our hearts. So, we have many parallel histories to the University, and our story has not largely been told by this University, because we're in the shadows. We have other, more personal stories and observances of people whom the world views with great prominence at the University, because my family were servants to these folks.

Figure 10.7 *Love and Critique, Together: Students' Reflections and Responses to Ms. Mason-Hogans' Talk.*

Love, critique, together.

"We all wanted to create a community from the predominantly white community … to celebrate our traditions." Chi

---

Showcasing how a community that has been targeted for oppression found resilience and inspiration when looking at/admiring the photos of African Americans protesting.

"These black and white photographs with words like resilience and rebellion proudly printed above them, ingrained a feeling of pride within me. Even though I had never known these people and was not even familiar with the particular strings of protests, I was inspired and felt connected to these protestors." Wyatt

---

A lot of the work that I do is to talk about the beauty and the majesty of the people who lived here and of the local Civil Rights era. Our segregated Black high school students organized, planned, and executed their own sit-in on February 28, 1960, all by themselves … and how beautiful, powerful women developed strategies to keep our community together and strong through the Civil Rights movement, and how they brought the first cadre of Black nurses to the university. There's so much to be proud of, and so many beautiful memories that we hold here at this big university that casts such a huge shadow.

Portraiture Assignment

We practiced using these resources together, in class, with video and textual artifacts. Following this work, students completed their portraiture assignments. Portraiture is a qualitative research methodology developed by Lawrence-Lightfoot (1983). We read Lawrence-Lightfoot's work and engaged together in learning about this research methodology. Davis (2003), who co-authored a book on portraiture with Lawrence-Lightfoot, wrote: "the research portrait, a written narrative, is imprinted with the researcher's understanding of, and relationship with, the individual or site that is represented in the test. Like the artist, the research portraitist works to balance elements of context, thematic structure, relationship, and voice into an aesthetic whole that is so carefully constructed that every part seems an essential ingredient in the clarity of cohesive interpretation" (p. 199). Students read sections of other students' written portraitures, guidelines of which are detailed in Table 10.2; these comprise the corpus of data for this analysis.

Table 10.2 *Portraiture Assignment.*

Portraiture assignment:
Practice exploring, recognizing, and naming the assets of a community
Guidelines:
(1) The purpose of this assignment is to give you practice viewing communities in asset-filled ways, beginning to build your capacity for understanding the social, cultural, and historical contexts of a community.
(2) Draw from Dr. Lawrence-Lightfoot and think about the structures and forces that might not be immediately visible when walking around a community. Ask yourself: "What is the social, historical, and economic history of the community?"
(3) Spend time observing people, businesses, flyers. Find local newspapers and neighborhood message boards to supplement your noticings.
(4) Consider: "Whose voices are highlighted? What details are provided?"
(5) Write your portraiture focusing on a facet of the community as seen by you, an outsider.

Methods

Guided by our research questions, our analyses interrogated students' trajectories of learning and unlearning, tracing the ideas we came with, and how we challenged these ideas and worked with criticality towards more racially-just understandings. As undergraduate researchers, Justin and Shelby simultaneously conducted research and learned what it is to *do* research. This dual process of learning is represented in Figure 10.8.

Figure 10.8 *Timeline of Student Growth and Research Methodology.*

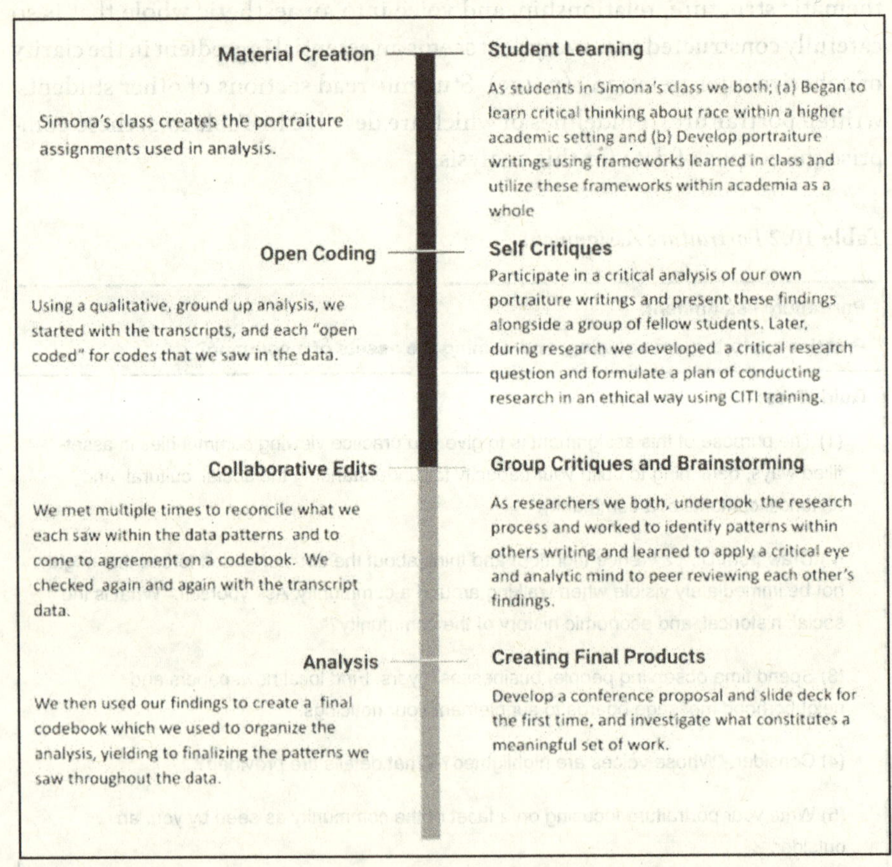

In Professor Simona's class, students both: (a) began to learn how to think critically about race within a university setting and (b) developed portraiture writings using frameworks learned in class and practiced using these frameworks. In class, students heard alternative viewpoints from each other, creating discourse and opening up opportunities to learn from each other. During class time students were given the opportunity to opt into sharing their portraiture assignments for this study. Per the stipulations of our IRB, the consent form was administered by an independent individual, and Professor Simona was not present at this time. The permissions were then held until after the grading period and were shared with Professor Simona only after the course grading period was closed. Twenty-two students participated in the study.

The research team de-identified the data, assigning pseudonyms, and paying careful attention to students' gender, ethnic, and racial identities. This was done to manage bias and maintain anonymity while safeguarding the identity-related associations of students' names.

The papers were read separately by the research team. Together, we developed an inductive and deductive codebook—beginning with Yosso's (2005) Community Cultural Wealth (CCW) capitals and looking for patterns in the data itself. The researchers repeated this process of identifying patterns, meeting bi-weekly to discuss and test emergent codes. We continued iteratively until no new codes emerged. The research team then worked to build a codebook and organize it. Again, this work was done separately and then together. Throughout this whole codebook-building process, researchers checked multiple times with transcript data to be precise and clear. The team then undertook the analysis process and worked to identify patterns within the data, applying a critical eye and analytic mind to coding the data. After finalizing our analysis, the research team developed a conference proposal and slide deck, something new to the two undergraduate researchers, and investigated what constitutes a meaningful set of work.

Three key themes emerged from our data: These are Race Talk (Naming Race), Interrogation of Community and University Histories, and CCW (Utilizing (2005) Community Cultural Wealth (CCWM)). These terms are defined in Table 10.3.

Table 10.3 *Pattern and Code Definitions.*

CODE		DEFINITION
Race talk (Naming race)	Erasure	Choosing to ignore/diminish the importance of race/ethnic groups in society, which thus removes the impact of marginalized groups of people from society.
	Highlighting	Acknowledging the presence of race/ethnic groups regardless of an environment, positive or negative, and work advocating for change.
Interrogation of Community and University Histories: Naming History (NH) University Questioning (UQ)	NH: Challenging	Using the naming of history to constructively criticize the community and recognize the impact of historical events on today.
	NH: Stagnation	Actively using history to disenfranchise meaningful change in the community and support the area's status quo.
	UQ: Challenging	Constructively criticizing the faults in the University to ensure future progression and diversity.
	UQ: Stagnation	Actively disregarding the racist history of the University and overlooking the change that needs to occur to produce an inclusive environment.
Community Cultural Wealth (Utilizing Community Cultural Wealth Model)	Truth-Telling	Using the methods of Community Cultural Wealth in a way that advocates for those of marginalized communities and how those communities used such tactics to persevere through adversity.
	Weaponizing	Falsely applying Community Cultural Wealth by undermining the methods in which marginalized communities have used CCW to navigate life, and incorrectly applying CCW to non-marginalized groups of people.

Results

Our research analysis revealed three patterns in the data: 1) *Naming Race— From Race Erasure to Race Highlighting*, 2) *Questioning University History— From Challenging to Stagnation*, and 3) *CCW— From Weaponization to Truth-Telling.*

Naming Race—From Race Erasure to Race Highlighting is a trend in the data in which the students named race along a continuum. On one end of the continuum, student writing featured the erasure of any mention of race, while other students chose to explicitly name race within the community. Another finding that emerged from data analysis was that students of color were more apt to name and analyze the role of race in their portraiture assignments whereas white students were more apt to be race-evasive, avoiding discussion about the complexity that race has at the University (Annamma et al., 2017). For example, in her writing, Adara names race in her observations of students in a campus setting, elaborating on moments of joy and celebration, and belonging: "I hear African music coming from the table advertising OASIS, the Organization for African Students' Interests and Solidarity, smell food from the Asian American Students Association and see numerous tables and people crowded around them, immersing themselves in their culture or learning about others right there in the pit." Adara pulls in many clubs and organizations from a variety of cultures while acknowledging their benefit. In contrast, Amelia states, "All I could see as I tried to study the atmosphere of the old drugstore was people from all walks of life enjoying a meal in a friendly and welcoming environment." This statement from, later in her writing, Amelia describes seeing a variety of people from all races, when in reality Amelia only states seeing one Asian woman and one African American woman in a diner with many people, the rest of whom were white.

The second pattern, *Questioning University History—From Challenging to Stagnation,* also is arrayed across a continuum. This continuum, *Naming History,* ranges from analyzing and holding the University accountable for its relationship with slavery, discrimination, and racism to not naming that history and instead presenting partial or incomplete historical tellings. Likewise, as in the first pattern, students of color often wrote about the University's racist past while white students more often resisted discussing the University's connection to slavery. In these instances, students honored the Uiversity founders for what they had done without addressing the discrimination and racism that they enacted. In the following example, Sophia, a white religious student, wrote about how she came to question the naming of a place that she loved, the Battle House:

> *I wondered if this Kemp P. Battle had anything to do with the beautiful Battle House which I had come to love over the past month. I assumed it had*

> *been named after some battle … but some quick research proved otherwise*
> *… not only was he an avid proponent of the institution of slavery, but he*
> *was a member of the Baptist church which twisted words in the Bible in*
> *support of slavery, something that [the Bible] definitely does not do. … He*
> *is also known for signing the secession papers for this state and his family*
> *being long-time slave owners who deeply mistreated those they enslaved.*

Here, Sophia challenges herself to investigate the naming of a place on campus that was meaningful to her. She does not shy away from this history. Nor, importantly, does she reject the Battle House. Instead, she plots a path forward to make this history better known. Meanwhile, Mackenzie clouds history's grievances as she dismisses segregation: "It housed the most African American students in comparison to other dorms in the 1970s, and it led to segregation accusations."

At the other end of the continuum, is *University Questioning*. Analysis of how students questioned and challenged pervasive issues and norms within the institution and its surrounding communities revealed that students discussed the history of the University in three distinct ways. These ways included: (1) Identifying injustices in hopes of creating change; (2) Naming ways in which improvements could be made; and (3) Remaining stagnant within the current culture (by not naming issues or by claiming that certain issues are historical and no longer relevant). Importantly, students' portraiture assignments (a) identified and/or (b) named language that was either explicitly or implicitly hateful. Instead, a feature of examples in this pattern was that students coupled challenges to the status quo with writing about their hopes to improve the University and town so it could be a place the community rallied around and drew inspiration from. We see questioning with love in another student, Justin's writings. He states, "Why is it that more people of color are not interested in attending [this University]? … To change the current … narrative … [we] must continue to advocate for the inclusion and immersion of more students of color as well as to hire staff that can relate to all students."

The third pattern of utilizing the *CCWM—From Weaponization to Truth-Telling*, examined how students used CCWM in their analyses. CCWM was introduced in class as a theoretical framework that could be leveraged to analyze the often-dismissed strengths of historically marginalized communities.

In this pattern, we saw that some students referenced CCWM in ways that illuminated the resilience of marginalized communities and the systems of oppression within institutions. In contrast, other students used the terms of CCWM in ways that were not congruent with the CCWM, and instead in ways that reinforced stereotypes. This misuse took on the form of weaponization (Goldin et al., 2021). For example, we see this in the following statement by Mark, "A potential catastrophe for the worker was avoided all because of the love and support shown from my peers, and I would even dare say this could tie into familial capital." Mark uses familial capital to describe an all-white space and promote the strengths of this space. Others, though, used the CCWM lens to see and name the strengths of communities of color. For example, Sage wrote: "Through the creation of the displays, the staff has chosen to highlight historically marginalized voices in multiple instances, such as with the National Hispanic Heritage Month display. … This accumulation of efforts to highlight the voices of minorities in the [local] community and the literature available to the public speaks to the type of environment that the staff is seeking to create." Here, Sage noted the ways in which the town library [the place Sage had chosen to write a portraiture of] was organizing its offerings in ways that reflected the CCWM extant in the community, not erasing those strengths but centering them.

Discussion: Questioning with Love

> *"I didn't know what to do with these negative histories,*
> *but something in me knew that it was the wrong choice*
> *to just stuff [them] away."*

We center what we have learned about theory, about this place's complicated and interwoven histories, and about schooling in the segregated south to see better, to name race and racism in our spaces. As students, teachers, and community members, we see our findings as illuminating the process of learning racial literacy. We also see that while arguments swirl around us about the "dangers" of critical race theory and the ways that it could incite hatred, our findings show the opposite. One consistent finding is that as students used critical frames to understand themselves and our institution, their commitment to that institution grew. This can be seen in this quote, which is a representative example of how students spoke about their commitments given their new knowledge and understandings: "Adjusting to the needs that many students of color lack will help create a better environment for all the students that [this University] welcomes while becoming the university that I am proud to be a part of on the inside and out."

Our analysis helps us to better understand trajectories of learning, and that students' racial literacy develops in uneven ways. The results highlight a pattern of duality—of questioning and reaffirming, of challenging and upholding. Inspired by the resources in the course itself, we conclude with the importance of bringing grace and opportunities to this endeavor. This research highlights promise(s): we see that education is effective at leading students to question, relearn, and create change. This is true, we saw, even while we also saw evidence of how systemic racism affected some of our uses of class resources. Learning is messy, which we saw especially in the ways in which some students used resources—such as CCW – to reinforce or uphold deficit frames. Some students did struggle in their attempts to bring resources from inside the classroom outside, into the world.

All students showed growth. Their growth, ultimately, falls on a continuum, from those who were, by the end of the class, still struggling and working to use asset-based frames with fluency to those who stumbled, and whose analysis and use of class resources was inconsistent or even damaging.

The student voices in this research team proclaim: Together we will be able to both teach one another and guide one another as we strive to create a better environment, locally and globally. "What is good here" (Lawrence-Lightfoot & Davis, 2002) is that there is a generation that is ready to learn and create the change that has been needed for decades. We have stretched ourselves to practice building criticality and racial literacy, not stopping at the porch steps, but naming the political in the personal. We are not there yet, but we are emboldened, and we have had important practice developing our own racial literacy in the service of disruption.

Implications for Learners and Critical Pedagogues

We conclude with implications, beginning with the research team's own reflections on what made speaking about race and racism difficult, and what enabled us, despite these difficulties, to have substantive conversations in our university classroom.

Figure 10.9. *Reflections: Implications for Learners.*

COMBINATION OF THESE THINGS MAKE SPEAKING ABOUT RACE AND RACISM DIFFICULT:	COMBINATION OF THESE THINGS ENABLED DIFFICULT CONVERSATIONS:
(1) ways that we do not talk about race in many white spaces, so there's little muscle memory/development of ability/nature of talking about race PLUS (2) the potential for harm is so great AND (3) we don't see this as something that can be learned, instead you have <u>it</u> or you don't	• Knowledge that everyone was coming from a place of understanding. Everyone there was there to collaborate. • Norms – norm of speaking in draft • Could participate when felt need to participate. Didn't feel compelled to speak for a grade • Asked to clarify, but not because I thought that that was the wrong answer… • Students also felt comfortable disagreeing w each other. Moments of tension where there was back and forth.

Our collective understandings, presented in Table 10.3 refract on and are extended by implications for critical pedagogues, summarized in Table 10.4 below.

Table 10.4 *Implications for Critical Pedagogues.*

Implications for critical pedagogues
Ground learning and inquiry in theory: including critical theories and asset-based theoretical frameworks
Scaffold learning practices, especially regarding leveraging theory in analysis
Disrupting hierarchies of knowledge: Provides multiple, rich opportunities to learn from and investigate primary source ephemera Studies, reads, and listens to counter stories and first-person testimonies
Construct and practice learning norms that: Reframe learning as a verb Enable students to learn from one another as the class community co-develops collective understandings Revise and improve students' ideas over time
Asset-frame learners will: Position learners as sense-makers Set ambitious learning goals (e.g., disruption of common patterns of color-evasion, paired with meaningful supports) Provide multiple opportunities to draft and redraft ideas, and to receive, give, and incorporate feedback

It is in the interactional and relational opportunities for learners and their teachers that freedom dreaming and radical imaginations engender change.

Reference

Annamma, S. A., Jackson, D. D., & Morrison, D. (2017). Conceptualizing color-eva-siveness: Using dis/ability critical race theory to expand a color-blind racial ideology in education and society. *Race Ethnicity and Education, 20*(2), 147-162.

Calfas, J. (2018, August 21). Why UNC's "silent Sam" statue was focus point of protest. *Time.* https://time.com/5373001/silent-sam-confederate-statue-unc-racist-history/

Chow, J. (2019, April 29). SPECIAL ISSUE: How generations of Cambodian Americans in Long Beach are embracing two cultures. *Daily Forty-Niner*

Davis, J. H. (2003). Balancing the whole: Portraiture as methodology. In P. M. Camic, J. E. Rhodes, & L. Yardley (Eds.), *Qualitative research in psychology: Expanding perspectives in methodology and design* (pp. 199–217). American Psychological Association.

Goldin, S., Khasnabis, D., O'Connor, C., & Hearn, K. (2021). Tangling with race and racism in teacher education: Designs for counterstory-based parent teacher conferences. *Urban Education, 56*(9), 1399-1428.

Lawrence-Lightfoot, S. (1983). *The good high school: Portraits of character and culture.* Basic Books.

Lawrence-Lightfoot, S., & Davis, J. H. (2002). *The art and science of portraiture.* John Wiley & Sons.

Love, B. L. (2019). *We want to do more than survive: Abolitionist teaching and the pursuit of educational freedom.* Beacon Press.

Tatum, B. D. (2007). *Can we talk about race?: And other conversations in an era of school resegregation.* Beacon Press.

UNCOFTHEPEOPLE. (2018, May 24). Old Chapel Hill Cemetery. *Reclaiming the University of the People.* https://uncofthepeople.com/2018/05/24/old-chapel-hill-cemetery/

Yosso, T. J. (2005). Whose culture has capital? A critical race theory discussion of community cultural wealth. *Race ethnicity and education, 8*(1), 69-91.

CHAPTER 11

Dreaming of Different Pasts, Presents, & Futures:
Filipino & Cambodian American Youth-Led Art & Organizing in California

Charlotee Austria, Chelsea Chhem, J Jimenez, May Lin, and Madison San Luis

Introduction

DREAMING TRANSPORTS US to another time. As Robin Kelley (2002) contends, radical imagination ignites our abilities to "see the future in the present" and to "realize that things need not always be this way" (p. 9). When daydreaming, we embrace an alternative reality as momentary respite from a present rife with drudgery or trauma. We are visited by ancestors we never had a chance to meet. Through dream-filled organizing, we can construct portals "into futures we cannot currently imagine" (Ritchie, 2023, p. 7) by foreshadowing those futures in our intimate, everyday practices. We build on Black, Indigenous, Southeast Asian, and Filipina/o/x scholar-organizers' feminist and queer conceptualizations of dreaming to show how youth organizing and art revive our ancestors' dreams, enact dreams through present actions, and facilitate dreams of more abundant futures.

We draw on our lived experience as youth leaders or alums from Filipino and Cambodian/Southeast Asian youth organizing groups (Char, J, Mady, and

Chelsea) and as a social movement-based educator at a university in California (May). We aim to rupture historical amnesia by extending the legacies of our ancestors', families', and community members' dreams. These dreams are found in lush gardens bursting forth from small plots of land juxtaposed with cracked concrete in Cambodiatown, and in the laughter of Filipino elders gathering for early Saturday morning strolls on a sidewalk that is freshly paved because of their organizing. Immigrant and refugee dreams of brick-and-mortar businesses, restorations of homes they were forced to leave, and political organizing have enabled their children to wonder, dream, and live out different futures.

We also discuss how we plant seeds for unapologetically hopeful futures through our art-making and organizing that reject the equation of dreaming with luxury. Daring to dream is an act of resistance when insidious ideologies of the American Dream and ageism conspire to ridicule young people's dreams as naive fantasies. As Chelsea once shared with May: "We deserve love and happiness, just as much as we deserve [the policies] we were fighting for." Young people's dreams of happiness are just as direly needed as policy change. This dream is realized as youth organize for a better collective future while refusing to defer urgently needed joy and healing through making art. By rehearsing the future we imagine, we pave the way to more capacious dreams of the future not confined to threadbare survival but abounding with creativity, collectivity, and joy.

Art as Dream-Making: Disrupting Stolen Time

We must dream to reclaim time because Filipino and Cambodian American communities have often been forced to live in dreams and times that are not of their own making. Allan Punzalan Isaac (2021) points out that "much migrant Filipino labor is paid to make time for others" (p. 9). For example, Filipina caregivers must sacrifice precious time with their loved ones as they labor to make time for others' ability to enjoy quality time with their families. Meanwhile, Cambodian refugees experience "refugee temporality:" an enduring "long and unbroken time and space of … captivity" that sustains rather than resolves the violence of U.S. imperialism (Tang, 2015, p. 21). Isaac and Tang point to how war, genocide, and militarism live on, albeit obscured by historical amnesia. We know this because we experience structural violence as stolen time—as young people expedited into adulthood, juggling caregiving responsibilities, work, and school. When deprived of time, our imaginations shrink, and it becomes "difficult to see anything other than the present" (Kelley, 2002, p. 11).

Through art, immigrant and refugee communities can re-claim ownership over time and dreams. Espiritu and Duong (2018) outline a feminist refugee epistemology that recalibrates time, when artists as "displaced people remember, forge, and transform a past that has been long suppressed" (p. 595). For example, Cambodian American artists revive cultural traditions pushed to the brink of extinction by the mass slaughter of cultural works during the Khmer Rouge: aided and abetted by U.S. militaristic bloodlust (Schlund-Vials, 2012). Filipino artists contest "the *erasure* of the extraordinarily violent historical circumstances surrounding the emergence of the Filipino's visibility" (See, 2019, p. 1). Yet time constraints also limit our ability to consume and create art. As Hayes and Kaba (2023) assert: "Capitalism robs us of our time, exhausting our bodies and minds. … How many times have you planned to check out a museum exhibit, a lecture, a podcast, an art installation … and found that you simply do not have the time or energy?" (p. 84).

This conundrum underscores why grassroots organizing is needed to reshape social, economic, and political conditions that inhibit dreaming. Youth and community organizing strategies to build power, such as leadership development, campaigns, critical consciousness, and identity development (Rogers et al., 2012), remain crucial. Yet organizing groups have increasingly recognized that we must dream bigger and experiment more boldly to rupture tired cycles of oppression that ensnare us. After all, freedom dreaming envisions a "total transformation of society," with "new social relationships, new ways of living and interacting, new attitudes towards work and leisure and community" (Kelley, 2002, p. 5). We cannot reproduce the same oppressions that we combat by glorifying constant work and urgency that foster burnout and compound trauma (Lee, 2014). Accordingly, art-making practice shows how we refuse the compounding of stolen time in organizing spaces to dream for different futures.

Context & Methodologies

To illuminate what dreaming and disrupting time look like, we draw on our experiences organizing in and supporting two youth-led organizing groups in California.

Anakbayan (Char, J, and Mady):

We have been leaders in our local chapter of Anakbayan ("Children of the People" in Tagalog) since 2022 and 2017. We draw from our perspectives as university undergraduates and alumni who are studying or have studied Asian American studies, political science, sociology, and/or studio art. We are also informed by experiences organizing academic student works (Char) and high school youth, LGBTQ+ communities, and renters (J). Char and J discuss our high school and college arts classes to reflect on tensions between the art world and community organizing. Meanwhile, Mady led the foregrounding of our experiences as children of migrants forced to come to the U.S. while making connections to the struggles of students from other backgrounds.

Anakbayan organizes Filipino youth and students from the working class, peasantry, and all sectors for national democracy in the Philippines. We are part of one of many overseas chapters addressing policies that displace Filipinos and compel them to work elsewhere while sending remittances back home. We focus on our university and other areas with large Filipino youth populations and organize with other groups in the Los Angeles metropolitan region, which is home to the largest Filipino diaspora (Budiman, 2021). We aim to liberate the Philippines from U.S. imperialism and to uphold the Filipinos' democratic rights against fascism and local puppet ruling classes, while building solidarity with students from all backgrounds to undo the shackles of U.S. imperialism and capitalism. For example, in fall 2023, our chapter engaged in student coalitional campaigns, conducting educational workshops and mobilizing students and community members to protest tuition hikes in our state university system, U.S.-funded occupation and genocide of Palestinians, and anti-worker policies and environmental plunder across the global south at the Asia-Pacific Economic Cooperation (APEC) summit.

Khmer Girls in Action and Invest in Youth (Chelsea and May)

We reflect on artmaking in Khmer Girls in Action (KGA) and the Invest in Youth (IIY) coalition. Chelsea is a daughter of Cambodian refugees and was a KGA leader during high school from 2015-2019, including leadership in IIY from 2017-2019. She is an artist deeply committed to preserving the power of the people and restoring art in uprooted communities. May volunteered with KGA and IIY, including at college preparation workshops and the Khmer Justice Program for juniors and seniors, where she worked with Chelsea (2018-2020). She is also a KGA board member (2021-present).

KGA is a Southeast Asian young women-led organization that builds power through grassroots community organizing, full participation of young women, and creating cultures of healing. Youth leaders participate in tiered leadership development programs that include political education, where they critically analyze histories that led to our city in California becoming home to the largest population of Cambodians outside of Cambodia (Chow, 2019). KGA also anchors Invest in Youth (IIY), a coalition of multiple organizations led by low-income Black, Latina/o/x, queer, and/or gender non-conforming youth. These youth discovered that in fiscal year 2018, their city allocated $204 per youth on positive youth development compared to $10,500 per youth arrest. Yet their action research found that the city's residents preferred programs that "support the mental, physical, and holistic well-being of youth and teens to reach their full potential and thrive" rather than policing (Invest in Youth, n.d.). Employing multiple strategies (e.g., leadership development, Integrated Voter Engagement, storytelling, political education, and relationship-building with decision-makers), this chapter of IIY has raised funds for and implemented an Office of Youth Development guided by principles of youth co-governance and equity.

Motivation and Methodologies

May has taught and learned from Char and Mady in her Asian American studies classes and supported Chelsea with college and internship applications during and since her time at KGA. Char, Chelsea, J, and Mady teach May about international solidarity and the power of art in their respective communities.

We have all experienced the dismissal of dreaming and political organizing in educational contexts where communities are pressed for survival. For example, students consistently ask May what the "use" of ethnic studies is. We believe that uplifting our unapologetic dreaming and organizing could propel others to dream different possibilities beyond the suffocating constraints of racial and ethnic capitalism.

We foreground Char, Chelsea, J, and Mady's lived experiences and knowledge drawn from writing prompts informed by *testimonio*. Rooted in Latin American and Third World decolonization struggles, Freirian liberationist pedagogy, Chicana/o/x/Latina/o/x studies, and especially feminist epistemologies, *testimonio* situates personal testimonies of oppression within critiques of systemic injustices and possibilities for social change (Delgado Bernal et al., 2012). *Testimonio* intervenes in hierarchical knowledge production—here, uplifting queer, low-income, immigrant/refugee youth, and/or young women and People of Color's lived experience as powerful knowledge. May developed initial and follow-up questions rooted in context from experiences as a movement-based researcher and educator, guided by principles of critical community engaged scholarship (first conceptualized by Cynthia Gordon da Cruz) wherein university researchers partner with communities for broader aims of racial justice, radical love, and care (Gordon da Cruz, 2017; Lin, 2023). May drew on experiences supporting and attending KGA and IIY events and meetings and conducting staff and youth interviews (including one with Chelsea) from 2018-2019. Meanwhile, her conversations with Char, Mady, and J were guided by faculty-staff solidarity around the aforementioned issues of focus (e.g., tuition hikes, Palestine). We draw on individual and collective memories shaped by these contexts and our relationships to illuminate how we reclaim ownership over our own time and our own dreams through art.

Dreaming of Our Ancestors & Reclaiming The Past

May: Dreaming of our ancestors is key to our presents and futures. My only sibling, Hong, died in 2015. He unapologetically voiced and chased his dreams despite our family's desperate entreaties to be "practical;" he created the possibilities for my own dreams. Though he didn't live to see how I

*brought some of those dreams to fruition, the dreamworld is a place where
he isn't lost forever, where we can still meet, where I can tell him about my
hopes and struggles that he was integral to seeding.*

Chelsea, Char, J, and Mady's art and organizing, too, remake and live out
the dreams of their ancestors. They pierce through historical amnesia, embodying feminist refugee epistemologies, by calling attention to persistent refugee
temporalities and time stolen from Filipino migrants that have threatened to
sever them from rich histories. Their art also visualizes how Filipino peasants and Cambodian cultural workers continue resisting structural violence,
from state committed or sanctioned slaughter to wanton theft and erasure by
western institutions. Importantly, they are not reviving static notions of his-
torically-steeped cultural traditions but claiming ownership in ways relevant
to young people in their communities today.

Chelsea: Activating the Past

*In KGA, I learned about histories of displacement, war, and imperialism
that led to my family escaping the Khmer Rouge and resettling in Little
Cambodia in a city within California. I grew up in a tight-knit community,
where we could walk to neighbors to exchange persimmons for lemongrass
or meet up with aunties for a bowl of boat noodle soup. But I have witnessed gentrification erase the beauty of my community, causing people and
neighborhoods to disappear. This connection between history and present
informs my desire to become an art historian, curator, and illustrator who
protects and creates culturally sensitive and historically important art
forms. I joined KGA because in middle school, I saw KGA members proudly
marching during the Cambodian New Year parade, wearing bright teal
shirts and joining hands. I had never seen young women like me representing
our community, and I wanted to recreate that feeling of empowerment and
being seen for other young Cambodian women.*

*KGA gave me that opportunity in my first year, when I co-illustrated a col-
oring book called "InHer Bloom:" a play on the idea of inner blooming and*

radical transformation. I imagined young people dreaming and reconstructing ideas as they filled the pages with color, finding power in their identity, locality, and history. My own dreams came true when we went to the house of KGA's executive director, and I saw her young daughter coloring in our book. It was all I ever wanted. This dream continues as I seek to connect young Cambodian Americans to history through reviving vibrant Khmer imagery, such as apsara mermaid filigrees, temple etchings of Angkor Wat, and the textiles of Cambodian ballet dancers.

Figure 11.1 *Activating The Past*

Note 11.1. A digital illustration by Chelsea Chhem depicting Sophiline Cheam Shapiro performing a Cambodian classical dance, praying for the return of statues of Cambodian gods looted by British collectors.

"Activating the Past" (Figure 11.1) conveys the dual existence of how Cambodian objects and people are received in elite institutions. In 2023, Sophiline, who co-founded a California Khmer Arts Academy, was stopped by security guards while performing a dance for the return of god statues on display at the Metropolitan Museum of Art. These statues are there for visitors to see as sacred objects, as artifacts of the past. Contemporary Cambodian dancers are an integral part of paying tribute to the old gods; they activate the space through movement and prayer, usually within a temple setting. I illustrated an exchange of gazes locked between Sophiline and the statues: an intimate exchange between dancer and ritual object, recreating a connection to resemble rituals in the temple. I drew Sophiline wearing a black and gold traditional Cambodian textile that was refashioned into a modern silhouette.

In contrast, I emphasize the Met's display of the objects in a white cube. This cube de-contextualizes history and the spiritual, cultural, and political presence of the ancient gods: deactivating their spiritual resonance, with no future promises of repatriation. But Sophiline's performance sparked the urgency of Cambodia's request that its objects be returned, re-coining their status as what she described as "Blood Statues." I visualized her dancer's scarf in a fitting shade of blood red to reference the statue's stolen nature. I am inspired by her brilliant strides to recontextualize Khmer art in museum spaces. Her bravery is evocative of ancient ancestral respect—an ethos that I carry into shaping museums and other art spaces in my own future.

Char, J, and Mady: Land to the Tillers

In Spring 2023, members of our chapter created a patch to display at the BAYAN 2023 Congress, where other Anakbayan chapters also shared cultural works. Our "Land to the Tillers" patch (Figure 11.2) pays tribute to peasant struggles for agrarian revolution and genuine land redistribution (Figure 11.2). This patch underscores historical and ongoing conditions of neo-colonialism, semi-feudalism, and imperialism behind land theft from peasant farmers, Indigenous people, and farmworkers. For example, intersecting feudal land policies and failed land reform have led to *haciendas* (family estates) holding thousands of hectares of land, and multinational corporations and foreign governments plundering natural resources (Ocasiones, 2018). In this patch, we tell the stories of Filipino peasants who are forced to serve imperialist interests while living and working in extreme poverty and the conditions that link us as diaspora in the U.S. to the Philippines, even while tearing our families apart physically.

Figure 11.2 *"Land to the Tillers" Patch.*

Note 11.2. Our Anakbayan chapter-created patch depicting a *carabao* (water buffalo) holding a *kampilan* (sword) in its mouth.

This patch also tells stories of pride in histories of peasant-led revolution. For example, farmers demanding land reform have taken over haciendas, bearing signs with the slogan "Land to the Tillers, Not to their Killers" to condemn extractive practices and remember those murdered by the state during past uprisings (Ocasiones, 2018). To develop the patch, Char drew inspiration from famous artworks of Filipinos waging militant revolution. The *carabao*, which helps farmers till the land to prepare the soil for planting crops, has been used to represent peasant and farmer Filipinos in revolutionary art. For example, in the *May 1ˢᵗ Mural* by Kalipunan ng Damayang Mahihirap, a militant alliance that fights for the liberation of the Filipino urban poor, multiple figures representing various sectors unite against their exploiters. A peasant figure rides a *carabao*, representing the peasant class's resiliency, power, and vital role in waging revolution and liberating the Philippines. Meanwhile, the *kampilan* was used by various ethnic groups in pre-colonial Philippines, fashioned specifically for warfare. Char was inspired by Manuel Panares's painting, (2008), which depicts the warrior Lapu-Lapu from Mactan and other Filipino soldiers fighting Spanish conquistadores. Panares captures the moment when Lapu-Lapu is about to behead Magellan, leader of the conquistadores. The staging emphasizes the power of the Filipino figure raising the *kampilan* high above their heads, about to strike down the colonizer now in a position of submission.

Our patch depicts the historical, lasting power of the Filipino peasantry. Honoring our history and culture, telling stories of our resistance traditions, rejects the pressures of assimilation that surround us. For example, Char and J's required arts classes overwhelmingly focused on white, European and American men. Our curriculum subtly scripted artists from the Global South as "primitive," stuck in the past, while equating Western art with modernity. Our patch rejects this idea of history, instead recontextualizing our lives to paint a broader picture of our shared histories.

Present

Creating Time to Dream and Enact a Different Present for Youth (May)

This section discusses how the local Anakbayan Long Beach (ABLA) Khmer Girls in Action (KGA) members make time for art and practicing collectivity through art-making. By rejecting oppressive ideals of individualism and constant urgency, they rehearse their dreams of a future beyond imperialism and capitalism that they aim to bring into fruition. To contextualize Chelsea's discussion of the Invest in Youth logo, I provide background from my work with KGA and IIY in Spring 2019. Starting fall 2018, our IIY chapter had meticulously plotted a thoughtfully timed plan for a ballot initiative campaign to secure funding for an Office of Children and Youth for our city. But city decision-makers caught wind and requested that the organizers hold off. Although disheartened, organizers did not want to burn bridges with powerful allies and decided to shift spring and summer programming to focus on cultural work as a space of imagination. As KGA's executive director, Lian told me that KGA recognized the need for different rhythms of organizing, including necessarily fast-paced and activity packed times, and "slow down" times. Instead of long days of door-knocking and collecting signatures, youth leaders and staff took a breath and made the time to dream. Organizers recognized that this could be a welcome relief from the frustrations of trying to enact change on timelines dictated by stubbornly slow-moving institutions.

Khmer Justice Program (KJP), where I volunteered and got to know Chelsea, decided to develop a zine (do it yourself magazine) highlighting personal stories, photographs, artwork, and comic strips to personalize and visualize why it was important to invest in youth. During one workshop, the lead organizer Jenn drew out a butcher paper (Figure 11.3) to illustrate how dreaming, creativity, and imagination could break free from the constraints of what others deemed "practical" or "possible." They elaborated that,

> *a lot of time in action space … we're reacting … someone says something and then we're limited in what's possible. Like someone says … immigrants should go to jail and we're like oh, immigrants shouldn't go to jail! But in an ideas space, we're envisioning more what's possible; we can lean into that, yes … the world looks more beautiful, we have more space to envision it.*

They explained that KJP's zine and work on a summer annual arts showcase embodied this ideas space, where they would visually depict youth as lovable and worthy of care and investment.

Figure 11.3 *"Action Space" vs. "Idea Space"*

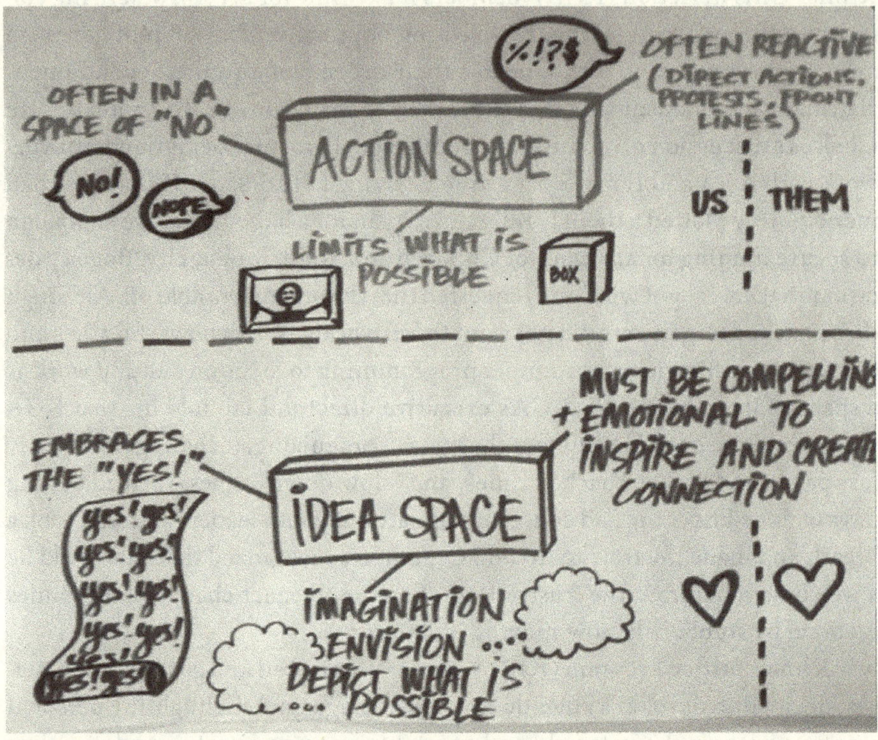

Note 11.3. Butcher paper illustrated by KGA organizer Jenn in spring 2019

Jenn's juxtaposition shows how dreaming carves out an alternative timeline, rupturing a sequence where decision-makers employ hegemonic discourses to set the possibilities, with youth organizers' responses following. Youth were often told by City Council that there was not enough money, that money had to be spent on "public safety," that they needed to be patient and await their turn (Lin & Patraporn, 2022). Meanwhile, polling revealed that residents bristled at the language of "teenagers," which Joy, communications director, characterized as a racialized and classed stigma, assuming that teenagers are "troublesome" or not "worth the investment." These challenges hint at refugee temporalities, where claims of inevitable disinvestment extend violences of the past to the present and a future of deprivation that seems to stretch on forever. By making time for dreaming, KGA and the local chapter of IIY claimed present ownership of their own time and parameters of possibility. Furthermore, as Chelsea's discussion shows, the campaign uplifted the power, vibrancy, and culture of Black and Brown, queer, and low-income youth *now*—not just as an adult or future in the making.

Chelsea—the Invest in Youth Logo

Figure 11.4 *Invest in Youth Logo*

Note 11.4. Logo for the Invest in Youth coalition, designed by Chelsea Chhem

KGA staff invested in me when they saw my talents and interests as a budding artist in high school. Rather than paying an outside contractor, they gave me my first digital art tools to develop a logo for the Invest in Youth campaign (Figure 11.4). I was inspired to develop my own typeface by the rebellious nature and stylized bold lettering of youth graffiti art on my high school walls, freeway ramps, and hidden between the buildings I walked by on my way to school. I also wanted to integrate KGA's symbolism and logo. The teal color represents the water of the rising lotus flower, referencing KGA's anthem, "Like a Lotus, We Rise." To visualize youth empowerment, I transformed the apex and tail of each letter into arrows, creating a sense of movement and energy in youth-led protests that I attended as part of KGA and IIY. In an earlier design, I drew a young person spray painting an institutional building in direct reference to dismantling larger systems of oppression. Here, I recreate the visual of dismantling institutions by combining arrows from the typology with vertical bars of the dollar sign to mimic a Greco-Roman building. The stylized dollar sign is an overt symbol of money and how we contested budgets. In place of the letter "o" is a prominent fist of solidarity with a bracelet to represent the diversity and coalition building in IIY that has historically existed in our city.

The graphic visualization of "Invest in Youth" reinforced the spirit of the campaign. Its jagged imperfections reminded seers that this was made by youth, for youth. The logo was featured in posters and banners and screen-printed on campaign t-shirts. During campaign events, we wore the shirts in masses, creating a sea of solidarity in support of young people. Volunteers and teachers from my high school wore the t-shirts, even on non-campaign days, to demonstrate their allyship to support how young people matter now and in our dreams for our futures.

Practicing Collectivity (Char, J, and Mady)

While making our patch, we made time to practice the collectivity and interdependence we dream of on a societal level. This is an alternative to the individualistic dreams of upward mobility and isolating, competitive education.

For example, our peers see college as merely a gateway towards lucrative jobs and scoff at the idea that college could be valuable as a genuine learning experience or time to build community. This message was reinforced in art classes that did not make time for collaboration. In Char's required studio drawing classes, student interactions (except for informal chatting before and after class) occurred only as infrequent critiques lasting around five minutes, usually once or twice a semester or, at most, every few weeks. In J's experiences, art labeled "bad" assumed that working class individuals were not dedicated enough to their craft: obscuring how they are denied time, resources, and energy to adhere to elitist standards.

Instead, we developed our practice of cultural revolution that involves the blooming of the creativity of masses, of every single activist and comrade. For example, members suggested different chants, such as *"Lumalaban, Anakbayan!"* (resisting, Children of the People) or *"Lubog sa masa!"* (immerse in the masses). The collective decision of "Land to the Tillers" was informed by Char's proposal of *carabao* imagery and AB's dedication to peasant empowerment. We intentionally made time to collectivize labor by teaching each other skills. For example, J guided members (including Char and Mady) who had no prior experience in printing through the often time-intensive, physically laborious, sometimes tedious process of carving the stamp and printing patches. Although each individual member had limited time as full-time students and workers, collaboration enabled us to create 50 patches.

During this process, we built new worlds that we continue to practice. Jaz, another long-time member, shared that creating cultural work together is "an opportunity to share ideas, discuss [them] passionately, build up excitement together and contribute to something larger than one's own self." We have applied and deepened these skills in later projects. The patch itself was meant to be an accessible form of political education that can be enjoyed by everyday people and can open up a dialogue. Developing the patch and discussing the patch with others who asked questions after seeing our patch on our jackets and backpacks helped strengthen and sharpen our political points. We connected to new potential members and took ourselves out of the deprivation of Filipinos' current living and working conditions. The patch was just one example of how we live out or dreams of a world where all are capable of art and social change, and where we dedicate our time for broader purposes rather than individual glory. The time we made for the patch mirrors how we make the time for camaraderie, relationship building, and honoring our culture as a political act: for example, through communal cooking sessions and practicing Tagalog. This practice shows us the joy and satisfaction of dedicating one's life to the genuine liberation of oppressed people both in the Philippines and around the world.

Future

Reconfiguring Dreams & Futures (May)

Char, Mady, and Chelsea discuss how their organizing spaces have enabled them to dream different futures for themselves and their communities. In doing so, they build on the dreams of ancestors while breaking with a cyclical past and the far-reaching tentacles of imperialism and refugee temporalities that have colonized their dreams. They also highlight how encouragement of art-making practice and their power as political actors enables them not only to redefine success and dream bigger, but to make collective dreams such as land redistribution and full investment in youth possible.

> *Char: My future and my goals for my life have always been up in the air. I knew that there was something fundamentally wrong with the way our world and society are structured, so it felt useless to go to college and focus on finding a job. Even in the art department (a field where I feel most comfortable in my skills), it was a lonely and directionless experience. After joining AB, I realized that my dreams don't need to center around finding a career. My dreams don't even focus on myself as an individual. They're rooted in my core belief of wanting more for my community and all people who suffer under imperialism and capitalism. My work in AB has been far more fruitful than any career or academic achievement, and I have faith in a free and just world within our lifetime because of it.*

> *Mady: Despite my efforts to "try" to be one, I have been an on-and-off artist for many years because of how isolating and discouraging it felt. As I integrated into AB, I saw how creating art and other forms of culture work*

together is important to sustaining joy within our movement. Those who are responsible for our conditions deem what is considered reasonable, rational, and successful. My comrades' focus on collective life has shown me that it is absolutely necessary for us to encourage the use of imagination for world-building in our collective spaces together, especially as we mirror the world we want to build.

Chelsea: I never wanted a career in medicine or law. KGA was the only place where I could express this and find support in staff and other girls who felt the same. I always felt guilt and trauma about my dream, knowing what my parents went through to come here and give me the American Dream. When my parents said they didn't want me to go far away to college and to spend all this money on a major they didn't even know about, it really hurt. I thought they couldn't understand my happiness. But KGA helped me understand my parents do want me to be happy; they just have a different definition of happiness. It helped me heal the guilt I had for pursuing higher education.

KGA staff helped me follow my dreams of becoming the first in my family to attend university. In college preparation workshops, they helped me fill out my FAFSA, essay intensive applications, and secure student housing and funding. Khmer-speaking staff members visited my parents and helped me persuade them to follow my dreams of going to [university] and studying art history. They explained the admissions process, logistics of housing, and assured my parents that I would be safe. My mentors, first generation Khmer and other People of Color, were also models of dreams realized—dissolving my belief that higher learning wasn't for people like me.

At its core, KGA truly took the time to invest in my future and [those of] the other young folks around me. Before, I always felt a lack of investment in my community. As a young person, budget cuts were felt in my school programs, every time a local business closed, and [among] my peers who were anxious for their futures. I had always assumed that this was a fixed reality: mobility just does not happen for people like me. But in KGA, I learned what it meant to truly fight for justice as I spoke at City Hall and went door-knocking. When our communities have been told that there is not enough and that youth are incapable of understanding or weighing in on a complex budget, KGA taught us that we deserved these dreams and that we had the knowledge and power to create a more just budget.

Conclusion

Art and dreaming are fundamental to youth-led social transformation. Art-as-dreaming connects us to ancestors who have always waged resistance against enduring legacies of imperialism and neo-colonialism. By making time to practice art in a loving and supportive collective space, we practice our dreams for the future in the present. Young people are not only the future, but powerful in their creativity and strength now. Through art, we imagine and make possible for ourselves futures that are grounded in joy and possibility rather than hampered by the fear of scarcity. While art and dreaming remind us of the need to experiment with new modalities of change, we cannot abandon strategic power-building. However, there are also tensions and challenges involved in integrating art and dreaming with more commonly understood forms of political action.

Our stories show that youth organizers and educators must refuse the constant urgency imposed by oppressive systems and make time for art and dreaming. AB, KGA, and IIY's recognition of the need to slow down mirrors a broader understanding in youth and community organizing that we must embody a refusal of white supremacy in all ways, including slowing down for joyful practices and embodied healing (e.g., Corpuz & Bell, 2021). Educators and organizers—often burnt out, overworked, and underpaid—can find inspiration in groups practicing holistic visions of social transformation that both heal individually felt trauma and bring about social change (e.g., Lee, 2014). Yet, limited funding, capacity, and structural conditions can suffocate creativity for youth and community organizing groups that are best positioned to win systemic change necessary to create time for art and dreaming. Everyone is a potential ally who can increase overextended groups' capacities to make time for creativity and dreaming. Funders who support youth and community organizing can bring arts funders into the fold. Arts education must become sites of politicization and dreaming in tandem with organizing spaces, so that J and Char's experiences will become the anomaly rather than the norm.

While the challenges are daunting, our experiences show that the forces of violence we endure are not permanent but already shifting. Through our art and organizing, we disrupt cycles of displacement and trauma. We know deeply that our dreams of a world abundant with Filipino and Cambodian cultural wealth, of land redistributed to those who cultivate it, and of full investment in and resources for young people; of a world where our creativities are nurtured, is not only possible but a reality that we cultivate now.

Reference

Budiman, A. (2021, April 29). *Filipinos in the U.S. Fact Sheet.* Pew Research Center. https://www.pewresearch.org/social-trends/fact-sheet/asian-americans-filipinos-in-the-u-s/

Corpuz, G. M., & Bell, S. (2021, August 18). *From demanding to commanding power.* The Forge. https://forgeorganizing.org/article/demanding-commanding-power

Delgado Bernal, D., Burciaga, R., & Flores Carmona, J. (2012). Chicana/Latina testimonios: Mapping the methodological, pedagogical, and political. *Equity & Excellence in Education, 45*(3), 363–372. https://doi.org/10.1080/10665684.2012.698149

Espiritu, Y. L., & Duong, L. (2018). Feminist refugee epistemology: Reading displacement in Vietnamese and Syrian refugee art. *Signs: Journal of Women in Culture and Society, 43*(3), 587–615. https://doi.org/10.1086/695300

Gordon da Cruz, C. (2017). Critical community-engaged scholarship: Communities and universities striving for racial justice. *Peabody Journal of Education, 92*(3), 363–384. https://doi.org/10.1080/0161956X.2017.1324661

Hayes, K., & Kaba, M. (2023). *Let this radicalize you: Organizing and the revolution of reciprocal care.* Haymarket Books.

Invest in Youth Coalition. (n.d.). *Invest in Youth Survey Results (2018).* Invest In Youth LB. https://www.investinyouthlb.org/invest-in-youth-survey-results-2018

Isaac, A. P. (2021). *Filipino time: Affective worlds and contracted labor.* Fordham University Press.

Kelley, R. D. G. (2002). *Freedom dreams: The Black radical imagination.* Beacon Press.

Lee, N. (2014). *Healing-centered youth organizing: A framework for youth leadership in the 21st century.* Urban Peace Movement.

Lin, M. (2023). "Actually changing our way of being": Transformative organizing and implications for critical community-engaged scholarship. *Social Sciences, 12*(10). https://doi.org/10.3390/socsci12100562

Lin, M., & Patraporn, R. V. (2022). The Invest in Youth Long Beach coalition: Youth of color at the forefront of anti-racist governance and planning. *Journal of the American Planning Association, 89*(4), 540-553. https://doi.org/10.1080/01944 363.2022.2123023

Ocasiones, L. G. (2018). "You can't have our land": Land grabbing and the feminization of resistance in Aloguinsan, Cebu. *Philippine Sociological Review, 66,* 35–60.

Ritchie, A. J. (2023). *Practicing new worlds: Abolition and emergent strategies.* AK Press. https://www.akpress.org/practicing-new-worlds.html

Rogers, J., Mediratta, K., & Shah, S. (2012). Building power, learning democracy: Youth organizing as a site of civic development. *Review of Research in Education, 36*(1), 43–66. https://doi.org/10.3102/0091732X11422328

Schlund-Vials, C. J. (2012). *War, genocide, and justice: Cambodian American memory work.* University of Minnesota Press.

See, S. E. (2019). Filipino American visual culture. In S. E. See (Ed.), *Oxford Research Encyclopedia of Literature.* Oxford University Press. https://doi.org/10.1093/acrefore/9780190201098.013.867

Tang, E. (2015). *Unsettled: Cambodian refugees in the New York City hyperghetto.* Temple University Press.

CHAPTER 12

A Collective Dreaming Process:
Reimagining Youth Space to Facilitate Latinx Youth Critical Consciousness Towards Educational Injustice and Anti-Immigrant Politics

Carlos R. Casanova, PhD and Eric Alvarez

Introduction

MANY YOUTH PROGRAMS tend to embrace deficit narratives and promote positive youth development ideas. This approach in youth spaces perpetuates marginalized youth, such as Latina/o/x youth, as the "problem to be fixed" and focuses on reducing youth violence, increasing academic performance, or preparing youth for gainful employment (Ginwright, 2010). In a political era where Latina/o/x youth are dehumanized by educational injustice and viewed as problems to be fixed, they need a space that develops their capacity to critically critique social injustice, and fosters hope for a more socially just world (Casanova, 2023). The focus of this chapter is on three program practices that emerge from a two-week collective dreaming session between adult staff and Latina/o/x youth at *Movimiento La Libertad* (MLL), a community-based youth program in Iowa. The aim of the collective dreaming session was to engage youth in a process where they could re-frame or reimagine what society should and could look like. What emerged from the collective dreaming session was their vision of a youth space that supports their critical understanding of systems of oppression and fosters a social justice vision of society and sociopolitical systems. In what follows, we present three practices Latina/o/x youth imagined for MLL and offer examples of each practice. First, we start with a brief overview of key conceptual ideas that guide this study, followed by methods, with a deep dive into the research setting and sociopolitical context of the study. The chapter ends with findings that highlight three MLL practices and examples of each program practice.

Background Literature/Conceptual

Agencies of Transformational Resistance

The Agencies of Transformational Resistance (ATR) framework is grounded on critical race theory and Latina/o/x critical race theory, pilot studies, and Covarrubias and Revilla's (2003) own personal and professional experiences within organizations. The ATR framework is guided by four tenets. First, ATRs raise participants' multi-dimensional and critical consciousness through formalized training sessions and opportunities to engage in dialogue and praxis. Second, there is a focus toward nurturing participants' commitment to dismantle all relations of power that create inequality that impact one's own life and beyond. Third, there is a focus on cultivating participants' skills and expanding resources, including an asset-based approach to community and youth development and meeting the personal needs of youth. Finally, ATRs foster an evolving network of resistance that offers opportunities to gain political and personal support to transform various forms of social injustice. We use this framework as a lens to examine the nuances and interconnectedness of the pedagogy, curriculum, and co-conspirators to understand the ways these three key processes facilitate Latina/o/x youth critical consciousness in MLL.

Co-Conspirators

Love (2019) outlines five tenets of co-conspirator behavior and values:
1.) Understanding where one stands in relation to privilege and oppression,

unlearning habits that protect those systems, which is a lifelong commitment; 2.) Building authentic relationships based on solidarity and mutuality, which is only possible when we do not avoid or transcend those imbalances; 3.) Honestly acknowledging and confronting those imbalances to create authentic relationships; 4.) Social change work that is rooted in collaboration, humility, and accountability; and 5.) The interior journey into silence, meditation, inner wisdom, and deep joy is inextricably linked to the outer work of social change (p. 17). Love (2019) explains that a co-conspirator is someone who is willing to use their intersections of privilege and leverage their power to stand in solidarity with Black people while confronting anti-Blackness. A co-conspirator is a verb, not a noun, thus it requires action and responsibility (Love, 2019). We view allies as those who may passively vocalize or express support for social movements and oppressed people; co-conspirators are allies who actively align themselves both publicly and behind-the-scenes with social movements or oppressed groups, leverage their privilege for justice, and take risks beyond personal interest or gain (Love, 2019).

Liberating Pedagogy of Praxis

Liberating Pedagogy of Praxis (LPP) is a pedagogical approach that aims to disrupt dominant ideologies, which contributes to eliminating oppression and empowering marginalized youth (Casanova & Cammarota, 2019; Casanova & Dominguez, 2023; Casanova et al., 2023). Also, LPP views race and racism as (a) embedded into social institutions; (b) intersecting with other social identities and systems of oppression; and (c) critical to understanding, analyzing, and teaching about racial subordination through dialogue. LPP emerged from a three-year critical ethnographic study at a Latina/o/x youth community organization in a large urban city in Iowa that took place within the social and political context of heightened state and federal level anti-immigrant politics and racist nativism within their educational system (Casanova & Cammarota, 2019; Herrera & Obregón, 2018; Rodriguez, 2019). LPP is guided by three intersecting principles: 1.) Knowledge holders—the belief that true knowledge, expertise, and assets already exist with Latina/o/x youth, which have been accumulated through their life experiences; 2.) Shared knowledge—dialogue with youth that demonstrates hope, the use of their voice, love for each other, their community, and history; and 3.) Co-construction of knowledge—youth build a community grounded in love and trust among themselves through collective authentic reflection, which guides how youth and adults teach and learn from and through each other, which promotes collective action. Casanova & Cammarota (2019) suggest that an LPP creates spaces for Latina/o/x youth to reflect, ask questions, face the oppressor, and resist the prescribed behaviors of the oppressor. Moreover, an LPP recognizes Latina/o/x youth as holders and creators of knowledge that is linked to their community, local history, and socio-political context. Furthermore, LPP validates Latina/o/x youth experiences and empowers Latina/o/x youth to engage in transformational resistance (Solórzano & Bernal, 2001) and achieve academic success.

Methods

Methodology

This study employed a critical ethnography because of the researcher's ethical commitment to work closely with a group of Latina/o/x youth for an extended amount of time to challenge oppressive schooling practices. This three-year critical ethnography fostered authentic relationships with participants through extended time in the field, engaging in participatory research and ongoing reflection, dialogue, and action with participants about their lived experiences, community, family, and injustice they experienced in school. Through these ethnographic methods, the researcher and participants critiqued oppressive school practices, policies, and culture, and cultivated individual, societal, and institutional change (Palmer & Caldas, 2015). This critical ethnography involved a process that cultivated spaces for the researcher and participants to create their own knowledge and share and co-create power (Guajardo & Guajardo, 2002).

The study was conducted when the researcher was a doctoral student. His major professor introduced him to MLL, and he spent five months with the youth prior to the start of the study. The early stages of the research served to build trust and familiarity with students and parents. Parents and students attended program events such as college night, know your rights training, and end of school year program celebrations. The researcher interacted with parents at these events, which included food and guest speakers.

Research Site and Participants

This study was situated in one of MLL's high school programs. During the academic school year, MLL youth and adult staff met once a week for at least two hours in the cafeteria of a local church. The church served solely as a meeting site for youth and was offered through a friendship between the MLL director and a church pastor. Program meetings followed the MLL 4-stage circle program model. In the MLL curriculum, the circle model is described as: The circle has been a symbolic representation of wholeness, inclusion, and equality in many cultures, including native cultures of Latin America. The use of a circle represents cycles in North, Central, and South American native cultures. Ceremonies, celebrations, *temazcal* (sweats) all happen in a circle for our Indigenous culture. It ties all participants together and creates safe and secure spaces where all students, adults, and visitors are equal and respected. Each program meeting used the model throughout the year. The circle model observed at MLL is similar to sharing circles described by Tachine et al. (2016). Guided by the circle model, each weekly program session started with an opening circle ritual activity (e.g., sit in silence). This was followed by a check-in, which offered youth the space to reflect on the last program meeting and to share any thoughts or questions. Then, a program activity was selected. All meetings ended with one youth counting down ("three, two, one") while all members were in a circle holding hands and arms crossed with the person next to them. When the youth reached "one," everyone shouted, "¡Sí Se Puede!" as we raised our hands and turned toward the outer part of the circle.

MLL was created to serve Latina/o/x youth in particular, but it was open to all high school students. Roughly 25 Latina/o/x youth attended weekly MLL meetings. Participants were high school students who attended four campuses in one school district in Iowa. Citizenship status among participants varied and included 1st generation, 1.5 generation, 2nd generation, and undocumented–all with some ties to Mexico/Latin America. Most participants were born and lived their entire life in Iowa. Others were born in other states, such as California, but moved to Iowa at a young age. The participants in this study were consistent members of MLL and participated in weekly program meeting activities. Many of them served as youth leaders of MLL for one academic year and helped develop the program curriculum and facilitate meeting activities. Their roles as youth leaders and consistent participation in meeting activities fostered opportunities for me to develop an authentic relationship with participants, which created opportunities for collective reflection and trust. Participants spent much of their time at MLL interacting with each other. They established close friendships, attended school together, as well as MLL events beyond programming time. Participants were recruited to join MLL by close friends. I also developed a trusting relationship with participants' parents through conversations at family events. Participants described MLL as a space that nurtured their professional and academic goals and empowered them to be proud of who they are.

Data Collection and Analysis

The data in this study involved intensive participant-observations outlined by seminal studies on urban Latina/o/x youth (Cammarota, 2008; Moya, 2017; Valenzuela, 1999). The field work documented observations of the activities, behaviors, the nature of conversations and dialogue, and the physical and social setting. Data was collected via audio recording and field notes. The recording device was placed directly in front of the researcher to capture his dual role as both facilitator and participant-observer. He also wrote field notes and recorded audio reflections after sessions ended and all youth had left the space. Field notes were typically short handwritten memos which were expanded on within 48 hours. He discussed fieldwork with a senior researcher who provided feedback and made suggestions related to assumptions, inferences, and ambiguities.

The theoretical framework provided the lenses for constructing meaning and writing. The first round of the analysis process was inductive as the researcher read and reread transcribed interviews. This process helped him to gain a deep understanding of the data and included writing interpretive memos. Most of the memos theoretically connected well with ideas and concepts in the theoretical framework. The researcher then reviewed, refined, and reorganized ideas and categories into subcategories to identify and understand the ways adult staff, curriculum, and pedagogy at MLL elevate Latina/o/x youth critical consciousness and their capacities for social justice activism.

Findings

Adult Youth Workers as Co-Conspirators

On a partly cloudy, rather warm day in February 2017, Latina/o/x youth from MLL joined an estimated 2,500 immigrant supporters on a two-mile march to the Iowa State Capitol Building. This was the first social protest for these Latina/o/x youth. Carlos joined the youth at this social protest and observed many of them carrying signs that read "Stop Separating Families" and "No Human is Illegal." He observed them engage in chants, and Leticia, a 16-year-old undocumented Latina/o/x youth, addressed the crowd with a powerful speech of unity and love for the immigrant community. At an MLL meeting a week before the protests, several Latina/o/x shared their concerns with adult staff about attending the protest. These concerns included doubts that social protest would create change, fear of ICE agents at protests, and concern for their safety and the safety of family members. In the collective dreaming session, Latina/o/x youth decided that all adult staff at MLL should have some experience participating in social movements and stand in solidarity with them at social protests. In other words, Latina/o/x youth called on MLL adult staff to be co-conspirators—adults who actively align themselves both publicly and behind-the-scenes with oppressed groups and use their intersections of privilege in ways that stand in solidarity and confront the oppression of marginalized youth (Domínguez & Casanova, 2023; Domínguez & Bertrand, 2023; Love, 2019). Co-conspirators nurture intergenerational relationships which foster authentic opportunities for adults and youth to learn from each other through practice and collaboration and undertake collective action toward a more socially just world. More importantly, co-conspirators enact authentic caring (Valenzuela, 1999)—youth and adults commit to a relationship that is nurtured on the foundation of trust and vulnerability.

Adult staff answered the call to be co-conspirators and stand in solidarity with Latina/o/x youth. The excerpt shared next comes from a group discussion that happened one day before The Day Without Immigrants March. The march was organized to challenge state and federal anti-immigrant politics. The march was a two-mile loop to the State Capitol building, where guests would speak.

Cynthia (youth): "How are we going to get the attention of our family members and friends and make them go to the protest? How are we going to do that?"

Gilbert (youth): "Our friends and family members don't have the same views that adults here have. How are we going to make them go to the protests ... do something they don't want? They're not going to want to go 'cause some of them don't care and are scared."

Leticia (youth): "At that march, do you think immigration will show up there? Because some people are saying that."

Maria (adult): "ICE isn't going to show up. Police are there. And the majority of the police don't want this either. Honestly, because they know that if something happens to you guys, you're not going to go to them. It makes their job harder."

Juan (adult): "You know, we are at a strategic advantage; the Capitol is right there, walking distance. I'm going to be there. And it's important for you to be there and have your voices ... heard."

Cynthia: "Then let's go to the protests tomorrow. I don't know, we can stand as a group and talk to as many people as we can. We can meet up tomorrow at the protest and just talk to the people, to Latino people, people who can understand English and Spanish. If we really want our voices to be heard. Why don't we do that? It's only going to be adults speaking, but they also want to hear from us, like you said, right?"

Joaquin (adult): "They do. I think they would rather hear from you."

Gilbert: "I say we go to the march tomorrow and speak to all the people."

Juan: "Being there together will be a powerful moment. You got to remember that. You have to remember that this is just the beginning. We're there tomorrow in solidarity. That's important. That way your voices can be heard, and your voices need to be heard, but we have to continue to fight. They call it a struggle. They don't call it a picnic, right? They call it a struggle. It's a struggle. It's going to be hard. But if you allow other people to decide things for you and speak for you, it's going to go against your interest. It's going to go against what you need. You gotta speak up for yourself. And Joaquin is right. It's like once you do something for yourself, then you get in a habit and a pattern of speaking up for yourself and you can bring that anywhere. So tomorrow at 12 o'clock, we will meet and be there together in *solidarity*!"

Maria: "Make sure to wear your MLL shirt. See you tomorrow!"

The dialogue above is an example of co-conspirators and Latina/o/x youth learning from each other to undertake collective action toward a more socially just world. What was apparent here is that Latina/o/x youth had internalized doubts and fears related to attending social protests. These doubts and fears are rooted in the fact that Latina/o/x youth have never attended social protests, and many of them are undocumented and have family members who are undocumented. The dialogue offers an example of co-conspirators as youth workers who demonstrate a deeper ethic of care and political commitment to Latina/o/x youth. This dialogue took place in an afterschool program, which can be understood as "behind the scenes" youth work by co-conspirators. For example, co-conspirators listened to Latina/o/x youth share concerns and doubts related to social protests. When adult staff listen, it cultivates authentic opportunities for adult staff and Latina/o/x youth to learn from each other. Co-conspirators demonstrated political solidarity by meeting Latina/o/x youth at the protests and marching the two-mile loop with them. For example, when the march reached the State Capitol Building, adult staff and Latina/o/x youth gathered with a group of people next to the area where the microphone and guest speakers were. After a few guest speakers, Cynthia made her way to the microphone. We all followed her lead. She gripped the microphone with one hand, and Maria held the other hand as she gave a powerful speech about solidarity and the power of immigrants.

Liberating Pedagogy of Praxis

The Liberating Pedagogy of Praxis (LPP) approach is influenced by tenets and principles of Latina/o/x critical race theory (LatCrit) and humanizing pedagogy (Casanova & Cammarota, 2019; Casanova & Dominguez, 2023; Freire, 1970; Solórzano & Yosso, 2000). These two frameworks were used to facilitate weekly MLL lessons and activities that would move students toward critical consciousness with the aim of challenging oppression and empowering Latina/o/x youth. A transdisciplinary perspective was used to position social and political institutional practices and policies in historical and contemporary context. There was a focus on intersectional forms of oppression that Latina/o/x youth experience, including language, ethnicity, race, gender, and citizenship status. There was an emphasis on Latina/o/x youth sharing their experiential knowledge through dialogue and storytelling, which were used to understand and analyze social injustice. These tenets and principles guide the pedagogical approach at MLL.

To apply an LPP approach with Latina/o/x youth, we co-created MLL lessons and activities so that youth and adults were engaged in an interdisciplinary analysis of oppression through dialogue and storytelling. One example happened when 25 Latina/o/x youth and adult staff participated in a weekend retreat. On the last night of the retreat, youth and staff gathered in the community room to watch a film produced by Edward James Olmos titled *Walkout*. The HBO production is based on the 1968 protest by thousands of Mexican American students from five East Los Angeles High Schools. The movie shows how Mexican American students organized a walkout to protest anti-immigration legislation, racial injustice, discrimination in the school system, and lack of equal opportunities. Adult staff member Juan started the activity by presenting national-level college enrollment rates based on student race and ethnicity. Juan shared, "nationally, about 35% of Latinos who graduate from high school and who are eligible to go to college, 65% of them are not going. And, 15% complete a four-year college degree." Joaquin, another adult staff member, posed a question to Latina/o/x youth, "Why do you think there is a low percentage of Latino students in college?" Gilbert, a Latina/o/x youth, replied quickly, "It's because of the school system. The counselors don't meet with us and give us information about college or scholarships." Margarita, an adult staff, follows with the question, "How many of you have met with your school counselors and feel like they are looking out for your best interests?" Many of the youth stated that they do not have a counselor who cares and that school counselors are never there when they try to go see them. The conversation ends, and just as Juan prepares to push the play button to start the movie, he looks at the group of Latina/o/x youth and says, "Think about how you feel while watching the movie and what connections you can make related to your school experiences."

In the collective dreaming session, Latina/o/x youth called for MLL to use a pedagogy approach that countered the banking pedagogy model (Freire, 1970) Latina/o/x youth often experience in schools. Banking pedagogy is where teachers lecture, tell students what to think, and seldom facilitate student discussions. LPP challenged the banking model by asking Latina/o/x youth questions that facilitate deep reflection on their public school experiences. The LPP model described here used a film about the Chicana/o/x youth movement as a backdrop to engage Latina/o/x youth in critical collective dialogue and analysis on college access and school counselors. Asking Latina/o/x youth questions promotes dialogue which challenges the silencing many Latina/o/x youth encounter in school. LPP encourages Latina/o/x youth to make connections between their schooling experiences and the long history of oppressive school practices Latina/o/x youth have experienced and challenged through direct action.

Social Justice Curriculum

In the collective dreaming session, it became clear that Latina/o/x youth history and culture were not taught in school, and students wanted to learn more about these topics. Several Latina/o/x youth spoke openly about how their schools' history books omitted Latina/o/x peoples' history and contributions to this country. Latina/o/x youth spoke often about school lessons that focused only on the history of white people and left out lessons related to Latina/o/x people, along with racism, immigration, and social movements. Latina/o/x youth's interest in learning about their history and culture resulted in the re-imagination of an MLL Latina/o/x-focused curriculum. The aim of the curriculum was to nurture Latina/o/x youth's critical understanding of social injustice and promote critical action.

To help reach this aim, Latina/o/x youth and adults imagined an MLL curriculum with a focus on Latina/o/x identity, immigration, educational injustice, and youth empowerment. To support Latina/o/x youth identity development, lessons were created so that Latina/o/x youth had time to reflect on their intersecting identities and engage in dialogue. One lesson involved having Latina/o/x youth write and share "I Am" poems with the entire group. "I Am" poems provide Latina/o/x youth with the opportunity to explore their social injustice and reimagine a more socially just society and education system. Latina/o/x youth and adult staff discussed each identity in detail. Some students and adult staff asked questions and discussed challenges students raised. One line of the poem asked students to describe what they hoped for. Examples from poems include, "I hope the world will someday see people of color as beautiful," "I hope that after years of organizing there will be social change," "I hope the education system changes to include people of color and also get more teachers who are people of color." In relation to education, Latina/o/x youth designed a lesson that included an excerpt by Gándara and Contreras (2009) about the Latina/o/x education crisis. The excerpt describes Latina/o/x students as the largest and most rapidly growing ethnic group in the country, but academically, they are lagging dangerously far behind their non-Latina/o/x peers. The excerpt argues that the Latina/o/x education crisis is the result of circumstances encountered by Latina/o/x students when they enter the education system.

The lesson uses large sheets of paper hung on the walls with headings that include a) my culture is valued at my school; b) I can see myself and my family/friends in the information I receive at school, especially history and arts; and c) I believe Latina/o/x students have equal opportunity to do well in school. Students have the opportunity to write a response or drawing to each statement and respond to another student's comment. When all students are finished, everyone goes around and reviews the finished comments. This is followed by students breaking into small groups with the task to create and present to the group their ideal school situation with subjects that they would like to learn. To nurture Latina/o/x youth's understanding of social movements, they imagined lessons related to the 1960s Chicana/o/x youth movement. One lesson included the HBO film *Walkout.* This lesson included an open dialogue on the history of educational injustice and Latina/o/x youth's role in social movements to expose injustice and abuse, and inspire people to keep hope and demand social change for a better society.

A Collective Dreaming Process: Reimagining a Youth Space to Facilitate Latina/o/x Youth Critical Consciousness

This chapter helps us think about what is possible when Latina/o/x youth come together to reimagine a positive vision for what the world could and should look like. What we learned is that for Latina/o/x youth, their vision includes a youth space rooted in and guided by ideas, values, and practices of co-conspirators, Liberating Pedagogy of Praxis, and social justice curriculum, moving beyond the traditional positive youth development processes that oftentimes overlook the role of power and oppression on young people's development and lived experiences (Gonzalez et al., 2020). The three interconnected processes were co-created in a collective dreaming session during a historical period when Latina/o/x communities were experiencing heightened social and political attacks in public schools and by federal and state governments. Immigration raids were happening across the country, public schools were upholding ideas and values of white supremacy, and Latina/o/x students experienced verbal and physical attacks motivated by the Trump administration's rhetoric of Mexicans destroying the United States. At the same time, Latina/o/x youth and adult staff came together in solidarity to reimage and co-create a youth space with practices that provide Latina/o/x youth with the opportunity to nurture authentic relationships with adult staff, develop a deep understanding of their history and culture through a pedagogy guided by practices of dialogue and problem-posing, and engage in critical action to challenge social injustice. Adult staff stood in solidarity with Latina/o/x youth at social protests to challenge anti-immigrant politics, the LPP promoted collective dialogue and critical analysis related to educational injustice, and the curriculum provided opportunities to learn about the important history of Latina/o/x youth activism.

The three interconnected processes highlighted in this chapter can be implemented and adjusted to meet the local needs of Latina/o/x youth in after-school programs across the country. It is time for afterschool programs to focus not only on academic success but to work closely with youth to co-create a youth space that facilitates the development of marginalized youth—specifically Latina/o/x youth—critical consciousness and promote social justice. As practitioners and researchers of youth development, this chapter challenges us to focus on youth spaces and practices that youth imagine when they think about a vision of what society should and could look like.

Reference

Cammarota, J. (2008). *Sueños Americanos: Barrio youth negotiating social and cultural identities*. University of Arizona Press.

Casanova, C. R. (2023). The development of Latinx youth critical consciousness in an afterschool program: Insights from Latinx youth critical reflection and critical action toward educational injustice. *Youth & Society, 56(2)*. https://doi.org/10.1177/0044118X231171609.

Casanova, C. R., & Cammarota, J. (2019). "You trying to make me feel stupid or something?": Countering dehumanization of Latin@ youth through a liberating pedagogy of praxis. *Journal of Latinos and Education, 18(4)*, 363-375.

Casanova, C. R., & Domínguez, A. D. (2023). Countering racist nativism through a liberating pedagogy of praxis. *Anthropology & Education Quarterly, 55(1)*, 43-64.

Casanova, C. R., Silver, J., & Domínguez, A. D. (2023). Social protest as a liberating pedagogy of praxis: Insights from Latina youth critical action toward anti-immigrant politics. *Social Justice, 49(1/2)*, 135-197.

Covarrubias, A., & Revilla, A. T. (2003). Agencies of transformational resistance. *Florida Law Review, 55*, 459.

Domínguez, A. D., & Bertrand, M. (2023). Where are the coconspirators?: Examining performative youth allyship and opposition by educational leaders in K-12 schools. *The Urban Review, 55*, 559-582.

Domínguez, A. D., & Casanova, C. R. (2023). School leader lotería: How school educators respond to Latinx student performances of (their) lived experiences with racism in school. *Journal of Research on Leadership Education*. https://doi.org/10.1177/19427751231175926.

Freire, P. (1970). Pedagogy of the oppressed. Continuum.

Gándara, P., & Contreras, F. (2009). *The Latino education crisis: The consequences of failed social policies*. Harvard University Press.

Ginwright, S. A. (2010). Peace out to revolution! Activism among African American youth: An argument for radical healing. *Young, 18(1)*, 77-96.

Gonzalez, M., Kokozos, M., Byrd, C. M., & McKee, K. E. (2020). Critical positive youth development: A framework for centering critical consciousness. *Journal of Youth Development, 15(6)*, 24-43.

Guajardo, M. A., & Guajardo, F. J. (2002). Critical ethnography and community change. In Y. Zou & E.H.T. Trueba (Eds.), *Ethnography and schools: Qualitative approaches to the study of education* (281-304). Rowman & Littlefield Publishers.

Herrera, L. J. P., & Obregón, N. (2018). Challenges facing Latinx ESOL students in the Trump Era: Stories told through testimonios. *Journal of Latinos and Education, 19(4), 383-391.*

Love, B. L. (2019). *We want to do more than survive: Abolitionist teaching and the pursuit of educational freedom.* Beacon Press.

Moya, J. (2017). Examining how youth take on critical civic identities across classroom and youth organizing spaces. *Critical Questions in Education, 8(4),* 457-475.

Muñoz, S. M., Vigil, D., Jach, E., & Rodriguez-Gutierrez, M. (2018). Unpacking resilience and trauma: Examining the "Trump Effect" in higher education for undocumented Latinx college students. *AMAE Journal,* 12(3).

Palmer, D., & Caldas, B. (2015). Critical ethnography. *Research methods in language and education: Encyclopedia of language and education,* 1-12.

Rodriguez, L. V. (2019). *Navigating a climate of fear: Adolescent arrivals and the Trump Era* [Doctoral dissertation, UC Santa Barbara]. eScholarship.

Solórzano, D. G., & Bernal, D. D. (2001). Examining transformational resistance through a critical race and LatCrit theory framework: Chicana and Chicano students in an urban context. *Urban education, 36(3),* 308-342.

Solórzano, D., & Yosso, T. (2000). Toward a critical race theory of Chicana and Chicano education. In C. Martinez, Z. Leonardo, & C. Tejeda (Eds.), *Charting New Terrains of Chicana (o)/Latina (o) Education,* 35-65. Hampton Pr.

Tachine, A. R., Bird, E. Y., & Cabrera, N. L. (2016). Sharing circles: An Indigenous methodological approach for researching with groups of Indigenous peoples. *International Review of Qualitative Research, 9(3),* 277-295.

Valenzuela, A. (1999). *Subtractive schooling: US-Mexican youth and the politics of caring.* State University of New York Press.

Valenzuela, A. (Ed.). (2016). *Growing critically conscious teachers: A social justice curriculum for educators of Latino/a youth.* Teachers College Press.

CHAPTER 13

Reimagining Life After High School:
Black and Latinx Students' Experience in a (Virtual) Counter-Space

Olga M. Correa

Introduction

THE ONSET OF the COVID-19 pandemic and subsequent shift to remote instruction in March 2020 challenged educators to pivot their pedagogical practices to not only engage students with the ongoing curriculum, but to account for and be mindful of the tumultuous impact of isolation, health concerns, financial instability, and overall uncertainty. Moreso, the pandemic disproportionately impacted Black and Latina/o/x communities as Black and Latina/o/x people were more likely to catch COVID-19 due to their work environments, were less likely to have access to medical support, and were more likely to lose their employment due to strict safety protocols that nullified their work responsibilities (Pew Research Center, 2020). Black, Latina/o/x, and Asian students were more likely than white students to live in a remote-only school district during the initial shift to remote instruction (Smith & Reeves, 2020).

Engaging with remote instruction was more difficult considering the limited access to a personal computer or reliable Wi-Fi in their homes. For students considering post-secondary education during this time, the strict health and safety protocols led to limited in-person opportunities to engage in the college application process, thus exacerbating existing inequalities related to college enrollment trends among Black and Latina/o/x students. Camera (2021) highlights that the number of students that applied for undergraduate admissions in spring 2021 dropped significantly for the categories of students of color and low-income students. These circumstances necessitated the development of new outreach strategies and engagement initiatives to promote educational pathways for communities of color.

During the 2020–2021 academic year, a group of Black and Afro-Latina/o/x eleventh graders expressed their concerns about navigating these inequitable and unjust realities during the height of the COVID-19 pandemic at a New Jersey high school. The school is part of a Title-I funded district in northern New Jersey, serving approximately 1,038 students. Under Title-I, the district is provided with supplemental funding to cover the cost of resources to best support students who qualify for free or reduced lunch (U.S. DOE, 2018). The majority of the students identify as Black and Latina/o/x, making up 24% and 48% of the population, respectively. Additionally, almost half of the student body was identified as economically disadvantaged because of receiving free or reduced lunch (New Jersey State School Performance Report, n.d). The concern is that schools with such enrollment demographics face economic, social, and structural challenges that schools with a predominantly white student population do not (Orfield et al., 2012; Pattillo, 2015; McGrew, 2019). These schooling experiences reinforce stereotypes of inferiority among students, fosters racial biases about underrepresented groups, and perpetuates economic inequality.

The aforementioned Black and Latina/o/x students took it upon themselves to create a virtual space to meet and maintain a sense of community, despite the ongoing challenges. As former participants of a middle school youth services program that I managed, the students and I built a foundation where they safely expressed their emotions and critiqued the injustices they experienced in the school and local community. What began as conversations about the sudden shift to remote learning transformed into *Life After High School*, a (virtual) counterspace of community, engagement, and youth resistance. During our weekly meetings, students developed thoughtful plans for persevering in their remote academic years, identified resources to promote their academic, social, and emotional well-being, and refused to let the conditions of their racially and ethnically segregated circumstance define their post-secondary plans.

This chapter imagines the potential of youth-led spaces outside the traditional classroom that promotes Kelley's (2002) "freedom dreams" by historicizing the current conditions of racially and ethnically segregated schools and highlighting the strengths Black and Latina/o/x students embody (p. 6). I describe the pedagogical practices that engaged students for two academic years, including check-in meetings, digital vision boarding, and virtual scavenger hunts to solidify post-secondary plans. I also discuss the group's unwavering commitment to racial and ethnic justice by learning key terms and identifying how structural racism functions within the public education system. By conceptualizing education in a historical context, students learned the ways in which anti-Blackness, colonialism, and hegemony have influenced the education system. Lastly, the chapter will include a collection of narratives from the inaugural group of students as they reflect on their experience now that they are living their "freedom dreams" as second-year college students.

Setting The Content

The landmark *Brown v. Board of Education of Topeka Kansas* case (1954) is paramount to the history of educational civil rights in the United States. The Court ruled that separate education was "inherently unequal" and mandated integration (para. 21). As a form of court-ordered desegregation, the impact of *Brown I* (1954) outside of southern states was constrained due to a lack of *de jure* segregation, formal state legislation mandating racially and ethnically separate schools; by the time *Brown I* was decided, such state statutes in the North had been barred (Douglas, 2005; Sugrue, 2009). The North was distinguished for its practice of *de facto* segregation, or racial and ethnic separation that existed in fact but was not created by specific statutes nor enforced by statutes or judicial decisions (Douglas, 2005; Highsmith & Erikson, 2015; Sugrue, 2009). In *Black Segregation Matters,* a report by The Civil Rights Project at UCLA, Orfield and Jarvie (2020) explain that civil rights lawyers had to prove that the schools had been "intentionally segregated" by school officials through "decisions about buildings, attendance boundaries, teacher assignment, and many other elements" that were more difficult to try in court despite the *Brown* ruling (p. 5). The inability to challenge trends of racial and ethnic segregation over the years has resulted in the resegregation of many public schools across the nation, particularly in the northern U.S.

The problem is not that predominantly Black and Latina/o/x schools exist, but rather that predominantly Black and Latina/o/x schools continue to face economic, social, and structural challenges that predominantly white schools do not. Racially and ethnically segregated schools and schools of concentrated poverty often have teachers who are less experienced and less qualified, high levels of teacher turnover, less successful peer groups, and inadequate facilities and learning materials (Orfield et al., 2012). McGrew (2019) emphasizes that these schooling conditions can limit students' academic performance and future employment opportunities critical for economic mobility. School segregation reinforces stereotypes of inferiority among students, fosters racial and ethnic biases about underrepresented groups, and perpetuates economic inequality. What I hope to emphasize in this chapter is the value of resistance efforts that center youth voice and action, as they are often missing from educational policy discourse.

Challenges During Remote Learning

The COVID-19 pandemic prompted a sudden shift out of physical classrooms and to remote learning for K–16 students across the United States in March 2020. Divides in educational opportunity across classrooms and campuses were deepened due to lessened access to school-based resources and support in the form of reliable technology, stable workspaces, mental health services, and college counseling. Black and Latina/o/x families faced the brunt of these challenges as research shows that Black children were more likely to lose a parent to COVID-19, Black and Latina/o/x adults faced higher risk for contracting COVID-19, and Black and Latina/o/x students were less likely to be enrolled in in-person instruction during the pandemic (U.S Department of Health and Human Services, 2021). The realities of remote learning and living were extremely difficult to navigate.

For students considering post-secondary education during this time, strict health and safety protocols prevented in-person opportunities to visit college campuses, meet with school counselors, and request recommendations from teachers, thus exacerbating existing inequalities related to college enrollment trends among Black and Latina/o/x students. According to the National Student Clearinghouse Research Center, enrollment among first-year students across colleges decreased by 13% between fall 2019 and fall 2020 (Causey et al., 2021). In particular, college-going culture was impacted by the shift to remote instruction as many high school students who were already isolated from peers, teachers, and counselors took on additional responsibilities with work or caregiving at home because of the added hardships of the pandemic. Expectedly, students who were already attending schools with limited college-going resources were more likely to cancel plans to attend college or face additional barriers to pursue a college degree.

Conceptual Framework

This chapter draws on the concept of counterspace to understand how the Life After High School program became a space of resistance for students attending a racially and ethnically segregated high school. Solórzano and Villalpando (1998) define counterspaces as academic and social safe spaces that allow underrepresented students to promote their own learning wherein their experiences are validated and viewed as critical. Many scholars have utilized counterspace to analyze the experiences of Black and Latina/o/x college students who join organizations or create such spaces in search of community and to foster a sense of belonging to successfully earn their degrees (Brooms et al., 2021; Nuñez, 2011; Yosso & Lopez, 2010). Further, Hernandez Rivera (2020) found that participation in a Womxn of Color retreat aligned with the concept of counterspace by providing a space for womxn's experiences and stories to be validated, countering the dominant culture of the predominantly white institution they attend. Recently, Puente and Ramirez (2023) used a counterspace approach among summer bridge students of color and found that the intentional structuring and content strengthened students' awareness of dominant higher education ideologies, nurtured their multiple identities and expressions, and built a lasting community of support among the group. The surrounding literature makes evident that pushing back against hegemonic realities and deficit-based narratives that exist about communities of color is an ongoing responsibility for educators and researchers because of the prevalence of racism in education. Thus, the notion of dreaming and (re)imagination speaks to the concept of counterspaces in the sense that individuals who make up these spaces develop trust and comfort with one another and do the work of fighting and advocating for a different future or different reality.

The responsibility to create and maintain such spaces was intensified by the additional hardships and circumstances during the onset of the COVID-19 pandemic. For example, in K-12 settings, there exists a prevalent deficit model education that implies that students of color "enter school without the normative cultural knowledge and skills and parents/guardians neither value nor support their child's education" (Yosso, 2005, p. 75). Instead, using a counterspace approach among high school students, in particular, became a valuable tool to not only bring students together during an extremely isolating time, but also to highlight the strengths, assets, and capital that they provide educational spaces and the greater community to go on with dreaming of alternative futures and taking steps towards accomplishing those goals.

Program Description

In September of 2020, after a challenging end to the previous academic year, I was approached by two of my former students for a virtual *check-in* on Zoom. Although they successfully completed the previous academic year, Mia and Amari (pseudonyms) began to feel less connected to their academics and less motivated to face their junior year. As former participants of a middle school youth services program that I managed, the students and I built a foundation where they safely expressed their emotions and critiqued the injustices they experienced in the school and local community. They shared concerns because they knew their junior year was really important when thinking about going to college, but they felt as though they were being set up to fail.

Mia and Amari were students at the local high school. As the only high school in town, their high school served approximately 1,038 students with a predominately Black and Latina/o/x student body. Additionally, a large number of the students were eligible for Free or Reduced-Price Lunch. Comparatively, the demographics among the town's population are described as 48.4% white, 26% Black or African American alone, 26.1% Hispanic or Latino, with a median household income of $85,999. Mia and Amari, who both identify as Black/Puerto Rican and Black/Peruvian, emphasized how feelings of inferiority worsened during the COVID-19 pandemic and subsequent shift to remote learning due to interactions with teachers, administrators, and students enrolled in honors courses.

What began as an informal conversation about the overwhelming feeling of being a high school junior transformed into a virtual space of community, engagement, and support. The Life After High School program ran virtually from September 2020 to June 2022 on a weekly basis for 60–90 minutes via Zoom. My understanding of how sociohistorical factors create pathways and barriers to quality education among historically marginalized communities, along with ten years of experience developing and facilitating college readiness curricula to 7th–12th graders, allowed me to co-lead this space with students. Mia and Amari invited a few of their peers who were experiencing similar challenges, growing our group to six students and myself. The additional students also identified as Black and/or Latina/o/x and were eligible for Free or Reduced-Price Lunch. Developing our virtual space was aided by the fact that the students were also part of the middle school youth services program I managed, and thus previously developed a level of rapport and trust with me.

Our weekly meetings included discussions about the overwhelming logistics of the college application process, the non-existent college-going culture at their high school, and students' aspirations of being art therapists, chemists, business owners, and professional athletes. One student, Joshua, reflected:

> I participated in the Life After High School group because no one at the time showed value or interest in me going to a good school for college. I didn't have any financial support, I had no sense of direction or even believed in myself. I wanted to have an opportunity to change the narrative for all my younger family members.

Another student, Tonya, shared:

> Honestly, this whole remote learning thing was a set-up for students of color. How were we supposed to get any work done when we were home with our younger siblings and had to watch them and make sure they did

their work AND get things done around the house? I had to go to work too; it was a lot. I don't think they cared that we were living like that.

Life After High School quickly became a space where youth felt comfortable to show up authentically, felt supported in their post-secondary planning, and resisted the circumstances available to them as students attending a racially and ethnically segregated school. I led various practices during our meetings to foster this kind of space and to discuss factors related to racially and ethnically segregated schools while highlighting students' strengths and assets as they navigated the college application process.

Checking-In

As students joined our meetings each week, they were prompted with a *check-in* question to spark discussion among the group and help cultivate relationships with and among students. Engaging in a casual format allowed us to learn about each other's experiences and interests while promoting a sense of connection between students who were isolated from others due to COVID-19 safety protocols. The practice of checking-in was inspired by bell hooks's (1994) notion of the classroom as a communal place, and I wanted to ensure that students understood that their participation in the group was meaningful because they are choosing to bring their authentic selves and lived realities into the virtual space. Fostering a communal place during our virtual meetings is related to reimagination as students were participating in a practice different from those used in their traditional classrooms—a practice that brought them closer together to their peers in an effort to collectively take action against the inequalities they faced as students at the same high school. As our time together continued, students followed up on comments made during our *check-in*, to hold each other accountable and assess what more had to be done to reach overall goals for the academic year.

During one *check-in* session, I tasked students with outlining the skills they enhanced or developed despite the hardships they were facing in the midst of the COVID-19 global pandemic. Students reflected on their organizational skills, learning to advocate for themselves, and managing their responsibilities within and outside school. Mia explained that being home from school had not been easy:

> To be successful, I mean I had to create a safe space where I felt comfortable and confident. I purchased new posters and bullet journals, and I started drawing more, writing poems, watching new shows, and listening to new music.

Joshua has felt unmotivated and frustrated from having to do everything on his laptop. He explained that because his workspace was messy, he tried cleaning and organizing to be more productive:

> I got lost during class a lot when teachers shared their screen and told us to follow along because I had to switch back and forth between all these tabs. I remember sharing that in the [Life After High School] group, and I practiced how I could talk to my teachers and ask for more time to complete my work.

While the media painted a deficit-based picture throughout the shift to remote learning, namely a focus on learning loss, I took the opportunity to highlight how students worked together to identify ways to overcome the barriers they were facing. Their counternarratives served as a way to reimagine how students' experiences during such a tumultuous time could be highlighted.

Checking-in served as a method to build rapport among students to a point where students were oversharing because they felt so comfortable with each other and developed a level of trust within the virtual space we created together. Meeting virtually allowed us to check-in from different physical places and devices; students joined from within town or surrounding communities from their laptops, tablets, or cellphones—they were not pressured to meet in one place at a particular time. We were also afforded the opportunity to be fully present (cameras on) or establish a boundary (cameras off) during a particular meeting. The major constraint we experienced during our *check-in* was the inability to give someone a high-five or a hug when sharing an accomplishment or if they were having a hard day. The isolation was looming over the students and myself during the height of the pandemic, but the *check-ins* and the program overall filled a much-needed void to be surrounded by community.

Dreaming of Future Selves

While the strict health and safety protocols in place restricted our ability to engage in person, the virtual nature of the Life After High School program allowed us to be creative in developing our discussions and activities. I created a curriculum that focused on racial justice, developing social identities, academic and career goals, exploring college options, and reflecting on post-secondary dreams. One activity students engaged in was creating a digital vision board about their *future selves*, including photos, clip art, and text. Amari reflected on a future where, before attending college and starting her own businesses, she would be elected to serve as president of her high school's Black Student Union. She dreamed of the opportunity to advocate for Black students' rights on campus because she felt that Black students were disproportionately punished for infractions that all students commit.

Figure 13.1
Amari's Digital Vision Board

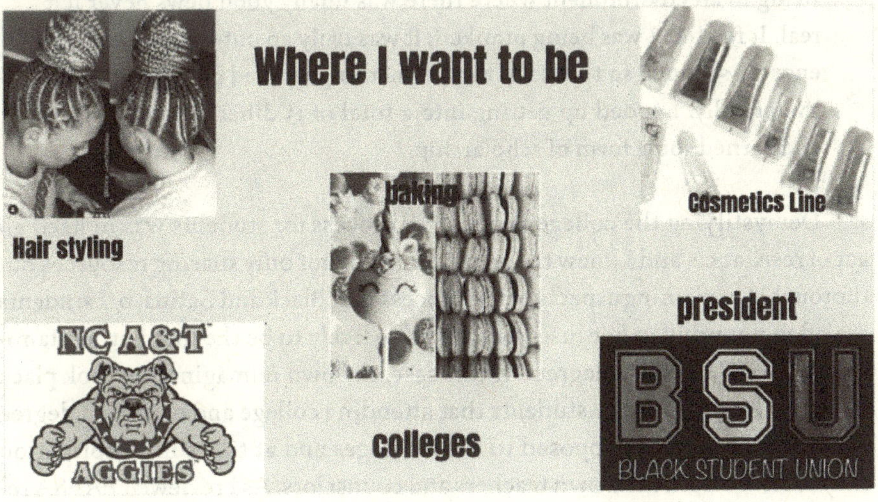

Amari went on to describe how the way Black students were treated on campus is similar to how the Black community is treated throughout society. She was motivated to attend college and continue being part of leadership opportunities that would help her make a difference.

As part of our college-going activities, I generated a Google Form for students to complete while navigating college websites to learn about campus features, student demographics, leadership opportunities, and cultural representation. During one of the virtual assignments, Joshua shared:

Being a first-generation college student is a huge deal. [Our high school] was not offering much help for students to prepare for college, or even to take the SAT. [The school's] students were only given the option of community college being their best option. So, learning about scholarships that I can apply for and getting support to work on my essays and help my peers with their applications really changed what our futures could look like.

Another student in the group voiced the challenge of believing good news was possible. Tonya shared:

Being in an environment where there was finally good news never felt real. It felt like I was being pranked; it was truly an out-of-body experience … so much so that each time something worked out, I would sob hysterically. I ended up getting into a total of 15 different universities and earned some form of scholarship.

Demystifying the college application process for students was in itself an act of resistance, and I knew the implications of not only sharing resources but thoroughly explaining aspects of the process that Black and Latina/o/x students are often not privy to because they are more likely to be the first in their families to pursue a college degree. In this case, my own reimagination took place in being able to show the students that attending college and earning a degree was a feasible goal, as opposed to the messages and at times misinformation they received from their own teachers and counselors. As I reviewed FAFSA requirements, local scholarship opportunities, and free SAT preparation courses, it was evident that students were not aware of available resources right in their community. Each activity and discussion became a tool in each student's toolkit for pursuing a college degree and staying on track to successfully graduate.

Resistance in Academic Settings

A primary practice in the Life After High School program was for students to understand the historical context of their high school and local community. During our first few meetings in 2020, we focused on defining key terms surrounding racial and ethnic justice in education and identifying how structural racism functions within the public education system. Our topics included racially and ethnically discriminatory policies and practices at the federal and state level, racial and ethnic segregation in housing via exclusionary covenants and redlining (Rothstein, 2017), and anti-Black sentiments that have transpired, painting the Black community as inferior (Douglas, 2005). I worked with the students to interrogate the racial and ethnic disparities we see today, across U.S. public schools and within their own school district. By conceptualizing education in a historical context, students were able to identify the ways in which anti-Blackness, colonialism, and hegemony have influenced schooling experiences for hundreds of years.

In one of our virtual meetings, Amari reflected on how frustrated she was with the double standard around discipline practices at her high school. She observed how Black girls were more likely to be kicked out of class or suspended for several days for minor infractions, compared to girls of other racial and ethnic backgrounds. The following week we focused on Monique Morris' (2016) scholarship surrounding the criminalization of Black girls in public schools, and made connections to what students experienced throughout their own K–12 journey. Amari used our discussion and reflection to organize a presentation for the campus's Black Student Union, where she highlighted how excessive punitive discipline disrupts Black girls' education, and she urged for this concern to be addressed by school administrators in the district. In a different session, Tonya shared about encountering numerous racially discriminatory experiences and microaggressions at the high school. She shared:

My intelligence and ability to participate in advanced classes [were] often questioned, by both students and teachers. They must've thought it was a compliment to say, "wait, you're actually smart?" It just made me feel like I didn't belong, but I can't even be mad because the teachers and administrators always made a distinction between us and honors students. It was hard to say anything at first, but I started to feel more comfortable making my voice heard whenever they made those comments because my voice should matter just as much as their voices, right?

Tonya's reflection is an example of how students gained more insight into how educational inequalities have transcribed over the years, and more importantly, began to develop strong feelings and arguments about their role in changing these realities for future generations. Our meetings and the conversations we shared became the foundation for students to begin to reimagine and envision themselves as agents of change within their school and the local community. Students earned leadership roles on Student Council and the Black Student Union, giving them the opportunity to advocate for equitable resources and speak up on behalf of the greater student body. Students also began to attend Board of Education and City Council meetings in an effort to gain a deeper understanding of the issues facing the school and community and were able to encourage their peers to attend to ensure that youth voice was represented during these meetings.

Key Takeaways

While the pandemic limited educators' ability to engage with students in-person and amplified the existing challenges-within public education, we were also encouraged to foster more culturally centered pedagogical practices. It has been evident that our practices prior to the pandemic were not sufficient for our students, and as Dr. Ladson-Billings (2021) encouraged us, it is time for a "hard re-set" to engage and support students in more innovative ways (p. 68). It is not that Black and Latina/o/x students do not want to do the work, engage in conversations about racial and ethnic discrimination and social justice, or advocate against the current educational inequities they are experiencing; rather, they may not have the time because of outside responsibilities, or they may not have the blueprint to even know where to begin. Life After High School became that blueprint and laid out various resources not provided by their teachers or counselors in their school environment.

When Mia and Amari first approached me for an informal *check-in*, I did not imagine that our conversation would grow into the Life After High School group. As I reflect on what we were able to achieve throughout our two years, I consider the potential our group has to inspire educators, practitioners, and scholars to be intentional in creating virtual support spaces for students of color. Connecting virtually allowed us to expand the boundaries of a space of learning, building community, and advocating for issues we care deeply about. An important aspect of Life After High School is that it was a youth-led space: Students determined the topics we discussed, evaluated the activities, and shared experiences. As students of color, these practices were vital to the success of our group, as often our lived experiences are not centered in the classroom.

During each meeting, I witnessed how much more comfortable students became with me and with each other; they were excited to join the Zoom room and share their responses to the *check-in* questions; they listened attentively and asked thoughtful questions. On multiple occasions, students expressed that the community we developed in such a short time was completely different from anything they had felt in a school classroom. I echo scholars and practitioners who have emphasized the importance of fostering a culture of care in their classrooms or other learning spaces where students of color are affirmed, valued, and uplifted on a daily basis. These practices, tied with disrupting power structures from traditional school settings, had a large impact on students choosing to enter the space with a willingness to engage.

Closing Thoughts

The inaugural Life After High School cohort are now pursuing their post-secondary goals at various public colleges and universities. They occasionally check-in with me individually and as a group to share updates, to seek guidance, and to encourage each other to stay on track with their academic and personal ambitions. As I look back, it is inspiring to see how the program and our consistent virtual meetings became a space for resistance and radical dreaming as youth developed thoughtful plans for persevering in their remote academic years; identified resources to promote their academic, social, and emotional wellbeing; and refused to let the conditions of their racially and ethnically segregated circumstance define their post-secondary plans. All students should be able to dream their future lives and not be burdened by the pervasiveness of racism and systemic oppression; all students deserve the ability to imagine the best version of themselves without the racial and ethnic biases of adults. My goal was to reinforce a space full of community, learning, and fun, where students began to live the dreams they were destined to live; the encouragement and support students received from each other and me aided in getting closer to those dreams. To witness their growth and hear about how influential participating in the program was for each student asserted Akom et al.'s (2008) thoughts about the importance of building such environments led by students where "young people have the ability to analyze their social context and resist repressive state and ideological institutions" (p. 2). The students indeed overcame various barriers during remote instruction at their high school and continue to engage with social justice and educational equity initiatives to improve pathways for future generations of Black and Latina/o/x students.

Through Life After High School the students and I created a space where everyone came together as a group, and over time, dreamed of and created alternative futures for themselves. Importantly, students had the support to consider small and big dreams, problem-solve, and manifest their dreams alongside peers. Students uncovered their potential in a world where they were constantly being torn down and doubted. As a community of critical thinkers and learners, students found ways to advocate for their school to become a safer space and imagined new possibilities as student leaders and community members. While each of the students struggled with racially and ethnically discriminatory policies and practices, they developed the drive to learn about improving educational equity for Black and Latina/o/x youth and became eager to spread this knowledge with their own peers and adults.

Reference

Akom, A. A., Cammarota, J., & Ginwright, S. (2008). Youthtopias: Towards a new paradigm of critical youth studies. *Youth Media Reporter, 2*(4), 1-30.

Brooms, D. R., Clark, J. S., & Druery, J. E. (2021). "We can redefine ourselves": Enhancing black college men's persistence through counterspaces. *Journal of Black Studies, 52*(3), 277–295. https://doi.org/10.1177/0021934720976410

Brown v. Board of Education, 347 U.S. 483 (1954).

Camera, L. (2021). Financial aid applications drop among 2021 High School graduates. *U.S. News.* https://www.usnews.com/news/education-news/articles/2021-07-19/financial-aid-applications-drop-among-2021-high-school-graduates

Causey, J., Harnack-Eber, A., Ryu, M., & Shapiro, D. (2021), *A COVID-19 special analysis update for high school benchmarks.* National Student Clearinghouse Research Center.

Douglas, D. M. (2005). *Jim Crow moves north: The battle over Northern school segregation, 1865-1954.* Cambridge.

Hernandez Rivera, S. (2020) A space of our own: Examining a Womxn of Color retreat as a counterspace. *Journal of Women and Gender in Higher Education, 13*(3), 327-347, DOI: 10.1080/26379112.2020.1844220

Highsmith, A.R., & Erickson, A.T. (2015). Segregation as splitting, segregation as joining: Schools, housing, and the many modes of Jim Crow. *American Journal of Education, 121,* 563 – 595.

hooks, b. (1994). *Teaching to transgress: Education as the practice of freedom.* Routledge.

Kelley, R. D. (2002). *Freedom dreams: The Black radical imagination.* Beacon Press.

Ladson-Billings, G. (2021). I'm here for the hard re-set: Post pandemic pedagogy to preserve our culture. *Equity & Excellence in Education, 54*(1), 68-78. https://doi.org/10.1080/10665684.2020.1863883

McGowan, E.J.J. (2011). *A case study of Dwight Morrow High School and the academies at Englewood: An examination of school desegregation policy from a critical race perspective.* [Doctoral Dissertation, Rutgers University]. RU Core.

McGrew, W. (2019). *U.S school segregation in the 21st century: Causes, consequences, and solutions.* Washington Center for Equitable Growth. https://equitablegrowth.org/research-paper/u-s-school-segregation-in-the-21st-century/?longform=true#overview

Morris, M. W. (2016). *Pushout: the criminalization of Black girls in schools.* The New Press.

New Jersey State School Performance Report. (n.d). *Demographics.* https://rc.doe.state.nj.us/2020-2021/school/detail/03/1370/040/demographics?lang=EN

Nuñez, A. M. (2011). Counterspaces and connections in college transitions: First-generation Latino students' perspectives on Chicano studies. *Journal of College Student Development, 52*(6), 639–655.

Orfield, G., & Jarvie, D. (2020). *Black segregation matters: School resegregation and Black educational opportunity.* UCLA The Civil Rights Project. https://www. civilrightsproject.ucla.edu/research/k-12-education/integration-and-diversity/ black-segregation-matters-school-resegregation-and-black-educational-oppor tunity/BLACK-SEGREGATION-MATTERS-final-121820.pdf

Orfield, G., Kucsera, J., & Siegel-Hawley, G. (2012). *E pluribus … separation: Deepening double segregation for more students.* UCLA The Civil Rights Project.

Pattillo, M. (2015). Everyday politics of school choice in the Black community. *Du Bois Review: Social Science Research on Race, 12*(1), 41-71.

Pew Research Center. (2020). *Health concerns from COVID-19 much higher among Hispanics and Blacks than whites.* https://www.pewresearch.org/politics/ 2020/04/14/health-concerns-from-covid-19-much-higher-among-hispanics- and-blacks-thanwhites/#:~:text=About%20half%20of%20Hispanic%20 adults,and%20needing%20to%20be%20hospitalized

Puente, M., & Ramirez, B. R. (2023). Summer bridge as a counterspace: Redefining postsecondary success for students of color. *Journal of Student Affairs Research and Practice, 61*(3) 403-416. www.doi.org/10.1080/19496591.2023.2218303

Rothstein, R. (2017). *The color of law: A forgotten history of how our government segregated America.*: Liveright Publishing Corporation.

Smith, E., & Reeves, R. V. (2020). *Students of color most likely to be learning online: Districts must work even harder on race equity.* Brookings. https://www. brookings.edu/blog/how-we-rise/2020/09/23/students-of-color-most-likely- to-be-learning-online-districts-must-work-even-harder-on-race-equity/

Solórzano, D., & Villalpando, O. (1998). Critical race theory, marginality, and the experience of minority students in higher education. In C. Torres & T. Mitchell (Eds.), *Emerging Issues in the Sociology of Education: Comparative Perspectives* (pp. 211-224). State University of New York Press.

Sugrue, T. J. (2009). *Sweet land of liberty: The forgotten struggle for civil rights in the North.* Random House.

U.S. Department of Education. (2018). *Improving basic programs operated by Local Educational Agencies (Title I, Part A).* https://www2.ed.gov/programs/titleparta /index.html

U.S. Department of Health and Human Services. (2021). *More than 140,000 U.S. children lost a primary or secondary caregiver due to the COVID-19 pandemic.* https://www.nih.gov/news-events/news-releases/more-140000-us-children-lost- primary-or-secondary-caregiver-due-covid-19-pandemic

Yosso, T. (2005). Whose culture has capital? A critical race theory discussion of community cultural wealth. *Race Ethnicity and Education, 8*(1), 69-91. http:// dx.doi.org/10.1080/1361332052000341006

Yosso, T. & Lopez, C. B. (2010). Counterspaces in a hostile place: A critical race analysis of campus culture centers. In D. Patton (Ed.), *Culture Centers in Higher Education: Perspectives on Identity, Theory, and Practice* (pp. 83-104). Routledge.

CHAPTER 14

The Politics of Faith:
Father Luce and the 1968 High School Blowouts in East Los Angeles

David Flores

Introduction

Unfortunately, Chicana/o/x Studies, as a field of research, has long overlooked a spiritually centered social movement history. This is a surprising omission, considering a majority of Latina/o/xs have some type of religious identification (Pew Research Center, 2014). Of course, the field's allergy to religion is not without merit, considering that the church, generally speaking, has historically been a principal accomplice to colonization, genocide, and enslavement throughout the world. In response, when the Chicana/o/x movement developed as a field of research, it adopted Marxist principles that consider religion a barrier to class struggle. The founders of the field thus fostered a hostility towards religion and overlooked any role it might have played in supporting Chicana/o/x self-determination. This anti-religious tradition has largely been carried over to the present. For example, a pioneering architect of Chicanx studies published a conceptual map of the field, naming over a dozen dominant themes and sixty subtopics, yet failed to include religion or spirituality as an area of interest (Macias, 2005). Excluding religion as relevant to the study of the Mexican-origin population is telling of the kind of attitude that Chicana/o/x studies has maintained throughout its development.

On the other hand, Chicana/o/x religious studies scholars have long challenged this historical oversight. Scholars such as David Carrasco (2010), Lara

Medina (2004), Mario García (2008), Theresa Delgadillo (2011), and others have persistently examined, interrogated, and documented the role and relevance of religion to Chicanidad generally and to its social movements specifically. Romero (2020), for example, has stated that "[in] every instance of racial and social injustice in Latin America and the United States over the centuries, the Brown Church has arisen to challenge the religious, socioeconomic, and political status quo" (p. 11). Chao Romero points to figures such as Bartolomé de las Casas, Sor Juana Inés de la Cruz, Cesar Chavez, Dolores Huerta, or Salvadorean Archbishop Oscar Romero as both religious leaders and freedom fighters who used theological texts and narratives against the tendencies of the powerful to subordinate vulnerable populations. Many Latina/o/x scholars who examine social movements through a religious studies lens agree with Chao Romero, that throughout history, the U.S. Latina/o/x church has, in one way or another, sometimes en masse and sometimes on an individual level, challenged social inequalities. If these scholars are correct, we should be able to find a social justice religious praxis by examining the largest Mexican American civil rights movement in U.S. history.

Fortunately, the increase in Latinx movement scholarship over the last decade that centers religion offers strong support to Chao Romero's claim, that the church has also been a critical accomplice to Latinx liberation and self-determination. Cesar Chavez and the United Farm Workers (UFW) have received the lion's share of academic inquiry; scholars have examined the role of the Catholic church in the UFW boycott (Prouty, 2008), to the religious poetics of Chavez's speeches (León, 2014). Additional work has examined the Pentecostal influence and rhetoric of Reies Lopez Tijerina, another important figure in the Chicana/o/x movement who was fighting for the reclamation of land in New Mexico (Oropeza, 2020). Lara Medina (2004) and Richard Martinez's (2005) work on Las Hermanas and PADRES, respectively, are two important monographs that document the Chicana/o/x movement's influence on Latina/o/x priests and nuns in the Catholic church. In a sentiment that ran contrary to popular and scholarly belief, Medina (2004) stated, "Chicana/o and Latina/o religious leaders, sisters, priests, and laity fought valiantly in the struggle for civil rights and self-determination" (p. 6). Their critical, yet marginalized, work shows the impact *El Movimiento* had on religious leaders who began organizing for many of the same demands as were the focus of the High School

Walkouts, but within the context of the Catholic church. Whereas students and educational leaders were demanding more Mexican American teachers, administrators, and school board members, in the church, religious leaders were pressing for Mexican American priests, nuns, bishops, in addition to resources for Chicana/o/x communities.

While previous scholarship has skirted around the role of religion in the Chicana/o/x movement, the work of Mario García (2008) and Felipe Hinojosa (2021) is closer to the epicenter. Both have dedicated chapters, articles, and monographs on *Catolicós por la Raza* (CPLR), a short-lived but meaningful organization of Chicana/o/xs in East Los Angeles who protested against the Catholic church's conservative position when it came to housing, education, and Mexican American self-determination during the 1960s. CPLR held vigils and even burned their baptism cards to pressure the church to validate the material and spiritual needs of Mexican Americans. CPLR was one of the first Mexican American groups to cross the secular line and pressure the church to align itself with the working-class communities in Los Angeles, which then encouraged Chicana/o/x priests and nuns to demand more from within the church (PADRES & Las Hermanas). Thanks to Latinx scholars, it is becoming clearer that the church is, and has been, an important site of struggle—from *Catolicós por la Raza*, to Hinojosa's work documenting the Young Lord's occupation of church buildings (2021), to how churches became sanctuary spaces for Central American refugees (Gonzalez, 2022). Yet, outside of those who have either lived or studied Chicana/o/x history, without a total disregard towards religion, these important religious-political intersections are largely unknown.

This chapter presents but another example of how the church, through its social justice religious praxis, has supported the radical dreaming of Chicana/o/x youth to organize for change. It challenges the popular belief that the church is nothing but a passive institution but instead is often (not always) on the right side of justice. Although Chicana/o/x and social movement historians have documented the political, educational, and social gains that resulted from the Chicana/o/x movement, particularly in Los Angeles, few have examined the impact and influence of religion. Exploring the role of the Church of the Epiphany uncovers a critical and radical socio-political and religious relationship with the Mexican American community during a time of heightened injustice. This political spiritual intersection shows that self-determination and liberation does not solely exist in the secular arena but can be considered as a highly spiritual praxis.

Methods

To understand how the Church of the Epiphany stimulated the radical imagination of Chicana/o/xs during the Mexican American civil rights movement, I utilized qualitative research methods, principally oral interviews and archival data. The archival data collected from the University of California, Los Angeles's (UCLA) Chicana/o Studies Research Center, the UCLA Library Center for Oral History, and from the Episcopal Diocese of Los Angeles provided the material nuts and bolts of the pre, post, and aftermath of the Church of the Epiphany's impact on the Chicana/o/x movement. However, it is the 21 oral histories that truly speak to the ways the Church of the Epiphany facilitated a space for Chicana/o/x youth to imagine a resistance movement. The oral interviews were given by some of the most important organizers of the Chicana/o/x movement, with intimate knowledge of or relationship with the Church of the Epiphany. The author conducted 13 interviews between August 2020 and February 2021; six recorded interviews were from the private collection of Rocio Zamora in the early 2000s, and two were led by Virginia Espino for the UCLA Chicana/o Studies Research Center in 2012.

I use oral histories as, what Maylei Blackwell (2011) calls, a "historiographic intervention," listening to the ways memory functions as an archive. Blackwell recovers Chicana feminist histories that have been erased by the traditional telling of Chicano history. She argues that despite the rise of Chicana feminism throughout the 1970's and 80's, "histories of the Chicano and feminist movements have failed to fully record the vital forms of Chicana political consciousness and organizing that existed in this period" (Blackwell, 2011, p. 3). In this chapter, I borrow Blackwell's concept of historiographic intervention because, although the role of religion and spirituality has played a central role in the development and deployment of the Chicana/o/x movement, a spiritually centered social movement history, or archive, is still largely absent. The oral histories literally say what the archives cannot. Because the Chicana/o/x movement is remembered and documented as a secular event, the oral histories are a methodological tool to disrupt (intervene in) that long-assumed narrative. Chicana/o/x history is just beginning to meaningfully explore the religious or spiritual nature of Chicanismo; therefore, these oral interviews will be extremely useful in developing a more holistic understanding of the development of the largest Mexican American movement in history, and specifically for this chapter, how the Church of the Epiphany supported the radical dreams of Chicana/o/x youth. They articulate the social justice religious praxis of the Church of the Epiphany to show that freedom itself is a spiritual endeavor.

The Parish of East Los Angeles

The Church of the Epiphany is the oldest standing Episcopalian church in Los Angeles and is situated in the Lincoln Heights barrio on Los Angeles's eastside. During the urban renewal of the mid twentieth century which caused economic changes and racial tensions, white families who once populated the area fled to the suburbs, and Mexicans filled the voids. Despite a growing Mexican presence in Lincoln Heights, the Church of the Epiphany largely maintained its Anglo identity. However, Episcopalian Bishop Robert E. Bloy, who was likely influenced, or pressured, by Catholic reforms like Vatican II, as well as the independence movements occurring all over the world, elected to experiment with a union of parishes in the impoverished communities of East Los Angeles. The coalition of eastside parishes was modeled after New York's "East Harlem Protestant Parish, a ministry founded by the President of New York Theological Seminary and two Union Theological Seminary graduates with the purpose of helping the poor and organizing social reform from the grassroots" (Wauters, 2013, p. 396). While the experiment was a proselytizing project to grow the Episcopalian flock, it also sought to improve the material conditions of the Mexican American barrio. The experiment was dubbed the Parish of East Los Angeles (PELA), and it launched in September of 1961.

After a slow start, in October of 1965, Father John B. Luce was tapped to lead PELA. No one could have imagined that Father Luce would become one of the most consequential figures and allies of the Chicana/o/x movement in Los Angeles. Little is known about Luce's history because he was such a reserved and private individual; he gave few interviews, and never wanted attention or recognition for his community work. As such, there is little documentation about his past, including his political trajectory. The gap in his history is noteworthy because his life contained the ingredients of a conservative destiny. Father Luce was born in Boston, Massachusetts, came from a family of wealth, and graduated from Harvard University. Not much suggests that he would become a principal accomplice to the Chicana/o/x movement in the coming years. However, while at Harvard, he was encouraged to join the priesthood by Paul Moore, a progressive Episcopalian priest who had a social justice religious praxis of his own. Moore is remembered for marching alongside Martin Luther King, Jr. in Selma and as the bishop who ordained Ellen Barret, the first openly gay priest in the Episcopal tradition. According to Lydia Lopez, a lifelong friend of Father Luce, Moore, who carried a lot of weight, had mentioned to the young Luce, "the action is in the cities … you should go to seminary and come work with me" (Personal communication, September 21, 2020). After attending seminary, and surely following Moore's footsteps, Father Luce was placed in New York where he became active in the Departments of Urban Work and Christian Social Relations, learning how to connect people to the church and vice versa. It was there that he gained his Spanish language chops as a youth minister in the diverse Chapel of the Intercession in New York City. Before coming to Epiphany, Luce served congregations in New York City, Milwaukee, WI, and Jersey City, NJ. It was these early experiences that prepared him to have such a profound impact when he moved west.

Dreaming on a Sea of Culture

Whereas the early stages of PELA were largely focused on social programming and becoming familiar with the sister churches, Luce considered himself an organizer. When he arrived on the west coast, he familiarized himself with the socio-political realities facing Mexican Americans. He sought mentorship from established organizers of the time, such as Cesar Chavez, Dolores Huerta, and especially, Bert Corona, a longtime Mexican American civil rights organizer. The plight of Mexican Americans, educational inequities, and police brutality were obvious areas of contention in the barrios. Additionally, Father Luce was told that there was a deep level of political apathy. He remembered, "In 1964 people told me you couldn't get a Mexican-American anywhere to carry a sign" (Andrade, 1979, p. 27). These comments were substantiated by Chicana/o/x activists, such as Carlos Montes, who stated, "Back then, young Chicanos were trying to be white. Girls would dye their hair blond. You know, I'm white, white is right. All that kind of stuff" (Wauters, 2013, p. 399). Father Luce realized that to inspire the community to imagine themselves as agents of change, he would have to make them feel proud of who they were. He stated, "You can't give what you haven't got. You have to know who you are or you won't do anything" (J. Luce, personal communication, n.d.). For a religious figure, Father Luce's praxis was unconventional: He blurred the lines between the material and spiritual. Rather than pray for favor from God to help Mexican Americans, Father Luce put significant effort into instilling ethnic pride as an important component of their political, social, and spiritual self-realization. His idea was to build Mexican American power on a sea of culture.

Father Luce's first order of business was to inspire the political imagination of the community. He drastically transformed the church to better represent the ethnic make-up of the barrio. He decorated the church with *papel picado*, hung culturally relevant banners, began celebrating *Dia de los Muertos*, served Mexican food, and erected a large portrait of La Virgen de Guadalupe by the main altar, an image not normally seen in Episcopalian churches in the 1960s. Luce commissioned Chicana/o/x artists to paint the skin of the religious motifs in the church from pinkish to brown, "to not make them look like white people," said Ricardo Reyes, an 18-year-old Chicano at the time (Personal communication, July 9, 2021). Reyes remembers Father Luce asking him to create new stationary materials for Epiphany that had more of a Chicano look. Father Luce also commissioned Benny Luna, another community artist, to paint a mural of the biblical story of the Epiphany to be the centerpiece of the church. Luna created a cubist portrait of the Three Kings that Father Luce placed directly behind the altar, in full view of churchgoers.

The church soundscapes were also adjusted. The organ was replaced with the guitar, and Mariachi Mass was soon instituted. In fact, the Church of the Epiphany may be one of the first churches to play mariachi music in a Christian service in the United States. The following exchange between Father Luce and Natividad Cano, the director of Mariachi Los Camperos, expresses how radical the move was at the time. Luce asked Cano to play mariachi during a service; he replied, "You're crazy Father, pardon me, but you can't do mariachi in the church." Luce responded by telling Natividad, "[You're] right, we can't, but you're going to" (J. Luce, personal communication, n.d.) This shows how Father Luce was going against the norms of the religious order, traditions, and customs in order to show the Mexican American community that their cultural capital was valued. Mariachi became commonplace at Epiphany activities and is now a regular part of Latina/o/x church services across the country.

Culture was indeed the principal strategy to inspire the radical imagination of the Chicana/o/x community, but pedagogical dreaming was another. Because Luce had heard from local parents about the unequal and culturally deficient schooling their kids were receiving, he implemented relevant educational programming at the church. With help from fellow priests, his new program director, Virginia Ram, and the laity, PELA started, Barrio Union for Scholastic Community Act (BUSCA). BUSCA was a community-run project to give Chicana/o/xs what they were not receiving from their institutional schooling, including culturally relevant history, ethnic pride, and appreciation of their language. BUSCA's mission was published in the December 2, 1967, issue of *La Raza* newspaper:

> Barrio parents and their children can no longer wait on unfulfilled promises of programs to satisfy their needs and aspirations. They have decided to begin the search for their OWN answer to their problems. They have joined in a Union of parents, community people and other interested people; together they are laying the foundation of a community educational effort ... Self-identity and pride will be enhanced through cultural activities. Culture and history[,] music and dance, art and theater will be part of BUSCA. (p. 8)

Even before the Chicana/o/x arts and cultural renaissance of the late 1960s was in full swing, the Church of the Epiphany was implementing critical socio-cultural programming that included Mexican American art, history, dance, language, and theatre. The changing sights and sounds that Luce implemented were a symbolic flag that the church would now be responding to the dreams and passions of the Mexican American community. The church's dramatic transformation could no longer be ignored by the still largely white congregation that occupied the pews, causing many to leave. In a time of mass devaluing of all things Mexican in the social, educational, and religious sectors of society, Father Luce made a radical decision to positively represent them. Again, against his purported role of growing the Episcopalian flock, Luce inspired the political imagination of the Mexican American barrio, and it did not go unnoticed.

Dreams Planted

While the sea of culture brought the community in, it was the unique intersection of faith and politics that kept Chicana/o/xs coming back. Rudy Tovar, who became involved with the politics of the church and later the Chicana/o/x moratorium against the war in Vietnam, remembers, "all the guys were talking about him [Father Luce]," and "I came over here because the action was here and there was nothing … where I lived, except for a guy here and there, an outspoken person. But I heard about Epiphany and I got involved" (Personal communication, n.d.). For Father Luce, material freedom was a spiritual enterprise. He recognized his duty was not only as a religious leader, but to support the self-determination of the communities he served, allowing them to believe in themselves so that they could dream of a future where they felt included. He stated of his time in Los Angeles, "The church here has an exciting challenge and opportunity to serve suffering people, and to assist them in their legitimate aspirations to participate more fully in the freedom and abundance of this nation" (J. Luce, personal communication, n.d.). Father Luce took the opportunity to enact his own social justice religious praxis, to transform the Church of the Epiphany into a safe and radical incubator for Chicana/o/x youth. As a result, it became a nexus for Mexican Americans to convene and organize a resistance movement.

Two critical organizations soon emerged at Epiphany: the Young Citizens for Community Action (YCCA) and *La Raza* newspaper. YCCA was a youth group that began meeting after attending a Mexican American Youth Leadership Conference, a conference that had the purpose of getting attendees to encourage their peers to become positive role models in their communities (Muñoz, 2007). The newly organized group sought to "bring about political and social awareness in East Los Angeles through direct community action" (*La Raza*, September 16, 1967). While the group was meeting at a park, Paola Crisostomo, an early member of YCCA, remembers Father Luce inviting them to have their meetings at Epiphany. Soon thereafter, Luce, along with David Sanchez, who later founded the Brown Berets, accessed War on Poverty funds from the Lyndon Johnson administration to hire YCCA members to meet at the church daily as Vista Volunteers, a branch of the domestic Peace Corps. In 1967, while YCCA was meeting at Epiphany regularly, Father Luce exposed them to and encouraged their participation in the organizing and political activity of the farm workers, the campaign of the first Mexican American on the school board, Julian Nava, the Community Service Organization, the Welfare Rights Organization, the Crusade for Justice, the Black Panthers, and more. Victoria Castro, first president of YCCA stated, "if I had to say there was a center of the Chicano movement, it was Father Luce's church. It was a fabulous personal wonder that this man gave us a location to blossom and develop and actually challenge your thoughts and let you organize towards them" (V. Castro, personal communication, August 27, 2020). As Castro stated, the political and civic engagement YCCA was exposed to at Epiphany triggered the radical dreaming of those youth in profound fashion.

While YCCA began meeting at the church regularly, a Chicana/o/x underground publication was developing in the basement of Epiphany: *La Raza* newspaper. The formation of *La Raza* was another critical advancement in the development of a Chicana/o/x resistance movement that had its beginnings at Epiphany, and with the behind-the-scenes support of Father Luce (Wauters, 2013). During the 1960s, media coverage of Mexicans articulated the same biases held by society. Raul Ruiz (2020), early editor of *La Raza,* stated, if Mexican issues were covered at all in the English media, they were often "sensationalist reports of crimes that allegedly had been committed by Mexican Americans or Spanish-surnamed people" (p. 56). There was little communication or sources of primary information coming from the community itself to resist these negative representations. Father Luce had been whispering to Elizear Risco and Ruth Robinson, two former UFW organizers, about creating a communications arm because they had experience with *El Malcriado,* the official newspaper of the UFW. While Risco and Robinson jumpstarted *La Raza,* Luce offered them the basement and financial support to publish it.

La Raza became one of the most critical organizations that came out of Epiphany during Luce's tenure. It was the first time Chicana/os were in a position to tell their stories, on their terms, and through their eyes. The publication was a physical materialization of the early dialogues, trainings, and exposure that Chicana/o/xs were immersed in, and it became the sound horn articulating those early Chicana/o/x movement dreams. Additionally, and critically, the founding of *La Raza* in the basement of Epiphany centralized the meeting points for Chicana/o/xs in Los Angeles. Moctesuma Esparza remembers, once the basement of Epiphany "became *La Raza* newspaper, then it really was a nexus" (Personal communication, August 25, 2021).

During the summer and fall of 1967, just months before the High School Walkouts, there was no shortage of activity at Epiphany. Luce hosted Black organizations and leaders at the Church, such as the United Slaves (US), the Black Panthers, and Stokely Carmichael. The socio-political activity was radical and vibrant: "every night was a graduate course in organizing and understanding what was to be known as 'La Causa'" (Wauters, 2013, p. 402). Esparza remembers, "Luce would just say come on over, or tomorrow, or the next day, so and so was going to be here, or this weekend we are going to take a trip or we were going to visit some people and there was a car, or there was a van, and three, four, or five of us would jump in and they would take us places" (M. Esparza, personal communication, August 25, 2021). In one case, Luce rented a bus and took a delegation to meet Reis López Tijerina and La Alianza Federal de Mercedes in New Mexico, a movement trying to reclaim disputed land taken after the Mexican and American War. Montes remembers the impact that trip had on him: "We were talking about better schools, civil rights, police abuse ... and all of sudden this guy is talking about the land, taking back the land, this is our land ... and that like radicalized us, politicized us, like shit! This is not about civil rights, this is about taking our land back" (C. Montes, personal communication, October 8, 2020). As Montes articulates, the radical dreaming of those Chicana/o/x youth was intensifying.

A clear sign of the heightened politicization of YCCA was their name change. While at Epiphany, they were exposed to the farmworker movement, the land struggles in New Mexico, and the Black freedom movements in the South. Soon, the Young Citizens for Community Action changed their name to the Young Chicanos for Community Action, and a few months later, voted to change their name again, to the Brown Berets. The Brown Berets remain active to this day and are largely remembered as the militant arm of the Chicana/o/x movement (Espinosa, 2001). The radicalization of these Chicana/o/x youth, with ever-increasing organization, infrastructure, and communication, along with support from college organizations, adult educators like Sal Castro, community leaders like Virginia Ram, religious leaders like Father Luce, and the inspiration from the Black Power movements helped them to realize that the time was right to materialize a Brown Power movement of their own.

Dream Walking

It was the social justice religious praxis of Father Luce that positioned the Church of the Epiphany to develop into the locus of struggle for a developing Chicana/o/x movement. At Epiphany, Chicana/o/xs combined their collected visions to manifest a pedagogical dream—educational equity. While supporting and organizing for other movements, these Chicana/o/x youth began to ask, "What about us? What about Chicana/o/xs in the southwest? What about urban Chicana/o/xs? What about our schools?" The consistent engagement with each other caused them to question the educational inequalities so prevalent in their barrios, to which they turned their attention. With the organizing momentum growing, and with Sal Castro, a supportive Mexican American teacher at the local high school, who planted the seed of organized resistance, those Chicana/o/x youth began dreaming of a walkout.

Within the first two and half years of Father Luce's arrival, many of those youth who were meeting at the Church of the Epiphany staged the largest student walkout in United States history. *La Raza* published the events, "La Causa that Cesar Chavez started in Delano gained a new stronghold in East Los Angeles" (*La Raza*, 1968). The walkouts triggered, energized, and solidified a Brown Power movement across the southwest that joined the freedom struggles happening around the country. Chicana/o/xs began meeting nationally to organize around a unified cultural front, a self-determining identity, for access to higher education, for their own anti-war movements, political parties, and more meaningful representation in the national polity. The manifestation of these Chicana/o/x dreams are more profound when considering that only months earlier, a United States Commission on Civil Rights stated that Mexican Americans lacked any real organization, making it "extremely difficult for the leadership to develop and pursue strategies which would force public agencies and institutions to pay greater and more intelligent attention to Mexican

American needs and to make changes" (Rowan, 1968, p. 14). Yet, inspired by the political courage and radical dreaming of Mexican American youth in East Los Angeles, Chicana/o/xs were now an organized and unified front that put real pressure on institutions to meet their unique needs. It was these seeds of radical resistance that advanced what today we call the Chicana/o/x Movement.

Dreams Realized

The 1960s were a heightened political moment, and Mexican Americans had not yet solidified their role in the national freedom movements stemming from virtually all communities of color. It was a period where radical dreaming spaces were necessary, particularly for Mexican Americans whose political activity was lukewarm. I have intended to state in this chapter, that for Chicana/o/xs in East Los Angeles, the Church of the Epiphany became, albeit unconventional, one of those radical dreaming spaces. Father Luce put aside much of the proselytizing responsibilities of a religious figure and maximized on his positionality to facilitate a space for Mexican Americans to dream about the kind of future they wanted to construct, and it largely materialized. The Church of the Epiphany was transformed from a strictly religious space into one that appreciated the cultural capital of the barrio, including its artistic and spiritual expressions. Gaye Theresa Johnson (2013) would suggest that Father Luce understood the "power of popular music and of popular culture to envision and create new political possibilities" (p. xiii). The space and moral support from Father Luce and the Church of the Epiphany allowed for Chicana/o/x youth to imagine an alternative future where they could live in a community where their language and culture were respected; where they had political representation; where there was no police brutality; where their educators, teachers, and administrators looked like them, and came from the same socio-cultural experiences as them; and where they could learn about their own history and contributions to society. It was this space and this moral and spiritual support, I argue, that facilitated the radical dreaming, the inspiration to ask the radical question, "what about us?" that became the impetus for Mexican American youth to morph into a self-determining Chicana/o/x identity, to organize, and to resist their marginalization. It was the intersection of faith and politics and the social justice religious praxis of the Church of the Epiphany that supported the escalation of the political imagination and pedagogical dreaming for Chicana/o/x youth.

In *Freedom Dreams*, Robin Kelley (2022) states, freedom is itself a spiritual endeavor, and "I would go so far as to say that freedom and love constitute the foundation for spirituality" (p. 12). This was the social justice religious praxis of Father John B. Luce. Esparza has called Father Luce the most egalitarian person he has ever met: "this guy was there for us, it was his actions that completely won us over, I never had any doubts about his commitment, his authenticity, and his willingness to take risks" (W. Wauters, personal communication, December 10, 2020) It was a spiritual labor of love.

There is no doubt that the elevation of Father Luce in the historiography of the Mexican American Civil Rights Movement introduces an unlikely ally. Father Luce is a white, East Coast native, comes from wealth, graduated from an Ivy League university, and was the head of a historically conservative institution. Naturally, and appropriately, issues of race and ethnicity, class, and the white savior complex are raised. As a Chicano social historian interested in the development of the Chicana/o/x Movement, I treaded cautiously in my examination of Father Luce. Yet, it was the Chicana/o/x participants I interviewed here that quickly put any idea of a white savior to rest. Reyes, a Chicana/o/x artist said, the biggest tragedy of the movement "is that Father Luce is not known, because we owe him so much" (R. Reyes, personal communication, July 9, 2021).

Radical dreaming spaces can happen or be housed anywhere; they can be facilitated by anyone willing to stand against inequity and injustice, and indeed they have. They can be triggered by a football player taking a knee; by a community garden in south central Los Angeles; or by a mural on a housing project, a musical album, or a church offering sanctuary. This research confirms what Chao Romero (2020) has argued, that in every instance of social injustice, the deep faith of Latina/o/x communities has stood head-to-head against *injusticia* and inspired the radical freedom dreams of the Latina/o/x community.

Freedom is indeed a practice of the spirit, and I hope that this research serves as a critical lesson for religious figures, social movement activists, and historians to look more deeply, but no less critically, at religious institutions, spaces, and figures—to examine how they have historically stood, and can still stand, alongside communities of color during moments of injustice, rather than as passive observers, or worse, complicit in the denial of justice. To recognize

Chicana/o/x religion and spirituality as a practice of freedom is to unearth an alternative lens by which to understand and appreciate the dynamic, inventive, and resilient nature that has characterized Mexicana/o/s and Chicana/o/xs for over 500 years.

Reference

Andrade, F. M. (1979). *The history of "La Raza" newspaper and magazine, and its role in the Chicano community from 1967 to 1977* (Publication No. 1312637) [Master's thesis, California State University, Fullerton]. ProQuest Dissertations Publishing.

Blackwell, M. (2011). *Chicana power!: Contested histories of feminism in the Chicano movement*. University of Texas Press.

Carrasco, D. (1982). A perspective for a study of religious dimensions in Chicano experience: bless me, ultima as a religious text. *Aztlán: A Journal of Chicano Studies, 13*(1-2), 195-221.

Delgadillo, T. (2011). *Spiritual mestizaje: Religion, gender, race, and nation in contemporary Chicana narrative*. Duke University Press.

Espinoza, D. (2001). "Revolutionary Sisters": Women's solidarity and collective identification among Chicana Brown Berets in East Los Angeles, 1967-1970. *Aztlán: A Journal of Chicano Studies, 26*(1), 17-58.

García, M. (2008) *Católicos: Resistance and affirmation in Chicano Catholic history*. University of Texas Press.

González, S. M. (2022). Political fellowship and the sanctuary movement: Central American refugees and practices of religiopolitical accompaniment, 1982–1990. In F. Hinojosa, M. Elmore, & S. González (Eds.), *Faith and power: Latino religious politics since 1945* (pp. 211-232). New York University Press.

Hinojosa, F. (2021). *Apostles of change: Latino radical politics, church occupations, and the fight to save the barrio*. University of Texas Press.

Johnson, G.T. (2013). *Spaces of conflict, sounds of solidarity: Music, race, and spatial entitlement in Los Angeles* (Vol. 36). University of California Press.

Kelley, R. D. (2022). *Freedom dreams: The Black radical imagination*. Beacon Press.

La Raza [Newspaper]. (September 16, 1967) Volume 1, Number 1. La Raza Publication Records, 1001. Chicano Studies Research Center, University of California, Los Angeles.

La Raza [Newspaper]. (December 2, 1967). Volume 1, Number 6. La Raza Publication Records, 1001. Chicano Studies Research Center, University of California, Los Angeles.

La Raza [Newspaper]. (October 15, 1968). Volume 2, Number 1. La Raza Publication Records, 1001. Chicano Studies Research Center, University of California, Los Angeles.

León, L. D. (2014). *The Political Spirituality of Cesar Chavez: Crossing Religious Borders*. University of California Press.

Macías, R F. (2005). El Grito en Aztlán: Voice and presence in Chicana/o studies. *International Journal of Qualitative Studies in Education, 18*(2), 170.

Martínez, R.E. (2005) PADRES: *The national Chicano priest movement*. University of Texas Press.

Medina, L. (2004) *Las hermanas: Chicana/Latina religious-political activism in the U.S. Catholic church*. Temple University Press.

Muñoz, C. (2007). *Youth, identity, power: The Chicano movement*. Verso Books.

Oropeza, L. (2020). *King of adobe: Reies López Tijerina, lost prophet of the Chicano movement*. The University of North Carolina Press.

Pew Research Center. (2014). *The shifting religious identity of Latinos in the United States*. Pew Research Center's Religion & Public Life Project. https://www.pewresearch.org/religion/2014/05/07/the-shifting-religious-identity-of-latinos-in-the-united-states/

Prouty, M. G. (2008) *César Chávez, The Catholic bishops, and the farmworkers' struggle for social justice*. University of Arizona Press.

Romero, R.C. (2020). *Brown church: Five centuries of Latina/o social justice, theology, and identity*. InterVarsity Press.

Rowan, H. (1968). *The Mexican American: A Paper Prepared for the US Commission on Civil Rights*. Creative Media Partners, LLC.

Ruíz, R. (2020). Chicanos and the underground press: A perspective on La Raza. In L. Garza, A. Scott, & C. Gunckel (Eds.), *La Raza* (pp. 52-62). UCLA Chicano Studies Research Center Press.

Wauters, W. (2013). The borderland cultures encounter the church and a church gave birth to a new Chicano culture. *Anglican and Episcopal History, 82*(4), 393-408.

CHAPTER 15

Dreamers Rise:
A High School Pre-College Program for Undocumented Students in Wisconsin

Gerardo Mancilla

Introduction

ACCORDING TO THE Higher Ed Immigration Portal (2023a), Wisconsin is considered a "locked-out" or a "restrictive" state because there is no in-state tuition or state financial aid for undocumented students. According to the Migration Policy Institute website (n.d.), 300,760 out of 5,595,148 (5.1%) of Wisconsin's population were foreign-born in 2021. They further state that about half (49.1%) of the foreign-born population are naturalized citizens, while half (50.9%) are noncitizens. In 2023, An estimated 3,000 undocumented students graduated high schools in Wisconsin (Connor, 2023). These students are not eligible to apply for the Deferred Action for Childhood Arrivals (DACA) program because, at the time of this study, the U.S. Citizens and Immigration Service (USCIS) is not accepting any new applications. Many educational and community-based organizations have worked on programs to support students in their transition to college. However, there is a need to address this support with a lens focused on the undocumented student perspective, honoring their unique experiences and helping them navigate the college transition process considering the implications of their immigration status. The Dreamers Rise program was developed to build on undocumented students' resistance and persistence as they continue their education. This program allows us to continue dreaming and developing sustainable approaches to address the challenges that undocumented students face as they pursue higher education.

The Dreamers of Wisconsin is a nonprofit organization that advocates for and supports undocumented students pursuing higher education. They noticed a need to explicitly support undocumented students in their college-going application process. In dreaming of possible solutions, they came up with the idea of creating a pre-college program. The organization secured a grant to establish the program and make this dream a reality.

The organization reached out to me based on my personal and professional experiences navigating the educational system as an undocumented student. I developed the curriculum and facilitated the program. Ten students participated in the program which took place during the fall 2021 semester. The goal of the program was to explain the college-going preparation process for undocumented students through a complex immigration status lens.

Literature Review

The following section will discuss the policies that are impacting undocumented students. This review will cover more of the national policies. The introduction addressed the current policies in Wisconsin. Additionally, this section will discuss freedom dreaming and resistance as it relates to the development of this pre-college program.

Policies Impacting Undocumented Students

An undocumented individual is a person who entered the United States without lawful inspection or someone who has overstayed their visa (Passel, 2006). According to Van Hook et al. (2023), there were approximately 11.2 million undocumented immigrants in the U.S. in 2021. Connor (2023) estimates that there are more than 600,000 K–12 undocumented students enrolled in U.S. schools. Jach et al. (2024) discuss how to support undocumented students pre-college, during college, and post-college. The U.S. Supreme Court case *Plyler v. Doe* (1982) established that undocumented youth have a constitutional right to a free and appropriate K–12 public education. In 2014, the U.S.

Department of Justice and the U.S. Department of Education released the *Plyler Dear Colleague Letter* (Lhamon et al., 2014) to remind educational agencies of their federal obligation to provide a public education for all students regardless of the students' or their parents' actual or perceived citizenship or immigration status. Plyler protects undocumented students up through their senior year of high school. As students transition to higher education institutions, each state may have different tuition and state-based financial support for undocumented students (Jach et al., 2024).

In 2012, President Obama established the Deferred Action for Childhood Arrivals (DACA) program through an Executive Order. DACA beneficiaries are protected from deportation and receive work authorization. The program has specific restrictions on age, residency, and educational/military requirements to be eligible (USCIS, n.d.-a). The DACA program has remained in limbo due to challenges in the courts (Valverde, 2018). DACA beneficiaries can petition for Advance Parole (AP) from the United States Citizenship and Immigration Services (USCIS) for educational, humanitarian, and employment purposes. AP allows DACA beneficiaries to travel outside the U.S. and return with a lawful entry (USCIS, n.d.-b). According to the American Immigration Council (2021), there were 590,070 active DACA recipients in 2021. As it currently stands, DACA beneficiaries can renew their DACA, but new applications are not being accepted.

Unfortunately, undocumented students and DACA beneficiaries do not qualify for federal financial aid (Serna et al., 2017). They can be accepted into institutions of higher education; however, many face financial challenges to pay for school. Each state can set its own state financial aid support for undocumented students and DACA beneficiaries (Olivas, 2004). According to the National Conference of State Legislators (2021), 24 states and the District of Columbia offer in-state tuition to undocumented students through either state legislative action or through higher education governing boards. According to the Higher Ed Immigration Portal (2023a), three states (AL, GA, and SC) have policies that prohibit undocumented students from enrolling in public colleges. Additionally, six states (IN, MO, NH, NC, TN, and WI) have policies barring access to in-state tuition or state financial aid for undocumented students.

As mentioned in the introduction, Wisconsin is considered a "locked-out" or a "restrictive" state because there is no in-state tuition or state financial aid for undocumented students. Previously, Governor Jim Doyle passed in-state tuition for undocumented students as part of the 2009–2011 biennial state budget. However, on June 18, 2011, Wisconsin Assembly Bill 40 barred undocumented students, including DACA recipients, from accessing in-state tuition (Higher Ed Immigration Portal, 2023b). For refugee students, Wisconsin Senate Bill 360, signed in 1992, provided expanded access to in-state tuition.

Freedom Dreaming and Resistance

Kelley (2002) describes the concept of freedom dreaming as the desires, hopes, and intentions of people to change the world. He explains, "And yet it is precisely these alternative visions and dreams that inspire new generations to continue to struggle for change" (p. ix), to fight for freedom from oppression and discrimination. He explains how his mother influenced his thinking: "She dreamed of land, a spacious house, fresh air, organic food, and endless meadows without boundaries, free of evil and violence, free from toxins and environmental hazards, free of poverty, racism, and sexism … just free" (Kelley, 2002, p. 2). Dreaming and radical imagining allow people to work towards change.

Tuck and Yang (2018) encourage us to dream and work toward justice. Their book highlights justice projects on abolition and decolonization. They explain that "[a]bolition is shaking the antiblack institutions that underwrite whiteness as property … that sanction murder, captivity, torture, and disposal: namely, the prison industrial complex" (p. 9). Similarly, they explain that "Decolonization is the rematriation of Indigenous land and life" (Tuck & Yang, 2018, p. 9). These projects call for radical social change, which starts with dreaming about that change.

Undocumented youth have also been freedom dreaming and resisting. Negrón-Gonzalez (2017) shares three lessons of resistance from undocumented youth in their struggle for a just immigration policy. The first lesson focuses on how undocumented youth put pressure on the Obama administration to pass DACA after the 2010 version of the DREAM Act did not pass in Congress. The second form of resistance focused on how undocumented youth protected all immigrants by denouncing narratives that blamed their parents, which had been used to promote the DREAM Act campaign. Their parents had a right to belong, as well. The last example of resistance focused on the more than 20 years of struggle to fight for recognition, visibility, and support for undocumented students. By publicly sharing their stories, undocumented youth have been able to push for in-state tuition and state-based financial support.

Methodology

The Dreamer Rise program started through the freedom dreaming of members of the Dreamers of Wisconsin. The group has worked towards immigration justice for undocumented students in Wisconsin. To take the program from dreaming to actualization, the organization collaborated with me in developing the program, enacting the collaborative imagining that Kelley described. The following section will focus on how the program was developed and implemented.

I begin this section with a statement on my positionality. A researcher's positionality refers to the various social identities that may interact with the research being presented. In a different article (Mancilla & Uy, 2024), my colleague and I discuss how our positionality is important to address when we conduct research with our communities as we are impacted by what we are researching. Our paper focuses on the emotional labor that goes into our work and how our lived experiences are intertwined with the projects in which we are doing research. In freedom dreaming, we are part of the people who imagine a more just world.

Positionality

The Dreamers of Wisconsin reached out to me because of my lived experience as a formerly undocumented individual and based on my professional work supporting immigrant communities. I navigated elementary school, high school, college, and graduate programs, all while being undocumented. There were many challenges that I faced, and I missed out on many opportunities, due to my immigration status. One of the most difficult challenges was applying for college, being undocumented. I was applying for college at the same time that the Development, Relief, and Education for Alien Minors (DREAM) Act was first introduced in 2001. For over 20 years, different versions of this legislation have been introduced to Congress, but none of them have passed. I applied to college ten years before DACA was enacted, so there was limited information on how to apply to college while being undocumented. I researched and navigated the college application process, finding private scholarships, and figuring out how to pay for college.

My lived experience propelled me to focus on working with pre-college programs. Additionally, when I was an assistant professor, I helped establish an undergraduate program for students to travel to the U.S./Mexico border to learn more about immigration (Mancilla & Vukelich-Selva, 2024). Most recently, I was also part of the steering committee which started a study-abroad program for DACA beneficiaries to apply for advance parole to travel to Mexico and return to the U.S. I also started the *Educators and Immigration* podcast (Mancilla, 2021), to have more in-depth conversations about immigration and supporting students. Throughout my professional career, I have worked on ways to continue addressing and supporting the needs of undocumented students.

Participant Vignettes

I applied to college more than 20 years ago, while being undocumented. I had to be persistent, resilient, and resourceful. Twenty years later, we had undocumented students in the program who experienced similar challenges while applying for college. Although we had ten students in the program, I shared Lorena and Miguel's stories to illustrate some of these experiences. Both of the students' names are pseudonyms.

Lorena's Story: Researching undocumented opportunities by herself.

Lorena was a senior Latina from Mexico who had grown up in the U.S., at least since middle school. She came to the program with a lot of information about being undocumented and the college-going process. Her knowledge came from the research she had completed on her own for the last two years. She researched various institutions, the lack of in-state tuition support, and scholarships to support her when applying. She had been a part of a scholarship program that supported her in high school and was in a college preparation program through her high school. However, the programs did not explicitly address how to apply for college being undocumented, which led Lorena to do additional research. By the time she participated in the program, she had already applied to several schools and was waiting to hear about her applications. She became a leader in the group and often shared her experience in finding information with the rest of the group. She also shared resources that she had used and started a messaging group to create a community for the program participants. At the end of the program, she reflected on being thankful that the program helped her know that more scholarships, resources, and people were available to help her with the process.

Lorena received a scholarship to attend an out-of-state university. The scholarship was one of the many she had researched on her own. Although she had applied to several in-state colleges and universities, the scholarship provided her with the best financial support to continue her studies. She recently completed her second year of college.

Miguel's Story: Looking for opportunities and pathways.

Miguel was also a senior during the program. He was Mexican and had grown up in the U.S., at least since middle school. I had developed trust with Miguel from a previous educational experience, and he shared his story with me. Like many undocumented students, Miguel shared about not being able to participate in a previous program due to his immigration status. The program required students to be permanent residents or U.S. citizens. This experience deeply impacted him and made him wonder about his future educational opportunities. In my own story, I had experiences that were similar to that of Miguel. There were several occasions when I could not participate in a program because of my immigration status. I remember feeling like it was unfair. The decision was not based on my ability but on my status. I remember thinking *"y todo esto para que?"* [translation: and all this for what?]. I wasn't sure if college would be an option for me. Miguel's experience discouraged him from trying in school.

Miguel then shared about what helped him change his mindset as it related to trying in school. He saw opportunities and possible pathways. He shared that a school member reached out to him and encouraged him to apply for a new program that they were starting. Although he was hesitant, Miguel agreed to apply for the program and was accepted. Miguel participated in a dual-credit program where he would take courses at the community college during the last two years of high school. The program greatly motivated him and offered a new pathway forward. Miguel graduated from high school with several college credits in December 2021. Like Lorena, he was grateful for the Dreamers Rise program, as it provided another community of support.

Program Development & Radical Dreaming

Our stories demonstrate some of the challenges that undocumented students experience when trying to apply for college. The Dreamers Rise program is one example of how radical dreaming can create change in our communities through collaboration and intentionality. We built the program specifically for undocumented students, most of whom are growing up in a post-DACA generation (Connor, 2023). The program is one form of resistance, and we need to continue working on making it sustainable for future generations.

Undocumented students are often the first in their families to go through the college application process in the U.S. Understanding the steps that are needed to apply for college and how being undocumented will impact them is important in the process. Dreamers Rise aimed to make these processes explicit and visible with a focus on being undocumented. There are many high school and community-based programs that effectively prepare students for the college application process. However, the programs and programming often approach this with a general lens for all students and may not explicitly address how being undocumented may impact the process. While community and educational groups may be getting better at addressing the college application process, undocumented and *DACAmented* students often find themselves trying to learn and navigate these processes on their own. The Dreamers Rise program aimed to create a space to normalize the understanding of the college application process while undocumented, and to provide students with information to help them.

The Dreamers of Wisconsin and I collaborated in making decisions about the program structure. We decided a face-to-face format, rather than virtual, would lend itself to the sensitive and interpersonal nature of the topic. The program was open to all high school students in the area, grades 9–12. Freshman and sophomore students were encouraged to think ahead about what steps they needed to complete to prepare themselves for college. Junior and senior students were already in the college application process. The program's goal was to have students understand their undocumented status, how to apply for college, and their options after college. We also decided to have the program as a Saturday program model, where the students would come to campus for a half-day to engage in the workshops, visit the campus, and build their social networks.

Originally, I developed 12 modules that would explicitly address various steps that students, educators, and families should consider when applying for college in Wisconsin. The modules were based on the idea that students could participate in the program throughout the year. The modules were as follows: (1) undocumented and *DACAmented* students, (2) the adjustment of status process, (3) building networks of supports, (4) support during the high school years, (5) the process of applying for college, (6) Wisconsin higher-education institution options, (7) alternative FAFSA, financial support and scholarships, (8) parental/guardian support, (9) first-generation college students, (10) support during the college years, (11) graduate and professional programs, and (12) undocumented entrepreneurs. The modules were sequenced for students to build an understanding of higher-education issues and served as a foundation on which they would build their educational journeys.

Program Implementation

The COVID-19 pandemic greatly impacted the K–12 educational experience for all students. After schools had been closed and instruction had moved to a virtual model, many supports and resources that students normally access were not accessible. This also impacted students as they were preparing to apply for college. I wrote the curriculum and developed the modules during the spring and summer of 2021. Then, the program was implemented during the 2021 fall semester. We piloted the program during the fall semester to support any seniors who would be applying to college by December 2021.

Program Recruitment

Working with undocumented students required the group to be sensitive to students' legal rights. *Plyler v. Doe* (1982) makes it unlawful to ask K–12 students in the U.S. about their immigration status. Students and families may self-disclose their family's immigration status to teachers and educators when they have developed trust and may be seeking educational opportunities for their children. Educators need to make sure they do not share a student's immigration status, but they can share opportunities with families and allow them to decide if they would like to apply for the programs.

The application process was developed by the Dreamers of Wisconsin. After completing the application, outreach efforts incorporated social media and direct connection to high schools and educational organizations to elicit interest. I had experience in community-based outreach efforts and promoted the program on my social networks. Community members reported that I had an established sense of trust with the community as it related to issues impacting the undocumented. As I reached out, I informed my networks that I was teaching the program, which further established trust.

The Dreamers of Wisconsin reviewed the applications, which included several from applicants who were recent immigrants to the United States. These students had arrived during their junior or senior years, expressed interest in learning more about the college-going process, and reflected diverse language backgrounds. Most of them were Spanish-dominant and inquired about options in the program for content delivery in Spanish or for interpreting services. One applicant was bilingual in English-Arabic, while others were fully bilingual Spanish-English students. The group had to decide how to move forward with the language of delivery for the modules so that content was accessible to all. After consulting with me, we decided to have Spanish as the language of instruction for the program; in that way, the content would be accessible to most participants and would honor their cultural and linguistic identities. I translated the modules into Spanish and delivered the information in both English and Spanish, preparing along the way for accommodations for bilingual students of languages other than Spanish (e.g., Arabic-speaking students).

Program Participants

The program's goal was 20 participants for the first cohort. Ten students participated in the first cohort from four local high schools. Three had grown up in the U.S. and had attended K–12 schools, at least since middle school.

They were fully bilingual and bicultural. Seven of the participants had recently arrived in the U.S., and they spoke Spanish as their primary language. The participants were from Mexico, Chile, Nicaragua, Venezuela, and Ecuador. Three students in the program were male students and seven were female. Eight of them were in their senior year and two of them were in their junior year.

Program Curriculum

The program model was changed from 12 modules to four workshop days; in this way, students would only need to attend four days instead of twelve, accommodating their busy schedules. The group decided to offer the program on consecutive Saturdays in November and December. This timeframe benefitted students applying for early college admission. The workshops took place on Saturday mornings from 9:00 a.m. to 1:00 p.m., with two modules covered in each workshop. Full attendance was a goal, but full participation was not always possible due to students' work schedules and prior commitments.

Program Big Ideas, Structure, and Components

As I developed the program, I imagined and recalled what information was needed to be successful in applying for college. I dreamed about the ideal program that would be all-encompassing and address every situation that I had experienced growing up undocumented. Having personal experience and professional experience with helping others allowed me to imagine many possibilities. The 12 modules were the product of many of these possible topics to be covered during the program.

My goal was to create a safe space for the participants and name the challenges that students may experience. The workshops each followed a similar structure, and five main components were included:

- *Goals or Big Ideas:* Focus on three goals: (1) Explore cultural identity (and social identity) and immigration status as it relates to the college-going process; (2) Attend to emotional wellness including mental health; and (3) Focus on personal persistence and resistance.

- *Mancilla's Story:* I had grown up undocumented and brought this lived experience into each workshop. I was transparent in sharing various aspects of my undocumented experience based on the topic being discussed during each week's workshop.

- *Journaling and Reflection:* The participants were provided with a notebook for the program. During each workshop, there were quick writes, journal prompts, and reflections to allow students to process the information that was being shared.

- *Activities:* Because the workshops were taking place over four hours, activities were incorporated that would have the students moving. The activities occurred both inside the classroom and throughout the building and campus.

Workshop 1: (Module 1) Undocumented and DACAmented Students &
(Module 2) The Adjustment of Status Process.

The first workshop covered both information about undocumented populations in the U.S. and the adjustment of status process. These two topics were selected first, to set a common foundation for everyone in the program. This workshop started by defining what it meant to be undocumented, a refugee, an asylum-seeker, and the various types of visa status. The group also explored the history of DACA and its current status. Then, the group explored Wisconsin and local resources. For example, they learned about a free immigration clinic that takes place two times a month. Next, the group explored the pathways for adjustment of status including family-based, employment-based, and visa-based. The group also explored specific requirements for each category.

Workshop 2: (Module 3) Building Networks of Support & (Module 4) Support
During the High School Years.

After setting the foundational knowledge on being undocumented, the second workshop focused on how students can build their support networks and what they need to do during their high school years to be ready for the college application process. The first part of the workshop focused on students taking care of themselves, which included mental health. The group discussed family support, including challenges and opportunities. Educational and community-based trusted adults were also discussed in this session. One important lesson conveyed was that it is okay to ask for help. The second part of the workshop focused on actions students can take during their high school years to prepare for college applications. High school graduation requirements, volunteering, and extracurricular activities were discussed. Additionally, information about pre-college programs and opportunities was presented.

Workshop 3: (Module 5) *The Process of Applying for College* & (Module 6) *Wisconsin Higher-Education Institution Options.*

The third workshop focused on the college application process and institutions of higher education in Wisconsin. The workshop focused on timelines, application essays, and financial information for applying for college. The students were then provided with time to draft an essay or to bring in an essay they were working on. The session also covered applying to college while undocumented and how the process was different from that being undertaken by other students. Information on financial planning for college was presented. The second part of the workshop focused on college options, including community colleges, private colleges, and public universities. This section also covered the "residency for tuition purposes" policies and the governing boards for each type of institution. It was important to also address out-of-state options and scholarship programs.

Workshop 4: (Module 7) *Alternative FAFSA, Financial Support, and Scholarships* & (Module 8) *Parental/guardian Support.*

For the last workshop, the group focused on alternatives to the Free Application for Federal Student Aid (FAFSA) and financial support to pay for college. During the session, the tuition cost for various institutions was presented. Then, the group discussed how schools may have an alternative FAFSA form that allows them to calculate their financial need without filling out the official FAFSA form. This form is often created by institutions and is handled internally. Then, information about various types of scholarships was presented to the participants, and strategies were provided for them to prepare to apply for scholarships. Then, for the second half of the workshop, a college student and their parent were invited to share their story about their college application process. The parents of the participants were also invited to this session.

Discussion

The Dreamers Rise program was developed to support undocumented students with the college application process. The program was successful in re-imagining the support that can be available for the undocumented community. There were two major lessons that emerged from this program which caused us to continue dreaming. The first lesson learned focused on the language of instruction for the program. The second lesson learned focused on additional support needed for newer immigrant students as they get prepared for the college-going process.

Language of Instruction

The Dreamers of Wisconsin and I had originally selected English as the language of instruction during the program planning phase. When people think about immigration, they usually focus on Latina/o/xs as the largest population. However, it is important to acknowledge that anyone can be undocumented, and immigrants come from countries that speak a wide variety of languages. We decided to have English as the language of instruction to allow all undocumented students to participate in the program.

As mentioned earlier, during the application process, the group found out that several recent immigrant students had Spanish as their primary language. Additionally, there was one student who spoke Arabic. The group decided to change the language of instruction to Spanish and to provide an Arabic interpreter if the student enrolled. The change to having the program fully in Spanish allowed the students to understand all the information that was presented in each of the modules. The conversations centered on educational equity and access for the students, both in terms of high school completion and in thinking about higher education. The students and the program allowed the group to have broader discussions relating to the educational system and how to offer support in terms of immigration status and language, which were positive outcomes of the program. As we continue dreaming, it would be most helpful to offer the information in multiple languages. The English language is usually used to access information, but it is important to dream of alternate language possibilities for youth.

Recent Immigrants

In addition to considering the language of instruction, the students who participated in the program also brought up an important conversation about support for recent immigrant students in the transition from high school into higher education. Additionally, a question about how to consider educational equivalencies between other countries and the U.S. education system arose. For example, one student could have graduated [the high school equivalency] in her home county. This would mean that she could have the equivalent of a high school diploma from her country. However, the student decided to take one year of high school in the U.S. and then receive a high school diploma here. Although she had already made the decision, her situation allowed the group to consider what may be various pathways for immigrant youth when they immigrate during their high school years.

Another opportunity for freedom dreaming occurred as we discussed how to best support newer immigrant populations. This creates an opportunity to imagine collectively with schools, community-based organizations, and pre-college programs, dreaming of additional ways to support students academically and personally.

A different discussion revolved around opportunities for English language acquisition in the process of attending institutions of higher education. The two-year community college offers (a) general English as a Second Language (ESL) classes, (b) ESL classes for degree-seeking students, and (c) ESL classes for the workforce. Additionally, several community-based organizations offer ESL classes. The Dreamers Rise program allowed the group to have more in-depth conversations about their possible individual educational pathways.

These conversations were important as the majority of students were seniors who were considering their next academic steps.

Conclusion

Dreaming of educational pathways and opportunities is key to supporting the resistance of undocumented youth. The Dreamers Rise program is an example of freedom dreaming to create a space to validate and support the lives of undocumented youth in Wisconsin. The program provided vital information on, and promoted essential conversations about, how to navigate the college application process. A few participants had done their research and had already applied to colleges. These students shared their personal experiences, resources, and advice with others. Other students learned more about possible next steps that they could take. The goal of having the program in December was to have the seniors ready to apply to colleges by the end of the program. Additionally, the program created a social support network for them as they moved forward in their educational journeys.

Although high school students may have programs and school counselors who help them navigate the college transition process, undocumented students often face additional barriers. We need to continue dreaming of ways to support undocumented students in the college-going process. The Dreamers Rise program made explicit the conversations that are needed to support undocumented students in this process. These conversations need to happen regularly so that everyone can stay up-to-date with the best ways to support immigrant youth.

My ultimate goal was to develop a program that can serve as a template so that other institutions can create similar programs on their campuses, and thus, continue dreaming of ways to make this information accessible and sustainable for other students. An important part of freedom dreaming is to support youth in creating their own possibilities. This program template can be part of the youth's work to make a more just and compassionate world.

Unfortunately, many of the undocumented youth who are graduating from high school do not qualify for DACA. It is important to support these undocumented youth in their preparation for college, with the college application process, and with the transition to college. Colleges and universities also need to dream up support systems for them in their institutions.

The Dreamers Rise program allowed us to dream up ways to support recent immigrants in high school. The program includes considering high school course equivalency, scholarships, and graduation requirements. Additionally, the conversation around English language acquisition and educational resources was important. Educators and programs need to have ways to support recent immigrants with this transition.

Reference

American Immigration Council. (2021). *Immigrants in the United States.* https://www.americanimmigrationcouncil.org/research/immigrants-in-the-united-states

Connor, P., (2023, May 23). *The Post-DACA generation is here.* fwd.us. https://www.fwd.us/news/undocumented-high-school-graduates/

Higher Ed Immigration Portal. (2023a). *U.S. state policies on DACA & undocumented students* [Data set]. https://www.higheredimmigrationportal.org/states/

Higher Ed Immigration Portal. (2023b). *Wisconsin* [State data]. https://www.higheredimmigrationportal.org/state/wisconsin/

Jach, E. A., Corral, D., Mancilla, G., & Hansen, S. R. (2024). Supporting undocumented students through pre-college, college, and post-college transitions. In B. R. Silver, & G. P. McCarron (Eds.), *Supporting college students of immigrant origins: New insights from research, policy, and practice* (pp. 376-399). Cambridge University Press.

Kelley, R. D. (2002). *Freedom dreams: The Black radical imagination.* Beacon Press.

Lhamon, C. E., Rosenfelt, P. H., & Samuels, J. (2014). *Plyler Dear Colleague Letter.* U.S. Department of Education and U.S. Department of Justice. https://www2.ed.gov/about/offices/list/ocr/letters/colleague-201405.pdf

Mancilla, G. (Executive Producer and Host). (2021). *Educators and immigration podcast* [Audio podcast]. Educators and Immigration, LLC. www.educatorsandimmigration.com/podcast

Mancilla, G., & Uy, P. S. (2024). Two researchers' journey toward healing and safety doing community-engaged scholarship with immigrant and refugee populations. *Intercultural Education, 35*(2), 139-155. https://doi.org/10.1080/14675986.2024.2314426

Mancilla, G., & Vukelich-Selva, D. (2024). Developing action research projects for Latinx students in predominantly white institutions. In I. Martinez, I. Montelongo, N. Natividad, & A. D. Nieves (Eds.), *Crossing Digital Fronteras:*

Rehumanizing Latinx Education and Digital Humanities (pp. 199-237). State University of New York Press.

Migration Policy Institute. (n.d.) *Wisconsin: State immigration data profile.* https://www.migrationpolicy.org/data/state-profiles/state/demographics/WI

National Conference of State Legislatures. (2021). *Tuition benefits for immigrants.* https://www.ncsl.org/immigration/tuition-benefits-for-immigrants

Negrón-Gonzalez, G. (2017). Political possibilities: Lessons from the undocumented youth movement for resistance to the Trump administration. *Anthropology & Education Quarterly, 48*(4), 420-426.

Olivas, M. A. (2004). IIRIRA, the Dream Act, and undocumented college student residency. Part III: Admission and removal. *Immigration and Nationality Law Review, 25,* 323–352.

Passel, J. S. (2006). *The size and characteristics of the unauthorized migrant population in the U.S..* Pew Research Center. https://www.pewresearch.org/race-and-ethnicity/2006/03/07/size-and-characteristics-of-the-unauthorized-migrant-population-in-the-us/

Plyler v. Doe, 457 U.S. 202 (1982). https://www.oyez.org/cases/1981/80-1538

Serna, G. R., Cohen, J. M., & Nguyen, D. H. K. (2017). State and institutional policies on in-state resident tuition and financial aid for undocumented students: Examining constraints and opportunities. *Education Policy Analysis Archives, 25,* 18–18. https://doi.org/10.14507/epaa.25.2809

Tuck, E., & Yang, K. W. (Eds). (2018). *Toward what justice?: Describing diverse dreams of justice in education.* Routledge.

USCIS. (n.d.-a). *Consideration of Deferred Action for Childhood Arrivals (DACA).* United States Citizenship and Immigration Services. https://www.uscis.gov/DACA

USCIS. (n.d.-b). *I-131, Application for Travel Document.* United States Citizenship and Immigration Services. https://www.uscis.gov/i-131

Valverde, M. (2018, January 22). *Timeline: DACA, the Trump administration and a government shutdown.* Politifact The Poynter Institute. https://www.politifact.com/article/2018/jan/22/timeline-daca-trump-administration-and-government-/

Van Hook, J., Gelatt, J., & Ruiz Soto, A. G. (2023, September). *A Turning Point for the Unauthorized Immigrant Population in the United States.* Migration Policy Institute. https://www.migrationpolicy.org/news/turning-point-us-unauthorized-immigrant-population#:~:text=Approximately%2011.2%20million%20unauthorized%20immigrants,at%20any%20point%20since%202015.

About the Authors

Miguel N. Abad is an Assistant Professor in the Department of Child and Adolescent Development at San Francisco State University. For over a decade, he has been a youth worker collaborating with community-based and non-profit organizations in the Bay Area in numerous fields such as college access, career development, arts education, and social movement organizing. As a youth studies researcher, his scholarly work touches upon race and social justice, out of school time education, youth development, youth activism, and participatory action research. His work has been featured in publications such as *Race, Ethnicity and Education, Anthropology and Education Quarterly,* and *Race and Class.*

Orubba Almansouri is a doctoral candidate in Urban Education at the CUNY Graduate Center. She holds an M.A. in Near Eastern Studies from NYU. She is an author, educator, and researcher. Her interdisciplinary research experience, and her own experience as a language learner and immigrant youth prepared her to work as an educator across disciplines with students from various cultural, linguistic, and academic styles. As a researcher and educator, Orubba's work explores cultures of care in school settings that are co-created by the community members including its students. Her ethnographic work aims to highlight the experiences of schooling for Arab, Yemeni youth in NYC. Through her work, Orubba aims to push forward the importance of multicultural and translanguaging education in transforming academia into an environment where immigrant students are able to connect and thrive in the world that revolves around them. She holds the Provost Enhancement Fellowship from the CUNY GC and has held multiple fellowship awards, including Mellon Mays Undergraduate Fellowship. She is currently teaching at Barnard College Columbia University and a fellow at Baruch College in the City University of New York.

Charlotte (Char) Austria is an undergraduate student at California State University, Long Beach studying Asian American Studies, with a minor in Printmaking. Her involvement in student activism and past organizing with academic student workers informed her work as Vice Chairperson and

Propaganda Officer of Anakbayan Long Beach in 2023. Through ABLB, Char aims to organize and mobilize Filipino youth and students, alongside other youth, towards the genuine liberation of the Philippines and the rest of the Third World from plunder and Western imperialism. Char seeks to use his creative skills to bridge the gap between the art world and organizing, and showing people that art should be an accessible tool for fostering change in the world, rather than a luxury reserved for a small few. He aims to achieve this through contributing his work to serve various mass campaigns, leading committees for creating propaganda and media, and constantly learning new skills from other organizers and political creatives.

Rachel Brand (she/her) is a Postdoctoral Fellow and Adjunct Faculty member at Santa Clara University, where she works within the Center for Food Innovation and Entrepreneurship, and the Leavey School of Business. Rachel received her EdD from the University of San Francisco, where she served as an Adjunct Professor, Program Director, and Community Engagement Director in the Environmental Studies Department, while simultaneously working towards her doctoral degree. Rachel's teaching and research focus on humanizing education, critical food systems education, environmental justice, student centered research methods, and critical pedagogy. Additionally, she looks at the roles and responsibilities of innovation and business to work towards a healthy and just environment. In her work, Rachel seeks to connect students to real world experiences through relationship building and community engagement. She has found that learning through experiences and collaboration results in lasting impacts on her students. Rachel greatly enjoys time with her family exploring the endless beauty of California's natural environment.

Carlos Casanova is a first-generation Latino college graduate. He is an Assistant Professor at Arizona State University in the Mary Lou Fulton Teachers College. His academic background includes two years at Jackson Community College where he studied Sociology and Education, a bachelor's degree in Sociology and Family Studies from Western Michigan University, Master's degree in Sociology from The University of Texas at San Antonio, and a PhD. in Social and Cultural Studies in Education from Iowa State University. He has over 11 years of professional experience in youth programs that serve primarily youth of color, specifically Latinx youth. His research is guided by LatCrit theory, humanizing pedagogy participatory action research, and critical ethnography. His research focuses on critical youth studies, Latinx youth resistance and wellbeing, liberating pedagogy of praxis, and community-based youth programs. His research is published in the *Journal of Latinos and Education, Anthropology & Education Quarterly, Youth & Society, Social Justice,* and *Teaching and Teacher Education.*

Borodine Chery is a rising junior. She attends Clark University where she is double majoring in history and political science. She was born in Port-au-Prince, Haiti, and immigrated to the United States when she was three years old. Currently, she lives in Taunton, MA, with her parents and two sisters, where she also completed her secondary high school education at Taunton High School. She is interested in how we can discuss race, create scholarship, and foster dialogue to foster change, and too help push and challenge the understanding of the complexities surrounding diversity and inclusion, through her journey of dedication to fostering inclusive higher education and community spaces overall, especially in the areas she is passionate about, such as history, political science, and community engagement work. She hopes to create and better help programs and scholarships and ensure that her work can help contribute to nurturing positive and complex change.

Chelsea Chhem is an arts maker and emerging curator who studied Art History and Museum Studies at UC Davis and is currently receiving her master's at George Washington University for Museum Studies with a concentration on Public Engagement. She grew up in the heart of Long Beach, California in Little Cambodia. As the daughter of refugee parents, her art is linked to her identity as a Cambodian American. Through her academic and personal journey, her projects begin with a people-focused approach with the intention to understand and uplift marginalized communities. In her museum work, she explores and challenges the mechanisms that perpetuate exclusion, seeing museums as potent sites of liberation. Throughout high school, she was part of Khmer Girls in Action, a grassroots organization for Southeast Asian youth to fight racial, gender, and economic justice. For Chelsea, one of the most instrumental moments was giving her the opportunity to design their campaign logo and the first volume of their coloring book. Her art and museum works continue the core principles she learned from community organizing in her youth. For her, art must be political, representative, and insinuate a culture of change and progress.

Justin Clyburn is an African American student from Winston-Salem and is a current sophomore, soon to be rising junior at the University of North Carolina at Chapel Hill. He is double majoring in Political Science and Hispanic Linguistics with a minor in Translation and Interpretation. As a child, Justin's parents never shied away from the fact of telling Justin that society would look at him differently because of the color of his skin. Nevertheless, Justin realized that although he was new to "Tarheel Nation", he could not be naive thinking that discrimination did not exist on campus. Therefore, Justin began to view his new surroundings through more of a critical lens to investigate how some circumstances enable discrimination to be unnoticed. Justin both critically analyzed his new home in Chapel Hill while still embracing the positive aspects of UNC which he loved so much as a new Tarheel student. Justin's goal is to create a safe space for all people, in and outside of UNC Chapel Hill, where people can learn and grow from one another in respect, understanding, and love.

Gilberto Q. Conchas obtained a PhD and MA in Sociology from the University of Michigan, Ann Arbor and a B.A. in Sociology from the University of California, Berkeley. He is currently the Inaugural Wayne K. and Anita Woolfolk Hoy Endowed Chair of Education at the Pennsylvania State University and a Center for the Study of Higher Education (CSHE) research associate. Prior to Penn State, Dr. Conchas was Professor of Educational Policy and Social Context at the University of California, Irvine, Assistant Professor at the Harvard Graduate School of Education, and Senior Program Officer for the Bill & Melinda Gates Foundation. Conchas is an expert on qualitative research methods, with a particular focus on case study methodology. Conchas' research focuses on inequality with an emphasis on communities and schools. A sociologist, widely published scholar, and experienced university administrator, Conchas has designed and led mentoring programs, has a well-honed awareness of the experiences of racially minoritized students and faculty, and draws on these experiences to advocate for pathways to better diversify higher education institutions. Numerous scholarly journals have published his work. He is the author of thirteen books, including the award winning *The Color of Success: Race and High-Achieving Urban Youth,*

Small Schools and Urban Youth: Using the Power of School Culture to Engage Youth, StreetSmart School Smart: Urban Poverty and the Education of Boys of Color, and *Cracks in the Schoolyard—Confronting Latino Educational Inequality,* and *Race Frames in Education.* His current coauthored book, *The Chicana/o/x Dream: Hope, Resistance, and Educational Success,* was conferred the 2021 Book-of-the-Year Award from the American Association of Hispanics in Higher Education (AAHHE). Conchas was also named the 2022 Sylvia Hurtado University Faculty Award for teaching and research from AAHHE.

Olga M. Correa is a scholar/practitioner with over 10 years of experience working alongside youth, families, school administrators, and community members to promote educational justice. Olga began her professional career in her hometown of Englewood, New Jersey, creating and facilitating college readiness workshops for Black and Latino/a/x youth and families through her roles as Youth Development Specialist, Summer Program Coordinator, and eventually, Program Manager. She has since worked in various capacities in New York City, Western Massachusetts, and Pittsburgh to center community-based knowledge, particularly among Black and Latino/a/x youth and families. Olga currently serves as the Director of the Cesar Chavez Learning Center at Lansing Community College where she oversees multi-faceted comprehensive student support programs and implements strategies to promote a sense of belonging and inclusion for historically marginalized communities. As a first-generation student and daughter of immigrant parents to the U.S, Olga uses her platform to acknowledge the sociohistorical factors that influence students' pathways to quality education, while working collaboratively with campus and community advocates to reduce access barriers. Olga is a Ph.D. Candidate in Educational Leadership at the University of Massachusetts Amherst. Her research encompasses larger societal factors, namely race, class, and gender in the U.S and the influence that these factors have had on K-12 education policy and practice. She presently holds a B.A. from William Paterson University of New Jersey and an M.Ed. in Higher Education Administration from the University of Massachusetts Amherst.

Bernadine Cortina is a storyteller from Parañaque City, Philippines who migrated to Hayward, CA in 2018. Now in her senior year at Chapman University, she is pursuing a B.A. in English Literature with minors in Africana Studies, Ethnic Studies, and Women's and Gender Studies. Claiming a transnational community, she is moved and profoundly sustained by love for the Philippines and the people beloved to her there. As a writer, she remains committed to nurturing ecosystems of Filipina/x/o dreaming and storytelling through the literary arts and hopes to enter a career in publishing in the Philippines. Her work has been featured in the *Journal for the Motherhood Initiative for Research and Community Involvement,* the *Journal for Undergraduate Multimedia Projects,* Chapman's the Voice of Wilkinson blog, and *Chapman's Calliope Arts and Literary Magazine.* She is also a proud member of the Santa Ana Youth Media Project and co-founder of the Dreamweavers Initiative.

Victor DeAlba is a PhD Candidate and graduate research assistant at The Pennsylvania State University. He attended community college in his hometown of Lompoc, CA where he earned an A.A. in Sociology from Allan Hancock College. He went on to earn his B.A. in Sociology from UCLA. His current research includes the perceptions of school leaders and Latina/o/x students on school engagement and student voice. Gilberto Q. Conchas is the Wayne K. and Anita Woolfolk Hoy Professor in the College of Education at The Pennsylvania State University. He received his Ph.D. in sociology from the University of Michigan, Ann Arbor and his B.A. in sociology from the University of California, Berkeley. He is the author and coauthor of The Color of Success, Streetsmart Schoolsmart, Cracks in the Schoolyard, Educational Policy Goes to School, The Complex Web of Inequality, The Chicana/o/x Dream, Race Frames in Education, and The Color of Success 2.0. Miguel N. Abad is a San Francisco-based youth worker and an Assistant Professor in the Department of Child and Adolescent Development at San Francisco State University. As a youth studies scholar, his research touches upon race and social justice, out of school time education, youth development, youth activism, and participatory action research. His work has been published in Race, Ethnicity and Education, Journal of Youth Studies, Anthropology and Education Quarterly and Race & Class.

Eric DeMeulenaere is a Professor in Clark University's Education Department. Prior to joining Clark University's faculty, he taught middle and high school social studies and English in Oakland and San Francisco, CA. He also co-founded and served as the principal of an innovative small public school in East Oakland that focused on social justice and increased academic outcomes for youth of color. Before opening the school, Dr. DeMeulenaere earned his Ph.D. in the Social and Cultural Studies Program at U.C. Berkeley's Graduate School of Education. He has consulted with urban school leaders and teachers nationally and internationally to transform their organizational school cultures and address social and racial inequities. His research employs participatory action research and narrative inquiry methods and draws extensively from critical theory to examine how to create more effective and liberatory learning spaces for urban youth both in and out of school spaces. Dr. DeMeulenaere is the co-author of *Reflections from the Field: How Coaching Made Us Better Teachers* (2013) and *The Activist Academic: Engaged Scholarship for Resistance, Hope and Social Change* (2020).

David Flores is an East Los Angeles native and received his PhD in the Cesar E. Chavez Department of Chicana/o and Central American Studies at the University of California, Los Angeles. Dr. Flores is now an Assistant Professor and codirector of the Chicanx/Latinx studies program in the Department of Ethnic Studies at Sacramento State University. His current research examines the intersection of religion and social movements, specifically within the Chicana/o Civil Rights Movement in Los Angeles. He has recently published an original article and co-edited a dossier on Christianity and Chicana/o/x Latina/o/x Studies in *Aztlán*, the premier journal in the field of Chicanx Studies (2022). Dr. Flores is also a co-founder of Las Cafeteras, an East Los Angeles musical and cultural project that lifts the narratives of Chicanxs and Latinxs in the United States. Dr. Flores's diverse academic, cultural, and spiritual work are the foundations of his community engaged scholarship.

Elsabet Franklin is a college student entering her junior year at Clark University majoring in Sociology and Spanish with a concentration in Africana Studies. Prior to attending Clark University, she attended high school in the East Village in New York City. She devotes her time to social justice, prison abolition, and the liberation of Black and brown folks which she hopes to continue for a career path. She has interned at Vera Institute of Justice, written an op-ed about the meaning of Juneteenth in a society that incarcerates Black men disproportionately, and continues to volunteer at Colin Kaepernicks Know Your Rights Camp. She is currently working on a campaign for Keith LaMar, a Black man who was wrongly convicted and on death row in the state of Ohio. During her free time, Elsabet likes to read, try new food, cook, listen to music, and hang out with family and friends.

Shelby Freeman is an undergraduate researcher at the University of North Carolina at Chapel Hill. She is from Chapel Hill but spent a year working with City Year AmeriCorp in a Title I school in Boston prior to starting college. Shelby uses her experiences living in the South and working with fifth graders in Boston to help her with this research. Education and health reform are priorities for her as she moves into her career in public policy. She plans to continue doing work to disentangle the intricacies of racism in our school systems today and make our learning spaces more equitable for all people. Shelby hopes this work will bring attention within the academic and wider communities to our successes and the beauty of the learning process within our schools, while not diminishing the need for growth. This project will be her first published work and is an immense accomplishment for her and her co-researchers.

Dr. Simona Goldin is a Research Associate Professor at the Department of Public Policy at the University of North Carolina and at the Education Policy Initiative at Carolina. Dr. Goldin is a teacher education and policy scholar who utilizes qualitative methods to contend with systemic inequality and racism in U.S. public schools. She has studied ways to transform the preparation of beginning teachers to teach in more racially just and equitable ways and has elaborated the teaching practices that bridge children's work in schools on academic content with their home and community-based experiences. Her most recent work has looked at the ways that innovations are weaponized against the very communities they are meant to support. With colleagues, she has designed and studied innovative instructional resources and unique opportunities—namely, home visits, performance assessments, and new pedagogies of teacher education. Across each of these has been the focus on supporting novice teachers' capabilities to develop instructionally rich, respectful relationships with families.

Anna Mei Gubbins (she/her) is the Equity and Diversity Program Coordinator at the Harvard Foundation for Intercultural and Race Relations where she oversees the communications, branding, and digital strategy of the office. She is passionate about diversity education, intentional curricula development, and designing, implementing, and assessing programming to promote a sense of belonging through holistic support, student identity theories, and intercultural communication. She currently sits on the Global Respectful Disruption Summit planning committee and has since its creation in 2021. Prior to her involvement in higher education, she worked in the fields of psychology, travel, and K-12 education. She has a master's in International Education Management from the Middlebury Institute of International Studies and a bachelor's in Hispanic Studies from Davidson College. Gubbins positions herself as a Chinese American, transracial adoptee from a middle class family, raised in a Welcoming and Affirming (2SLGBTQIA+) American Baptist Church in New England in the late 1990s and early 2000s. Gubbins' passion for intercultural exchange led her to experiences living in Spain and Chile, but as a Spanish and English (but not Chinese) speaking woman, Gubbins continues to explore questions of authenticity and the gatekeeping of identity.

Dr. Ava Jackson is an Assistant Professor in the School of Education at Loyola University Chicago. Dr. Jackson received her Learning Sciences PhD at Northwestern University and was an AACTE Holmes Postdoctoral Fellow at Boston University. She is a Learning Scientist whose research examines the intersections of learning and identity development in critical pedagogical and disciplinary learning environments. Using collaborative ethnographic, micro-ethnographic, interaction, discourse, survey, and community-based methods of data collection and analysis, her work explores the developmental and learning processes that foster situated disciplinary, racial, and political identities in expansive disciplinary educational contexts. Specifically, she explores how these identities shape student participation and sensemaking over time and across contexts and vice versa. Dr. Jackson's research explores questions of teaching, learning, identity, and design across a variety of formal and informal educational contexts, including high school History classrooms, STEM tinkering and making programs, hip-hop after-school programs, and arts-based design programming.

Reva Jaffe-Walter is an Associate Professor in the Department of Counseling and Educational Leadership and Research Faculty in Educational Foundations at Montclair State University. She is an anthropologist of education exploring questions related to nationalism, the education of immigrant students, educational policy, and school leadership. Through comparative international ethnographic research in schools serving immigrant youth in Europe and the United States, she explores questions related to how schools provide access to educational resources, promote feelings of belonging or marginalization, and support post-secondary transitions. Engaging the anthropology of policy, her research has focused on how nationalist and neoliberal policies materialize and are resisted by school leaders, teachers, and youth in schools serving immigrant youth. Her current research funded by the the Spencer foundation examines how teachers, of immigrant-serving schools in Denmark resist nationalist policies. Her book *Coercive Concern: Nationalism, Liberalism and the Schooling of Muslim Youth* is published with Stanford University Press and her work has been published in journals such as *The Harvard Educational Review,* and the *American Journal of Education and Race, Ethnicity and Education* and with Teachers College Press.

Emanuel (J) Suarez Jimenez is a doctoral student in Education at the University of California, Santa Cruz. His journey into the field of education was driven by a desire to become the teacher he never had. This led him to a career dedicated to promoting social justice and educational equity by critically exploring the pedagogical implementation of digital technologies among historically racialized and marginalized teachers in various educational and community-based contexts. He places a strong emphasis on the sociopolitical implications of emerging digital technologies, such as AI, chatbots, and surveillance technologies, and their impact on historically marginalized communities. Additionally, Emanuel's scholarship is influenced by his experiences as a substitute teacher in the San Francisco Bay Area and his collaborative work with Indigenous educators in Oaxaca, Mexico. These experiences have provided him with unique insights into how digital technologies can be leveraged for social and political transformation. His current work aims to explore how educators can make informed pedagogical decisions regarding digital tools and design teaching practices that foster equitable and culturally responsive learning environments. Emanuel's work seeks to deepen the understanding of educational equity in the digital era, particularly the pedagogical potential of digital technologies to support linguistically and culturally diverse students.

Leyla Shirley Knight completed their bachelor's degree in 2024, majoring in Media, Culture, and the Arts with a minor in Entrepreneurship & Innovation. In undergrad, they were a fellow with Difficult Dialogues and facilitated in specialized multiracial queer spaces and BIPOC spaces which discussed the complexities of race, love, community, and intersectionality in 2023 and 2024. They were also a fellow with the Mosakowski Institute for Public Enterprise in 2023- 2024 which specializes in mental health for young people of color. They aided in developing the institute's first Womxn of Color group on campus. They were also on the e-board of the Clark University Black Student Union as treasurer (2023) and outreach chair (2024). Leyla is native to Harlem, NYC, and loves healthy, happy, interdependent communities at heart, with interests in education and community organizing in the non-profit sector. They laugh loudly and enjoy volleyball and writing, with a passion for art, social activism, and loved ones.

May Lin is a community rooted educator and researcher who teaches Asian American Studies at CSULB through a lens of liberation, solidarity, and intersectionality. She aims to bridge classrooms/academic learning with community & social movements, drawing on her background in youth development, grassroots media, graduate student unionizing, resisting gentrification in New York City and Los Angeles, queer internationalist solidarity organizing, and local efforts to divest from policing and invest in life-affirming resources. She has conducted collaborative research with organizations including Californians for Justice, Youth Organize! California, Center for Empowered Politics, Gender and Sexualities Alliance Network, and Chinese Progressive Association-San Francisco to uplift youth/community organizing campaigns around healing, racial, gender, and social justice. Her peer-reviewed research has been published in venues such as *Health Affairs, Journal of Ethnic and Migration Studies,* and the *Journal of the American Planning Association.* May is also a proud board member of Khmer Girls in Action, Long Beach Forward, and an active member in the Long Beach People's Budget Coalition.

Ma. Glenda Lopez Wui is an Assistant Professor at the Department of Sociology and Anthropology, Ateneo de Manila University. She has conducted research on education in Singapore, the United States, and the Philippines. She co-authored (with C. S. White) the book *Civic Engagement of Asian American Student Leaders* (2022, Lexington Books), and served as the Principal Investigator for the project *"Letter to the Next President of the Philippines: Examining the Civic Writing of Filipino High School Students."* She recently completed the writing project, *"Civic Education in the Philippines: Confronting the Challenges of the Present Times"* with the Rosa Luxemburg Stiftung Southeast Asia Manila Office. Her current research project is on *"Governance Cultures, Perspectives and Practices in Philippine Basic Education Settings: Focus on Teacher In-Service Training and Development"* funded by the University of the Philippines President Edgardo J. Angara (UPPEJA) Fellowship under The Second Congressional Commission on Education (EDCOM II) of the Philippines. Her research interests include the civic engagement of culturally diverse youth, civic education, sociology of education, and school culture.

Gerardo Mancilla is an Associate Professor of Education at Edgewood College. He holds a B.S. in Elementary Education, M.S. in Curriculum & Instruction, M.S. in Counseling Psychology, and Ph.D. in Curriculum & Instruction, all from the University of Wisconsin-Madison. Prior to working at Edgewood College, Mancilla worked for the Madison Metropolitan School District where he was a Dual Language Immersion teacher. At Edgewood College, Mancilla teaches both undergraduate and graduate courses in the Elementary Education program, ESL, and Bilingual Education program. Mancilla's research interests include critical race theory, LatCrit, the school-to-prison pipeline, bilingual education, program development, and immigration. In 2021, Mancilla launched the *Educators and Immigration* podcast, where he interviews various guests about ways to support undocumented and immigrant students. He has also helped develop several educational programs for youth, including the Latino Youth Summit, Dreamers Rise Precollege program, Leadership Institute for Borderlands Research and Education (LIBRE), and the Mexico International Study Opportunity for Learning (MISOL).

Danita Mason-Hogans is an oral historian, memory worker and native of Chapel Hill, NC. She uses oral histories to advocate for informed collaboration, repair, reconciliation, and policy change. She works in partnership with veterans of the Student Nonviolent Coordinating Committee (or SNCC), and today's activists to center equity when documenting national and local movement history at Duke University. Her TED talk provides an explanation of the Critical Oral History methodology which she helped to adapt. The first *Chapel Hill Civil Rights Task Force*, a podcast series on Chapel Hill history, the Chapel Hill Nine Monument, the James Cates Memorial, and the Black Women in the Movement historical documentary series are a few projects that she has been involved with. In 2023, she was a part of a documentary entitled *Gaining Ground, the Fight for Black Land* with Al Roker and John Deere. She also serves on the University of North Carolina at Chapel Hill's History, Race and a Way Forward task force. and her current avocation is for a no-cost education program and cost-free college tuition for the descendants of the enslaved laborers at UNC.

Jie Park is an Associate Professor of Education, and advisor of the Difficult Dialogues Program at Clark University. She holds a B.A. and M.A. in English Literature from Stanford, and a Ph.D. (2010) in Education from the University of Pennsylvania. A language and literacy scholar, she studies immigrant youth and their literacy and language practices in out-of-school and school-based settings. Currently, she is involved in a variety of research projects around teacher and youth-research, antiracist teaching in higher education, multicultural and multilingual curricula in high school classrooms, and the intersection of youth literacy, language, and identities. Her most recent work has been published in *Anthropology and Education Quarterly*, the *Journal of Adolescent and Adult Literacy*, *English Education*, and the *International Journal of Multicultural Education*. She is also the author of *Learning about Academic Literacies from Urban Immigrant Youth*, published by Routledge in 2018, and *Educating Emergent Bilingual Youth in High School: The Promise of Critical Language Pedagogy*, published by Routledge in 2023.

Brianna R. Ramirez (she/her/ella) is the oldest daughter of Mexican immigrants with familial roots in Guanajuato and Jalisco, Mexico. Through critical race feminista and Chicana/Latina feminist perspectives and methodologies,

Brianna explores how higher education systems, structures, and practices uphold systems of marginality that shape Chicanx/Latinx student pathways, opportunities, and experiences. Her research centers Chicanx/Latinx student navigation and negotiations to make visible the everyday forms of student agency and resistance within and against the inequitable, unjust educational system and institutions. Brianna received her master's degree in the Social and Cultural Analysis of Education program at CSU Long Beach. She earned her Ph.D. in Education Studies with a specialization in Critical Gender Studies from UC San Diego. She is currently a postdoctoral scholar at UC Irvine, where she advances graduate student training in community-based research with BIPOC communities, and she teaches ethnic studies and education courses in the California State University (CSU) system.

Zabrina Richards is a university student at Clark University majoring in Political Science on the American government track, minoring in Community Youth Education Studies (CYES), and a concentration in Comparative Race and Ethnic Studies (CRES). Prior to attending Clark University, she grew up in Maine. Growing up in a predominantly white state, it encouraged her to participate and initiate projects focused on amplifying racialized people's experiences. Some examples include testifying against legislation, speaking at local rallies, creating a social media account for Asian American youth in Maine to share their experiences, planning/organizing/participating in a panel discussion focusing on Maine Asian American youth's experiences during the height of COVID-19, and interned in Los Angeles in the summer of her junior year to collaborate with community members in Los Angeles' Chinatown community. She is passionate about amplifying Asian American/Pacific Islander voices, dismantling white supremacy, and community organizing efforts that put the concerns of the community at the forefront.

Jorge F. Rodriguez is an Assistant Professor in the Integrated Educational Studies program within the Attallah College of Educational Studies at Chapman University. His interests include a critical examination on how culture, privilege, and power intersect within school systems and their larger community environments. His work explores the politics of knowledge, funds of knowledge, critical media literacy, ethnic studies, and the praxis of centering counter narratives within his scholarship. Jorge is passionate about creating spaces for youth and students around social justice, self-determination, and cultural resistance. His teaching and research experience demonstrate his ability to both create and operationalize culturally responsive curriculum and reflective learning environments. Jorge comes from an immigrant family from Coahuila, Mexico. His interest in schools and culture comes from his experiences growing up on the south side of Santa Ana, CA. His inspiration and commitment come from lessons and struggles learned being raised by a determined and visionary Indigenous mother. Jorge considers himself a scholar activist, constantly looking for ways to engage in the process of dialogue, critical questioning, and unlearning.

Kathleen Rucker is the principal of The Brooklyn International High School (BIHS), a public high school for newly arrived immigrants. BIHS is a member of the Internationals Network for Public Schools (INPS) and the New York Performance Standards Consortium. She has worked in education for over 25 years as a Peace Corps Environmental Education Volunteer (Senegal), science teacher, assistant principal, and principal. As school leader, she seeks to create the conditions for imaginative, intellectual, and socio-emotional growth for adults and students alike. She has presented on multiple panels covering a range of educational issues related to serving immigrant youth, including restorative justice, work-based learning, performance-based assessment, and alumni leadership programs. She also co-authored a chapter with BIHS alumni entitled "Adopt Intentional Staffing" in *Humanizing Education for Immigrant and Refugee Youth* (Bajaj, Walsh, Bartlett and Martinez, 2023).

Madison San Luis (Mady) was born and raised in Santa Maria, California, one of the centers for agricultural work on the Central Coast. They are a Political Science and Asian American Studies graduate from Cal State Long Beach and a community organizer with Filipino student and youth fighting organization, Anakbayan Long Beach. Mady's drive as a life-long learner and community organizer is fueled by their experiences growing up as the middle child of Filipino immigrants, witnessing the roots of their family's forced migration to the United States. This, with the lessons and tools they've learned from their peers, educators, and other community organizers in Long Beach, Mady links the personal and political through their integration and work with local Filipino communities. Wherever they are planted, Mady's unwavering commitment to continue agitating, organizing, and mobilizing the communities they serve will not end until the genuine liberation of the Philippines.

Aubry Threlkeld (they, them, theirs) is the Associate Director of Academic and Student Programming for the Harvard Summer School, Division of Continuing Education, Faculty of Arts and Sciences, Harvard University. Dr. Threlkeld has given more than 100 invited talks internationally in pedagogy, disability studies, 2SLGBTQIA+ studies, Mad studies, and cultural studies. During the last 19 years, Dr. Threlkeld has taught at Endicott College; Pace University; the Experimental College at Tufts University; and as a lecturer in Studies of Women, Gender and Sexuality at Harvard University. They advise a number of national projects including the Collaborative on Racialized Disability (CORD) where they focus on improving the lives of Black children with disabilities. They have twenty-five publications focused primarily on the practical work of curriculum development for children and youth with disabilities, trauma-informed pedagogy, and more recently, Mad studies. They have a doctorate in education from Harvard University, a master's in science from Mercy College, a master's in business administration from Endicott College, and a bachelor's of arts from Middlebury College. They position themselves as MadQueer, Genderqueer, Neuroqueer, Disabled, and as a white person of Romani descent. They live in Boston with their spouse and two cats where they can be found reading, writing, cooking, and going to see art in all of its forms.

Jessica Tonai is a musician and aspiring educator from Orange County, California. She holds a Bachelor of Music in Vocal Performance and Music Education and is currently a student at Chapman University working towards a Master of Arts in Teaching and a teaching credential to teach music in K-12 schools. She performs a wide variety of types of music, including classical/opera, jazz, and mariachi. She began working with the Santa Ana Youth Media Project two years ago as a coordinator and composer and has been constantly inspired and changed by the creativity of our youth. Jessica also serves as the marketing officer for another grassroots organization active in Orange County and the California Bay Area, Musicians of Color Association, which works to provide inclusive and accessible arts programming in schools and for the greater community. Through these spaces, Jessica hopes to continue to build transformative community that allows for radical dreaming.

Corey Winchester (he/him) is a Chicago-based, Philly-born educator with over a decade of experience serving in various roles as a veteran classroom teacher, professional developer, coach, mentor, coordinator, fellow, consultant, and student. Corey has worked for several local, state, and national organizations such as Breakthrough Collaborative, Northwestern Academy for Chicago Public Schools, Evanston Township High School, Loyola University Chicago, the Golden Apple Foundation, the Aspen Young Leaders Fellowship, and the Gilder Lehrman Institute of American History. He has been recognized as an Excellent Early Career Educator by the Illinois State Board of Education in 2013, a Distinguished Alumni from Loyola University Chicago's School of Education in 2016, received the Golden Apple Award for Excellence in Teaching in 2019, and was honored as Illinois History Teacher of the Year by the Gilder Lehrman Institute of American History in 2020. Corey is currently pursuing a PhD in Learning Sciences at Northwestern University (NU) and has dual appointments as an adjunct instructor at NU and Saint Louis University's respective schools of education.

Chloe Wing Ching Yau is a recent graduate of Clark University majoring in Community, Youth, and Education Studies, with a concentration in Comparative, Race, and Ethnic Studies. Originally from Hong Kong, China, she attended high school at United World College Changshu China, and went to Switzerland for her first year of college. At present, she is a master student pursuing a degree in Master of Arts in Teaching at Clark University, hoping to become an elementary teacher afterward. She was one of the Difficult Dialogues fellows for the past one and a half years, and she was also a co-founder of Asian/Asian American Undergraduate Student Caucus on campus. During her leisure time, she enjoys binge-watching K-dramas, hand-feeding her guinea pig (named Junior!) and holding a facetime-marathon with her younger sister. She also enjoys trying new Asian dish recipes! As a soon-to-be elementary teacher, she hopes to inspire students to be proud of their cultural heritage, utilize their lived experiences, and diverse identities to engage in learning altogether in loving, collaborative ways!